PROPOSITIONAL
ATTITUDES

CSLI
Lecture Notes
Number 20

PROPOSITIONAL ATTITUDES

The Role of Content in Logic, Language, and Mind

edited by
C. Anthony Anderson
and
Joseph Owens

CENTER FOR THE STUDY
OF LANGUAGE
AND INFORMATION

CSLI was founded early in 1983 by researchers from Stanford University, SRI International, and Xerox PARC to further research and development of integrated theories of language, information, and computation. CSLI headquarters and the publication offices are located at the Stanford site.

CSLI/SRI International   **CSLI/Stanford**   **CSLI/Xerox PARC**
333 Ravenswood Avenue   Ventura Hall   3333 Coyote Hill Road
Menlo Park, CA 94025   Stanford, CA 94305   Palo Alto, CA 94304

Printed in the United States

98 97 96 95 94 93 92 91 90   5 4 3 2 1

Library of Congress Cataloging-in-Publication Data

Propositional attitudes : the role of content in logic, language, and
  mind / edited by C. Anthony Anderson and Joseph Owens.
      p.   cm. -- (CSLI lecture notes ; no. 20)
    Includes bibliographical references.
    ISBN 0-937073-51-2
    ISBN 0-937073-50-4 (pbk.)
    1. Language and logic. 2. Proposition (Logic) 3. Semantics
  (Philosophy) 4. Philosophy of mind. 5. Attitude (Psychology)
    I. Anderson, C. Anthony. II. Owens, Joseph, 1943- . III. Series.
BC57.P76 1990
128'.2--dc20   90-34223
                                                                    CIP

Contents

Contributors

TYLER BURGE is Professor of Philosophy at UCLA. He has written articles in the philosophy of language, philosophy of mind, philosophy of logic, and the history of philosophy.

KEITH S. DONNELLAN is Professor of Philosophy at the University of California, Los Angeles. He is the author of a number of articles in philosophy of language and related areas.

KIT FINE, Professor of Philosophy at UCLA, has written papers in philosophy, logic, and related areas. He is the author of *Reasoning with Arbitrary Objects* and a co-author (with A. N. Prior) of *Worlds, Times, and Selves*.

KEITH GUNDERSON is Professor of Philosophy at the University of Minnesota and a member of the Minnesota Center for Philosophy of Science. He is author of *Mentality and Machines* (1985) and is editor of *Language, Mind, and Knowledge* (1975), a volume in the Minnesota Studies in Philosophy of Science series. He is currently working on *Interviews with Robots*.

HANS KAMP is Professor of Philosophy at the University of Texas, Austin.

ERNEST LEPORE is Associate Professor of Philosophy at Rutgers University. He has written on philosophy of language, mind, and logic.

BARRY LOEWER is Professor of Philosophy at Rutgers University. He has written on philosophy of language, mind, and physics.

H. E. MASON is Professor of Philosophy at the University of Minnesota. He has written on moral and political philosophy and on the philosophy of Wittgenstein.

JOSEPH OWENS is Assistant Professor of Philosophy at the University of Minnesota, Twin Cities. He has published papers in the philosophy of language, mind and psychology.

NATHAN SALMON is Professor of Philosophy at the University of California, Santa Barbara. The author of numerous articles in analytic metaphysics amnd the philosophy of language, he has written two books, *Reference and*

Essence (1981) and *Frege's Puzzle* (1986), and is co-editor of an anthology on *Propositions and Attitudes* (1988). A former Fulbright distinguished professor, Salmon received the "Gustave O. Arlt Award in the Humanities" from the council of Graduate Schools in the U.S. in recognition of his contributions to the field.

STEPHEN SCHIFFER is Professor of Philosophy at CUNY Graduate Center. His publications include *Meaning* (1972) and *Remnants of Meaning* (1987).

JOHN R. SEARLE is a Professor of Philosophy at the University of California at Berkeley. He has written widely about the philosophy of language and the philosophy of mind. Among his recent books are: *Intentionality* and *Minds, Brains and Science*. He is currently working on a book tentatively titled *What's Wrong with the Philosophy of Mind*.

ROBERT STALNAKER is Professor of Philosophy at MIT. He is the author of articles on the logic of conditionals, pragmatics, the semantics of propositional attitudes, and the foundations of modal semantics, as well as a book, *Inquiry*.

JOHN WALLACE is Professor of Philosophy at the University of Minnesota. He has written on the philosophy of language and is currently working on political philosophy and the philosophy of language.

Introduction

IN SPITE OF the title of this volume it is not really possible to sharply divide the papers below into those that are concerned with issues involved in formulating a logic of propositional attitudes, those that concern the attitudes as an issue in philosophy of language, and those that concern the philosophy of mind. The problems are too closely interconnected. Nevertheless, we make a rough cut into those that bear more or less directly on the question of treating such matters formally (or semi-formally), logic, and the others: those that concern the semantics of natural language and matters in the philosophy of psychology or mind. These last two *really are* too closely connected for any surgery. So we don't even try. But we find some ways to internally group the papers in this second category.

Logic

In the first, "logic," group, we find the papers of Kit Fine, Hans Kamp, and Ernest LePore/Barry Loewer.

Kit Fine's "Quine and Quantifying In" is a careful and imaginative examination of Quine's well-known arguments against combining quantification and intensional contexts. Fine focuses on modal contexts but much (though not all) of his critical analysis is obviously of direct relevance to the case of the propositional attitudes.

Fine's discussion concerns logical necessity (to be contrasted with natural and metaphysical necessity) but he takes it to bear also on analytic necessity. He considers two different arguments for Quine's famous transition from the failure of substitution (of co-designating terms to preserve truth-value) to the conclusion that objectual quantification is incoherent for such contexts. The "Special Argument" questions the possibility of finding a notion which will stand to satisfaction as logical truth stands to truth—necessary satisfaction. Fine concludes that Quine's misgivings, while they do have some force against metaphysical necessity, are without foundation as applied to the *de re* application of logical necessity.

The "General Argument" concerns the coherence of the ideas of satisfaction conditions and quantification for the disputed contexts. Fine considers each step in Quine's argument, proposes counterexamples, makes distinctions, and generally brings the logical possibilities into unusually clear focus. As applied to the project of constructing a logical symbolism which is free from anomaly and is syntactically perspicuous relative to the semantical functions of its terms, Fine concludes that a sound form of Quine's argument goes through. And this, he thinks, is not utterly damning but does impose substantial limitations on the form of a quantified intensional logic. But as applied to quantification in ordinary language, the theoretical presuppositions of Quine's argument must give way to direct intuitions of intelligibility.

Hans Kamp's "Prolegomena to a Structural Account of Belief and Other Attitudes" develops the ideas of *Discourse Representation Theory* into a detailed and subtle theory of the structure of complex propositional attitudes. Discourse Representation Theory conceives of the process of interpretation (and hence of communication) as dynamic—information is received and interpreted in the light of semantic connections to previous data. The theory articulates a set of rules, a *construction algorithm*, which maps a given segment of discourse onto certain formal structures, the latter representing the truth-conditions of the discourse segment. The content-carrying structures which thus develop are called "Discourse Representation Structures" (DRS's) and take the traditional place of propositions as the units of information. The basic DRS consists of a specification of the *discourse referents*, constituents which represent the individuals, events, times, places, and other entities explicitly mentioned or implied by a given discourse, together with a set of *conditions*, property and relation specifications providing information about the represented entities. Given one such, together with, say, a new sentence of the discourse, a new DRS will be generated which may well be constrained by anaphoric and other connections with the initial structure. In this way the contained information is represented as a developing structural "web" rather than in the traditional conjunctive proposition-by-proposition conception.

Kamp's present paper deals especially with the elaborations and refinements required in order to represent particular complex propositional attitudes such as belief or desire. To distinguish attitudes with the same content, DRS's are paired with *mode indicators*, markers indicating the state which they constitute—belief or desire, say—to produce *articulated* DRS's. In order to represent direct reference and attitudes de re, Kamp introduces the idea of *anchors* (of two kinds, internal and external) which tie the formal structures to the world. Ultimately, anchored articulated DRS's are suggested as (partial) formal representations of the properties of complex attitudes, and the resulting theory is applied to illuminate a number of topics in the philosophy of language.

In "A Study in Comparative Semantics" LePore and Loewer compare the semantical approaches of Frege and Davidson, especially as these pertain to sentences expressing propositional attitudes. Frege claimed that such sentences as

(a) Galileo said that the earth moves

assert a relation between Galileo and the ordinary sense of "the earth moves" (or, what he takes to be the same, the proposition that the earth moves). LePore and Loewer explain the virtues and shortcomings of this approach but with particular emphasis on the way the Fregean theory deals with substitution on, and quantification into, such contexts and with such inferences as that from (a) and

(b) Everything that Galileo said is true

to

(c) The earth moves.

They conclude that initially the Fregean account has considerable plausibility.

Davidson's "paratactic" analysis is considered in special detail, objections are stated and countered, and the ideas are extended to give a formal account of the validity of such inferences as that just explained. The authors conclude about this approach that it too "on first pass" has intuitively impressive credentials and can deal persuasively with a number of initial worries about adequacy.

LePore and Loewer then address in turn Davidson's objections against the Fregean theory and Fregean objections against the Davidsonian theory. They conclude that the objections can be rebuffed in both cases and that if a preference for one approach over the other is to be justified, it will be on the basis of their respective metaphysical and epistemological commitments. The Fregean theory may well strike contemporary philosophers as *unnaturalistic*. But whether this is really so and whether this indicates a telling point in favor of the Davidsonian account is a matter which needs further discussion.

Language and Mind

The papers on language and mind fall naturally into three broad groups: (1) Burge, Stalnaker, Owens, and Wallace/Mason, (2) Donnellan, Salmon, and Schiffer, and (3) Searle and Gunderson.

(1) The first four papers, of Burge, Stalnaker, Owens, and Wallace/Mason, all focus on the role of contextual elements in determining mental content. The issues here were given prominence in a series of articles by Burge, in which he argued that contextual factors contribute to the *individuation*

of mental content (and states) in ways not previously appreciated. According to Burge, mental content is importantly non-individualistic in that subjects ensconced in different environments can differ in their mental states (such as belief) *even though they do not differ in any intrinsic physical properties*. This important and controversial thesis is supported with a series of ingenious thought experiments, of which the following is but one example. Bert, an English speaker, has acquired the word 'arthritis' in a fairly familiar way. He says, and apparently believes, that elderly people are especially afflicted with it, that he has it in his knees, and so on. Experiencing pain in his thigh, and not knowing that arthritis is by definition a disease of the joints, he concludes that the disease has spread to his thigh. Consider now a counterfactual situation in which Bert satisfies all the same nonintentional (and nonrelational) characterizations: he has the same physical makeup, the same experiential state, hears the same sounds, is disposed to the same (nonintentionally characterized) behaviors. In both situations he is disposed to utter, "I have arthritis in my thigh." The only relevant difference between the two situations is in the communal use of the term 'arthritis'. In the counterfactual community it is used to designate a variety of ailments, including that which afflicts Bert. The terms have different meanings in the two communities and we must take this into account in interpreting Bert. In both situations, he utters the same-sounding sentence, "I have arthritis in my thigh." In the actual situation he thereby expresses his belief that he has arthritis in his thigh. In the counterfactual situation he expresses a different belief with this utterance. Thus Bert's belief apparently changes from the one context to the other despite the fact that he remains physically unaltered. To use the current philosophical jargon: beliefs and their contents do not "supervene" on the physical. This "externalist" conception of belief content is at odds with long-standing Cartesian models of the mental. It is thus highly controversial and allegedly even inconsistent with the methodological commitments of recent cognitive science.

In his contribution, "Wherein Is Language Social," Tyler Burge considers once again the role of social context in determining psychological and semantic content. He addresses two specific issues. First, his account of semantic and psychological content is, he argues, compatible with most of the rationalistic and individualistic elements in Chomskian linguistics. Second, he takes up the question of individual psychology in detail, offering a new argument for the anti-individualistic conception of content in a way that makes no essential appeal to the notion of a shared linguistic community. Even if one restricts oneself to content *in a subject's idiolect*, that too appears to be socially determined.

A familiar response to Burge-style arguments has been to grant that he is correct so far as belief *attribution* goes, but to deny that this tells in favor of contextually determined *content*. Simplifying somewhat, we can describe the reply thus. Such theorists readily concede that the propositional (or "wide") content designated by the 'that'-clause in belief ascriptions is contextually determined. But, they argue, genuine psychological content, the content to which we have introspective access, the kind of content that figures in psychological explanation, *that* content, is not contextually determined. This latter, typically now called "narrow content," is constant across the sort of counterfactual contexts described in the Burgian Gedankenexperiments. Thus it is claimed that while Burge's examples do spotlight *one* element in our practice, we can do justice to fundamental intuitions regarding psychological explanation and introspective access to belief only if we employ a different, context-invariant notion of content.

In his paper "Narrow Content," Robert Stalnaker agrees that there is a need for a notion of content which is quite different from full-fledged propositional content. But, he argues, there is no reason to suppose that this other kind of content will be "narrow." There is in fact no reason to think we have a notion of content which is such as to supervene on the physical. Furthermore, he rejects the claim that the wide-content of the kind espoused by Burge is somehow counterintuitive, and urges in particular that such content poses no special problems for our intuitions regarding introspection.

Owens also focuses on the issue of cognitive access, on the kind of access a subject has to such contextually determined content. He agrees with Stalnaker that the contextual determination of content does *not* undermine the access a subject has to the contents of her beliefs. But, he urges that social determination of content does tell against a further kind of access; it tells against the subject having "introspective" access to sameness and difference in her beliefs. The contextual factors that determine wide content will likewise determine sameness and difference in wide content, and, hence, a subject's ability to determine such sameness and difference is contingent upon her awareness of these external factors. Owens argues that full appreciation of this epistemic point opens the way to the resolution of puzzles such as Kripke's well-known conundrum about the semi-bilingual Pierre.

Wallace and Mason object to some basic assumptions implicit in these disputes. They don't deny the anti-individualistic conclusion, and they don't charge Burge and other anti-individualists with actual fallacy. But, they argue, the counterfactual style ("Twin Earth") arguments all rest on the supposition that propositional attitudes have "sharp content," on the supposition that beliefs and other attitudes are states "individuated by content." The supposition of sharp content, which they reject, manifests itself in the assumption (of Burge and other parties to the debate) that there is usually a correct, unqualified, simple "yes" or "no" answer to questions of the form, "Does subject S believe that P?" and "Is S's belief that P the same as S^*'s belief that P^*?" They marshal a number of examples in support of their claim that the assumption of sharp content is unwarranted, that in many cases a flat "yes" or "no" is simply not adequate. Often one can convey the subject's perspective only by telling a fairly complex story, and this story is essential to capturing the subject's perspective; it is not a mere embellishment. The authors recognize that in opting for this more complex account, they are sharply at odds with traditional accounts of belief as a two-place relation.

(2) Donnellan, Salmon and Schiffer are also concerned with problems that plague our understanding of the propositional attitudes, but their specific concern is with the much more familiar problem deriving from Frege: How should the theorist account for the apparent differences in truth conditions between (i) and (ii)?

(i) The ancient astronomer believed that Hesperus is Hesperus.

(ii) The ancient astronomer believed that Hesperus is Phosphorus.

The story, of course, is that (i) appears to be true and (ii) appears to be false, despite the fact that 'Hesperus' and 'Phosphorus' are simply names for one planet.

This problem is particularly acute for Donnellan and Salmon who favor the Millian thesis that proper names are like mere tags in having no semantic value over and above reference. If Mill is correct, proper names should be everywhere interchangeable *salva veritate*, and, in particular, (i) and (ii) should necessarily agree in truth value.

In a famous paper, "A Puzzle About Belief," Saul Kripke sought to undermine Frege's objections to such interchanges. Kripke recognized the fact that interchanging names in such sentences does generate puzzles. How, for example, can we say of the ancient astronomer that he believed that Hesperus is Phosphorus given that he would staunchly dissent from "Hesperus is Phosphorus" (on its translation)? Kripke's argument was that this should not be taken to tell against interchange since the same kind of puzzle can be generated without any reliance on interchange; all one needs are some relatively uncontroversial principles of translation and disquotation. And, furthermore, the Fregean needs these same principles to mount his objection to interchange. There is no reason, Kripke suggests, to think that interchange poses any special problems; the problems arise not from interchanging proper names, but from the very concept of belief itself.

In "Belief and the Identity of Reference," Keith Donnellan reexamines Kripke's conclusion that our concept of belief is itself problematic, a source of possible confusion, and he sees this as important in defending Millian intuitions. He rejects, however, Kripke's contention that the Fregean objection relies on the linguistic principle that Kripke employs in his new puzzle. The Fregean puzzle, Donnellan argues, arises from our concept of belief and should not be construed as depending on linguistic principles of disquotation and translation. Donnellan goes on to draw some metaphilosophical parallels between Kripke's puzzle about belief and a more familiar puzzle of identity, the Ship of Theseus.

In his recent book, *Frege's Puzzle*, Nathan Salmon argued that Frege's problem poses no special problems for Millian theorists. If the sentences P

and P^* differ only in having co-designative names interchanged, then the Millian must suppose that they don't differ semantically, that they express the same proposition, and he must treat sentences of the form "S believes that P" and "S believes that P^*" (e.g., (i) and (ii) above) as necessarily equivalent. They assert that the subject stands in the believing relation to one and the same proposition. We can still accommodate our intuition that (i) is appropriate in a way that (ii) is not by introducing a *nonsemantic* value—by recognizing that such sentences may pragmatically convey information that they don't assert. In particular, a belief ascription not only asserts of a subject that he bears the believing relation to a proposition, it also pragmatically suggests or conveys the mode or guise under which the subject accepts the proposition. This is how (i) and (ii) differ, and this is why (ii) is misleading but not false. It *suggests* that the ancient astronomer would have accepted the proposition when it is put to him under the form 'Hesperus is Phosphorus'. He did accept that very proposition, of course, and that is why (ii) is true, but not under that guise or form.

In "A Millian Heir Rejects the Wages of Sinn," Salmon elaborates on some central elements in his theory, offering new examples in support of the analysis and responding to some recent challenges. Of special interest is a new argument for the Millian construal of proper names based on the kinship between ordinary names and individual variables.

Schiffer is also concerned with the Fregean conception of the propositional attitudes, but with something much more fundamental than interchange. He argues that any account of belief which treats belief as a relation between a subject and a proposition (whether the account be of a Fregean sort or of the kind favored say by Salmon) is doomed. Each one of these accounts, different though they be, must do justice to the kind of phenomena Frege cited and, Schiffer argues, they can do this only by introducing "modes of presentation." The problem is that there are no modes of presentation. Something qualifies as a mode of presentation only if it satisfies two constraints (the "Fregean constraint" and the "intrinsic description constraint") and none of the things appealed to as modes of presentation (individual concepts, names, causal claims, stereotypes, functional roles, etc.) satisfy both requirements. There is, he argues, no reason to think anything satisfies these constraints; no reason to think that there are modes of representation. He concludes with some remarks on what he calls a "Pickwickian" version of propositional theory, one that does not require modes of presentation, but which abandons some other elements in the traditional approach, e.g., compositionality.

(3) The final two papers, those of Searle and Gunderson, are concerned with issues in the foundations of cognitive science.

In his paper "Consciousness, Unconsciousness, and Intentionality," John Searle takes the cognitive theorist to task for attempting to provide accounts which make essential appeal to intentional, representational states, while at the same time giving consciousness no explicit role. This theorist works on the assumption that we can come to an understanding of intentionality, of how it as a subject represents her world, without getting mired in problems of consciousness and subjectivity. This Searle rejects: it is, he argues, a conceptual error to think that we can come to an understanding of intentionality without reference to consciousness. Something counts as "intentional" only if it has "aspectual shape," and to have this it must be a possible object of consciousness. Attempts to push consciousness aside as a mere epiphenomenon, as being of little theoretical interest, are, Searle argues, badly mistaken. Consciousness is a necessary ingredient in any plausible account of intentionality.

Gunderson's paper touches on a variety of issues, but, like Searle, his primary concern is to insist on the essential role of consciousness in any adequate accounting of the mental. He looks to both intentional and nonintentional psychological phenomena and argues that a proper understanding of either is possible only if consciousness is given its due. He defends (against Dennett) the intuitive distinction between intrinsic (original) and derived intentionality, and then uses this distinction to attack the adequacy of Artificial Intelligence models of linguistic understanding and communication. There is, he argues, no reason whatsoever to think that these programmed systems, which lack consciousness, have anything other than derivative intentionality. The conscious production and understanding of speech is, for example, characterized by certain deep asymmetries which fail to find any reflection in the AI models. He closes his paper with a discussion of nonintentional psychological phenomena such as pain.

Most of these papers were presented at a conference held at the University of Minnesota, Twin Cities Campus, during October 14–16, 1988. A paper presented at the conference by Aldo Bressan, "New Semantics for the extensional but hyper-intensional part $\mathcal{L}_\alpha$ of the modal sense language $\mathcal{SL}_\alpha^\nu$," was of a rather more technical character than the others and will appear in *Notre Dame Journal of Formal Logic*. The conference was supported by NEH Grant RX-20961, by a generous gift from D. Michael and Sarah Rand Winton, and by the Graduate School and the College of Liberal Arts of the University of Minnesota. For this support the conference organizers (the editors of this volume) are grateful. Special thanks go to Anne Dickason and Debra Dykhuis for their superb help in organizing and running the conference.

C. ANTHONY ANDERSON AND JOSEPH OWENS

1

Quine on Quantifying In

KIT FINE[1]

QUINE'S ARGUMENT AGAINST quantifying into modal contexts can be presented in the following way. Suppose that a statement like $\exists x \,\square\, (x > 7)$ makes sense. Then one should intelligibly be able to ask: for which objects x is the condition $\square\, (x > 7)$ rendered true? But one cannot so ask. Specify the object as '9' and the condition is apparently rendered true; specify the object as 'the number of planets' and the condition is apparently rendered false. Fail to specify the object one way or another and there is no saying whether the condition is rendered true or rendered false.

Central to the argument is a fact about substitution. Upon substituting '9' for 'x', the condition $\square\, (x > 7)$ becomes a true statement; upon substituting 'the number of planets' for 'x', the condition becomes a false statement. Call an instance of such a fact a *failure of substitution*. Call the notion of an object rendering a condition true independently of how it is specified *objectual satisfaction*. Then it is because of the failure of substitution that there is thought to be no coherent notion of objectual satisfaction.

However, there are two quite separate accounts of why the one is a reason for the other. According to the first, the failure of substitution provides a general reason for rejecting the notion of objectual satisfaction. Given such a failure, the occurrence of the term upon which a substitution is made will not be purely referential, it will not be used solely to pick out its object. But given that this is so, we can have no understanding of what it is for an object to satisfy the corresponding condition.

On the other account, the failure of substitution provides a special reason for rejecting the notion of objectual satisfaction in its application

---

[1] I should like to thank the members of a seminar on the philosophy of language at the University of Michigan for many helpful discussions on the topics of this paper; I should also like to thank Graeme Forbes for some helpful remarks. Some of the topics, and some related topics, are discussed at greater length in my "The Problem of *De Re* Modality" [54]. I have allowed myself to be careless about use-mention when nothing turns on being careful.

to necessity conditions. For there is no understanding of *de re* necessity except in terms of *de dicto* necessity, no understanding of what it is for an object to satisfy a necessity condition $\Box\ \psi(x)$ except in terms of the truth of the instances $\Box\ \psi(t)$ (or perhaps of comparable closed sentences in which terms give way to predicates). So given a failure of substitution, the satisfaction of such a condition will arbitrarily depend upon the term (or predicate) by which the object is specified.

The two accounts give rise to very different considerations. The first belongs to the philosophy of language. It is part of the general question of what, if anything, accounts for our understanding of quantification and satisfaction. The second belongs to metaphysics, loosely construed. It is part of the general question of what, if anything, accounts for the existence of necessary *de re* connections.[2]

It is my aim in this paper to evaluate Quine's argument against quantifying into modal contexts, dealing first with the peculiarly modal considerations and then with the more general logical considerations.

The Special Argument

I follow Quine in distinguishing between the strict and the non-strict modalities. The strict modalities include logical and analytic necessity, while the others include natural and metaphysical necessity. I also follow Quine in confining my attention to the strict modalities. Indeed, I shall concentrate on the case of logical necessity, though most of what I want to say will apply without essential modification to the case of analytic necessity.

There is a general difficulty in defending or challenging the intelligibility of any notion. For if the dispute is to have any point, it must be possible to identify the notion in such a way as to not presuppose its intelligibility. One cannot therefore identify the notion in the usual way as "the concept so and so"; for the objector to the notion will fail to attach any reference to the phrase and so will fail to say, in the intended sense, that anything is unintelligible.

The obvious way out of this difficulty is to make the dispute about words. The proponent of the notion will have his chosen way of expressing it. He will therefore take the chosen form of words to be intelligible, while his opponent will not.

But there is a danger in this way out. For it mixes up two distinct questions: one is the intelligibility of an idea without regard for how it might be expressed; the other is the intelligibility of a form of words without regard

---

[2] It was Kaplan, in "Quantifying In" (p. 41 of Linsky [112]), who first made explicit the different considerations to which the two kinds of reason give rise. See R. Barcan Marcus's "A Backward Look at Quine's Animadversions on Modalities" (forthcoming) for an account of the transition from one reason to the other in Quine's work.

for what it might express. It is perfectly conceivable that a philosopher might find the chosen form of words intelligible, not because he found the notion under dispute intelligible, but because he took the words to express some other notion altogether. Likewise, it is perfectly conceivable that a philosopher might find the chosen form of words unintelligible, not because he found the notion unintelligible, but because he thought the words incapable of expressing the notion or, indeed, any notion at all.

These possibilities need to be taken seriously in the case of *de re* necessity. For suppose our chosen form of words is '$\Box\ \psi(x)$'. Then someone who accepts Quine's general argument from substitutivity may find these words unintelligible and yet still believe in necessary fulfillment. Indeed, Quine was in this position in *Word and Object*, though in regard to belief and not modality. Or again, someone who rejects Quine's general argument from substitutivity may find the words intelligible and yet disbelieve in necessary fulfillment. Indeed, Carnap was in this position in *Meaning and Necessity*, since the satisfaction of the condition $\Box\ \psi(x)$ would depend upon the intension associated with the variable x.

If a particular form of words gives rise to a possible misunderstanding, then another form of words may be chosen in its place. So in the present case, instead of saying 'x satisfies $\Box\ \psi(x)$', we may use a relational idiom and say 'x necessarily fulfills $\psi(x)$'. Indeed, it was just by means of this alternative wording that I attempted to draw the contrast between the acceptance of the original form of words and the acceptance of the notion.

Now it is true that the peculiar difficulties concerning substitutivity are avoided upon the adoption of this new form of words. But the general difficulties in identifying the notion under dispute are not so readily avoided. For either the chosen form of words is simple or it is complex. Suppose it is complex. Then there are again two cases; either the construction from simpler elements is problematic, or it is unproblematic. If the construction of problematic, then there is the danger of interference from the different ways in which the expression might be understood. If the construction is unproblematic, then the question reduces to the intelligibility of the simpler elements and might as well have been stated in those terms in the first place. Suppose, on the other hand, that the expression is simple. It is then hard to see what the dispute is about. For what common understanding of the simple expression is it that falls short of a grasp of its meaning and yet enables the parties to the dispute to sensibly debate its intelligibility?

Suppose, for example, that we take the predicate for necessary fulfillment to be primitive. Then what is to stop someone saying that the predicate is intelligible on the grounds that an object necessarily fulfills a condition just in case it actually fulfills the condition, or even just in case it fails to fulfill the condition? What is it in our common understanding of the predicate which serves to rule out such interpretations?

It is clear, once this line of reasoning is pursued, that the proper formulation of disputes over intelligibility is in terms of an identifying set of desiderata. The question is ultimately not about a form of words, but about the existence of an intelligible notion which conforms to certain desiderata. Traditional disputes over intelligibility are best seen in this way. Infinitesimals are what conform to the demands of proof in which they are used; the self is something which, in an appropriate sense, is "beyond" experience; and so on.

In the present case, it seems possible to give a rather sharp formulation of the desiderata by which the *de re* notion of logical necessity is to be identified. There are notions of truth and of satisfaction. There is also a notion of logical truth, which stands in a certain relationship to the notion of truth. The question then is whether there is anything that stands in the same relationship to the notion of satisfaction. Is there anything that is to satisfaction what logical truth is to truth?[3]

Other issues of intelligibility also take this special form. We may ask: is there an intelligible notion of subtraction on the real numbers, or on the cardinal numbers (transfinite or finite)? This question may then be put in the form: is there a notion that is to addition on the reals (or on the cardinals) as subtraction on integers is to addition on integers?

Of course, we have here only a scheme. To get a definite question, we must say what relationship it is that holds between the original pair of notions, and in such a way as not arbitrarily to limit its application. This can be done for the case of numbers. For the result of subtracting b from a should be the solution x of the equation $b + x = a$. We see then, on this construal of the question, that there is an intelligible notion of subtraction for the reals but no intelligible notion of subtraction for the cardinals (even with the restriction that $a \geq b$).

Something similar can be done for the logical notions. Logical truth is truth that can be determined on the the the basis of logical form. Logical satisfaction is therefore satisfaction that can be determined on the basis of logical form. Our question is therefore whether we can meaningfully single out a special subclass of the relationships of satisfaction, those that can be determined on the basis of logical form.

Now it might be thought evident, once the question is put this way, that there is no such intelligible notion of logical satisfaction. For the notion of logical form only properly applies to sentences and to other parts of speech (or perhaps to what they convey). So how can we even talk of logical form for a relationship of satisfaction that is capable of holding between an ordinary physical object, let us say, and a condition?

But matters are not so simple. Suppose that we have a relationship of satisfaction, one that holds between a single object a and a condition $\phi(x)$. Then the question is: when we attempt to determine whether the relationship holds on the basis of logical form, what is it that is meant to

---

[3] We shall not make anything of a distinction, which might be drawn, between logical truth and logical necessity.

have the logical form, what should we look at? Now one might wrap up the object and the condition into a single entity, perhaps the ordered pair $\langle a, \phi(x) \rangle$, and scrutinize that for logical form. And one might then decide, given the non-linguistic nature of the object a, that the single entity had no logical form and that there was therefore no logical form on the basis of which the relationship of satisfaction could be determined to hold.

But such a response cannot be right. For there is a notion of logical implication which stands to material implication as logical truth stands to truth. Now suppose we follow the same strategy in determining whether the sentence ϕ logically implies the sentence ψ. We will then wrap up the two sentences into a single entity, say $\langle \phi, \psi \rangle$, and go by the logical form of that single entity. But if logical form only properly applies to entities of a linguistic nature, then the non-linguistic nature of the ordered pair, or some comparable entity, is as much an impediment to crediting it with logical form as is the non-linguistic nature of one of its constituents. We will therefore incorrectly conclude that there is no coherent notion of logical implication.

It is clearly arbitrarily restrictive to suppose that the logical form on the basis of which a logical relationship is determined to hold should be that of a single entity. We should instead be allowed to look separately at the logical form of the relata. Thus if the sequence of relata is $a_1, \ldots, a_n$, then the information we should extract is a corresponding sequence $\alpha_1, \ldots, \alpha_n$ of logical forms.[4]

There still remains a difference, under such an approach, between the relations of logical satisfaction and of logical implication. For with the case of implication, both relata possess logical form; while in the case of satisfaction, only one of the relata will.

However, it is not clear that this should count as a reason for ignoring the logical form of *both* of the relata; it might simply be regarded as a reason for taking account of the logical form of only one of the relata. We thus arrive at what I call the *object-blind* account of logical satisfaction. A condition will be satisfied by an object and, in general, by a sequence of

---

[4] This raises another problem, for the sequence of forms needs to be properly coordinated. If, for example, '$\neg$(2 is even)' is to logically imply '$\neg\neg\neg$(2 is even)', then we need to know that the constituents in the logical forms that correspond to the two occurrences of '2 is even' are appropriately correlated. It is usual to think of the (most Fine-grained) logical form of an expression as unique. But this is not a conception of logical form which will permit the proper coordination. For we must then say that '2 is even' and '2 is odd' have the same logical form and so will be incapable of distinguishing between '2 is even' logically implying '2 is even' and '2 is even' logically implying '2 is odd'. What then distinguishes the two cases is that in the first we have the same duplicate forms, while in the second we have appropriately different duplicate forms. However, this is a general problem about the concept of form, and has no special bearing on the particular problem at hand.

objects just in case it can be determined to be so satisfied on the basis of the logical form of the condition alone.

On such a conception, many conditions will be logically satisfied; for example, a condition of the form '$Fx \lor \neg Fx$' will be logically satisfied by any object. However, there will be no distinction among satisfiers; if one sequence logically satisfies a condition, then so does any sequence. Indeed, a condition $\phi(x_1, \ldots, x_n)$ will be logically satisfied by a sequence just in case the universal sentence $\forall x_1 \ldots \forall x_n \phi(x_1, \ldots, x_n)$ is logically true.

So we see that even if we restrict logical form to linguistic items, it is still possible to make out an intelligible notion of logical satisfaction.

However, I am inclined to think that the principal assumption of the object-blind account, that the objects make no contribution to logical form, is itself in error and that the account is therefore to be rejected. The issue turns on what should be taken to be the more basic bearers of logical form—physical tokens or abstract types (or meanings). All can agree that there is a sense in which sentence tokens have logical form and also a sense in which sentence types have logical form. But do we attribute a logical form to a sentence token because it is a token of a type with that form or do we attribute a logical form to a sentence type because it is a type of a token with that form? Should we think of the types as codifying the logical form of the tokens or, alternatively, should we think of the tokens as representing the logical form of the types?

If we adopt the former view, that the tokens come first, then it does indeed seem reasonable that the objects should be ignored in any account of logical satisfaction. For take satisfaction, logical or otherwise, to be a relation between a sequence of objects and a condition. (It would not matter, for my purposes, if we took the first relatum to be something like an assignment of objects to variables). In a sequence $a, a, \ldots$ beginning with an identical pair of objects, can we now recognize the re-occurrence of the object a as part of the logical form of the sequence? Should logical form be primarily attributable to tokens, then re-occurrence, in the sense that is relevant to the determination of logical form, would appear to consist in the occurrence of appropriately similar physical tokens: in an identity sentence '$t = t$', for example, it is the occurrence of two appropriately similar tokens of 't' that helps define its logical form. But it is not in this way that we have a re-occurrence of objects in the sequence; and so it is not clear that the re-occurrence of objects in the sequence can, with equal legitimacy, be taken to help define its logical form.

Suppose, on the other hand, that we adopt the much more plausible view that it is the types (or the meanings) that come first. Then there would appear to be no good grounds for distinguishing between the re-occurrence of an object in a sequence and the re-occurrence of a constituent in a sentence-type (or proposition). Indeed, if we took a sentence-type simply to be a sequence of symbols, then the two notions of re-occurrence would be exactly the same. But even without such a conception of sentences, it would still appear to be in the same abstract sense that we may talk of re-occurrence in the two cases.

We are therefore led, on this alternative view, to what I call the *object-sensitive* account of logical satisfaction. A condition will be satisfied by a sequence of objects just in case it can be determined to be satisfied on the basis of the logical form both of the condition and of the objects. The logical form of the sequence will be given by the pattern of identities and difference, i.e., by which members of the sequence are the same and which distinct. So the condition '$x = y$' will be logically satisfied by the sequence a, a, since it is part of the logical form of the sequence that its two members (which are respectively assigned to x and to y) are the same; and similarly the condition '$\neg(x = y)$' is logically satisfied by the sequence a, b, for a distinct from b. In general, let $\pi(a_1, \ldots, a_n)$ be the statement that says which of the objects $a_1, \ldots, a_n$ are the same and which distinct. Then the condition $\phi(x_1, \ldots, x_n)$ will be logically satisfied by the sequence $a_1, \ldots, a_n$ just in case the sentence $\forall x_1 \ldots \forall x_n(\pi(x_1, \ldots, x_n) \to \phi(x_1, \ldots, x_n))$ is a logical truth.

We therefore see that there is a perfectly intelligible notion of logical satisfaction, even if there is some doubt as to whether it should be object-sensitive or object-blind.

What then of Quine's objections? He has argued that such a notion can only be purchased at a certain cost, the commitment to Aristotelian essentialism. One must adopt "an invidious attitude toward certain ways of uniquely specifying" an object, seeing these ways, rather than others, "as somehow better revealing its 'essence'" ([142], p. 155; [143], pp. 173–4).

But the force of the objection in the present case is far from clear. First, we may note that if it is the logical satisfaction of a condition by a *single* object that is in question, then no discriminatory, let alone invidious, attitude toward ways of specifying the object is required. An object will logically satisfy a condition $\phi(x)$, on either the object-blind or the object-sensitive account, just in case the corresponding closed sentence $\forall x \phi(x)$ is logically true, and hence regardless of how the object might be specified.

When we turn to logical satisfaction by a sequence, the situation is somewhat different. On the object-blind account, again no discrimination is required. But on the object-sensitive account, it is. For the specification of a pair of objects as the same, should they be the same, or as distinct, should they be distinct, will possess a special status; such specifications can indeed be seen to somehow better reveal the essence of the objects.

So such an attitude is discriminatory. But is it invidious, without good reason, and therefore bad? If we were simply to stipulate that certain specifications were to be given a special status, then that would be objectionable; or if we were arbitrarily to presuppose that certain specifications were special, then that again would be objectionable. But we do neither. We explain the notion of logical satisfaction in terms of logical form; no special specifications of objects are either stipulated or presupposed. Rather, it is a natural consequence of the account, not an arbitrary feature of its formulation, that identity and distinctness turn out to have a special status.

Quine's misgivings do indeed have some force in regard to the *de re* application of *metaphysical* necessity. We may want to say that 9 is necessarily greater than 7, but not necessarily the number of planets. And how can this be so unless a special status of the one specification of the object over the other is somehow presupposed? But in regard to the *de re* application of *logical* necessity, the very kind of modality that is Quine's primary concern, it would seem that similar misgivings are without foundation.

The General Argument

I turn now to the logical version of Quine's argument against quantifying into modal contexts. The argument may be broken down into five steps:

(1)   It is claimed that occurrences of singular terms within modal contexts are not open to substitution—replacement with co-referential terms will not in general preserve truth-value.

(2)   From this it is inferred that such occurrences of terms are not purely referential—they are not used solely to pick out their object.

(3)   From this it is inferred that the corresponding occurrences of variables are not purely referential—they are not used solely to pick out their values.

(4)   From this it is inferred that the concept of objectual satisfaction is not meaningfully applicable to the condition formed with the help of the variables.

(5)   From this it is then inferred that quantification with respect to these variables is incoherent.

I should first like to discuss some of the general issues raised by this argument, considering each of the steps in turn. The main upshot of the discussion will be that the argument only goes through once a certain requirement of uniformity is presupposed. With this and other qualifications in mind, I would then like to discuss the application of the argument to the question of quantifying into modal and other problematic contexts.

Step (1). *The failure of substitutivity.*

Quine's standard example concerns the number of planets: it is necessary that 9 is greater than 7 and yet not necessary that the number of planets is greater then 7, even though 9 is in fact the number of planets.

To such examples it is often objected that they depend upon adopting a narrow scope reading of the critical terms. Employ a wide scope reading instead and the failure of substitution disappears. It will be necessary that 9 is greater than 7; and it will also be necessary that the number of planets is greater than 7.

Since this point has been the source of so much misunderstanding, it may be worthwhile to consider it with some care. It may be agreed that the intelligibility of the wide scope reading and of the quantification into the modal context stand or fall together: if the one is intelligible then so is the other. If therefore Quine's argument has depended upon excluding the wide scope reading, i.e., if it had been one of its assumptions that the wide scope reading was not available, then the argument would clearly have been circular. But it depends upon no such assumption. For the purposes of his argument, Quine can afford to be agnostic about the existence of the wide scope reading; he need merely insist on the legitimacy of the narrow scope reading and on the consequent failure of substitution for it.

Of course, if the argument succeeds, if it is shown that quantification into modal contexts is unintelligible, then the wide scope reading is thereby also excluded—but as a consequence of the argument, not as an assumption. Someone who holds to the intelligibility of the wide scope reading is therefore objecting to the conclusion of the argument. If he would maintain his position, then it remains incumbent upon him to show what is wrong with the argument itself.

Step (2). *The inference to the irreferentiality of singular terms.*

The reader could be forgiven for thinking this step innocuous. For does not the irreferentiality of the occurrence of the given term simply follow by definition from the failure of substitution?

But it has to be recognized that there are two concepts of referentiality, one informal and the other technical. According to the technical concept, an occurrence of a singular term in a sentence is purely referential if the truth-value of the sentence is preserved upon the substitution of co-referential terms. According to the informal concept, an occurrence of a singular term in a sentence is purely referential if it "is used purely to specify its object, for the rest of the sentence to say something about" (Quine [141], p. 177). These two concepts are different in character: one concerns the behavior of the sentence under substitution; the other concerns the role of the singular term.

If referentiality is taken in the technical sense, then irreferentiality of the occurrence of the term does indeed follow by definition. However, it is irreferentiality of the occurrence in the informal sense that is relevant to the cogency of the argument; it is this that makes the unintelligibility of quantifying in plausible. And it is therefore for this sense of referentiality that the validity of the present step needs to be considered.

But once it is, we see that there are clear counter-examples. I shall present four cases in all, each illustrating a somewhat different way in which a term may occur referentially in the face of a failure of substitution.

(1) The first example comes from arithmetic (with the usual conventions governing the scope of '+' and '×'). The sentence '$2 \times 2 = 4$' is true; the terms '2' and '$1 + 1$' are co-referential; and yet the result '$1 + 1 \times 2 = 4$' of substituting one term for the other is false. So there is a failure of substitution, even though the initial occurrence of '2' is referential.

(2) For the purposes of the next example, we must imagine that three men are in a line, with Bill at the back and Fred at the front. Suppose now that Fred leaves. Then the sentence 'The man behind Fred saw him leave' is presumably true; the terms 'The man behind Fred' and 'The man before Bill' are co-referential; and yet the resultant sentence 'The man before Bill saw him leave' is false. So again there is a failure of substitution, even though no one would doubt that the initial occurrence of 'The man behind Fred' was referential.

(3) The third example is taken from the old notation for pounds, shillings, and pence (which some of us still remember). Under this notation, '1d' would be used to denote one pence, and '1/1d' would be used to denote one shilling and one pence, or thirteen pence in all. Bearing this in mind, we have the following: the sentence '1d was Kit Fine's pocket money in 1952' is true; the terms '1' and '1/1' are co-referential, at least in the sense that the identity sentence '$1 = 1/1$' is unequivocally true; and yet the sentence '1/1d was Kit Fine's pocket money in 1952' is, alas, not true. So substitution fails with the initial '1' referential.

(4) The final example comes from Hebrew (and was produced to my specifications by Ran Lahav). In Hebrew the word 'TSAFA' can either be the present, third person, feminine form of a verb meaning to float, or it can be the past, third person, masculine form of a verb meaning to observe. The word for moon can either be 'YARE'ACH', which is in the masculine, or 'LEVANA', which is in the feminine. So we see that: the sentence 'The moon (LEVANA) floats (TSAFA) in the sky (RAKEIA)' is true, with the occurrence of 'LEVANA' referential; the terms 'LEVANA' and 'YARE'ACH' are co-referential; and yet the sentence 'The moon (YARE'ACH) observed (TSAFA) the sky (RAKEIA)' is false.

It is tempting not to take these examples seriously, since they are clearly not the kind of case that Quine had in mind in formulating his test for irreferentiality. But in fact the examples pose a serious challenge to the intended applications of the test. For how do we know that they are not similarly aberrant, though in a less blatant way?

So what has gone wrong? When we examine each example in turn, we see that the substitution for the given singular term has unintended consequences. In the first example, '$2 \times 2 = 4$', there is a shift in the syntactic status of the subject-expression. Upon substitution, it changes from occurring as a constituent singular term to not even occurring as a constituent at all.

In the second example, 'The man behind Fred saw him leave', there is a shift in the syntactic status, not of the the subject-expression, but of the remaining predicate-expression. Upon substitution, the pronoun 'him' in 'saw him leave' gets to stand in an anaphoric relationship to 'Bill' rather than to 'Fred'.

In the third example, '1d was Kit Fine's pocket money in 1952', there is no external shift in the syntactic status of the subject-expression and no internal shift in the syntactic status of the predicate-expression. Instead, the referent of the subject-expression changes from being the number 1 to being the vector of 1 and 1.

In the final example, 'LEVANA TSAFA RAKEIA', there is a semantic shift in the predicate-expression; 'TSAFA' goes from meaning *float* to meaning *observe*.

In each of the counter-examples, there is an unintended shift in either the syntactic or in the semantic analysis of the given sentence. So if the counter-examples are to be avoided, a certain requirement of uniformity should be imposed; it should be insisted that the given and the resultant sentences "work in the same way." If the given sentence is $\phi(s)$ and the resultant sentence is $\phi(t)$, then the syntactico-semantic analysis of the context $\phi(\ )$ of $\phi(s)$ should be the same as the syntactico-semantic analysis of the context $\phi(\ )$ of $\phi(t)$, with the one context "feeding off" its term s in exactly the same way the other context "feeds off" its term t.

Step (3). *From the irreferentiality of the term to the irreferentiality of the variable.*

We may take the occurrence of a variable in a formula to be referential if it is used solely to pick out its value (for the rest of the formula, under an assignment of values, to say something about). This is the analogue of the informal concept of referentiality for closed terms. There is also an analogue of the technical concept. The occurrence of a variable x in $\phi(x)$ is referential in this sense iff the sentences $\forall x \forall y(x = y \rightarrow (\phi(x) \leftrightarrow \phi(y)))$, for y any variable distinct from x, are true (cf. Quine [141], p. 167).

Just as with the term-to-term case, several examples of anomalous contexts can be given to show that irreferentiality of a closed term does not imply irreferentiality of the variable. One example, amusingly enough, derives from Quine's notation for quasi-quotation. Under this notation, the metalinguistic variable 'α' has a referential occurrence in '$\ulcorner \alpha \urcorner$ is a term', but the corresponding term '0' in '$\ulcorner 0 \urcorner$ is a term' has an irreferential occurrence.

Another example, discussed as such by Kaplan in "Opacity" [93], arises from the "suggestion for notational efficiency" from footnote 3 of his earlier paper "Quantifying In" [90]. According to this suggestion, 'the number of planets' will have an irreferential occurrence in 'Necessarily, the number of planets is greater than 7', but 'x' will have a referential occurrence in 'Necessarily, x is greater than 7', since it is treated as shorthand for 'x is such as to be necessarily greater than 7'.

A third example comes from arithmetic. The variable 'x' has a referential occurrence in '$2 \times x > 0$', but the term '$1 + 1$' does not even have a constituent occurrence in '$2 \times 1 + 1 > 0$'.

Again, I would propose getting around such counter-examples by imposing a requirement of uniformity. The syntactico-semantic analysis of the context must remain the same under substitution and must operate on the variable in the same way that it operates on the term.

Step (4). *From the irreferentiality of the variable to the non-objectuality of satisfaction.*

The terms 'referential' and 'objectual' are often used interchangeably in connection with the variables of quantification. But given the natural explanation of these terms, it is possible to draw a subtle but significant distinction between them.

A variable is referential, it will be recalled, if it is used solely to pick out its value. On the other hand, for satisfaction to be objectual it must be a relation that holds between a condition and an assignment of objects from the domain of quantification to the variables. Such a constraint on the form of the relation excludes two main possibilities. The first is that satisfaction should depend upon the manner in which the value of the variable is specified. The second is that the value of a variable should be anything other than an object from the domain; it should not, for example, be a term or a concept for such an object.

However, such a constraint does not guarantee that the variables should be referential. True, satisfaction cannot depend upon the manner in which the value of a variable is specified nor upon a non-objectual value. But it may depend upon the variable itself; and so the variable, through its very identity, can make a contribution to the conditions of satisfaction that goes beyond its value.

Variables which are objectual without being referential I call *literalist*. It is important to appreciate that the use of literalist variables gives rise to a genuinely new form of quantification. Philosophers are familiar with various non-objectual alternatives to referential quantification, such as the substitutional interpretation or Carnap's method of extension and intension. But the literalist quantifiers provide an objectual alternative to referential quantification. The values of the variables are standard. The clause for the quantifier is standard; an existential formula $\exists x \phi(x)$, for example, is satisfied by an assignment just in case the condition $\phi(x)$ is satisfied by an appropriate variant of the assignment. It is just that the variable, through its own identity, can make a contribution to the satisfaction conditions.

We shall later give some modal examples of literalist quantification. A simple non-modal example, suggested to me by Allen Hazen, arises from the use of a many-sorted language in which the domains can overlap. Perhaps we have a sort for numbers and a sort for sets under a logicist construal of numbers as sets. Notwithstanding the overlap of the domains, we may wish '$x = n$' always to be false when the 'x' and 'n' are of different sorts. In such a way, we could permit within the meta-language ("off-stage") a reduction of numbers to sets and yet not accept within the object-language ("on-stage") that any number was identical to a set. On a referential treatment of the variables, no such account is possible. But on a literalist treatment, it offers no special difficulties; for we can take it to be part of the satisfaction conditions for the identity formula '$x = n$' that the variables 'x' and 'n' should be of the same sort.

Another non-modal example, though of a more sophisticated kind, arises from the theory of truth. We may so use the truth-predicate T that the formula $T\alpha$ is satisfied by an assignment θ just in case (i) a formula ϕ of the object-language is assigned to the meta-linguistic variable α, (ii) individuals from the domain of the object-language are assigned to the free variables $x_1, \ldots, x_n$ of ϕ, and (iii) the assignment of those individuals to $x_1, \ldots, x_n$ satisfies ϕ. (Succinctly put, $\theta \models T\alpha$ iff $\theta \models \theta(\alpha)$). On a referential treatment of variables, such an interpretation of the truth-predicate is incoherent, since the satisfaction of the formula $T\alpha$ does not simply depend upon the formula assigned to α. But on a literalist treatment, in which α serves not only to contribute the formula which is its value but also the assignment of values to the free variables of that formula, the interpretation is unproblematic.

It is not necessarily possible to tell from the content of the satisfaction conditions alone whether or not the variables are referential. The point may be illustrated by means of our previous example concerning a many-sorted language. Where α and β are any two variables, an identity formula $\alpha = \beta$ will be said to be satisfied by an assignment just in case (i) the objects assigned to both α and β are the same, and (ii) the sorts of α and β are the same. But how does this result come about? What is the division of linguistic labor? One view is that the variables have a double linguistic role: to pick out their value and to pick out their sort. The identity predicate then picks out a relation that holds of object, sort and object, sort just when the objects are the same and the sorts are the same. The other view is that the variables have a single linguistic role: to pick out their value. However, it is part of the linguistic role of the identity predicate to "look at" the sorts of the variables. It is not that the variables supply the sorts; the identity-predicate takes its own initiative in seeking them out.

On the first of these views, the variable is literalist; but on the second, it remains referential. The notion of a literalist variable stands in contrast, if you like, to the technical and the informal notions of referentiality. So a variable may be literalist in contrast to the technical notion of referentiality and yet still fail to be literalist in contrast to the informal notion.

Step (5). *From the non-objectuality of satisfaction to the impossibility of quantification.*

Several philosophers have attempted to disarm Quine's argument by appeal to a non-objectual account of quantification. They have supposed, for example, that the quantifiers should be substitutional or that the variables should be assigned both a sense and a reference as values. The question therefore arises as to whether it is just a matter for decision how the quantifiers are to be interpreted or whether it is in some sense an objective matter.

It is hard to extract from Quine's writings any compelling reason for taking the quantifiers to be objectual; and so his arguments would only appear to show that objectual quantification into modal contexts is to be rejected, not any kind of quantification whatever. However, there seems to be a way of giving objective meaning to the question of how the quantifiers are to be interpreted. For we may require that the interpretation of the quantified statement, $\exists x\phi(x)$ let us say, should be uniform with that of its instances. Our understanding of the general use of variables should conspire, along with our understanding of a particular closed sentence $\phi(t)$, to produce the required understanding of the quantified sentence $\exists x\phi(x)$.

But in what does that uniform interpretation consist? The closed term t will make a certain contribution to our understanding of the sentence $\phi(t)$. We may now recognize a certain range of variation, not in how the contribution is made but in what it is. The variable will then make an identical contribution within the given range of variation in a way that is fixed, not by the language itself, but by a hypothetical specification or assignment.

However, this construal of the issue is not one that especially favors the objectual interpretation of the quantifier. Insofar as it is recognized that a closed term can occur irreferentially, it should equally well be recognized that a quantifiable variable can occur irreferentially; for the variable may work, relative to an appropriate kind of assignment, in the same way as the term. It is therefore perfectly conceivable that the resulting interpretation of the variable should be non-objectual. Suppose, for example that we follow Carnap in taking a term to pick out both an intension and an extension. Then on the corresponding uniform interpretation of the quantifier, the variable will be assigned both an intension and an extension as values, and so is clearly non-objectual.

Cases

We come finally to the application of the considerations of the previous section. We take up three kinds of question in all. First, are terms within the given problematic contexts referential? Second, is formal quantification into the context possible? Third, is ordinary language quantification into the context possible? In the case of each kind of question, we consider three kinds of context: those generated by quotation; those generated by Quine's Giorgione-example, 'Giorgione is so-called because of his size'; and those generated by modality. Each kind of context has a certain intrinsic interest and serves to illustrate somewhat different points.

Two novel aspects of our approach should be noted. The first is that the application of Quine's test for irreferentiality will be made to depend upon the appropriate uniformity assumption, either from term-to-term or from term-to-variable. Although this qualification may appear slight, it makes an enormous difference to the epistemological status of the test. For its application now depends not only on the "empirical" matter of the truth-values of certain sentences, but also on the "theoretical" matter of how they function.

Secondly, we shall be careful to distinguish between three sources from which the problematic cases can come. The first is ordinary language, in our case English; the second is Loglish, the result of adjoining variables and formal quantifiers to English; and the third is Modalese, the "pure" language of quantified modal logic. These source languages differ in the extent to which their interpretation is "up to us" and hence differ in regard to how the appropriate uniformity assumption might plausibly be maintained.

Referentiality of Terms

It will be recalled that the inference from the failure of substitution to irreferentiality only goes through under the assumption of uniformity. This may make one wonder whether the substitution test for irreferentiality is ever of any use. For how can one tell that $\phi(s)$ and $\phi(t)$ are uniform unless one already knows how s and t are functioning in their respective sentences?

But the fact remains that one may know (or have good reason to believe) that the terms s and t function in the same way without knowing what that way is. A good illustration is provided by the case of quotation. The sentence " 'Tully' has five letters" is true; the corresponding sentence " 'Cicero' had five letters" is false. But it is plausible to maintain that the two sentences are uniform, especially under the assumption that one of the terms is referential. It may therefore be argued that neither term is referential, that neither term is being used solely to refer to the man.

But note that such an argument only makes plausible the conclusion that the terms are not *standardly* referential, that they are not being used within the quotation context to refer to what they standardly are used to refer to. The argument still leaves room for the Fregean hypothesis that the terms within quotation contexts are non-standardly referential, that they are being used to refer, not to their standard referents, but to the expressions themselves.

A case where the assumption of uniformity is much less plausible is provided by the Giorgione-contexts. Quine [139] (p. 140) asks us to consider the sentence 'Giorgione is so-called because of his size'. This is a truth. But upon substitution of the co-referential term 'Barbarelli', it converts to a falsehood. Should we therefore conclude that the given occurrence of 'Giorgione' is not purely referential?

Quine thinks we should. Indeed, he suggests that the term is only partly referential: it is used to pick out its object; but it is not solely so used. It seems that the term makes a double contribution to what the sentence says: it picks out its object; and it picks out, or presents, itself. The rest of the sentence then says of the two things picked out by the subject-term that the first is called the second because of its size.

But there is a far more plausible account of how the sentence functions, one that would make the term referential and would consequently lead us to reject the assumption of uniformity upon which the inference to irreferentiality depends. On this alternative account, the term 'Giorgione' is used solely to pick out its referent. However, the expression 'so' in 'so-called' is used to refer to that term. So what the rest of the sentence says of the referent Giorgione is that it is called 'Giorgione' because of its size. The sentence attributes a property to a single thing picked out by the subject-term, not a relation to a pair of things picked out by the subject-term.[5]

The case of terms within modal contexts raises somewhat different considerations. When the terms are descriptions, as in 'Necessarily, the number of planets is greater than seven', there is the possibility of both a wide and a narrow scope reading. Should the descriptions be given a wide scope reading, there will be no failure of substitution and hence no way of establishing irreferentiality on the basis of the substitution test. However, one cannot conclude that the descriptions occur referentially, though this is a view with some independent plausibility.

Should the descriptions be given a narrow scope reading, then there may be a failure of substitution. For example, the substitution of 'the sum of seven and two' for 'the number of planets', in the above example, converts a falsehood into a truth. It seems plausible, in such cases, to suppose that the syntactico-semantic context remains the same. We may therefore conclude that the descriptions in these contexts do not occur as referential terms (though it is still possible, of course, that they occur as referential quantifiers).

When the term within the modal context is a proper name, it is not clear whether both a wide and a narrow scope reading are available. Is there a reading (wide scope) on which 'Necessarily, Cicero = Tully' is true, and also a reading (narrow scope) on which it is false? If one thinks there is, then there exist the same reasons as in the case of descriptions for denying referentiality to the names on a narrow scope reading. If one thinks otherwise, then the argument to irreferentiality from the failure of substitution will not go through.

It might be thought that, in such a case, one could argue for irreferentiality on the basis of the substitution of a description for a proper name. 'Necessarily, Cicero = Cicero' is true; 'Necessarily, the most famous Roman orator = Cicero' is false; and therefore the initial occurrence of 'Cicero' is irreferential. Indeed, Quine's original argument was of this sort, with the description 'the number of planets' being substituted for the name '9', although in fairness to Quine it should be pointed out that he took the sentence '9 > 7' to be analytic and so presumably regarded the numeral as an appropriately disguised description.

However, such an argument would be extremely weak. For it rests upon the assumption that names work in the same way as descriptions with narrow scope. And it is hard to see how this can be the case, even

---

[5] A similar suggestion has been made by R. H. Thomason in "Home is Where the Heart Is" [182].

with all other considerations put aside, given that substitution holds up for names but not for descriptions.

Autonomous Quantification

We wish to know what Quine's argument can tell us about the intelligibility of such statements as $\exists x\phi(x)$ where $\phi(x)$ is one of the problematic contexts. The question divides according to whether the interpretation of quantification is autonomous or uniform. Under a uniform interpretation, our understanding of the quantified statement $\exists x\phi(x)$ is implicit in the understanding of its instances; the condition to which the quantifier '$\exists x$' applies is determined in conformity with the meaning of its instances $\phi(t)$. Under an autonomous interpretation, on the other hand, our understanding of the quantified statement $\exists x\phi(x)$ is unconstrained by the understanding of its instances; we are free to let the condition to which the quantifier applies be anything we like.

Let us consider first the possibility of autonomous quantification. In this case, it is quite clear that Quine's argument from the failure of substitution or from the irreferentiality of the singular term is powerless to demonstrate the unintelligibility of the quantification; for, as we have seen, it is critical to the argument that the quantified statement should be uniform with that of its instances. Indeed, Quine himself concedes as much. For he writes ([139], p. 150): "Nonsense is indeed mere absence of sense, and can always be remedied by arbitrarily assigning some sense." Here, we may suppose, the absent sense is that which should have accrued from a uniform interpretation, and the assigned sense is that which could accrue from an autonomous interpretation.

But arbitrary as they are, autonomous interpretations are not without their interest; and we would do well to consider some of the different ways in which they might be provided. Under the substitutional account of the quantifier, there is a single natural way of providing an autonomous interpretation for all contexts. For we may so understand $\phi(x)$ that $\exists x\phi(x)$ is true iff some instance $\phi(t)$ is true. Of course, there is uniformity here of sorts. But it applies across contexts and not, in the required way, from quantified statement to instance.

For other conceptions of the quantifier, such sweeping generality is not attainable; so let us consider the case of the autonomous referential account as standing in greatest contrast, in this respect, to the substitutional account.

Since the quantifier $\exists x$ is to be referential, the satisfaction of the condition $\phi(x)$ depends only upon the values assigned to its free variables. But the question is: what are the satisfaction conditions for $\phi(x)$, given that they are not implicit in our understanding of the instances $\phi(t)$? The problem can be represented as one of translation: how can the condition $\phi(x)$ be "reorganized" so that the satisfaction conditions are now apparent from the instances?

It may well be possible to deal with this question in a highly systematic and rigorous manner; but let me limit myself here to making some general remarks and considering some suggestive cases. It should be noted that our concern is to provide interpretations of quantification *without regard* for considerations of uniformity. It is therefore possible, in a case that was susceptible of a uniform interpretation, that the autonomous and the uniform interpretations should coincide.

If our concern were only to obtain *some* account of the satisfaction conditions, then this could readily be done. For we could stipulate that no assignment was to satisfy the condition $\phi(x)$. However, such an interpretation would not respect the meaning of the truth-functional connectives or of the other unproblematic constructions. If this is also to be arranged, then we can stipulate instead that no assignment is to satisfy any of the immediately problematic contexts and then let "recursion" do the rest. But even so, it is doubtful whether such an interpretation would be of much interest.

There are perhaps two main factors which make for the interest of an autonomous interpretation. They usually go together, but may sometimes come apart. The first is that when $\phi(x)$ is the immediate context for which there is a failure of substitution, then the concept of truth for $\phi(t)$ should cohere or "be of a piece" with the concept of satisfaction for $\phi(x)$. It is hard to say more exactly what this coherence amounts to, but we may take it to be typified by the connection that was previously argued to exist between the concepts of logical truth and satisfaction.[6]

The second factor is that the logic of the quantifier should approximate as closely as possible to the classical logic of referential quantification. Indeed, often what makes an autonomous interpretation of the quantifiers "workable" is that, but for some readily understood restriction, we can reason with them as if they were referential.

However, it is never possible to get the whole of classical logic, given that there is an underlying failure of substitution. For suppose that there are terms t_1 and t_2 and a condition $\phi(x)$ for which $t_1 = t_2$ is true but for which $\phi(t_1) \leftrightarrow \phi(t_2)$ is false. Then we cannot accept both Specification, $\forall x \Phi(x) \to \Phi(t)$, and Substitutivity, $\forall x \forall y (x = y \to (\Phi(x) \leftrightarrow \Phi(y)))$, for arbitrary terms t and contexts $\Phi(x)$. For let $\Phi(x)$ be the particular condition $\phi(x)$. Applying Specification to the resulting instance of Substitutivity as antecedent yields $\forall y (t_1 = y \to (\phi(t_1) \leftrightarrow \phi(y)))$; and applying Specification once again then yields the falsehood $t_1 = t_2 \to (\phi(t_1) \leftrightarrow \phi(t_2))$.

We are therefore forced to make a choice between the principles of Specification and Substitutivity; and, indeed, one useful way of classifying quantification theories which have been "imposed" over a failure of substitution is in terms of how they make this choice. Very roughly, we may

---

[6] I assume that it is coherence in this sense, rather than the earlier concept of uniformity, that corresponds to Kaplan's notion of coherence in "Opacity" [93].

say that referential interpretations, of the type we are considering, favor the retention of Substitutivity, whereas substitutional-type interpretations favor the retention of Specification.

Quine's argument itself may be understood in these simple formalistic terms: quantified modal logic is to be rejected since it is incompatible with the standard principles of quantification theory. This is not how Quine would want to be understood or how he should be understood; for in case the instancing term is irreferential, the principle of Specification itself stands in need of justification. But the formalistic argument does serve to highlight the purely logical problems which must be overcome if a workable form of quantification is to be sustained.

After these general remarks, let us turn to some examples. Perhaps the best known case of autonomous quantification is provided by Quine himself. Quine has enjoined against quantifying into quotes; but his device of quasi-quotation, as expounded in *Mathematical Logic* [138] (Ch. 1.6) and elsewhere, enables us to do just that. It may be objected that this device only allows us to quantify into quasi-quotes, not into quotes. But quasi-quotes behave just like quotes in the absence of free variables; and, indeed, the reasons Quine has, from the failure of substitution, against quantifying into quotes apply equally well to quasi-quotes.

It might be thought that the method of quasi-quotation is geared to the special case of quotation contexts, but in fact it is generalizable to any context whatever. For let $\phi(x)$ be an immediately problematic context. Then we may re-interpret $\phi(x)$ as a condition on expressions: 'the result of substituting x for 'x' in $\phi(x)$ is true'. And similarly when the context is a term $t(x)$, as in the case of quotation.

Substitutional quantification may also be regarded as referential quantification over expressions. We therefore see a close connection between quasi- quotation, once it is suitably generalized, and substitutional quantification. The main difference is that, in the case of substitutional quantification, the meta-linguistic device is applied across the board to all of the contexts, whereas in the case of quasi-quotation, the meta-linguistic device is only applied to the immediately problematic contexts. The method of quasi-quotation is, if you like, a half-hearted version of substitutional quantification.

In one respect, though, the two methods are not on a par. The variables of substitutional quantification apply straightforwardly to the ordinary predicates of the language. The variables under quasi-quotation do not; for their values are expressions rather than objects from the given domain. As a consequence, atomic combinations of ordinary predicates with the quasi-quotational variables must either be excluded or some special interpretation for them must be proposed.

These difficulties are avoided under the method of arc-quotation of Kaplan's "Opacity" [93]. Under this method, it is the objects, and not the expressions, which are assigned to the variables. There is therefore no difficulty in interpreting the application of ordinary predicates to those variables. The innovative step comes in the interpretation of the open quotational terms. The term '$\langle x$ is a philosopher$\rangle$', for example, will denote the result of substituting Quine (the man) for 'x' in the expression 'x is a philosopher' under an assignment of Quine to 'x'. Thus the referents of arc-quotation expressions may be hybrid objects, consisting of both linguistic and non-linguistic material.[7]

Natural as this method is, it is not generalizable to arbitrary contexts. Suppose that we have a problematic open term $t(x)$. Then we might try saying that the denotation of $t(x)$ under an assignment of a to 'x' is the denotation of the result of substituting a for 'x' in $t(x)$. But it is not in general clear what the denotation of the resulting "expression" should be. It is a peculiarity in the case of quotation-mark contexts that there is something which we can naturally take the denotation to be, viz., the "expression" which falls under the quotes.

An interesting feature of arc-quotes is that they may be used to legitimate what would otherwise be illegitimate clauses in the truth-definition. Suppose we so use the truth-predicate T that '$T\langle x$ is a philosopher$\rangle$', for example, is true under an assignment of Quine to 'x'.[8] Then we may correctly assert:

$$T`\exists x(x \text{ is a philosopher})' \leftrightarrow \exists x T`\langle x \text{ is a philosopher}\rangle'.$$

Note the essential use of arc-quotes to the right. It may even be possible, under suitable conventions of disambiguation, to make reasonable sense of such general assertions as $\forall\alpha\forall\phi(T`\exists\alpha\phi(\alpha)' \leftrightarrow \exists x T`\phi(x)')$ and thereby to vindicate what are normally regarded as sloppy habits of use-mention.

Let us pass over the question of autonomous quantification for Giorgione-contexts as being of no independent interest and move directly to the case of modal contexts. Perhaps the best known method of autonomous quantification in this case consists in associating with each object of the domain a unique standard term or name. A modal condition $\square \ \phi(x)$ is then taken to be true of an object just in case the result $\square \ \phi(s)$ of substituting the standard name of the object for the variable is true.

In a way, such a method combines the advantages of purely substitutional methods, like quasi-quotation, and of purely objectual methods, like arc-quotation. In contrast to quasi-quotation, it avoids embarrassment over the interpretation of variables in ordinary contexts; and in contrast to arc-quotation, it avoids the embarrassment over the interpretation of the variables in problematic contexts. But the element of artificiality is

---

[7] A related procedure was adopted, at my suggestion, by B. Richards in "A Point of Reference" [150], pp. 431–441.

[8] As Kaplan has observed in Appendix C of "Opacity" [93], this requires, in case the values of the variables include expressions, that some method be used to distinguish between the substitution of a value *qua* object and *qua* expression.

not avoided altogether, since the association of objects with names must somehow be given.

The method is capable of considerable variation. (1) Instead of associating a single name with each object in the domain, several names may be associated. Of course, many pairs of names will be intersubstitutable *salva veritate*; but there is no need for the several names associated with a given object all to be equipollent in this regard. (2) Sequences of names may be associated with sequences of objects in a way that is not generable from the simple association of names with objects. (3) Predicates (or "incomplete" names) may be associated with the objects or with the sequences of objects. (4) Given the association, either of several names or of predicates, there are two different ways in which satisfaction can be explained. We may say, for example, that $\phi(x)$ is true of an object iff $\phi(s)$ is true of *all* of the associated names or, alternatively, of *some* of the associated names s.

The previous object-sensitive account of modality can be regarded as a special case of this method. Suppose that with each sequence $a_1, \ldots, a_n$ of objects there is associated the identity-type predicate $\pi(x_1, \ldots, x_n) =_{df} \bigwedge_{i,j}(\pm x_i = x_j)$, where the $\pm$ is blank if $a_i = a_j$ and $\neg$ if $a_i \neq a_j$. We may then say that the modal condition $\Box\, \phi(x_1, \ldots, x_n)$ is true of $a_1, \ldots, a_n$ just in case $\Box\, \forall x_1 \ldots \forall x_n(\pi(x_1, \ldots, x_n) \to \phi(x_1, \ldots, x_n))$ is true.

The object-blind account may be obtained in a similar way, simply by letting the predicate associated with an n-tuple being a trivial predicate, true of all n-tuples whatever.

The method is generalizable to all contexts and is in no way peculiar to the modal case; although, of course, which names or predicates are appropriately associated with the objects may well vary from case to case. The method is, in particular, applicable to the earlier example of quotation. It might be thought odd that quotation contexts should be equally susceptible of an "essentialist" interpretation as modal contexts. But many domains of objects are conceived in terms of a canonical system of notation which may then be exploited to this end. With each natural number, for example, may be associated its designation in the Arabic notation. We may then take 'n is even', say, to designate '12 is even' under the assignment of 12 to 'n'. In such a way, we obtain a highly natural account of quantification into quotation contexts, one that is actually of use in the interpretation of some programming languages.

Uniform Quantification

The autonomous interpretations of the previous section call for an innovative act of understanding. Our question now is: what understanding of the problematic quantified statements is already implicit in the understanding of their instances? Is Quine right when he states in "Reference and Modality" ([142], p. 150):

> But the important point to observe is that granted an understanding of the modalities ..., and given an understanding of quantification ordinarily so

called, we do not come out automatically with any meaning for quantified modal sentences ...

Granted this requirement of uniformity, it appears that Quine's argument can get a grip. For given that the instancing terms are irreferential, the corresponding variables cannot be referential and so quantification into the context is unintelligible.

But our earlier discussion prepares us for several ways in which this line of reasoning might be challenged. In the first place, the irreferentiality of the instancing term does not simply follow from the failure of substitution. The case for irreferentiality will vary from context to context. For the Giorgione-example, 'Giorgione is so-called because of his size', it seemed most plausible to maintain that the term 'Giorgione' was referential. What explained the shift in truth-value under substitution was the shift in the reference of 'so'. Uniform quantification, of a standardly referential sort, would then also be possible, if only this referent could somehow be kept fixed.

For the modal and quotational examples, it did not seem plausible to maintain that the terms were standardly referential. Uniform quantification, of a standardly referential sort, would therefore appear to be barred. However, it was still left open whether the terms were non-standardly referential. If they were, then the variables would likewise by non-standardly referential. Thus quantification over a non-standard domain of entities, far from being a subterfuge, would actually be dictated by the requirement of uniformity. It is in some such way as this that one can understand Church's Fregean proposal in his early review [26] of Quine: quantification into modal contexts is permissible, but with respect to senses not objects.

In the case of quotation, the non-standard entities are expressions and the quantification is similar in effect to the quasi-quotational method of Quine. We therefore have an example of quantification which seen from one point of view is uniform and which seen from another point of view is autonomous. Indeed, part of the appeal of the quasi-quotational method is that it enables us to engage in the fiction that the quantification is uniform.

The second challenge to the Quinean line of reasoning depends upon being more sensitive to the exact content of the requirement of uniformity. May a quantified statement be uniform with only one of its instances or must it be uniform with all of them? If the reason for insisting upon uniformity is that our understanding of a quantified statement should issue from our general understanding of quantifiers and variables, then one instance should suffice; for our general understanding will apply in this one case, regardless of how it may apply or fail to apply in other cases.[9] So in demonstrating the unintelligibility of a quantified statement, it is not

---

[9] Even in the bizarre case in which different instances with a referential term produce different conditions, the resulting quantified statement will be ambiguous rather than incoherent.

sufficient to establish irreferentiality for one of the instances, as Quine's argument would lead us to suppose. Irreferentiality must be established for them all.

For the quotation and Giorgione contexts, the point is of no real significance. For the instances themselves are uniform; if one of the instancing terms is irreferential then so are the others. But for the modal and other such contexts, the matter is different. For them it is plausible to draw a distinction between names and descriptions with wide scope, on the one hand, and descriptions (and possibly names) with narrow scope on the other. Even it is conceded that descriptions with narrow scope are irreferential in the given contexts, it is still possible that either the names or the descriptions with wide scope are referential; and if this is so, then they may be chosen as a basis for a uniform understanding of quantification.

I have so far assumed that if we find anomalies in the linguistic function of the singular terms of ordinary language, then we should accept them. But our aim may be to construct a logical symbolism that is free from such anomalies, that is syntactically perspicuous in regard to the semantic function of its different terms. For such a symbolism, a sound form of the Quinean argument goes through. Its upshot will be that it is impossible to have a language in which: (a) there are terms subject to failures of substitution in modal or other problematic contexts; (b) there is uniformity from term-to-term and from term-to-variable; and (c) the variables of quantification are (standardly) referential.

This, it seems to me, is the only negative conclusion of any real value to emerge from the logical argument. The conclusion is indeed not damning; but it does impose a substantial limitation on the form that the symbolism for quantified intensional logics can properly take.

The third challenge to Quine's argument resists the restriction to referential quantification. It is conceded, if only for the sake of argument, that there are instances of the problematic contexts with irreferential terms; and it is also conceded that referential quantification, at least when grounded in those instances, is therefore impossible. But it is denied that quantification *simpliciter* is impossible; for the quantification may be uniform and yet not referential.

One way for this to happen, with which we are already familiar, is for the instancing terms to be non-standardly referential. The corresponding uniform quantifiers will then range over the appropriate domain of non-standard entities.

But another way is for the terms to have double or multiple roles. An example, *for Quine*, is provided by the occurrence of 'Giorgione' in 'Giorgione is so-called because of his size'. For there the term has two roles: it picks out the man; and it picks out the name itself.

In such a case, it may not always be clear what the requirement of uniformity amounts to. For there is the uniformity of variable-to-term and of term-to-term. So if a term has several roles, then is the variable to occur *as* a variable with respect of all of these roles or only with respect to some of them?

At one extreme is the view that the variable is to serve as a variable with respect to all of the roles. The uniform interpretation is therefore one in which the variable simultaneously takes several values, one for each of the roles. In the Giorgione-case, this means that the variable which supplants 'Giorgione' will take two values, one a term and the other an individual. As a consequence, the existential sentence '$\exists x(x$ is so-called because of his size)' will not only be meaningful but true; for under the simultaneous assignment of Giorgione and his name 'Giorgione' to 'x', the open sentence 'x is so-called because of this size' will be satisfied.

A more significant example is provided by Carnap's method of extension and intension, as propounded in *Meaning and Necessity* [20]. Carnap takes a singular term to have a double linguistic role: one given by its extension; and the other by its intension. The corresponding interpretation of variables therefore requires the simultaneous assignment of an extension and an intension; and under such an interpretation, quantification into the appropriately intensional contexts will be unproblematic.

At the other extreme is the view that the variable is to serve as a variable with respect to only one of its roles, presumably the one that for the term is most unproblematically referential; with respect to the other roles, the variable will function exactly like an ordinary term. As a consequence, the variable will be single-valued, but the satisfaction of an open sentence may depend not only on the value assigned to the variable but also on the relevant aspects of the variable itself. We will have what amounts to a literalist use of variables and quantifiers.

In the Giorgione case (again under Quine's construal of it), the variable 'x' in 'x is so-called because of his size' will take a single object as its value, but the open sentence will depend for its satisfaction upon the identity of 'x' in the same way that an instance depends for its truth upon the identity of the corresponding term. So the existential sentence '$\exists x(x$ is so-called because of his size)' is still meaningful, but presumably false: for even if there is someone called by the *name* 'x', he is not likely to be called by the *variable* 'x'; and even if he is called by the *variable* 'x', he is not likely to be called by the variable 'x' because of his size.

A more significant example is provided by modality. Let us suppose that the terms within modal contexts serve as contributors to logical form in such a way that 'Necessarily, Cicero = Cicero' comes out true while 'Necessarily, Cicero = Tully' comes out false. Under a corresponding interpretation of the variables, in which the role of contributor to logical form is kept fixed, the open sentence 'Necessarily, $x = x$' will be satisfied by any assignment of objects, while the open sentence 'Necessarily, $x = y$' will be satisfied by none. We thereby obtain a uniform and literalist account of quantification into contexts governed by an object-blind operator for necessity.

Ordinary Language Quantification

Finally, let us consider the question of whether *ordinary language* quantification into the problematic contexts is intelligible.

It is important to distinguish the question of intelligibility for ordinary language quantification from the corresponding question for formal quantification. If it could somehow be assumed that the ordinary language constructions were to be rendered in terms of the formal ones, then the two questions would be the same. But this is not something that can simply be taken for granted.

What can Quine's argument show us, then, about the intelligibility of such sentences as 'Something is such that necessarily it is greater than seven'? It is evident that the argument cannot even get off the ground unless it is assumed that the quantified sentences are appropriately uniform with their offending instances. So what reason is there for making such an assumption?

There is some plausibility to the view that we understand quantified statements and their various instances on the basis of certain general principles concerning the meaning of the relevant operators, quantifier constructions, and types of terms. There is indeed a preference for general principles over special cases. But it is far from clear that such an amorphous requirement of uniformity would lead to the specific requirement of uniformity from quantified statement to offending instance. On a Russellian conception of language, for example, it would be part of our understanding of the problematic operators that we understand how they apply to singular "objectual" propositions; and so there would be no difficulty in seeing how the quantified sentences could be understood, no matter now aberrant the behavior of the unquantified substructure.

But even if we decided, at the end of the day, that no general explanation of the meaning of the quantified statements and their various instances was forthcoming, this still would not provide us with a strong argument for the unintelligibility of the quantified statements. For given a conflict between a direct intuition of intelligibility and a theoretical presumption of uniformity, it seems clear that it is the theoretical presumption that should be given up.

2

Prolegomena to a Structural Account of Belief and Other Attitudes

HANS KAMP[1]

1 Introduction

CALVIN AND KEVIN, friends, and as sensible as boys of ten can be expected to be, are dropped by Kevin's father at the entrance of Disneyland. He makes them promise to be back at the entrance by 5:30, when he will come to collect them, and gives each twenty dollars for the afternoon. The lads stick together and spend their money on exactly the same rides. By 5:20 they are back at the appointed spot, tired and hungry. Both remember exactly which rides they took and what each ride cost.

Near the place where they are waiting for Kevin's father there is a hamburger stand. Hamburgers, a sign informs the potential customer, can be had at $1.50 apiece. Both boys feel very much like a hamburger. But only one of them, Kevin, goes up to the stand to order one. When he wants to pay for the hamburger that the attendant hands him, he finds to his mortification that he has only 60¢ left and thus cannot pay for it. Calvin, who wants a hamburger just as badly, spares himself this embarrassment. He never goes up to the stand, for, unlike Kevin, he *knows* he has only 60¢ left.

---

[1] This paper consists mostly of points and ideas that can be found in earlier work, most of it unpublished and some of it dating back to 1980, in which I have made various attempts to come to grips with the problems touched on below. I have included some of the relevant papers and manuscripts in the bibliography. In recent years a number of papers by other authors have appeared, most notably by Nicholas Asher and Henk Zeevat, which contain many of the proposals I will be making here too. As the similarities between their papers and the present essay are numerous and obvious, it would be both onerous and tedious to point them out individually at every turn. My indebtedness to these authors should be evident however to anyone familiar with their work. I record it here once and for all.

There is nothing very remarkable about this story. Calvin and Kevin behave differently, but the difference is readily explained: Calvin is aware of something of which Kevin is, at the crucial moment, not aware. And the thing of which he is aware keeps Calvin from doing that which gets Kevin into trouble. Both act rationally, and their desires coincide. That there is nevertheless no coincidence of action is because the boys differ in what, at the crucial time, they are conscious of.

Indeed, Kevin's behavior is no less *rational* than that of his friend. The only point on which one might fault him is that he *could* have realized he had only 60¢ left, either by checking his pocket, or—and this is the consideration that matters here—by recalling what he paid for each of the rides he took and doing the necessary sums. For, as we assumed, both he and Calvin know exactly what they spent when and where, and a sensible boy of ten can, if he puts his mind to it, surely figure from this what is left of the amount with which he set out.

To the unbiased observer this account of the difference in their behavior would seem to be perfectly straightforward: One of the boys has the belief that he doesn't have the money to pay for a hamburger, and the other lacks such a belief. Surely a decent theory of belief should be able to make sense of such an explanation and of the role belief plays in it. A theory according to which the doxastic difference between Kevin and Calvin, which is needed in the explanation of their behavior, does not really exist is surely too much at variance with our apparent use of the concept of belief to be acceptable!

Theories that analyze belief as a relation between the believer and a set of possible worlds (the set of possible worlds in which any sentence expressing the belief is true) are unacceptable in just this way. To be precise, if we attribute to Kevin the complex belief (call it B_1) that he started out with \$20, spent x¢ on his first ride, y¢ on the second and so on, and identify this belief with the set of all possible worlds in each of which all this is true, then this set of possible worlds is exactly the same as the one in which all these things are true and in which, *moreover*, he has only 60¢ remaining (let us refer to this second proposition as B_2). For the conjuncts that make up B_1 logically entail that Kevin has only 60¢ remaining and so this last proposition is true in just those worlds which also verify B_1. Thus, if Kevin does have the belief B_1, he also has the belief B_2. For, according to the possible worlds account, B_2 *is the very same belief* as B_1. But B_2 is (mutatis mutandis) just the belief which, as I have told the story, kept the sagacious Calvin from going up to the stand. So, if we are to trust the possible worlds account, there is no difference between the boys' beliefs that could explain why there is a difference in their behavior.[2]

---

[2] The difficulty which such cases present for the possible worlds approach can be brought out in a number of related ways. For instance, we could marginally extend the story by specifying that at the time when he goes up to the hamburger stand Kevin believes that he has enough money to pay for a hamburger. (As I

The point is an overly familiar one: Theories of belief that identify beliefs with sets of possible worlds cannot differentiate them finely enough to do justice to our common understanding and use of the notion. As it is most often put: Possible worlds accounts entail that belief sentences—i.e., sentences of the form "A believes that s"—are truth-invariant under substitution of necessarily equivalents for the embedded clause s, and this does not appear to be the way in which belief sentences are actually understood. The trouble which the possible worlds account encounters with the case presented here is arguably of just this sort. For, as we have just seen, it boils down to the identification of B_1 and B_2, whereas it is precisely the difference between those beliefs that is essential to the explanation of why the two boys behaved differently. Nevertheless I feel that the case presented here illustrates the predicament in a particularly striking way. Let me explain.

Advocates of the possible worlds approach often argue against theories which identify beliefs with sentences of a natural language (or with "syntactic" structures belonging to some other formalism) on the ground that belief is *intentional*. Belief, it is argued, is always directed at a certain domain or subject matter, most commonly at the world in which the believer himself exists. The intentionality of belief (and other propositional attitudes) is especially important if we think about the relation between belief and action. Our beliefs can guide our actions in and on the world precisely because and insofar as those beliefs pertain to that same world. It is by virtue of the information they carry about that world that they enable us to infer how the actions we contemplate will affect it, and thus they guide us in choosing the action that seems best to us. Moreover, since we have an idea of how such choices are made, we can make predictions about the actions performed by others, provided we know enough about their desires and beliefs; and, similarly, explain some of the actions that we have already observed. Evidently this is one of the main reasons why we are interested in ascribing beliefs to others.

If it is one of the main points of attributing beliefs that it enable us to account for rational action as resulting, via certain processes of deliberation

---

told the story, it isn't clear that this belief should be ascribed to Kevin; it may be that he simply did not consider the question whether there was enough left). This belief is incompatible with the (true) beliefs he had about the money he began with and his various expenses during the afternoon. So the combination of these beliefs corresponds, according to the simple possible worlds account, to the empty set of worlds. Alternatively, suppose that Kevin almost went up to the stand, but, at the last moment, ran through the calculation which showed him that he wouldn't be able to pay; and so he checked himself just in time. There is a natural inclination to say of this case that what decides him against going up to the stand is a change in his beliefs. But according to the possible worlds theory there has been no change: For strictly speaking it does not allow for the possibility of acquiring new beliefs by means of deductive reasoning only; valid deduction never changes the set of worlds to which our beliefs commit us.

and decision, from those beliefs, then a theory of belief cannot pass unless it gives a proper account of its intentionality. The possible worlds theory does provide such an explanation, it has been claimed, in that it identifies a belief with the set of worlds that are compatible with it. This makes it possible to construe the having of a belief P about the actual world as a relation between the believer and the world, a relation which can (perhaps not very helpfully) be described as that of "taking the world to be one of those belonging to the set P." In contrast, "syntactic" theories of belief, which identify beliefs with sentences or other syntactic objects, have been accused of failing to explicate the intentional nature of belief.[3]

In a context where beliefs are attributed for the sake of explaining overt behavior their intentional character would thus appear to be of paramount importance. Yet, as we have seen, in the context of our example the identification of beliefs with sets of possible worlds causes the relevant explanation to collapse. What is needed therefore is a theory of belief which does justice both to (i) the intentionality of beliefs and (ii) to the fact that their identity conditions are stricter than those of the corresponding sets of worlds.

The second of these requirements is closely connected with a point which has been made, urgently and repeatedly, by Jerry Fodor. Attitudinal states, Fodor has argued, must be *computational* in the sense of having some kind of finitary structure on which the inferencing mechanisms of the ratiocinating believer can operate. The importance of this point becomes evident as soon as we reflect on what a detailed theory might be like of the processes by which belief guides action. The central part of such a theory ought to be an account of practical reasoning—an account, that is, of the cognitive dispositions which permit rational agents to form intentions in the light of their beliefs and assumptions, and of the ways in which these dispositions are applied to the task of determining actions that, within a realm of possibilities defined by the agent's beliefs, optimally realize his goals. These dispositions should be conceived as inference principles and rules, like those which we find in formal logic (at least, it is hard to see what else they could be like!). This entails that the items to which these dispositions are applied in individual cases of practical reasoning must, just as logical formulas, have a "syntactic" structure, which the agent's inferencing module can identify as suitable input for particular inference rules.

The desiderata for a theory of belief that are implied by these observations have long been recognized, and they have led to a variety of proposals

---

[3] When it is addressed to theories which offer a merely syntactic analysis of belief, and have nothing to say about the semantic connections between the structures in terms of which belief is analyzed and the world, this accusation is justified. But no such objection can be levelled at theories which combine proposals concerning the syntactic structure of belief with an account of the intentionality of those structures.

that circumvent the embarrassments of the simple-minded possible worlds account, while satisfying the intentionality requirement. Within philosophy the most familiar—and probably the most successful—strategy has been that of identifying beliefs with structures of some natural or partly synthetic language for which there exists a truth definition that assigns to each of those structures an *intension*, viz., the set of all possible worlds in which the structure is true, or satisfied. A well-known example of such a proposal is the one due to Rudolf Carnap [20] and David Lewis [106], according to whom beliefs might be identified with what Lewis calls *meanings*, i.e., syntactic configurations the end nodes of which are intensions. Another proposal, often dismissed as naive and obviously wrong, but recently revived by, in particular, Igal Kvart, is to identify beliefs with sentences of a natural language such as English, while recognizing the need to explicate the intentionality of that natural language, presumably by providing a truth- or model-theoretic semantics for it.

As the suggestions I will put forward below bear a certain similarity to this last proposal, I want to take time out at this point to make a preventive strike against an argument that is sometimes cited against the identification of propositional attitudes and sentences of natural language. The argument goes back a fair way, and, to my knowledge, was first given by Church [27]. It rests on the simple observation that the beliefs of someone whose only language is, e.g., English can as a rule be described just as easily in a language other than English as in English itself. Thus a German speaker could report Calvin's belief with the sentence: "Calvin ist sich bewusst dass er nur 60¢ in der Tasche hat," although Calvin himself would not be able to recognize this as a correct expression of something he holds true.

This observation is sometimes thought to show that belief cannot be construed as a relation between a believer and a sentence. But surely that does not follow. Whatever the observation shows, it certainly does *not* show that Calvin's believing that he has only got 60¢ in his pocket cannot consist in his standing in a "belief" relation to a certain natural language sentence. In particular, the observation does not tell against the claim that his belief consists in his standing in such a relation to the English sentence "I have only 60¢ in my pocket." At best, it shows that *if* it is true that believing is, or involves, standing in a certain relation R to a sentence, and that *if*, moreover, standing in that relation presupposes that one understands that sentence, then there will be cases in which the sentence to which one stands in the belief relation will not be identical with the complement clause of a statement used to report one's belief.[4]

---

[4] For reasons that will become evident later I do not think that the simple identification of attitudinal objects with sentences of a natural language like English can produce a theory of propositional attitudes that is particularly useful or plausible. But the argument just mentioned has next to nothing to do with the considerations that have led me to this conviction.

I will return to this issue later. But before leaving it now, I want to make explicit something that is implicit in what I have just said about Church's argument, and which will be a central presupposition to the attitude theory that I am going to sketch. It is—I will argue this point below—crucial to distinguish carefully between:

(i) The question of what form, structure or organization must be assumed for the beliefs and other propositional attitudes that are held by the various organisms capable of such attitudes; and

(ii) The question of how an attitude report, i.e., a sentence in which an attitude is *attributed* to such an organism, must be related to the reported attitude for the report to count as correct.

Sometimes these questions are not distinguished; or, alternatively, only one of the two is being addressed. This is true in particular of those philosophical accounts of propositional attitudes which confine themselves to the study of the semantics of attitude reports.[5]

In many instances the refusal to try and do more than develop a semantics of attitude reports is born out of wisdom. At present there isn't much that we can say with any precision or certainty about the way in which the human mind represents and processes information (not to speak about the minds of the various kinds of animals which we also judge capable of belief and desire, and perhaps other sorts of attitudes as well). And there is little hope that this situation will significantly improve in the foreseeable future. So for the time being theorizing about these matters is bound to be speculative, and devoid of a proper empirical basis; it is something one had better stay away from. As regards the practice of *attributing* attitudes the situation is quite different. People have attributed propositional attitudes to other people (as well as to many kinds of animals) as long as anyone can remember; and those who have engaged in the practice have been no better informed about the inner workings of the mind than we are at present. Nonetheless, attitude attribution is a highly developed practice, about which many of us have firm and detailed intuitions. As such it is a proper and promising subject for philosophical analysis. And since the practice does not seem to require detailed knowledge of the mind's inner workings, a theory of it should have no need to refer to those inner workings either. Thus, a theory of attitude reports ought to be independent of any specific assumptions about the organization of mental states and the mechanisms which transform them.

---

[5] Attitude reports come in a number of different syntactic forms; but the most prominent form in philosophical and logical discussions has been that which consists of (i) a subject term referring to the possessor of the attitude, (ii) a verb denoting the attitude (e.g., *believes*, *desires*, *doubts*, etc.) and (iii) a *that*-clause identifying the content of the attitude form. It is to this type of sentence that I will be referring henceforth when using the term "attitude report."

Up to a point this is right. Yet, the methodological constraints that some have inferred from these considerations are, I think, not really workable—not even when the semantics of attitude reports is declared to be the only going concern. In particular, many of the outstanding puzzles relating to belief attribution—on which much of the recent philosophical debate about belief has focused—cannot be addressed within the austere frameworks to which these constraints condemn us. The difficulties those puzzles have been thought to present are only symptoms of the more fundamental problem we have already identified: Any attitude theory that fails to put forward substantive hypotheses about the structural properties of propositional attitudes thereby prevents itself from saying anything of substance about how attitudes are *cognitively active*. And so it cannot say much either about the ways in which attitudes issue in overt behavior (including that behavior, much of it verbal, against which the correctness of attitude reports is to be measured.) Without certain assumptions about attitudinal structure we will never get very far.

I already noted that theorizing about attitudinal structure is a hazardous business, and hard-pressed for an empirical basis. Indeed, it has been surmised that a careful study of the medium in which we express our attitudes, i.e., natural language, provides perhaps the only significant lead that can assist us in this effort.[6] Whether this is really so I do not know for sure; but I am inclined to believe it, and certainly I am like most linguists and philosophers in that I would not have anything else to go on.

I believe that it is possible to extract from the analysis of natural language important clues about the likely form and organization of our attitudes but that the aspects of language which are the most revealing in this regard have long been overlooked. It has only been in the course of the past decade that these aspects have become the subject of a more systematic and formal analysis. Their study has led to what might be termed a "dynamic" theory of the semantics of natural language, which was first developed, in at least two different forms, in the early eighties. One of these has come to be known as Discourse Representation Theory (DRT).[7]

In the next section I will give a brief sketch of DRT, focusing on those features of it that are relevant to the theory of belief and other attitudes

---

[6] I suspect that this judgment has somehow contributed to the austere view that all a theory of the attitudes could hope to accomplish is to formulate a semantics for attitude reports. Nevertheless, the two should be carefully distinguished. In fact, the austere view is compatible with the opinion that even the study of language will not yield any structural insights into the propositional attitudes of its users.

[7] The semantic approach which DRT exemplifies has been developed also in other ways, most notably in the form of Heim's File Change Semantics, which was conceived at roughly the same time as DRT. (In fact, Heim's theory appears to have been worked out slightly before the first explicit version of DRT saw the light). Since the early eighties a number of further variants of the approach have

which it has inspired. In Section 3 I will draw out the implications of
DRT, as presented in Section 2, for a theory of the attitudes. Section
4 discusses direct reference and the related concept of an attitude de re,
and then proceeds to discuss some issues relating to indexicality and the
relation between linguistic meaning and verbal communication. In Section
5 the suggestions for a theory of communication of Section 4 are elaborated
further and issue in a view about the form of shared information which
involves a component of shared reference as well as common knowledge of
the sort first discussed at length by Lewis in his book *Convention* [105].
Section 6 is no more than a preview of the treatment of three topics, (i) the
semantics of the attitudinal structures proposed in the preceding sections,
(ii) the analysis of attitude reports and (iii) the treatment of attitudes that
are "self-reflective" in the sense of being about one or more of the subject's
other attitudes (Such as the belief that a certain belief you have rests on
what you read in the Times, or the desire not to have a desire you do have
and can't get rid of. Each of these three topics is of primary importance
for the theory outlined in Sections 1–5, but spatial as well as temporal
constraints prevented me from allotting them the treatment they clearly
deserve.

2 Dynamic Semantics and Discourse Representation Theory

It has long been obvious to students of natural discourse that discourse
understanding proceeds incrementally: What the hearer or listener has
learned from the first n sentences of the discourse helps him in interpreting
the $n+1$-st sentence; more often than not this help is essential.

   In fact, it may be essential in two different ways. First, the sentences which make up a coherent discourse usually contain elements—
demonstratives, definite descriptions and pronouns, tenses and temporal
adverbs, "discourse particles" like 'however', 'hence', 'moreover', 'yet', etc.
—which can only be interpreted with reference to the context which the
preceding sentences of the discourse have established. Second, the intended
interpretation of such elements typically links them, and therewith the content of the sentence in which they occur, with the interpretation of the
sentences preceding it, thus creating a semantic "web" that cannot in general be equated with a simple conjunction of propositions expressed by the
individual sentences.

---

appeared, most notably the relational approach of Barwise [6] and the development of Dynamic Predicate Logic of Groenendijk en Stokhof (see Groenendijk
and Stokhof [69]). If I confine my discussion of the central ideas to the format of
DRT, this is partly out of habit and partly because I do not quite know how to
state some of the points I want to make within the alternative frameworks.

One type of example that demonstrates the connectedness of discourse, and which has been pivotal in the original development of DRT, is illustrated in (1):

(1)   Last month a whale was beached near San Diego. Three days later it was dead.

The information this sentence pair conveys is that there was (i) a time somewhere inside the month preceding the one containing the utterance time of (1), (ii) a place in the vicinity of San Diego, and (iii) a whale, such that that whale was beached at that time and died within a period of three days from that time. In (rough) predicate logic notation:

(1') $\exists t \, \exists t' \, \exists p \, \exists x \, (\mathit{Time}(t)$ & $\mathit{Time}(t')$ & $\mathit{Place}(p)$ & $\mathit{PrevMon}(t, n)$ &
      $\mathit{Whale}(x)$ & $\mathit{Beach}(x, p, t)$ & $\mathit{Near}(p, sd)$ & $t \leq t' \leq day(t) + 3days$
      & $\mathit{Dead}(x, t'))$[8]

One could quarrel with certain details of this formula, in particular with the precise form of some of its conjuncts. But these do not matter here. What does matter is that the conjuncts which originate in the first, and those originating in the second sentence are all inside the scope of the same existential quantifiers. Thus the content of the two sentences together is that there exist times, a place and an individual which satisfy both the conditions imposed by the first sentence and those imposed by the second. This implies that the truth conditions of (1) cannot be represented as the conjunction of a pair of separate propositions, each one expressed by one of the two sentences.[9]

---

[8] "$\mathit{PrevMon}$" stands for the relation that holds between times t and t' iff they belong to successive months, "$\mathit{Beach}(x, p, t)$" stands for the three place relation which means that x is beached in place p at time t, "$t \leq t' \leq t{+}3$ days" expresses that the time t' lies between t and the end of the third day after the day containing t, and n and sd are constants denoting the utterance time of (1) and the city of San Diego, respectively.

[9] There is an ongoing debate over the question whether a sentence pair such as (1) entails that the time t and the whale x are uniquely determined. Arguably the subsequent reference, by means of the pronoun 'it', to the whale introduced by the indefinite description of the first sentence implies that there must be some particular whale that the two sentences are about. It need not be the case that only one whale was beached near San Diego last month, nor even that only one was beached near San Diego and dead within three days. But nevertheless, the argument goes, the utterance should be linked (in some appropriate causal way) to one particular such whale if it is to qualify as entirely felicitous. Similarly the time of the beaching, which is picked up by the adverb 'three days later', should be fixed by some such causal connection. This observation might be taken to imply that the content of (1) can be seen as the conjunction of two separate propositions, each expressed by one of the two sentences, after all. The first proposition is that the whale in question was beached at the relevant time, and the second is the proposition that that whale was dead within three days after

Such connections are largely responsible for the cohesiveness of discourse, which, discourse theorists have recognized for a long time, it is one of principal tasks of discourse analysis to describe and explain.[10] But in more formal approaches towards semantics, in particular those which have followed Davidson and Montague in the methodological conviction that the principal task of a semantic theory is to articulate how syntactic form determines truth conditions, this kind of connectedness was ignored until quite recently. DRT arose as an attempt to fill this gap, by providing an explicit account of the kind of discourse connectedness which (1) exemplifies, while preserving the achievements of truth-conditional semantics.

Informal reflection about what goes on when someone reads or hears a sentence pair like (1) suggests the following: The recipient starts by taking in the first sentence. Let us assume he understands it. This means for one thing that he has grasped (in some appropriate sense) the conditions under which the sentence is true. But in addition it gives him a basis for making sense of the second sentence. His making sense of the second sentence involves linking its anaphoric elements to the interpretation he has already formed of the first sentence, in such a way that a new interpretation emerges, this time for the two sentences combined. The most natural way, it would seem, to analyze this interpretation process is to assume that the recipient builds, step by step, an interpretative structure of the discourse that reaches him, repeatedly relying on the structure he has built already in deciding what further pieces are to be added.

It is this model of natural language understanding that DRT has tried to develop in detail. To accomplish this, one articulates a system of rules—the

---

that time. According to my own intuition this is true: Sentence pairs such as (1) presuppose some relation which links the utterance to a particular whale and time. However, this relation can be arbitrarily indirect. For instance, (1) might be said by a person who read a short note to this effect in the daily paper a few days earlier; and that note, though ultimately going back to an eyewitness report, may itself have found its way into the newspaper in as roundabout a way as you like. I think that even in such cases the hearer of A's utterance is entitled to infer from the assumption that (1) was felicitously used that there must be some such link to a particular whale and time, even though he has no way of knowing, or even of finding out, what the link in this particular case is. It seems to me that in such cases the *information* which the hearer gets from the utterance is indeed correctly captured by $(1')$. But there is also a sense in which the utterance can be construed as carrying, in virtue of the *complex* causal chain that connects it with the particular whale and time, additional information; and when this additional information is taken into account as well, the total content can factored as a conjunction of the two singular propositions about the whale and time that are expressed by, respectively, the first sentence and the second sentence. For discussion of the matter see in particular Chastain [21], Evans [48], Heim [79], and Kadmon [84].

[10] See, e.g., Haliday and Hasan [74].

so-called *construction algorithm*—which maps discourses belonging to the language, or language fragment, under study into certain "interpretative structures." The formulation of the construction algorithm presupposes a certain syntax for the language which assigns to each of its sentences a syntactic structure on which the algorithm can operate. The output structures are called "Discourse Representation Structures," or "DRS's." Each DRS represents certain truth conditions which are assigned to it by a general truth definition. The empirical adequacy of the theory is determined largely in terms of whether the construction algorithm transforms each syntactically admissible discourse segment D into a DRS whose truth conditions match those which are associated with D by competent speakers. The principal challenge to DRT, experience indicates, is the exact formulation of the construction algorithm.

Since an important aspect of the construction algorithm has to do with how anaphoric sentence elements are linked with components of the previously constructed DRS (for it is this which accounts for the aspect of discourse cohesion that DRT was designed to explain), the construction of DRS's from syntactic inputs must be seen as an operation which always applies to a *pair* of input structures—on one hand the syntactic description of the sentence under consideration and on the other the DRS as it has been constructed so far. This DRS functions, one might say, as the *context* in which the new sentence is being interpreted. This second role which DRS's play in the theory, i.e., as inputs, not outputs, of the interpretation process, imposes on them certain special structural constraints which have no direct equivalents within earlier theories of natural language semantics.

Particularly important in this regard are *discourse referents*. Discourse referents are DRS constituents which represent individuals and other entities that are mentioned, or otherwise implied, by the processed discourse. For instance, the first sentence of (1) introduces, according to one of the construction algorithms currently in use, (i) a discourse referent corresponding to the indefinite description a whale; (ii) a discourse referent for the event of the whale's beaching which the sentence reports; (iii) a discourse referent for the place where this event takes place; (iv) a discourse referent representing the city of San Diego; (v) a discourse referent for the intended time of evaluation of the DRS, here (as normally) the utterance time of the represented discourse; (vi) a discourse referent for the time at which the event occurred; and (vii) a discourse referent for the calendar month preceding that of the evaluation time. In addition, the resulting DRS contains *conditions*, which specify certain properties of and relations between these discourse referents, and thus provide descriptive information about the represented entities. In the diagram-like form in which DRS's are most commonly presented, the DRS looks like this:[11]

---

[11] The meanings of these conditions are, I trust, intuitively clear: "$whale(x)$" means intuitively that the discourse referent x stands for a whale, "$Event(e)$"

(2)

$$
\begin{array}{|l|}
\hline
\quad x \quad e \quad p \quad z \quad n \quad t \quad t' \\
\hline
whale(x); \quad Event(e); \\
Place(p); \quad In(e,p); \quad San\ Diego(z); \quad Near(p,z); \\
Bef(e,n); \quad Time(t); \quad Time(t'); \quad calendar\ month(t'); \\
Succ(t', calendar\ month[n]); \quad At(e,t); \quad Incl(t,t') \\
e\ldots \boxed{Beached(x)} \\
\hline
\end{array}
$$

When the second sentence of (1) is processed in the context which (2) provides, the construction algorithm can link the discourse referents introduced by certain elements of that sentence—the pronoun 'it', the past tense 'was' and the prepositional phrase 'three days later'—with the relevant discourse referents of the context DRS (2). We will represent these links as conditions involving a new discourse referent, introduced by the anaphoric sentence constituent, and the already existing discourse referent with which that constituent is being linked. The resulting DRS is the following extension of (2):

(3)

$$
\begin{array}{|l|}
\hline
\quad x \quad e \quad p \quad z \quad n \quad t \quad t \quad t' \quad y \quad s \quad t'' \\
\hline
whale(x); \quad Event(e); \\
Place(p); \quad In(e,p); \quad San\ Diego(z); \quad Near(p,z); \\
Bef(e,n); \quad Time(t); \quad Time(t'); \quad calendar\ month(t'); \\
Succ(t', calendar\ month[n]); \quad At(e,t); \quad Incl(t,t') \\
e\ldots \boxed{Beached(x)} \\
y = x; \\
State(s); \quad Bef(s,n); \quad Time(t''); \quad day[t''] = day[t]+3; \\
Overlaps(s,t'') \\
s\ldots \boxed{dead(y)} \\
\hline
\end{array}
$$

The truth definition for DRS's has the following general form: A DRS K is true (with respect to a world w) iff it is possible to correlate entities (of w)

---

conveys that e represents an event, and similarly for the predicates "*Place*" and "*Time*." "*San Diego(p')*" means that the discourse referent p' stands for San Diego, "*In(e,p)*" that the event represented by e occurred within the place represented by p, and similarly for the conditions that relate e to n and t, and t to t'. The last condition specifies that e stands for an event of x getting beached. For our present purposes many of these details are not important. What is important is the general organization of the DRS into (i) discourse referents and (ii) conditions.

with the discourse referents of K such that the conditions of K are satisfied (in w) by the entities correlated with the discourse referents occurring in those conditions. Thus (2) will be true provided there are individuals a and b, an event E, a place P and times T and T', such that a is a whale, b is San Diego, E is an event of a getting beached, E precedes the utterance time N, E occurs in place P and at time T, T' is the month preceding that of N, and T is temporally included in T'. Note that the definition does not require that the entities correlated with the discourse referents be uniquely determined by the associated conditions. In general these conditions only constrain the choice of the corresponding entities up to a point, without fixing them completely.

Much the same considerations apply to (3). (3) will be true if there are entities corresponding to *its* discourse referents which satisfy all *its* conditions. Note that the choice of entities correlated with, say, x and e is now more severely restricted than it was by the conditions of (2). For instance, the individual corresponding to x must now be a whale which not only was beached at the right time and place, but which moreover should have been dead within three days of the time at which it was beached. Still, the conditions need not fix this individual completely, any more than this need be so for the conditions of (2). It is for this reason that the truth conditions represented by (3) cannot be reduced to a conjunction of two sets of truth conditions, one for each of the two constituent sentences of (1). In particular, it seems impossible to find a separate proposition which reflects just the content of the second sentence. Evidently this impossibility is a consequence of the circumstance that the two parts of (3) which derive from the first and the second sentence, respectively, have certain discourse referents in common. (This is so for x, which occurs in the condition "$y = x$" of the second part, and for t which figures in the condition "$day[t''] = day[t]+3$".)

Many of the details of these DRS's are of no relevance to what I will have to say about the attitudes.[12] What will be important is their organization into discourse referents and conditions—formally a DRS is defined as a pair consisting of a set of discourse referents and a set of conditions—and in particular, the fact that the discourse referents can act as links between conditions that originate in distinct sentences.[13]

---

[12] I should add that some of the details—especially those pertaining to the treatment of time and tense—are still a topic of debate: Thus, for all I can see at present, the temporal information conveyed by text segments such as (1) can also be represented in DRS's that look rather different from (2) and (3). So long as the methodological constraints under which DRT operates do not force a choice between such alternatives, the question whether attitudes might be organized in accordance with one of those alternatives or with another would, from the methodological perspective of this paper, be idle speculation. I have done my best to steer clear of such speculations.

[13] Many of the interesting issues in DRT have to do with the representation of universal and generic quantification and of sentence modifiers like negation,

3 First Suggestions for a Theory of Attitudinal Structure

The main reason why DRT appears to be a useful point of departure for a theory of attitudinal structure lies in its concern with the incremental character of language interpretation, and, therewith, of the assimilation of information by verbal means. Indeed, it is tempting (and, I think, up to a point legitimate) to see DRT as providing a model of the process by which the recipient of a discourse acquires new beliefs as he takes in its successive sentences. Consider someone who is reading a certain text—say, a newspaper report about a recent air show. He has full confidence in the paper's reliability and so accepts everything he learns. Each time he reads a new sentence, his information—or, if you prefer, his array of beliefs—about the show increases. DRT implies that the growth of information which the reading of each new sentence s produces corresponds to the change which processing s according to the construction algorithm in the light of the already erected DRS produces in that DRS. But it implies more—and here I recall the remarks about discourse coherence in Section 2: In general, we saw, the contribution made by a new sentence to the content of a discourse or text cannot be logically detached from the content of the preceding sentences. Therefore, insofar as that which the reader learns from the new sentence is to be considered a new separate belief of his,[14] we must be

---

disjunction and conditionality. These notions require complex conditions, conditions which themselves have DRS's as constituent parts. (The discourse referents of these constituent DRS's act essentially as bound variables!) In the present paper this aspect of DRT is entirely ignored. Nevertheless it is important to the attitude theory proposed here. For attitudes whose content involves the logical concepts (quantification, negation, etc.) for whose representation complex conditions are needed, should, if the general approach of the present paper is correct, have structures which involve these same complex conditions.

[14] It would be implausible to hold that every new sentence of a discourse produces in the trusting reader a distinct new belief. Precisely how beliefs are to be demarcated and counted is a difficult question to which I doubt that any categorical answer is possible: whether we see a certain amount of information as representing a single belief or as being constituted of two or more distinct beliefs is a matter that may depend on the context of the particular use which the believer is, at any one time, making of the belief(s), and, as a reflection of this factor, also on the explanatory purposes for which we, who attribute the belief(s) to him, make these attributions. Nevertheless there are many cases where the presumption must be that a number of sentences give rise to a single new belief. However, the point is not affected by this qualification. For, first, a segment consisting of several sentences will often hang together with preceding segments in the manner illustrated by the example of Section 2, and second, there are at least some cases where a new belief derives from a single sentence and hangs together with earlier beliefs in the indicated way. One such example would be that where two people, A and B, are both present when (1) is uttered, but where B for some reason does not hear the second sentence, while A hears both. Assuming

prepared for the possibility that the content of this belief is inextricably interwoven with his other beliefs. The doxastic commitments which the reader makes by adopting the new belief impose additional limitations on the set of worlds compatible with his beliefs. But these commitments are associated with the entire *family* of beliefs he holds; there is no way of construing the set of worlds as the intersection of a number of world sets, each of which corresponds exactly to one of the beliefs in the family.[15] As we have seen in the preceding section, the formal reason DRT offers for this connectedness is that the (structures identifying) the different beliefs share certain discourse referents.

This brings us to two assumptions concerning beliefs and other attitudes which will be basic to all else I will have to say in this paper:

(A1) In general it is not possible to specify the truth-conditional content of each of the individual beliefs that are held by a given person; only the belief state as a whole (or, at any rate, substantial parts of it, which comprehend a large number of his beliefs) determine well-defined truth conditions. The same goes for attitudes other than belief. (For instance, desires are often inextricably connected with beliefs, as well as with each other.) Therefore, a theory of the attitudes must concern itself with analyzing the intentionality of such complex propositional states, and with the ways in which their constituent attitudes are interconnected.

(A2) The connectedness of different attitudes that are part of the same state is an effect of certain intentional elements which they share, and which play conceptual roles comparable to those played by discourse referents in the DRS's of DRT. Therefore, complex attitudinal states must be assumed to be organized "around" such elements. These

---

that they both believe all they hear, it would seem correct to say that there is one belief that A and B share, but another which A has and B does not have. This second belief, moreover, is linked with the first belief of A in just the way the DRS (3) makes explicit. (This last example raises a further question about *shared* belief which I will take up in Section 5.)

[15] In a way the interconnectedness of discourses such as (1) does not capture the full extent of the interconnectedness of belief. In connected discourse there is an apparent asymmetry between the earlier and the later parts. In our analysis of (1) for instance we found that the second sentence could not be considered to determine a separate, proposition that is logically independent from that expressed by the first sentence. But with regard to the first sentence this difficulty did not arise. In the case of belief, in contrast, the situation appears in many cases to be fully symmetric. For instance it may be true that the different beliefs of a connected family were acquired in a certain temporal order, but that the believer does not recall anything about this order. Here the earlier formed beliefs will have come to depend for their intentional significance just as much upon those formed later as the latter are dependent upon the earlier ones.

elements represent entities in the world (or, more generally, in whatever domain the relevant attitudes happen to be about). They are accompanied by "attributions" of certain properties and relations, which act as attributions of properties and relations to the entities which the elements are taken to represent. These elements and the "attributions" which accompany them determine the state's intentionality.

Assumption (A2) appears to be little more than a prolix way of repeating what I had already said, viz., that attitudinal states are structured like DRS's. My reason for spelling matters out once more, and in this manner, is this. I am persuaded that some of the features of the DRS's that are used in current DRT correspond to important structural properties of attitudinal states. Yet I think we should not take it for granted that *every* feature which is needed in a semantic theory such as DRT must necessarily have its psychological counterpart.[16]

Before proceeding further I want to briefly raise a general methodological issue, which is related to what I just said. Someone persuaded that beliefs and other attitudes have a structure which resembles that of DRS's (or, for that matter, of any other class of formal objects) can express this thesis in one of two ways. He can either propose a theory which, in a certain sense, *models* the relevant doxastic phenomena, by positing that propositional attitudes are relations between individuals and DRS's (or whatever other formal objects). (Such a theory would be a direct alternative to any theory which analyzes propositional attitudes as relations between individuals and sets of possible worlds). Alternatively, one may postulate that (cognitively capable) individuals are, at any one time of their existence, in certain cognitive states, and further that these states have structural properties analogous to, or exemplified by, DRS's (or other formal objects). On this second alternative the role of the formal objects is not that of *being* the attitudinal objects themselves, but rather of specifying complex structural predicates which given attitudinal states do or do not satisfy.

The two alternatives differ more in style than in substance, and there is not much to motivate a choice between them. If I have opted for the second alternative, this is primarily because I do not in general want to exclude, by ascribing some particular structure to a given state, the possibility that the state may have various other properties as well, either properties not yet revealed by current research or else properties that are irrelevant to the explanatory goals at hand. Strictly speaking, if one proceeds in the

---

[16] It should be noted in this connection that the present state of development of DRT still leaves a range of questions pertaining to the form of DRS's unsettled. It is to be hoped that continuing research will provide answers to these questions. But as long as we do not know the definitive forms of DRS's, it is pointless to try and to assess whether all their properties can be meaningfully transferred to the psychological domain.

first way, and *identifies* attitudinal states, or their objects, with DRS's, one thereby precludes the possibility of these states or objects having additional structural properties, which the DRS's do not display. Treating DRS's as complex predicates does not have this consequence.

On the second approach one cannot say literally of a given state that it contains discourse referents or conditions. Speaking exactly, it is only the DRS characterizing the state which can be said to have such constituents. The state only functions "as if" it had such constituents—for instance, if the state is a belief state (i.e., it consists exclusively of beliefs) then the person who is in this state will expect the world to be one of those in which the DRS holds. It will be both convenient and harmless, however, to speak informally of the state as *having* the kinds of constituents that make up DRS's.

What distinguishes the two approaches is hardly significant in comparison with what they have in common. It is important in this connection to note that they are similar not only in that they postulate similar attitudinal structures, but also in the obligations which they thereby incur. Either must, if it is to earn its keep, relate those structures in an explanatorily significant way to the phenomenology of belief and the other attitudes. In particular, it must be able to tell us how certain complex states consisting of beliefs, desires and possibly other attitudes lead to new beliefs, desires, intentions and plans.

As I intimated already in Section 1, a theory capable of this would have to include, at the very least, a detailed account of practical reasoning. This is more than any current theory of belief has accomplished yet, or, for that matter, that any could hope to accomplish in the near future. In fact, not many of the extant theories of propositional attitudes have made serious attempts to address this problem.

This is no less true of the theory presented here than it is of any others with which I am familiar. No detailed account of practical reasoning based on the structural proposals I will be making exists. However, even in the absence of such an account we should at least reflect on the minimal conditions which a structural description of attitudinal states must satisfy if it is to be capable of providing the foundation on which such an account would have to rest.

Perhaps the most obvious implication of this general requirement is that structural descriptions of complex attitudinal states distinguish between those components of the state that function as beliefs and those that function as desires. For it is obvious that in practical reasoning these two types of attitudes play entirely different roles. This is not a matter of their content. For instance, once a desire has been fulfilled, it typically makes place for a belief with the same content. In such cases the cognitive role of the belief is utterly different from that of the earlier desire, notwithstanding the fact that their contents coincide. The difference between desires and beliefs is a matter of, as I will call it, *attitudinal mode*.

Among the attitudinal modes are, first and foremost, belief and desire.
However, an explicit theory of cognitive processes will certainly have to
distinguish many more. Doubt, hope, fear, regret are just some of many
that come to mind. Another mode—which has received far less attention
than I think it deserves, as it seems to me to be of paramount importance
to a theory of cognition—is the one I will refer to as *wonder*. This is the
attitude someone has towards a given content if he is aware of this content
but totally uncommitted towards its *alethic status*—i.e., if he is entirely
neutral as to whether it is true or false, or, for that matter, even whether it
is possible.[17] The classification of attitudinal modes is a substantial task.
It is one I could not undertake here. For the task of classifying cannot
be separated from that of making explicit what role each mode plays in
practical reasoning and other forms of reasoning, and, as I have already
said, this is something that exceeds our present capacities.[18]

Even a superficial reflection on the question of what factors influence
the roles that the different parts of attitudinal states play in the processes of
practical and theoretical reasoning, and through which they are continually
transformed, makes us realize that there are many more ways in which
attitudes are discriminated than is suggested by the small list of attitudinal
modes I just gave. Moreover, many of these factors do not seem to be
a matter of mode, in the way in which the difference between desire and
belief is. For instance, people frequently associate with the beliefs they hold
further beliefs about how they came to hold the first beliefs, e.g., about who
gave them the information the beliefs embody, or in what other way that
information was picked up. Many such associations have an important part
to play in determining the cognitive roles of the attitudes in question. Thus
if you associate with a belief of yours assumptions concerning its origins,
this will as a rule influence how confident you are in that belief: To a belief
that as far as you can remember comes from a source you have learned to be
reliable you tend to attach a higher degree of certainty than to one whose
pedigree is more dubious. In their turn degrees of confidence are crucial
inputs to our procedures of belief revision. For instance, if you receive new
information which you regard as trustworthy, but which is incompatible
with the conjunction of two beliefs you already have, and if you attach to

---

[17] By and large this is the attitude of one who asks the corresponding question; but not quite, for questions are often asked by people who already regard
their content as possibly true, but want to know whether it is really true. The
attitudinal mode of someone who asks a question regarding the content of that
question and thereby manifests his ignorance concerning truth or falsity as well
as his commitment to possibility, is to be distinguished from belief on the one
hand and from mere wonder on the other.

[18] I suspect that subjective probability should also be seen as giving rise to
distinct attitudinal modes, each one of which would reflect a particular probability
commitment of the subject with regard to the relevant content.

one of these two beliefs a high, and to the other a low degree of confidence, then it is to be expected that you will give up the second of those two beliefs.

Similarly with wishes and desires. Desires come in varying degrees of intensity and they are accompanied by varying assumptions concerning the likelihood or the preconditions of their fulfillment; both intensity degrees and assumptions affect what plans we form for satisfying those desires. The examples can be extended ad libitum. There appears to be a vast spectrum of conditions which people associate with their various attitudes, and many of these influence the roles those attitudes play in the development of the attitudinal states of which they are part.

The conclusion we are forced to draw from this is that a complex attitudinal state will as a rule have a large part that is "higher order" in as much as it consists of conditions on the basic components of the state. This is an aspect of such states which DRS's of the sort presented in Section 2 are unable to represent. So, to arrive at an appropriate theory of attitudinal structure we will have to extend the structural descriptions which those DRS's provide in such a way that they capture this aspect as well.

The term 'higher order', which I used in the preceding paragraph, suggests a fairly traditional solution to this problem, in which the "higher order" attributions are represented, in the spirit of higher order predicate logic, as conditions which combine attitudinal predicates with discourse referents that represent propositional attitudes. This is indeed how we will represent them. However, we must realize from the outset that by proceeding along these lines we will be able to provide only part of the solution. In particular, we cannot hope to distinguish desire and belief in this way. We cannot, for trying to do so would get us into an infinite regress.

To see that this is so we argue as follows. Suppose that a given state were to identify one of its parts as a belief by virtue of containing a condition consisting of the appropriate predicate—let us designate it as "Bel"—and a discourse referent, p say, representing that part of the state. Would this establish the relevant component as a belief? Well, we can't say yet. For we didn't say anything about the mode of the "second order" condition "$Bel(p)$". Is it a belief? A desire? Or what? Intuitively it seems to be more like a belief than a desire. For in general people act as if they know—and thus believe—that their beliefs are beliefs, and not desires (and similarly that their desires are desires and not beliefs, etc.). So let us suppose it is a belief (but the assumption is not essential; if we were to assume a different mode we would run into the same trouble). If, as we are assuming, attitudinal modes are identified via conditions on the attitudes of which they are the modes, then the belief whose content is the condition "$Bel(p)$" will require another condition, in which the predicate "Bel" combines with a discourse referent, q say, which represents the condition "$Bel(p)$." But then exactly the same problem will arise in connection with this new condition "$Bel(q)$": What determines its mode? Presumably a further condition. And so on ad infinitum.

In order to see how this regress might be avoided it is important to recognize that attitudinal *modes* like belief and desire are fundamentally different from the *attributions* we often make to our attitudes. Given that a certain attitude is part of your attitudinal state you can make it the subject of further predications. Thus when you remember of a certain belief of yours that you got it when you read yesterday's Times, you genuinely attribute to that belief a certain property.[19] But I have the intuition—although I would not know how to prove this—that such predications presuppose their subjects to be full-blown attitudes, each with a particular mode as well as a particular content. Your remembering that you got a certain belief from yesterday's Times can be analyzed as involving the belief that the first belief satisfies a certain condition. But knowing that the first belief is a *belief*—and not a desire, say, or an intention—is not like this. Its identity as a belief, i.e., as an attitude with that particular mode, is given as an inseparable aspect of the attitude itself.

These considerations and speculations have led me to a solution for the problem of "higher order" attitudinal structure which consists of two parts. The first part concerns the representation of attitudinal mode. Intuitively, what I would like to say is that complex attitudinal states have the structure of DRS's the components of which "come in different colors." Each such component represents one of the constituent attitudes of the state; its conditions and discourse referents identify the attitude's content while the color determines its mode (e.g., blue for belief, red for desire, black for regret, and so on. But feel free to pick your own). In the less colorful setting of set theory this proposal comes to the following:

(A3) Complex attitudinal states have the structure of sets of pairs, where each pair consists of (i) a *mode indicator* and (ii) a DRS. The different DRS's may share the same discourse referents, and this may be so even when their modes differ. Such sets of pairs of mode indicators and DRS's are called *articulated* DRS's.[20]

Eventually, I already surmised, a substantial range of distinct mode indicators will be needed, but only further research into the workings of practical reasoning and other cognitive processes can tell us what that range is like in detail. At the very least we will have to distinguish between belief and

---

[19] For the most part such second order attributions take the form of further beliefs. But it is also possible to make such attributions in desire. For instance I may desire of a given belief I have that you share that belief. And I, for one, desire of quite a few of my desires that I may be free of them.

[20] See also Asher [2] in this connection. It should be noted, however, that Asher sometimes uses the term *delineated* DRS in the sense in which I am using *articulated* DRS.

desire, and so we need at least different indicators for those two modes. I will use *Bel* as the indicator for belief and *Des* as that for desire.

Mode indicators are not constituents of the contents of attitudes. Hence they cannot be expected to have meaning in the way of sentence constituents, or of the constituents of other truth condition representing structures. Nevertheless, modes have something partly similar to constituent meaning. I will refer to it as *logical force*. It is the logical force of each mode which determines the inferential role which attitudes with that mode play in the various processes of practical and theoretical inference. (Thus logical force is partly similar to the meanings of sentence constituents, insofar as the latter also (help) determine, via the contributions they make to the truth conditions of the sentences in which they occur, what inferential roles those sentences can play.) As the analysis of logical force evidently belongs among the tasks of the theory of practical reasoning, it falls outside the scope of this paper.

As (A3) explicitly says, different components of the same complex attitudinal state may be connected in that they share one or more discourse referents. In fact, this is an exceedingly common phenomenon, and it arises both in cases where the sharing components have the same attitudinal mode and in cases where they do not. Instances of the second kind are especially important, as they are crucially involved in virtually all processes of practical reasoning. Usually, when we move from a set of beliefs and desires to an intention (to act in such a way that the desires are likely to be optimally satisfied given what we believe the world to be like), the desires and the beliefs are connected in just the way that discourse sharing components of complex attitudinal states seem to capture. Let me give a simple example. Suppose that I believe there is a cup of tea in front of me and that I have the desire to drink. I may then form the intention to pick up the cup and bring it to my lips. Here belief, desire, and intention are connected in just the way that the sharing of discourse referents suggests: They all contain the same discourse referent, representing the cup, and it is only because the belief and the desire are connected in this way that the mechanisms of practical reasoning may be expected to yield an intention which is about the same cup of tea in virtue of containing this discourse referent as well. (A proper treatment of this, and other cases of practical reasoning, should spell out the inferential principles which exploit the connectedness of belief and desire; but I think the point ought to be clear enough even without these details.) Note that it would not do to try and re-analyze this inference by construing belief, desire and intention as all being about the same external object, the cup of tea that is actually standing in front of me. For it might be that I am hallucinating (or wrong for some other reason) and that there isn't any cup in front of me at all. In that case none of the attitudes in question can be construed in the way this analysis would require. Yet it is obvious that the processes of practical reasoning will evolve just as they would in a case in which there is a real cup; from a cognitive point of view—i.e., from the only viewpoint that matters to questions of reasoning, whether theoretical or practical—the two cases are indistinguishable. Only a theory of belief and desire which allows for a notion of *intended coreference*, such as that embodied in the commonality of discourse referents, is in a position to explain how the two complex states can be intentionally identical, even though the one but not the other is directed at a real thing.

The first part to my proposal for dealing with higher order attitudinal structure does not deal with the higher order as such, but only with the form of those "first order" components of states which may, though they need not, figure as the arguments of higher order conditions. It is only the second part of the proposal that deals with higher order attitudinal structure itself. This part posits that higher order conditions have for their arguments discourse referents that represent components of attitudinal states. Superficially this might seem an entirely straightforward matter, given what has already been said, in Section 2, about discourse referents and conditions generally. However, there are some subtle questions about precisely how the attitude discourse referents, which this extension of the DRS formalism takes on board, are connected with the attitudes (or, more accurately, with the components of attitudinal states) they are meant to represent. Note in this connection that in the cases which motivated the adoption of such discourse referents—those where the subject attributes a property to one of his own attitudes—the discourse referent must be connected with a part of the attitudinal state to which it itself belongs. This situation is quite different from that exemplified by, say, the discourse referents x, t, and p of (2) and (3), which represent entities in the world, not components of the very same structure to which they themselves belong.

In fact, this is a problem which I will not be able to discuss in any depth in this paper. I will return to it only very briefly towards the very end, in Section 6.3; but a proper treatment will have to wait for another occasion. Instead of addressing it, we will, in Sections 4 and 5, look at questions which relate, some more some less directly, to the problem of higher order attitudes and which need to be addressed before we can deal with the problem of higher order attitudes in the way I think one should.[21]

---

[21] The representation of attitudinal states as articulated DRS's bears on a question which I have not raised explicitly in the text. This is the question how many distinct attitudes are contained in any given attitudinal state. Formally articulated DRS seem to provide a straightforward answer: The individual attitudes are its members (And so the number of them is its cardinality.) But this answer conceals a number of difficult issues which complicate the question. In fact, I doubt very much that the question permits more than a partial answer. Surely parts of an attitudinal state which either differ from each other in their modes or are the subjects of incompatible higher order attributions are thereby established as representing distinct attitudes. What is not so clear is whether attitudinal state should sometimes be regarded as subdivided over and beyond the divisions thus established. This question is complicated by two separate factors. First,

4 Direct Reference and Attitudes De Re

4.1 Direct Reference

In my discussion of the DRS (2) in Section 2, I emphasized that the real world correlates of the discourse referents x, e, p, and t are not necessarily fixed. The content of (2) only requires that there be some set of entities a, E, P, and T which satisfy the given conditions. If there happened to be two whale beachings near San Diego within the indicated period,

---

attitudinal states are subject to continual change, both as a consequence of new inputs from outside and of the inner processes of the mind—in short, because creatures with attitudinal states think. These changes affect in particular the ways in which bits of information are grouped together and/or separated. So what at one moment acts as a single belief may the next moment act as two or more, and this may happen even though there is no change in content over all.

Second, whether we, as outside observers of a certain individual, should describe him as having, say, one single belief or rather as having two "smaller" beliefs whose conjunction is logically equivalent to the first may depend on our purpose in making such an attribution to him. (I suspect that there are important connections between these two factors, but I do not see my way through what they might be). The following case may give an idea of the complications that worry me. Suppose you and I are waiting at a zebra crossing when a shiny convertible sweeps past. I recognize Emma at the wheel, and the car strikes me as a Ferrari. So I form the belief that Emma just passed us in a Ferrari. You also recognize Emma, but you also recognize the car as a Fiat. And so you now have the belief reflecting that impression. When I exclaim: "Gosh, did you see Emma in that Ferrari!" you retort: "That wasn't a Ferrari, you twit. That was a Fiat." Suppose you persuade me that I was wrong: Certain features of the car, which in fact I did notice, are never found with Ferraris but only with Fiats. So I adopt your version, and adjust my beliefs accordingly. Question: Have I changed the one belief I had, viz., that Emma passed us in a Ferrari, into the (incompatible) belief that she passed us in a Fiat? Or did I really have two beliefs—one that Emma just passed us in a car, and the other that that car was a Ferrari—the first of which I shared with you, while you succeed in talking me out of the second? I just would not know how to answer this question and I doubt that an unequivocal answer could be found.

One would expect a similar difficulty to arise in relation to questions involving simple existential or universal quantification over attitudes. Consider for instance, the claim that immediately after Emma raced past us, but before I could comment on the event, you and I had a belief in common concerning the event? If my only belief at that point was that Emma passed in a Ferrari the claim should be regarded as false; for that is a belief you did not have. If it is correct to attribute both to me and to you more than one belief on the subject, one of which is, for each of us, the belief that she passed in a car, then the claim should count as true. Interestingly, the intuitions about this claim seem pretty clear. Surely we did share the belief that she passed in a car. The fact that our apparent uncertainty how beliefs should be counted goes hand in hand with much clearer intuitions about claims involving purely existential or universal

then either one would provide a satisfying correlation of real world entities with these discourse referents. This is just another way of saying that these discourse referents function, from the perspective of traditional formal logic, as existentially quantified variables.

But this is not true for all of the discourse referents of (2). In fact it is not true for any of the remaining discourse referents n, p', and t'. The reasons are different for each of the three cases. We shall have to go over each of these in turn.

Before we address the problems which these discourse referents raise, let us begin by noting that there is one very straightforward type of case in which a discourse referent can be said to represent a unique entity. This is when the conditions in which the discourse referent figures are true of exactly one thing in the world. Such discourse referents have a status like that of definite descriptions which are proper in the sense of the classical description theories of Russell and Strawson. Indeed, one way in which discourse referents with this property arise is when a proper definite description is processed by the DRS construction algorithm, yielding a discourse referent, together with conditions reflecting the description's descriptive content, and thus satisfiable by exactly one thing.

In real life, however, pure cases of this sort are not all that common: Very few of the definite descriptions we encounter in ordinary use are proper in the strict Russellian sense. Typically, descriptions succeed in denoting uniquely only by virtue of the support they get from other noun phrases. And when one pursues the support chains to their beginnings, one often finds noun phrases which act in a demonstrative or indexical capacity.[22] It is widely accepted nowadays that such indexical and demonstrative noun phrases succeed in picking out their referents in a non-descriptive manner, that they *refer directly*. The classical account of this is that an assertion containing such a noun phrase puts forward a so-called *singular* proposition, in which the property expressed by the remainder of the asserted sentence (i.e., by that which remains when the noun phrase is removed from it) is attributed to the individual which the noun phrase picks out. The noun phrase does not furnish the proposition with a description of

---

quantification suggests that belief is conceived more as a homogeneous than as a countable category. Independent evidence which points in this same direction is that in many languages, including for instance German and French, the closest translation of the English noun belief is a mass noun, not a count noun.

[22] The simplest sort of example illustrating what I have in mind is provided by descriptions which embed demonstrative or indexical noun phrases. Take for instance the description 'my father's second wife'. This description uniquely identifies a certain individual as the only one who stands in a certain relation— that of being a second wife—to another individual which is uniquely identified as the only one standing in some other relation—that of being a father—to the individual denoted by the indexical pronoun 'my'.

the individual, but rather, the individual is itself a constituent of the proposition. This does not mean that the noun phrase lacks all descriptive information. It only means that whatever descriptive information it has serves exclusively for the *identification* of the individual; it is only in this indirect way that the descriptive content of the description can affect the proposition the sentence expresses; it does not enter into the proposition directly.

By what means different types of directly referential noun phrases succeed in picking out their denotata is a subject about which there is a good deal to say and about which, in fact, much has already been said.[23] I will address certain aspects of this problem later. But for now we will leave the issue aside.

What does the doctrine of direct reference come to in DR-theoretical terms? The first point to observe is that DRS's of the sort considered in Section 2 cannot do justice to direct reference as is. For the information such DRS's contain is purely descriptive, and so their truth conditions are always those of strictly general propositions. What is missing is some direct link with the world within which the DRS is situated—the world, that is, in which the sentence or discourse from which the DRS derives is uttered. To endow a DRS with the truth conditions of a singular proposition we must connect it with the appropriate entity or entities in the domain about which it intends to speak. Such connections are called (*external*) *anchors*. I will sometimes use the term *anchor* also for the individual with which a given discourse referent is connected, and, more specifically, refer to this individual as an *anchor for* the discourse referent, or *for* the DRS in which that discourse referent occurs, and I will call both the discourse referent and the DRS *externally anchored*.

Formally an external anchor is simply a pair consisting of a discourse referent and an entity. Besides unanchored DRS's, such as (2) and (3), DRT also admits *anchored* DRS's, which consist of an unanchored DRS together with one or more anchors. Given the motive for introducing them, the semantic role of external anchors should not be hard to guess. They serve to constrain the admissible correlations between discourse referents and entities in the world: Each of the anchored discourse referents may be correlated only with the entity to which it is already anchored. It is easily seen that this rule affects the truth conditions of the DRS in just the way the doctrine of direct reference requires. By way of an example, consider the case where someone says, pointing at a man standing on a street corner,

(4)   That man is a cocaine dealer.

This utterance contains two directly referential elements. The first is the demonstrative noun phrase that man, which refers directly to the man at which the speaker points; the second is the present tense of the verb;

---

[23] References are the familiar works of Kripke [96], Kaplan [91], and others.

this is an indexical element, which refers directly to the time at which the sentence is uttered. So the DRS that represents this utterance has two anchored discourse referents, as shown in (5) below:

(5)

$$\boxed{\begin{array}{ccc} x & n & s \\[4pt] \multicolumn{3}{c}{Incl(n,s)} \\[4pt] s\ldots\ \boxed{cocaine\ dealer(x)} \end{array}}\qquad \{\langle n,T\rangle,\langle x,a\rangle\}$$

Here the expression on the extreme right specifies the two anchors. It is important not to misunderstand what this expression is doing. It is not part of the DRS itself, but should rather be seen as a reminder that its truth conditions are not those of an unanchored DRS, but the modified truth conditions that are obtained when T is the only permissible correlate for n and a the only permissible correlate for x.[24] Thus, anchored DRS's express what Kaplan, following Russell, has termed *singular propositions*.[25]

Anchored DRS's capture the truth conditions which the doctrine of direct reference stipulates. But it is not clear how they fit into the picture of DRT that I sketched in Section 2. Recall that DRS's were supposed to result as representations of discourse, derived from them by a mapping (the

---

[24] I have chosen the terms, here 'T' and 'a', which are used to denote the entities to which the discourse referents are anchored, arbitrarily. Any terms (of the metalanguage in which the analysis of (4) is being carried out) which denote the right man and time will do here. Of course, I am not really in a position to provide the correct terms. For as the case has been presented, it leaves open when the utterance really occurred, or who the man was that the speaker pointed at.

[25] In fact, the structure of DRS's makes it easy to articulate in which respects singular propositions are singular. The proposition expressed by an anchored DRS is *singular with respect to* each of the individuals that anchor one of its discourse referents. Evidently, and as required by the accepted use of the term *singular proposition*, any proposition p that is singular with respect to the individual a can be understood as the attribution of a certain property P to the individual a— where p is expressed by the anchored DRS $\langle K, A\rangle$ and A contains the anchor $\langle x, a\rangle$, this is the property that, in any world w, is true of an object b iff the anchor $(A - \langle x, a\rangle)U\langle x, b\rangle$ can be extended to a correlation of the remaining discourse referents in K which satisfies all conditions of K in w (We say in this case that P is *expressed by* $\langle K, A\rangle$ *with respect to* x). If propositions are sets of possible worlds, then it is in principle possible that a singular proposition be expressed by an unanchored DRS. For instance, if p attributes the property P to the individual a, and there is a property Q such that (i) in each possible world w, Q is satisfied by a and only by a, (ii) P necessarily entails Q, and (iii) P is the property expressed by K with respect to x, then K expresses p. Intuitively this means that the conditions of K fix the possible correlate of x to be a in all possible worlds. But all this is thoroughly familiar from the work of Kripke [96], Kaplan [91], and others.

construction algorithm) which uses as inputs (i) the (syntactic description of) the current sentence and (ii) the already constructed DRS. As I presented matters, the input DRS itself derives from the earlier parts of the discourse. At no point is there room, according to this picture, for the world that the discourse is about to make its impact on the emerging DRS directly. Construction algorithms so conceived can only produce unanchored DRS's.

Part of the difficulty is that in the sketch of DRT which I gave in Section 2 the context in which a sentence is interpreted was identified with the result of interpreting the predecessors of that sentence in the same discourse. While information deriving from the earlier parts of the discourse tends to be needed for the correct interpretation, it rarely suffices on its own. As a rule interpretation relies on a host of additional information, reaching from the most general knowledge about the rules and laws which govern our world to knowledge of incidental facts about particular situations. Much of this information is acquired by non-verbal means. In particular, when we try to make sense of a sentence about our immediate surroundings we rely at least as much on what we can see of them as on what we have been previously told.

This points towards a reassessment of the model that, I said, DRT offers of the process of discourse interpretation. If this model is to stand a chance of being even remotely realistic, we must assume that the contexts to which the DRS construction algorithm is applied in sentence processing contain much more information than is supplied by the antecedent discourse alone. And it must allow for the possibility that even while discourse interpretation goes on, additional information may be introduced into the context via other than verbal channels.

Since some of the information that these so much more comprehensive contexts include must be expected to be of non-verbal origin, the hypothesis that such contexts are structured like DRS's reaches well beyond our earlier assumption that DRS's capture the structure of belief states acquired on the strength of verbal inputs alone.[26] Nevertheless I will stick to the hypothesis that contexts of interpretation have the form of DRS's. However much of an idealization this may well prove to be, I believe it will serve us well enough for the problems I will be discussing in this paper.

4.2 The Anaphoric Dimension of Direct Reference

Now that we have thus revised the notion of context, it is time to return to our example (4). Let us make the plausible assumption that among the contextual information available to the recipient of (4), just previous to the moment when she receives and processes the utterance, there is

---

[26] In fact, I think the balance of probability is that visual information and verbal information are stored in very different forms, and that reasoning mechanisms typically exploit them in very different ways. How the two interact may well prove to be one the most challenging problems of cognitive science.

some pertaining to the man at whom the speaker points (because, say, the recipient had already noticed the man herself). In terms of DRT this means that the context DRS contains a discourse referent representing the man, together with certain conditions which reflect what properties the recipient sees the man to have (in the jargon of the philosophy of perception: What the recipient sees the man *as*).

Against the background of such a context it is possible to provide a more pertinent analysis of the interpretation of (4). In particular, we are now in a position to see the processing of the demonstrative 'that man' as involving, just like that of the anaphoric constituents of the second sentence of (1) in Section 2, the connection of the new discourse referent with one that is already in the context: The discourse referent introduced by the demonstrative noun phrase is connected with the discourse referent in the context DRS which already represents the demonstrated man.

According to this analysis, the DRS-construction for (4) involves the extension of an existing DRS, not, as (5) suggested, the construction of one *ab initio*. Displaying of the context DRS only that part which matters (and that part merely schematically) we can indicate the difference before and after the processing of (4) by the following pair of diagrams:[27](i) Here the conditions $V_1(x), \ldots, V_n(x)$ are those which derive from the recipient's earlier observation of the man on the corner. (ii) I have ignored for the moment all questions which have to do with the discourse referent n. These will be addressed below.

(6)   Before:

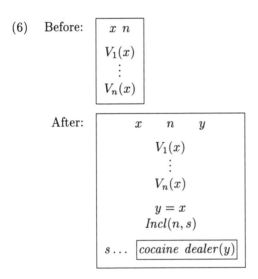

This seems to capture more of what goes on when an utterance like (4) is interpreted than did our earlier account, which led us to the DRS (5). Note however that the second DRS of (6) is *not* anchored. It is true that, as the direct reference account of demonstratives requires, the descriptive content of the demonstrative 'that man' has not become part of the content. Instead, the identity of the individual y represents is given via the conditions $V_1(x), \ldots, V_n(x)$, which reflect the recipient's antecedent observations about the man on the corner. But if we are to go by what was implied in Section 2, these conditions are once again descriptive. They represent the man as standing in a certain place, wearing such and such clothes, etc. There is no direct, non-descriptive link between y and the man at whom the speaker pointed.

I can see two different ways in which this problem could be overcome. I shall discuss them both. According to the first, the construction algorithm not only introduces a discourse referent x for each sentence contituent which it recognizes as directly referential, but also attaches to this discourse referent a "signal" that x is to be treated as directly linked to the entity that it represents. Which entity this is will, if all goes well, be determined by descriptive conditions on x of the sort with which we are already familiar. In the case of (4) the result will be a DRS looking like this:

(7)
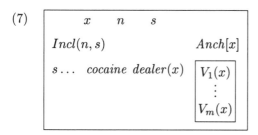

Here $V_1(x), \ldots, V_m(x)$ are the conditions which fix (if all is well!) the anchor of x. $Anch[x]$ is the signal that x is intended to function as anchored, via the descriptive conditions $V_1(x), \ldots, V_m(x)$.

It is important not to confuse DRS constituents like "$Anch[x]$" with conditions such as "$Incl(n,s)$," "$s \ldots$ cocaine dealer(x)" or "$V_i(x)$." The latter conditions are directed towards whatever it is that is represented by the discourse referents that occur in them. But "$Anch[x]$" does not have this kind of significance. It does not make an attribution to whatever object the discourse referent x represents, but rather imposes a special constraint on the role of the discourse referent itself (viz., that of being rigidly and directly linked to whatever object the descriptive conditions associated with x determine. Constituents with this kind of function, that of saying something about how discourse referents relate to what they represent rather than describing the represented entities themselves, will be termed *formal* conditions. In contrast, conditions of the sort considered so far will be called *descriptive*, or *predicative* conditions. (Often I will refer to both predicative and formal conditions simply as *conditions*.) Graphically, I will distinguish formal conditions from predicative conditions in that the former will be represented with their arguments enclosed within square brackets, while in the latter they are enclosed within parentheses.

If the condition "$Anch[z]$" is a constituent of the DRS K, then we will say of the discourse referent z that it is *formally anchored in K*.

The semantic significance of conditions of the form "$Anch[..]$" becomes explicit in the truth definition for the DRS's in which they occur. Recall that a DRS of the kind considered in Section 2 is defined as true in a world w iff it is possible to correlate its discourse referents with entities existing in w which satisfy the corresponding (predicative) conditions of the DRS. To adapt this definition so that it produces the right truth conditions for DRS's with occurrences of "$Anch[..]$," two things are necessary. First, the truth relation can now no longer be simply a binary relation between DRS's and worlds. We need, besides the world with respect to which the DRS is evaluated, also a world which provides the anchors for the discourse referents. (For the evaluation, as true or false, of DRS's representing purely extensional contents, the two worlds will coincide. But in general, when nonextensional information is represented, or when we are interested in the intension of an extensional DRS, this will not be so.) Second, we have to provide means that permit us to recognize those descriptive conditions which are ancillary to a formal anchor "$Anch[x]$" in that their role is to fix the entity to which x is externally anchored as playing this role. In (7) I have indicated this by placing those predicative conditions which serve to fix the anchor beneath the formal condition "$Anch[x]$." But we must make the division also formally precise.

What is needed here is something very similar to the articulated DRS's we found it necessary to introduce in connection with complex attitudinal states. Let us call the new structures *formally anchored* DRS's. The notion is defined as follows:

(8)   A *formally anchored* DRS K is a pair $\langle K, A \rangle$, consisting of (i) a DRS K, which may contain one or more conditions of the form "$Anch[..]$"; and (ii) a function A which assigns to each discourse referent z that is formally anchored in K. A DRS K_z not containing conditions of the form "$Anch[..]$." [28] K will be called the *principal* DRS *of K*.

The idea behind this definition is that the DRS K determines the content of the formally anchored DRS (modulo the individuals which the formally anchored discourse referents pick out), whereas the DRS's K_z have the function of picking out those individuals. Given what has been said about

---

[28] It is debatable whether the DRS's K_z should be permitted to contain formally anchored discourse referents in turn. If we were to permit formal conditions in these DRS's, then they should be made into formally anchored DRS's themselves. In that case the notion of a formally anchored DRS would have to be defined recursively, with the definition given in the text as the base case.

While I think there are linguistic constructions whose analysis requires such more complex structures, I feel that the inductive definition would have produced a formal complexity that would not bring us anything of substance here, and only confuse matters.

the truth conditions of such DRS's already, it should be clear that we can define the *truth value* of a formally anchored DRS K *with respect to* a world w *when anchored in* a world w' as follows:

(9)   a. K is *true with respect to* w *when anchored in* w' iff
    i. for each z such that "$Anch[z]$" occurs in the principal DRS K of K there is a unique entity a_z in w' such that there exists a correlation between the discourse referents of K_z and entities in w' which correlates a_z with z and satisfies all conditions of K_z in w', and
    ii. there is a correlation of entities in w with the discourse referents of K which correlates with each formally anchored discourse referent z of K the entity a_z, and satisfies all predicative conditions of K.
   b. K is *false with respect to* w *when anchored in* w' iff
    i. as (a.i) above, and
    ii. there is no correlation as described under (a.ii).

Note that this is a partial truth definition. K will come out as true or false with respect to w when anchored in w' only if it is "properly anchored" in w'—only, that is, if the descriptive conditions specified by the K_z single out unique individuals in w' for each of the formally anchored discourse referents z.

What sorts of conditions go into the DRS's K_z? This is a question that I do not intend to discuss in depth. But, to get at least an idea of the issues involved, let us return to our example (4). It is part of the meaning of a demonstrative noun phrase like 'that man' that the individual to which it refers is determined by a combination of two factors—first, the descriptive content of the NP itself, and, second, what might be called the "information content" of the demonstrative act (if any) which accompanies the utterance.[29] It is neither a simple nor, I believe, a particularly rewarding enterprise to spell out precisely how these two factors interact to produce, in all those cases where demonstratives are used felicitously, the descriptive conditions that identify the referent correctly.[30]

---

[29] Either of these factors may be vacuous. Thus demonstrative NP's can contain so much descriptive information themselves that there is no need for any disambiguating gesture. On the other hand there are the "pure" demonstratives 'this' and 'that' which have no descriptive content of their own and must rely entirely on the accompanying demonstration for referential success. (Actually this second claim isn't strictly correct, as even 'this' and 'that' contain a remnant of descriptive information: in cases where the referent is assumed to be a person, 'this' and 'that' are incorrect, except in a few special constructions such as 'That is a man'.)

[30] In the special case where the demonstrative act is a pointing, the descriptive condition should be something like "nearest thing of kind C lying in the indicated direction," where C gives the descriptive content of the NP and where "the

It is important to understand the difference between anchored DRS's such as (5) and formally anchored DRS's such as (7). Evidently an anchored DRS like (5) is not formally anchored, for there is nothing internal to the DRS to indicate that the relevant discourse referent, x, is anchored. Conversely, a formally anchored DRS need not be anchored, in the sense that there in fact exists an external anchor for each of its formally anchored discourse referents. For it may well be that one or more DRS's K_z fail to identify unique referents. Ideally, of course, this situation should never arise in the context of actual language use. For ideally directly referential expressions should always be used properly. And when a directly referential expression is used properly, then the discourse referent z it introduces into the formally anchored DRS K which represents that discourse will receive through the DRS K_z associated with it a unique individual a_z in the world w in which the utterance takes place. Thus a formally anchored DRS deriving from a discourse in which all directly referring elements are used properly is, according to the truth definition for formally anchored DRS's, always either true or false in the world to which the external anchors for its (formally) anchored discourse referents belong. We can represent the truth conditions of such a formally anchored DRS K in the form of an externally anchored DRS consisting of (i) the principal DRS of K and (ii) the external anchors which map each of the formally anchored discourse referents of K to the associated entities of w.

4.3 Formally Anchored Attitudes.

This first solution to the problem we encountered on page 55 has been largely based on our earliest discussion of (4), which led to the DRS (5). The second solution, which we will discuss now, relates more closely to the discussion which issued in the DRS's given under (6). This solution, moreover, will at last lead us to the subject announced by the second half of the title of this Section, *attitudes de re*.

According to the account associated with (6), a recipient of (4) who is in the epistemological position which the use of the demonstrative 'that man' presupposes, will connect the discourse referent y that the NP yields with another discourse referent, x, which is already part of the context provided by his background knowledge. By itself this does not supply y with an external anchor. But it will if there already is an anchor for the discourse referent x with which y gets connected. This, I want to suggest, is just what we have in the case of (6). The recipient of (4), who has been looking at the man standing on the corner, is thereby related to him in a

indicated direction" is a shorthand for some descriptive condition that specifies the direction in terms of a coordinate system to which the recipient has cognitive access in view of the position he himself occupies. But this could only pass as a first approximation, even if pointings were all we care about. More could be said on this point, but I won't bother.

way that puts her in an ideal position to have opinions that are directly about him, opinions which carry the commitment that it is *that* man— the one who is the actual cause of her perception, and no other—who has the properties attributed by those opinions. The content of such an opinion is, in the terminology of Russell and Kaplan, a singular proposition. Attitudes whose contents are singular propositions are sometimes referred to as *attitudes de re*. This is a term I will use also.[31] The proposal I made in Section 3 asserts that attitudinal states have the structure of articulated DRS's. That proposal did not allow for de re attitudes, and it is time to modify it in a way which makes room for these as well.

To arrive at a modification which does justice both to psychological and intentional aspects of de re attitudes it is important to keep in mind what was said in the last section about the difference between formal and external anchors. For it is crucial to distinguish between having, say, a belief that *is* about some external object (and whose content is thus a proposition that is singular with respect to that object) and having a belief that one *takes* to be directly about some external object. In particular, it is possible for someone to have a belief that he takes to be about some external object, and be mistaken about this. For instance he may be hallucinating, and thus be in a belief state which is psychologically indistinguishable from the state of someone who entertains a belief about an object he in fact sees, even though in his case there is no real object that he perceives.[32] When I say that in such a case the belief is psychologically indistinguishable from that of someone whose attention is directed towards an object which is actually there, I mean to imply in particular that the belief is qualitatively distinct from an existential belief—from a belief, that is, to the effect that there exists an object with such and such properties (including those which the subject hallucinates it to have) as well as the property of being seen by the subject.

This distinction—between believing that there is a thing with such and such properties and having a belief that the thing characterized by such and such properties, and to which, in particular, one stands in some special causal relation has certain other properties as well—I propose to represent by means of formal anchors: Where there is no anchor the attitude is existential, where there is one the attitude carries, as a kind of presupposition, the commitment that one is in fact standing in some suitable relation to some object answering the descriptive conditions associated with the anchor. This having been said, the following proposal follows straightforwardly from the earlier proposal (A3):

---

[31] The notion should not be confused—not at any rate in the theory developed here—with that of a *de re attitude report*. There are, it is true, close connections between the two concepts. But in the present theory they are nevertheless crucially different.

[32] Recall the comparison of the case with and that without a real teacup in Section 3.

(A4) Complex attitudinal states have the structure of *formally anchored articulated* DRS's, i.e., of sets whose members are pairs consisting of a mode indicator and a formally anchored DRS. In a DRS identifying such a state those and only those discourse referents are anchored that represent entities to which the possessor of the state takes himself to stand in some suitable causal relation.

Attitudinal states structured in the sense of (A4) raise a question of propriety which does not arise in connection with the simpler proposal (A3): It is possible for someone to be in an attitudinal state characterized by a formally anchored articulated DRS and fail to stand in some relation presupposed by one of the state's formal anchors. Where this happens—in other words, where a state has a formal anchor without a corresponding external anchor—the state strictly speaking misfires and lacks a well-defined truth-conditional content.[33] Of course this does not warrant the conclusion that, in such a situation, there is no attitude the subject could be said to have. Within the context of his own psychology the state is as real, i.e., as causally active, as it would have been had there no mismatch between formal and external anchoring.

We call an attitudinal state which is characterized by an articulated DRS that contains one or several formal anchors *formally de re*. Such attitudes, we have seen, may suffer from failure of presupposition. When there is no presupposition failure, and for every formal anchor there is a corresponding external anchor, the attitude will be called *truly de re*.

Whereas states that are formally but not externally anchored do in fact occur, states with external anchors unmatched by formal anchors, it seems to me, do not represent a possible category. The notion of such a state strikes me as incoherent: It makes no sense to describe an attitude as de re unless it is *taken to be de re* by the person who has it. Of course, it is possible to stand in the relevant causal relation to an object that does satisfy all predicative conditions associated with some discourse referent x of (the DRS identifying the content of) some attitude one has. But that is not enough to make the attitude into an attitude de re. For instance, I may have a purely existential attitude that happens to be satisfied, maybe even uniquely satisfied, by an object to which I stand in such a relation—I may, for all I know, be looking at it. The attitude is no less existential for that.

As a matter of fact, this kind of case is not uncommon. I may be looking for something of a certain kind, believing that there are such things and that I will eventually find one. At the same time I may in fact be staring at the one and only thing that, as it happens, is of this kind, and yet I need not realize that this in fact is the thing I am after. In this instance the belief that I will find something of the kind I want surely is as purely existential in content as it would have been had I not been staring at the object.

---

[33] Cf. the discussion of formally anchored DRSs and their truth conditions in the preceding Section.

Summarizing the last paragraph, we come to the following principle:

(A5) No external anchor without a formal anchor.

This principle does not play a central role in what I will have to say in the remainder of the paper. Nevertheless it seems to me to express an important intuition concerning the relation between the psychological (i.e., strictly internal) and the intentional (i.e., world-oriented) side of cognitive content, important enough to be mentioned, even if it has no implications for what is to come. In fact, the issue is delicate enough to warrant a much more careful and extensive discussion. But this too must wait for another occasion.

As it stands, (A4) is incomplete. For I haven't said anything yet on the question *which* relations give rise to anchored attitudes. This is a notoriously difficult problem, about which there appears to be a good deal of uncertainty and disagreement. Paramount among the relations which are thought to give rise to attitudes de re is that established by direct veridical perception, and especially, for those of us who can see, visual perception: If there are any cases at all in which a person qualifies as attributing in thought a property or relation to some individual other than himself, certainly thoughts that are directed towards individuals he is actually looking at should qualify as such thoughts. For other perceptual modalities the matter is perhaps not quite so clear. For instance, does hearing an alarm clock go off establish a direct link with it, in the way that (I think) looking at it would? Or is it more accurate to construe such a perception as involving an inference from the sound that one is hearing to the conclusion that there must be an alarm clock which is making it? I do not know how to answer such questions, and will have to leave them.[34]

Another type of relation which, I suggest, at least sometimes provides a sufficient basis for attitudes de re is memory. For one who has accepted that current perception provides such a basis, this seems to be especially plausible in the case of recent memories of perception: If a person can be said to have de re attitudes concerning an object while he perceives it, then it would seem unwarranted to deny he has de re thoughts about the individual as soon as ceases to perceive it even if the perception is still vivid in his mind. But memory is a matter of degree, and moreover, its degree is subject to change. As English puts it so well, memories *fade*. How vivid or accurate the memory of an object must be if it is to qualify thoughts about it as de re is a question that probably cannot be settled without some measure of arbitrariness.

---

[34] Perhaps the answer should depend in part on how well the various modalities of the perceiver work. For instance, a congenitally blind person, who has to rely on hearing and touch as his primary perceptual resources, should perhaps qualify as being directly related to the alarm clock he hears, whereas someone who relies primarily on sight (as I believe most of us do), would not. But this is all highly speculative.

I want to mention one other kind of situation which has been argued to give rise to attitudes de re. This is a case which is of particular importance for the relation between language and mind. It is where somebody forms a new belief (or other attitude) in response to an utterance which contains a directly referential expression. Note that, as with so many other concepts in the theory of language, there are two sides to the notion of direct reference. On the one hand there is the side of the speaker. He may use an expression e as directly referential, for instance, when he intends to express the content of one of his de re attitudes—a certain proposition p which attributes the property P to the individual a—and to this end utters a sentence which contains e and the remainder of which expresses P. On the other hand there is the side of the hearer. He may *take* an expression e to have been used as a directly referential expression, and represent, in the belief which the utterance produces in him, the referent of this expression e by means of a formally anchored discourse referent x. In other words, his belief will be formally de re. And presumably, if all goes well, it will also be truly de re.

But when will it be truly de re? That depends. If for instance the hearer recognizes the referent of e as something from his immediate surroundings, something to which he has independent access (e.g., because he is looking at it himself), then there is as much reason for attributing to him an attitude whose content is directly about that thing as there is in other cases where we form beliefs about things which we are directly observing. And, as I have just said, if there are any situations at all which lend themselves to the formation of attitudes that are truly de re, it is those in which the relevant objects are directly seen. In fact, it seems reasonable to assume that in the case we are considering the predicative conditions which support the formal anchor for x in K include those which derive from the direct perception, and which, as they do in other such cases, suffice to identify the external anchor unambiguously.

But not all cases are like this. For instance, the hearer's line of sight may be blocked, so that he cannot see the thing at which the speaker is pointing; or it may be that the referent is not part of the immediate surroundings at all; and if it isn't, it might be something to which the hearer is related through memory; or it might be something with which he has never had any dealings before, so that the expression e mediates their first and only contact. (The list could easily be extended, but these few examples suffice for the point). It is not easy to decide in which of these cases the resulting belief is truly de re and in which it isn't. Again the problem is that there appears to be no general agreement over which relations between believer and object warrant that an attitude that is formally de re is truly de re as well.

It would be foolish to legislate in this matter, and I won't try to do so. But I want to make two observations relating to it, but which are also pertinent to some points that are to be discussed later. In the first and the last of the three cases mentioned in the previous paragraph the predicative conditions supporting the formal anchor for x will, if they are to secure unique identification of the referent of e, have to involve reference to the expression e and/or to some intention of the speaker (and possibly to some other parts of his attitudinal state as well). For instance, the anchor's descriptive support might consist of a condition to the effect that "x is the direct referent of the expression e (as used by the speaker)" or "the object to which is the speaker is directly connected, via some discourse referent x' which gave rise to his use of the expression e"—or something to that effect; but without something of the sort unique reference cannot be assured. Thus, if it is possible in these cases for the hearer to acquire a belief that is truly de re, then, ipso facto, it is possible for the speaker to transfer his direct connection to external objects through the mere use of directly referential expressions.

In the above discussion I tacitly assumed that the hearer is correct in taking the expression e to have been used as a directly referential one. But of course, he could well be mistaken in this assumption—he may think the speaker used in this way, although as a matter of fact he didn't. In some cases this mistake gives rise to attitudes which, though formally de re, are definitely not truly de re. This may happen, more specifically, when the speaker is using an indefinite description non-specifically, and the hearer misinterprets his use of it as specific. In that case the relevant discourse referent in the hearer's belief will be formally anchored, and that anchor will be supported by some such descriptive condition as "x is the object the speaker had in mind and to which he referred with his use of e." Under the circumstances this condition is not satisfied by anything; so it fails to associate an external anchor with the given formal anchor.

We may sum up this discussion as follows: It is difficult, and perhaps impossible, to come up with precise and yet non-arbitrary criteria for when an attitude that is formally de re is truly de re as well. But there exist on the one hand clear cases where attitudes are truly de re, and on the other also cases of formally de re attitudes which nevertheless are not de re in the external sense.

Let us briefly compare the two solutions that we have sketched in this and the preceding section of the problem that we encountered in connection with (4). The first solution, that of Section 4.2, offers an extended DRS formalism which allows us to express (i) the intended content of an utterance like (4), and (ii) the content which such an utterance has in those situations in which the presuppositions of direct reference are fulfilled. The second solution, of Section 4.3, involves the same distinction—between formally anchored and externally anchored DRS's—but it recasts the analysis offered by the first solution as one concerning the structural and intentional properties of the attitude which a recipient would form in response to (4).

However, there are some further differences as well. First, the construction principles needed to arrive at the structures posited by the second solution must in general accomplish more than those which the first solution requires. Thus the second solution demands, for instance, that in processing a demonstrative such as 'that man' as it occurs in (4) one not only introduce a new discourse referent and anchor that discourse referent formally, but also that, in those cases where this is possible, the predicative conditions supporting the anchor are exploited to link this discourse referent internally to one already representing the demonstrative's referent in the context.

Another difference, this one of a more general and methodological nature than the one just mentioned, relates to the concepts of linguistic meaning (and, more specifically, of sentence meaning) that are implied by the two solutions. The first solution suggests, in line with what was said in Section 2, that the meaning of a sentence resides in its capacity for transforming truth condition bearing structures (DRS's) into other such structures. The second solution implies a somewhat different view, one on which the meaning of a sentence resides in its potential for transforming attitudinal states. This last difference carries a further implication which appears to be of particular importance for the theory of meaning and communication. Because different recipients of the same utterance may bring different attitudinal states—and thus different contexts of interpretation— to the same utterance, their interpretations of that utterance may yield significantly different results, even though both proceed in full accordance with the rules that govern the language to which the utterance belongs. Thus the second solution, but not the first, carries the clear implication that the meaning of an utterance, while itself independent of the individual properties of the actual or intended recipient, can nevertheless produce by equally legitimate means distinct messages in different receivers.

4.4 The Now and the Self

Up to now we have been looking in this section at direct reference by demonstrative noun phrases and by proper names. The direct referents of such NP's are, we saw, objects that are external to both speaker and hearer. (At least, this was so for the few examples we considered; but, in fact, as further reflection on the matter will readily reveal, with NP's of these types this is the norm.) The present section is concerned with direct reference as well, but with a form of it that is nevertheless importantly different form that considered so far. This is *indexical* reference. Indexical reference, as I understand the term, is always to an entity to which either the speaker or the recipient stands in some special direct relationship. Most languages have set particular words, suffixes or constructions aside for the purpose of indexical reference. Prominently among these devices are, in English and most other languages, the first and second person pronouns.

We will look at two types of indexical reference, to the present and to the self. We begin with reference to the present, for the representation of which we already introduced a special discourse referent, viz., n. The discourse referent n, I said, represents the utterance time of the represented discourse. Its role in DRS construction is that of guiding the interpretation of temporal constituents of the discourse. It enters into the analysis of all tenses and of a large number of different temporal adverbs. (The details of this are complicated but do not matter here). The truth conditional function of n is easily stated: Since it represents the utterance time it should always be correlated with that time.[35]

The discourse referent n also has a role to play in the characterization of attitudinal states. However, the semantic role which I propose that we assign to it when it acts as a constituent of an attitudinal state is somewhat different from the one just explained. For the possessor—call him B—of an attitude containing n, n is to represent, at any time t, that very time t (and not, say, the time at which B takes his belief to have originated). For instance, if a given person B has, at t, a belief characterized by the DRS (5), this is to mean that he believes the individual represented by x to be a cocaine dealer at time t. And this is to be the meaning, even if B knows that he formed his belief at some earlier time t_0, the time, say, at which someone said to him "That man is a cocaine dealer." There are some intriguing questions to which this proposal gives rise. But since they would lead away from the central topics of the paper, it would be unwise to try and explore those here.[36]

---

[35] Formally we can proceed in the ways familiar from tense logic: We define first what it is for a DRS K to be true in a world w with respect to a time t. This will be the case iff it is possible to find a suitable correlation of entities in w with the discourse referents of K which in particular correlates t with n. We can then define a DRS K deriving from a discourse D to be true in w iff K is, in the sense of the previous definition, true in w with respect to the utterance time of D.

[36] There is an important problem about identity and change of belief through time which relates to this proposal. (I have been aware of it for a number of years, on the one hand through the work of John Perry [128] and on the other through conversations with David Kaplan.) If someone who has formed a belief with the structure of (5) at t_0 retains the belief in this form the truth conditions to which he is thereby committed will in fact be subject to perpetual change. If on the other hand the truth conditional content of the original belief is to be preserved, the belief must be "re-registered" as a belief about the past. Such a belief has a quite different form—according to DRT, something like:

$$
\boxed{
\begin{array}{l}
\quad x \quad n \quad t \quad s \\
\qquad t < n \\
\qquad Incl(t, s) \\
\qquad W(t) \\
s \ldots \boxed{cocaine\ dealer(x)}
\end{array}
}
$$

where "$W(t)$" is meant to be some condition that identifies the past time at which B learned that the man on the corner was a cocaine dealer.

The upshot of this is that our beliefs about what is supposed to be the case now (i.e., at the very time of our having the belief in question) involve us in a

The relation in which we stand to the present time is not the only one which has a strictly non-descriptive character. There is at least one other, one's relation to the self. This is the relation which Lewis captured in his "Attitudes De Dicto and De Se" [107] by making the contents of beliefs properties that are self-attributed instead of propositions that are attributed to the world in which one lives. It is a relationship that is perhaps more easily perceivable in attitudes other than belief, such as, for instance, desire. Most of our desires are desires to the effect that something happen to *us*, e.g., that it is *we* who get the things that seem desirable. That the content of such a desire does indeed involve a direct connection to the self, and not simply an attribution to an individual that we could not distinguish from ourselves descriptively, is notoriously hard to prove. However, the matter has been argued in detail by Perry [128] and Lewis, and I have nothing to add to their subtle discussions.

I propose that just like the present the self be represented by a special discourse referent, for which we will use the symbol 'i'. Like n this discourse referent comes with its own formal condition, which distinguishes it from all others, and which is implicit in the use of 'i'.

The explication I gave of the role of n distinguishes between its role in representations of the content of discourse and that which it is to play in representations of attitudinal states. I want to make a similar distinction in relation to i. This time, however, it seems better to reverse the earlier procedure and to explain first its role as a constituent of an attitudinal state and then to define the part it is to play in representations of linguistic contents.

The first role is easily explained, and indeed there is nothing new in what it seems to me ought to be said here: i always represents the possessor of the state of which it is part (and does this in the particular way that gives rise to what Lewis [107] terms attributions de se). The implication of this for the truth conditions of DRS's containing i is straightforward: i must always be correlated with the possessor of the state of which it is a constituent.

---

perpetual tension between identity of form and identity of content. This tension gives rise, among other things, to the curious cognitive predicament that through mere intellectual apathy we may in actual fact allow the truth conditions of our beliefs to change, and thereby fall into error.

This is an intriguing topic in its own right, but not one to be pursued further here. I have mentioned it only to underscore my conviction that our relation to "now" is unlike any other cognitive relationship into which we enter with our environment. The special status of n is meant to reflect this. An important aspect of this relationship is that it is not mediated by any descriptive information. That n represents whatever time it happens to be is therefore a formal, not a predicative, condition. (I follow the existing practice in DRT of representing this formal condition by always using the symbol "n" for this discourse referent, and for nothing else).

It is important not to confuse what I have just said about i with the semantics of the pronoun 'I'. It has been suggested that all a semantic theory needs to say about 'I' is that the word refers in all cases in which it is used (except those where it appears inside direct quotation) to the person who uses it; and that is all there is to it. In a way this is clearly right. And yet I think I can see why such an account leaves some people dissatisfied. By relating 'I' to i we can, I hope, come a little nearer to the roots of that dissatisfaction. To explain what I have in mind I must say something about an aspect of language that we touched upon in passing in the last section, but about which I have not so far been explicit. This is its communicative aspect.

So far I have been concentrating on the interpretational side of language. But of course, as we noted already in Section 4.3, that is only one of its two sides. Before any bit of language can be interpreted, someone must have uttered it, must have chosen those words that make up the utterance to express the thoughts he wanted to convey. DRT suggests a very simple model for what goes on when someone puts his thoughts into words: The process is roughly the inverse of the interpretation process, one which turns DRS's into natural language rather than turning natural language into DRS's. I will refer to it as the *verbalization algorithm*.[37] Even so, the model of communication to which this simplifying assumption leads has turned out to be quite useful in a number of applications.

In simple situations, in which verbal communication involves just two participants, A and B, and in which A does all the talking, the model comes to this. Both A and B are in certain attitudinal states, characterized by articulated DRS's $K(A)$ and $K(B)$. Suppose A wants to communicate to B a certain bit of information. Typically this will be something that he himself believes; in other words, it will be some component of $K(A)$ of the form $\langle Bel, K_0 \rangle$. To communicate this belief to B, A has to find a sentence (or perhaps several sentences) which express it, i.e., which when processed according to the rules of the language in the context available to B will yield an addition to that context which captures the belief's content. If all goes well, B will, through processing the sentences that A speaks to him, add to his attitudinal state a new part which has the same content as the belief that A tried to put into words. The reason why we may expect this to happen is that B will be using the same rules that guided A in his choice of those sentences—A and B employ the same rules, since they are speakers of the same language.[38]

---

[37] The claim that verbalization and interpretation are inverses of each other is correct only in first approximation—there are many important asymmetries between language generation and language reception processes. One of these concerns the pronouns 'I' and 'you' and we will make its acquaintance shortly.

[38] In most ordinary speech situations B's context does not differ radically from A's own. In such situations it will be good enough if A's words produce, when

The only additional assumption needed for the point I wish to make here is that both $K(A)$ and $K(B)$ involve i (this is plausible enough; everyone has attitudes de se) and that the information A wants to communicate to B concerns himself, that is, A. To be concrete, suppose that A wants to tell B that he is a cocaine dealer. In $K(A)$, we may presume, this information is represented in some such form as this:

(10)

$$
\boxed{
\begin{array}{l}
\quad i \quad n \quad s \\[4pt]
\quad Incl(n,s) \\[6pt]
s \ldots \boxed{cocaine\ dealer(i)}
\end{array}
}
$$

and let us also suppose that the words he uses to convey this are

(11) I am a cocaine dealer.

In the last paragraph I said that to find the words which express this, A must apply a procedure, the verbalization algorithm, that is the inverse of the DRS construction algorithm. As a matter of fact, an analysis of the pronouns 'I' and 'you' shows that this cannot be not quite right. Thus, for instance, the verbalization algorithm must have a rule for 'I' which is not the inverse of the interpretation rule for 'I'.[39] To see this let us reflect on what the two rules should be like.

The verbalization rule for 'I' is extremely simple:

(12) 'I' may (again excepting occurrences within quotation contexts) only be used as designator for the individual represented by i.

---

interpreted in the context of the remainder of A's own beliefs—i.e., what remains of his belief state after the given belief has been removed from it—the very same belief that was just removed. But of course this condition isn't always fulfilled. When B's assumptions differ importantly from A's own, A will have to take this difference into account and rely in choosing his words, not on his own assumptions but on what he takes B's assumptions to be. If A is ignorant or mistaken about those assumptions, it may well happen that the message his words have for B is quite different from the effect they would have had on A himself had he believed all he does believe except for the particular belief he is trying to transmit. Various kinds of communication failure are likely to result in such cases. Precisely what kinds of failure arise through what kinds of utterances in the face of what kinds of discrepancies between the beliefs of speaker and hearer is a topic that deserves careful investigation, and that ought to hold a prominent place in any theory of verbal communication, (and especially one along the general lines sketched here). For what I have to say about the attitudes in this paper, however, the topic need not be explored further. (It is important in relation to the analysis of attitude reports, but since I won't have room to deal with attitude reports in the present paper, and have relegated them to its sequel, the analysis of communication failure can wait for a later occasion too.)

[39] This is one of the reasons why I qualified my claim, saying that the procedures are "roughly" inverses of each other.

In contrast, the interpretation (= DRS-construction) rule for 'I' is somewhat more complicated, and resembles fairly closely the processing principle for demonstratives which we discussed in Sections 4.1–4.3. To process an occurrence of 'I' in a sentence that reaches you, you must introduce a new discourse referent and anchor it by means of the descriptive information which the rule associates with 'I', viz., something like "whoever is, or was speaking (writing) what I am now hearing (reading)." Precisely how much descriptive information you will get out of this depends, as in the cases involving (4) which we discussed earlier, on the kind of access you have to the person who produced the sentence. If you face each other there will be a lot; when you read a letter or an autobiography there is often much less; and there are cases, as when you find a letter that was written by you know not who, nor to whom nor when, where it isn't even clear that the beliefs you form about the author on the basis of what you read could be construed as de re. But what matters is that in all these cases the new belief involves a formally and perhaps also externally anchored discourse referent for the presumed source of the utterance or text you interpret.

The asymmetry between the interpretation rule and the verbalization rule for 'I' suggests that there is more to the matter than the principle "I always refers to the speaker" reveals. To put it in Lewis's terms, the person who uses 'I' uses it to express self-attribution. But what an utterance containing 'I' conveys to the hearer is not a self-attribution; rather, it is an attribution to some external individual, albeit one to which he will typically stand in a relation that qualifies the attitude as de re. There is an intimate connection between the meaning of 'I' and the special access that we have to ourselves, but this connection is restricted to the context of language production. For the interpreter the word 'I' is much like a third person demonstrative such as 'that man' or the deictic use of 'him'. All these expressions lead to discourse referents which normally can be anchored descriptively, and often are connected with discourse referents that are already present in the processor's context DRS.

With 'you' the story is much the same, only reversed. 'You' also bears a special relationship to i. But here it is the construction rule, and not the verbalization rule that must exploit the special relation to the self. A minor difference between 'I' and 'you' is that the construction rule for 'you' is a little more complicated than the verbalization rule for 'I', since it must distinguish between the case where the interpreter identifies the utterance as addressed to him, and that where he takes it to be addressed to someone else.[40] It is the rule covering the first of these two possibilities that resembles the verbalization rule for 'I'.[41] It can be succinctly stated as:

---

[40] I am speaking here only about the singular pronoun. The analysis of plural 'you' is somewhat more complicated.

[41] The rule for the other case treats the pronoun as some kind of demonstrative; I will make no attempt here to state it.

(13) Represent the referent of 'you' by means of i.

The verbalization rule for 'you' resembles the construction rule for 'I' in that it is concerned with discourse referents other than i. It has some such form as :

(14) If z represents the person you are addressing then use you for the individual z represents.

So much about the role of i in characterizations of propositional attitudes. But what about its role in representations of linguistic utterances? The policy that seems to suggests itself here is entirely parallel to the one we adopted for n: i always stands for the one who produced the represented utterance. This means that in the context of discourse representation the construction rule for 'I' should not be the one described above, but rather the inverse of the verbalization rule for 'I':

(15) Always represent the first person pronoun by means of the discourse referent i.

I trust that in view of what has been said already it is evident at this point that the formal similarity between this new rule and the earlier verbalization rule for 'I' is largely illusory.

Let me summarize what I have done in this section. In Section 4.1 we discussed external anchors as a device for capturing the truth conditional content of discourse involving direct reference. In Section 4.2 we noted that an expression can be directly referential in intention without actually succeeding in (directly) referring. We introduced formal as opposed to external anchors to express this distinction. This apparatus, comprising external and formal anchors, can be used, we found in Section 4.3, to represent a parallel distinction within the realm of propositional attitudes: An attitude can be, just like an utterance, directly referential in intention— or, as we put it, formally de re—without being directly referential in reality, or truly de re. Precisely when a formally de re attitude does succeed in being truly de re as well is, I surmised, a question to which there may be no conclusive answer.

Section 4.4 dealt with indexical reference. We discussed the roles of two "indexical DRS elements," n and i, each of which has its own unique cognitive status. I argued that the DRS constituent i must be carefully distinguished from the pronoun 'I'. The two are connected in verbalization, but not in interpretation. In fact, i has as much to do with 'you' as with 'I', and in interpretation it is the first, not the second of these two connections which matters. To be able to articulate these connections we needed to take a first step towards a DRT based account of verbal communication.

5 Communication and the Intersubjective Dimension of Meaning

5.1 Internal Links

Among the expressions of natural language that have been claimed to function in a directly referential manner there are its proper names.[42] Whether proper names do indeed give rise to attitudes that are formally de re; if so, whether these formally anchored attitudes will also be truly de re; and, if only some of them are truly de re, under what conditions; these are important questions. But they have, in one form or another, been subjected to massive discussion in the philosophical literature, and I do not want to make the mountain any bigger as I would inflate it sideways, not upwards.

The feature of proper names that I do want to discuss is related to their directly referential character, but it is nonetheless a different one, which can be discussed only within a setting in which language is seen as a means of communication, not simply as a symbolic system which bears semantic relations to the world or subject matter that it is about.

So let us return to our simple-minded model of verbal communication, involving the two participants A and B, with their respective attitudinal states $K(A)$ and $K(B)$. Suppose that A utters a sentence containing proper names, e.g.,

(16) Mars is more massive than Venus.

Let us assume that this bit of information is new to B, but that he takes A's word for it, and thus that he adopts a new belief with the content of (16). According to our model this involves his adding to $K(B)$ a new component of the form $\langle Bel, K_1 \rangle$. I will assume that B already knew about Mars and Venus before the present exchange; in other words, that formally anchored discourse referents x and y for these two planets were already present in $K(B)$. Secondly, I assume that B understands 'Mars' and 'Venus' as proper names in Kripke's sense, so that K_1 contains formally anchored discourse referents to represent the bearers of these names. Finally I make the (DRT-internal, and conceptually unimportant) assumption that the discourse referents introduced for the occurrences of 'Mars' and 'Venus' in (16) are identified with x and y. From these assumptions it follows that x and y are components of the addition to $K(B)$ occasioned by (16) and that both are formally anchored.[43] So, in light of what has been

---

[42] In fact, the claim, first made in Kripke's *Naming and Necessity* [95], that names are directly referential seems to antedate similar claims about indexicals and demonstratives; but history is delicate in this particular domain, partly because it is sometimes difficult to decide whether certain claims really count as claims of direct reference.

[43] The directly referential view of proper names seems to entail that the discourse referents x and y are also externally anchored (to the planets Mars and

said about language processing and attitude formation so far, the formally anchored DRS K_1 will be of the following form:

(17)

x y	$Anch[x]$	$Anch[y]$
x is more massive than y	bearer of the name $Mars(x)$	bearer of the name $Venus(y)$
	$\boxed{\begin{matrix} V_1(x) \\ \vdots \\ V_r(x) \end{matrix}}$	$\boxed{\begin{matrix} W_1(y) \\ \vdots \\ W_s(y) \end{matrix}}$

If one reflects a little more carefully on what goes on in utterance interpretation, however, it is plain that even verbal communications of this exceedingly simple sort give rise to a good deal more in the way of attitude formation than is captured by (17). To begin with there is the well-worn pragmatic wisdom that when A says something to B and B accepts this as (probably) true, that acceptance is, in all normal cases, grounded in two separate assumptions, (i) that A is sincere, i.e., that he has a belief corresponding to what he is saying, and (ii) that A knows what he is talking about, i.e., that his belief is likely to be true. Let us suppose that the communication involving (16) is of this kind, and let us concentrate on the first of the two assumptions that, according to received pragmatic doctrine, underlie the acceptance of what one is told; let us, that is, ask: What would B's adopting the belief that A himself has a belief expressed by (16) come to within our model of communication?

It is clear that the theoretical vocabulary introduced thus far does not provide everything that a representation of this "second order belief" requires. So let us begin by filling this gap. We need to represent the belief content that A has a certain belief, with a certain structure and content given by (16). I propose that we take this literally: There is an object of a certain kind, viz., a belief, which is held by A and which has certain properties relating to its structure and content. Glossed in this way the content requires for its representation:

(i) a discourse referent p representing a belief,
(ii) a discourse referent a representing the speaker A,
(iii) a condition to the effect that p is a belief of a,
(iv) one or more conditions which specify the required structural and contentual properties of p.

Condition (i) demands that we add to our representational vocabulary discourse referents $p, q, r, \ldots, p_1, p_2, \ldots$ for attitudes; for us, for whom attitudes are components of attitudinal states, this means that the new

---

Venus). I am ignoring these external anchors as they are irrelevant to the central issue of this section.

discourse referents must be mapped onto such state components when the DRS's in which they occur are evaluated for truth or falsity.

Condition (ii) is unproblematic; discourse referents for persons have been available all along. We just note that in the case we are discussing B is bound to have a discourse referent for a which is both formally and externally anchored. Again, we will ignore the external anchor.

Condition (iii) will be given as $Bel(a, p)$. In general, we introduce for each mode indicator **M** which our theory admits a corresponding two-place predicate M which takes as first arguments discourse referents representing beings endowed with consciousness and as second arguments discourse referents representing components of attitudinal states.

And as for (iv), we specify the structural and contentual properties of p in one fell swoop, viz., by specifying p to have the structure of a certain formally anchored DRS. Graphically we do this by writing "$p\!:\!K$," where K is the specifying DRS. All that we have already said about the significance of DRS's in the specification of attitudinal content and structure can then be invoked to determine the truth conditions of conditions of this new form. More about this anon.[44]

Our earlier commitments determine virtually without remainder how this new notation is to be applied to the case under discussion. In particular, it seems clear that the DRS K which is to characterize the content of the belief which B attributes to A should be obtained from (16) by the same process as the representation of B's own belief of (16). Thus K will be isomorphic to that representation, for processing the sentence twice will yield DRS's that are isomorphic copies.

Proceeding along these lines we get for B's belief that A holds a belief he has expressed by (16) the representation:

(18)

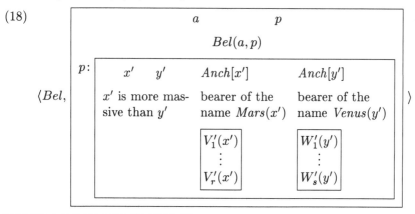

---

[44] Note that by adopting the notation "$p\!:\!K$" we are introducing an infinity of predicates in one go; in fact, since conditions of this form will themselves occur as components of DRS's, the addition of such conditions, in the sense in which we intend it here, leads to a recursive generation of DRS's containing such conditions on the one hand and on the other conditions in which such new DRS's occur on

Our account so far of the changes which B's reception of (16) occasions in $K(B)$ seems to come to this: B adds to $K(B)$ not only his own belief of (16), viz., $\langle Bel, (17) \rangle$; he also adds a belief to the effect that A holds a similar belief. According to what we have just said, this should be the pair $\langle Bel, (18) \rangle$. Thus the total change will consist in adding both these pairs. It seems to me however, that this representation misses something important. The intention behind (18) is that B attributes to A a belief with the very same content as that which he himself adopts. The representation we have just obtained appears to warrant this, as the two contents are given by isomorphic DRS's (viz., (17) and the DRS following "p:" in (18)). And yet there is some aspect to the identity of these two contents that this isomorphism fails to capture. In situations such as this one, in which one adopts a belief that one also attributes to someone else, the belief one adopts and the belief one attributes are, I contend, conceived as the same also in the sense of being *about the same things*. The word 'conceive' is crucial here. It is not just that the belief B adopts and the one he attributes to A are both about the actual Venus and the actual Mars, B *intends* that they be about the same things, and insofar as this intention is part of how he understands the two beliefs to be related, it ought to be captured by our representation of the over-all change to his attitudinal state.

The device we will use to represent this aspect of the identity of the two beliefs is that of what we call *internal links*. Formally an internal link is simply a pair $\langle x', x \rangle$ of two discourse referents which, roughly speaking, stipulates that these discourse referents represent the same individuals. In particular, with the use of internal links the change to $K(B)$ we have described can be represented as in (19). But what exactly could this stipulation, that x' and x (and y' and y) "represent the same individuals," mean? What, to put the question differently, could be meant by the intention that a belief of another person and one of one's own beliefs be about the same things?

The answer to this question that I want to proposes embodies what is perhaps the most radical of the various theses this paper puts forward. It is a thesis which I cannot hope to prove, but which has come to impress itself upon me as a crucial component to any account of the relation between thought and communication. Let me state it in summary form and then try to elucidate it:

(A6)   In many communicative situations we form beliefs and other attitudes that we intend to be about the same things as certain beliefs (or other attitudes) which we attribute to some other person. Such an intention carries the commitment that the content of the adopted attitude count as verified only in those situations which also verify the identifying conditions that the other person associates with the individuals he takes his attitude to be about.

---

the right hand side. In this way we have the formal means of expressing iterated belief (and other attitudes) of any finite depth.

(19)

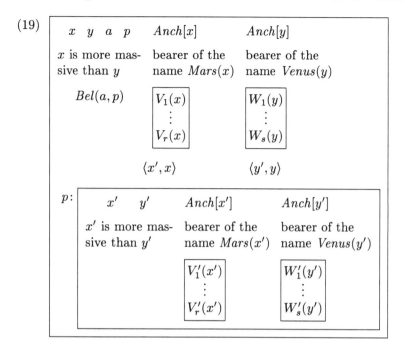

To express what (A6) tries to say in a more precise and comprehensible form I need to make use of the theoretical machinery we have been developing. Suppose that the attitude adopted by B is characterized by a DRS K_1, that the one which is attributed to the other person, A, say, has a content characterized by K_2, that K_1 contains the discourse referent x and K_2 the discourse referent x', that x' has in K_2 the anchoring DRS $K_{x'}$, and that the individual represented by x for B is intended to be the same as that represented by x' for A. Then only those correlations F of objects with the discourse referents of K_1 will count as verifications of the content of B's attitude which have the property that correlating $F(x)$ with x' yields a verification of $K_{x'}$.

Intentions of this sort render the contents of our own attitudes dependent on the attitudes of others, and so are responsible for a certain social dimension to the content of thought. In a case like the one we have been discussing in this section this effect is not visible. For, at least according to what we assumed about the case, the discourse referents x and y which represent Mars and Venus for B are formally anchored to these two planets, and the same is true for the discourse referents x' and y' with which x and y are linked and which, according to B, represent Mars and Venus for A. So B's commitment that whatever satisfies his belief content must also satisfy A's formal anchors for x' and y' does not add anything new to the truth conditions that his own belief would have had anyway. For the only correlations that could have verified that belief would have had to associate Mars with x and Venus with y in any case.

But it isn't always like this. Often the type of commitment described in (A6) does make a real difference to the truth conditions of the attitude with which it is associated. Typical cases are those where A uses an indefinite description which B takes to have been used *specifically*. Suppose for instance that A says to B:

(20) There is a man in my village who collects fossilized anteaters.

More likely than not B will take A to be talking about some particular man he knows, one for whom he, A, has a formally and externally anchored discourse referent. If so, and if B adopts what he is told as a belief, he is likely to associate with this belief the commitment that it be about the man the speaker had in mind when he said (20). In this case the link between the discourse referent x representing the fossil collector in B's new belief and the discourse referent x' playing the analogous role in the belief B attributes to A will make a difference. Without it the content of B's belief could in principle be satisfied by any man in A's village with the mentioned hobby (For all we know the place may have a secret society of fossilized anteater collectors, a circumstance of which A, even though he is from there, is ignorant). But with the commitment that only the man whom A had in mind qualifies as a verifier of B's belief this possibility is excluded. For only the man A had in mind will fit A's formal anchor for that man, and the internal link then guarantees that this man will also count as the only verifier of B's own belief that there is such a collector in A's village.

But is this really right? We are bound to ask this question when we recall what was said at the end of Section 4.3. There I suggested that the recipient of an utterance will under certain circumstances be induced to attach to a discourse referent x a condition saying something like "x is what the speaker referred to with his use of the expression e" or "x is what the speaker had in mind when he used e." Would such conditions not have precisely that effect on the truth conditions of the newly formed attitude that are now being attributed to internal links?

The answer to this last question is of course: Yes. But that does not really detract from the central point I am concerned to make. For, obviously, the effect of conditions of this kind would be precisely that they make the attitudes of which they are part dependent on the attitudes of others. Indeed, the device of internal anchoring can be seen as a first and limited explication of conditions which, like those informally described at the end of Section 4.3, create referential connections between one's own and others' attitudes.[45]

---

[45] In fact, in a more careful and formal definition of the theory as we have (informally) developed it up to this point, in which one spells out in full detail what DRS conditions are admitted, conditions of the sort discussed towards the end of Section 4.3 would not be admitted: The only permitted mechanism for making the values of discourse referents dependent on the attitude of others would

In Section 4.3 we were concerned with the question what kinds of utterance situations can give rise to formally anchored beliefs. In particular, we wondered whether there could be formal anchors which are supported by nothing more than identifying conditions which pass, so to speak, the burden of identification to someone else. By adopting (A6) I have in effect committed myself to a positive answer to the last question. For linking can produce precisely the effect of formally anchoring a discourse referent of the recipient's attitude via anchoring conditions that are directly accessible only to the speaker.

From the two illustrations of (A6) we have thus far considered it might appear that internal links always have this effect—that of making a formal anchor of one person available to another. But not all cases in which (A6) is operative are like this. It is also possible for B to establish an internal link with some discourse referent belonging to an attitude he attributes to A, but for which A (while having the attitude attributed to him) does not have a formal anchor (and for which B does not assume A to have such an anchor either). A typical sort of case where this seems to happen is that where A tells B of his future plans, say, his plan to buy a plot on the Riviera, build the bungalow of his dreams on it and then retire there. B may find this a wonderful idea, and start making plans of his own, for instance that of paying A an extended visit once he is properly set up. It seems to me plausible to maintain of this case that the intention which B forms, that of visiting A in his future bungalow, comes with a link between the discourse referent that represents the bungalow in B's own plan with the discourse referent representing the bungalow in the plan that he now attributes to A (i.e., the plan that A has just revealed to him). B's plan is, we might say, contingent on that of A, and this contingency manifests itself in part by his making the value of his discourse referent dependent on whatever may turn out to be the value of the corresponding discourse referent in the plan of A. Nevertheless it may be assumed that A's discourse referent for his future bungalow is not formally anchored. In fact, there is nothing that it could be anchored to. The bungalow is at this point only a dream, a dwelling of no fixed place, size or form, something with no other identity than that which accrues to figments of the imagination.

In a case like this B evidently cannot make the value of his discourse referent x for the bungalow dependent on the formal anchor that A has for the corresponding discourse referent x', for there is no such anchor. So the dependence must take a different form. My intuitions about the present case is that it is the conditions attached to x' in A's plan that will provide the support for the link. After all, B's plan presupposes the realization of that of A. But should all the conditions from A's plan be

---

be the internal links. Refinements of that theory might extend this mechanism and introduce notation that could be seen as corresponding more closely to the problematic conditions.

taken on board? In general this would not seem necessary. For instance, A may have been quite explicit to B on one or two points of detail, and it is conceivable that on those points his plan will later come to be modified (e.g., because he will find that those aspects of the original plan are not practical, or through a simple change of heart). B may envisage this possibility and while conceiving his own plan as contingent on that of A, yet not conceive of it as contingent on those details. In fact, it appears as if the question precisely to which conditions he should see himself as committed need not be fully determined. Whether there are any general principles for identifying the conditions (some or all of them) that B should commit himself to in cases such as this one I do not know.[46]

5.2 Sharing of Discourse Referents and Common Knowledge

The instances of referential dependence which we discussed in Section 5.1 were all one-directional: One person, B, makes the values of some discourse referents dependent on the attitudes of some other person, A. In some situations in which this happens it is all that happens—more precisely, the dependencies of B's discourse referents on the attitudes of A's are the only dependencies of one person's attitudes on those of another to which the communication gives rise. More often than not, however, what happens is more than this. Not only do some of B's attitudes become dependent on those of A, some of A's become conversely dependent on attitudes of B. The principal reason for this has to do with a feature of face to face communication which I did not mention so far, but which is as familiar as the principle I offered as motivation for (A6) (the principle that the hearer typically adopts the belief that the speaker believes what he says). When, in oral communication the hearer does not overtly object to or doubt what the speaker has just said, then the speaker assumes by default that his words have been accepted and thus that the hearer now has a belief reflecting what he has just told him. Thus, in the standard case the speaker comes away with a belief that the hearer has a belief corresponding to what was said, and the belief that the hearer believes that he, the speaker, has a belief reflecting his own words is equally available to him. It is an insight of long standing that these are the first steps in an unbounded hierarchy of mutual attributions of ever more complicated, nested attitudes.

---

[46] Another complication arising with the unanchored cases is that a good representation will in some way have to mark the conditions (from A's attitude) which are to support the link B establishes. One way to do this would be to associate with any link $\langle x', x \rangle$ a DRS $K_{\langle x', x \rangle}$ *supporting* it. This DRS would have to be drawn in its entirety from A's attitudinal state. In the cases where x' is formally anchored for A this DRS would be $K_{x'}$. In the cases where there is no formal anchor some more complicated procedure, which apparently could not be fully determinate, would be operative for culling $K_{\langle x', x \rangle}$s from A's attitudinal state.

It is a default assumption, operative in the standard case, that this entire hierarchy is in principle available and, moreover, that this assumption is itself one which speaker and hearer share.

There exist a number of theories which articulate the semantic and logical implications of this shared assumption, theories of, as it is usually called, *common knowledge*. These theories concentrate on common knowledge whose objects—in the sense of what is (commonly) known—are propositions. To that topic I have nothing to contribute here. However, there is a side to the phenomenon of shared information which relates directly to the issues that we have been talking about and which theories of common knowledge have so far ignored: The participants in a discourse may not only come to share the knowledge of, or belief in, certain propositions; the very identity of those propositions may be dependent on the very commitment which the sharing involves.

An example may help to explain what I mean. Consider the following case. A and B plan to write a joint paper. They once talk about this project, then go their own ways, and think more about what shape the paper should take. After that they talk about the project off and on. After a while their ideas about the paper diverge, but nevertheless it remains, in the minds of both, a joint project. Each knows that the other has a number of beliefs, desires and intentions relating to the paper. Or, put in the language of this essay, each attributes to the other a complex attitudinal state which contains a discourse referent representing the paper and which occurs as argument in a variety of conditions, some but probably not all of which are known to his partner. It is, I claim, an essential feature of such a situation that the two participants take their respective discourse referents for the paper to be linked, in the sense that they have a joint commitment to count any correlation of one of those discourse referents with a real object (in this case with some real paper written at some later date) also as a correlation for the other discourse referent. Thus verification of A's attitudes cannot be detached from verification of those of B nor vice versa. I will call this kind of joint commitment *sharing of* (the relevant) *discourse referents*.

This is not to say that either A or B will have to see his own beliefs about the paper as verified only in those cases where his partner's beliefs would be fulfilled too. On the contrary, it is in virtue of the joint commitment which A and B share that they can see conflicting beliefs about the paper as actually incompatible. Suppose for instance that A believes the paper will be more than 30 pages long and that B thinks it will be less, and that they reveal these beliefs to each other. These two beliefs are obviously incompatible, and A and B will surely see them as such. But their incompatibility presupposes that they are about the same thing. And if there is any sense in which they are about the same thing this can only be because A and B are committed to construing them so.

The point is a perfectly general one. But for the possibility of sharing discourse referents we could rarely, or at any rate in far fewer cases than we actually do, see ourselves as holding views that disagree with those of others; there would be virtually no scope for disagreement and debate. Perhaps there is no better way of realizing how pervasive the phenomenon of sharing discourse referents must be.

The description of shared discourse referents cannot take quite the same form as that in which we have represented internal linking so far (as for instance in (19)). For that representation is, as the term "internal link" implies, internal to the attitudinal state of one particular individual. What we need is a way of saying of two or more individuals that certain discourse referents which figure in their respective attitudinal states are shared by them. As this is a claim that is made "from the outside" about the two attitudinal states together, our device for expressing it will have to be external to each of the two states, too. Once this is realized, however, nothing seems to speak against using the same notation, involving pairs of discourse referents, to indicate sharing as well as internal linking; the place where the pair appears will make it clear how it is to be understood. The external claim (our claim) that A and B share the belief that Mars is more massive than Venus (in the sense that they take their beliefs to be about the same planets) may be represented as:[47]

(21)

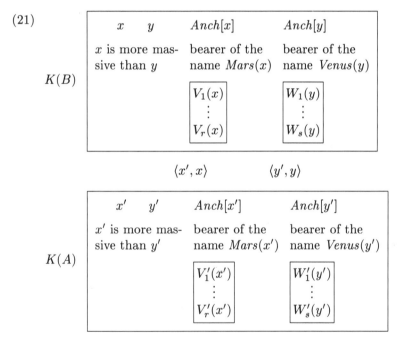

The pairs $\langle x', x \rangle$ and $\langle y', y \rangle$ stand here outside the representations of both attitudinal states. In view of this they must be understood as external

---

[47] Again ignoring what else may be part of the attitudinal states of A and B.

assessments of subjects and their states, which involve not only the individual psychologies of those subjects but also certain causal relations between them (having to do with their present and past communications and more generally with their interactions within the larger information exchanging community of which they are part), just as external anchors must be understood as claims based not only on a person's psychology but also on the causal relations in which he stands to the things towards which his thoughts are directed.

However, for reasons parallelling those which led us to the principle (A5) we may surmise that from a description such as that of (21) an essential bit is missing. What is crucial for sharing of discourse referents is that the participants *take* themselves to be sharing those discourse referents. Precisely how this psychological aspect of discourse referent sharing is best represented is something about which I have no definitive views, and what I shall propose in this regard should be seen as tentative.

In trying to decide how the psychological aspect of discourse referent sharing is best represented we do well to distinguish between two types of cases. The first, which is really a special subcategory of the second, is exemplified by the one we have been discussing and which found its (incomplete) representation in (21). Here the participants A and B take themselves to share a particular attitudinal content identified by a structure specifying the discourse referents that are taken to be shared. Both A and B have a commitment to this effect; and since these commitments may be assumed to be identical in form, let's concentrate on just one of them, say A's.

It is clear that the condition expressing A's commitment must specify (i) the content shared, (ii) the discourse referents occurring in this content that are shared, and (iii) who are doing the sharing. How these components should be represented follows more or less directly from the commitments already made: The content should be specified as a DRS, and the shared discourse referents can then be selected from that DRS. As regards (iii): One of the participants is A himself; in line with Section 4.5 he should be represented by the discourse referent i. The other participant will have to be represented by an "ordinary" discourse referent; in general A will, in the cases giving rise to shared discourse referents, have a formally and externally anchored discourse referent b representing his partner B.

What remains is the choice of a predicate that takes these different components as arguments. I propose the predicate "*Shared*." In general the condition expressing the subject's commitment to regard the content specified by the DRS K and the set D of discourse referents occurring in K as shared by him with the individual b will have the form

(22) *Shared*$(D, b, i) : K$

For the special case that was incompletely described by (21) the two relevant instances of (22) are as follows:

(23)

(A): $Shared(\{x'', y''\}, b, i)$:

x''	y''
x'' is more massive than y''	

(B): $Shared(\{x''', y'''\}, a, i)$:

x'''	y'''
x''' is more massive than y'''	

Evidently, somebody holding that he is sharing a certain attitude with someone else must indeed have this attitude. This imposes an obvious constraint on representations of attitudinal states in which conditions of the form (22) occur: Whenever the representation contains an instance $Shared(D, b, i) : K$, then it must also contain a component $\langle \mathbf{M}, \langle K', A \rangle \rangle$ where K' is an isomorphic copy of K.[48] Moreover, the representation should make explicit that K and K' represent the content of one and the same attitude. This means that each discourse referent in K' must be internally linked to the corresponding discourse referent of K.

Let us see what this means for the particular case of our example. To complete the description given in (21) in the spirit of what has just been said we must do the following: (i) we must add $\langle Bel, K_A \rangle$ to $K(A)$ and $\langle Bel, K_B \rangle$ to $K(B)$, where K_A is the DRS consisting only of the condition (A), and similarly for K_B. (ii) we must add all the internal links, i.e., $\langle x'', x' \rangle$ and $\langle y'', y' \rangle$ must be added to $K(A)$ and $\langle x''', x \rangle$ and $\langle y''', y \rangle$ to $K(B)$. If we once more ignore the mode indicators of the "sharing beliefs" (which in this as in earlier cases is unproblematic as all components are beliefs and thus have the same mode) we arrive at the expansion of (21) shown in (24).

Just as we stipulated, in (A5), that the description of a complex attitudinal state is incoherent unless for each external anchor there is a corresponding formal anchor, so we stipulate now that there can be no coherent representation of a system of attitudinal states belonging to distinct persons which contains claims of discourse referent sharing (i.e., pairs $\langle x, x' \rangle$ occurring outside the representations of each of those persons' states) unless each of the states that make up the system contains a corresponding instance of (22). Note that this stipulation makes sense provided each claim $\langle x, x' \rangle$ concerns discourse referents x' for person A and x for person B such that A and B share an attitudinal content K in which these discourse referents occur. In that case the representation of A's state will contain a component of the form $\langle \mathbf{M}, K_A \rangle$ and that of B a component of the form $\langle \mathbf{M}', K_B \rangle$ where both K_A and K_B are isomorphic copies of K, and thus also of each other, and where the isomorphism between the K_A and K_B carries x' over into x. That A and B take themselves to share this content

---

[48] By an isomorphic copy of a DRS K we understand any DRS which can be obtained from K by replacement of discourse referents.

is then manifest through a corresponding instance of (22) involving further copies of K internally linked to K_A and K_B, respectively.

(24)

$$
\begin{array}{lll}
x \quad y & Anch[x] & Anch[y] \\[4pt]
x \text{ is more mas-} & \text{bearer of the} & \text{bearer of the} \\
\text{sive than } y & \text{name } Mars(x) & \text{name } Venus(y)
\end{array}
$$

K(B)

$$
\boxed{\begin{array}{c} V_1(x) \\ \vdots \\ V_r(x) \end{array}} \qquad \boxed{\begin{array}{c} W_1(y) \\ \vdots \\ W_s(y) \end{array}}
$$

$Shared(\{x''', y'''\}, a, i):$

$$
\boxed{\begin{array}{cc} x''' & y''' \\ \multicolumn{2}{c}{x''' \text{ is more massive than } y'''} \end{array}}
$$

$$
\langle x''', x \rangle \qquad\qquad \langle y''', y \rangle
$$

$$
\langle x', x \rangle \qquad\qquad \langle y', y \rangle
$$

$$
\begin{array}{lll}
x' \quad y' & Anch[x'] & Anch[y'] \\[4pt]
x' \text{ is more mas-} & \text{bearer of the} & \text{bearer of the} \\
\text{sive than } y' & \text{name } Mars(x') & \text{name } Venus(y')
\end{array}
$$

K(A)

$$
\boxed{\begin{array}{c} V_1'(x') \\ \vdots \\ V_r'(x') \end{array}} \qquad \boxed{\begin{array}{c} W_1'(y') \\ \vdots \\ W_s'(y') \end{array}}
$$

$Shared(\{x'', y''\}, b, i):$

$$
\boxed{\begin{array}{cc} x'' & y'' \\ \multicolumn{2}{c}{x'' \text{ is more massive than } y''} \end{array}}
$$

$$
\langle x'', x' \rangle \qquad\qquad \langle y'', y' \rangle
$$

The general case is that where A and B share discourse referents but where there need not be a corresponding sharing of an attitudinal content of which these discourse referents are part. What I said about disagreement suggests that such cases do arise and in fact that they are quite frequent. At the moment I do not see how best to handle these cases. In fact I am not persuaded that such cases actually occur. Perhaps a more careful analysis of sharing will reveal that where there is sharing of discourse referents there is also always a shared propositional content, even if the epistemically or pragmatically most prominent attitudes in which those discourse referents figure conflict.[49]

---

[49] Sharing lies at the heart of the notorious Hob-Nob problem: How are we to explain that the sentence "Hob believes that a witch killed Cob's cow and

5.3 Sharing and Proper Names

I have argued that sharing discourse referents is a pervasive feature of human thought and that it arises typically (if not exclusively) through verbal communication. But I have said very little about the mechanisms through which verbal exchanges give rise to shared discourse referents. To provide a detailed account of these mechanisms appears to be a difficult task, which on the one hand requires an explicit theory of common knowledge, and on the other careful analyses of the contributions made by particular parts of speech to the interpretation of the utterances that contain them. There is no question of carrying out such a program here. But there is one aspect of it about which I want to say a few words. This is the question—which I raised at the beginning of Section 5.1 but which then disappeared from sight—how sharing arises through the use of proper names.

There is only one example that we have discussed in any detail and that is directly relevant to this question, viz., (16). We concluded that the acceptance of (16) would, under normal conditions, lead to a belief in which the discourse referents for the names 'Venus' and 'Mars' are shared with the speaker. But it never became fully clear what role the names themselves played in the process which produces the sharing, because the discourse referents for 'Venus' and 'Mars' were subject to so many other constraints as well: formal and external anchoring, as well as internal linking to discourse referents already present. In fact, the sharing might, in this particular case, be simply a side effect of linking; the new discourse referents might be shared through being linked to discourse referents that were shared already.

It is not hard to see however that proper names yield shared discourse referents also where there can be no question of their inheriting this status through linking. The clearest cases are those where a name is new to the recipient, and its referent unknown to him. Suppose for instance that you

---

Nob thinks she has blighted Bob's mare" does not commit the speaker to the existence of witches? In a nutshell, the solution to this puzzle that I would vote for is along the following lines. Members of a given community, in the present instance Hob and Nob, may come to share a discourse referent for a witch that they take to cause mischief in the region even if no such witch actually exists. This enables them to have beliefs "about the same witch," even if most of their beliefs concerning her aren't even the same. It is this kind of situation, involving two different beliefs concerning an individual that does not exist but a representation for which is nevertheless shared by the believers, that a sentence like the one above is designed to report. That a sentence of this particular form can be used to report just such a situation does of course not follow from these considerations. The principles which explain why the sentence might be used in this way, and precisely what sorts of situations can be described by such sentences, involve details pertaining to the interpretation of indefinites and the mechanisms of pronominal anaphora that we cannot go into here. See Asher [2] for a way of spelling out these details.

tell me about Thomlinson, a colleague of yours, who has, say, just won an important prize. I have never heard of Thomlinson, but I believe what you tell me. The belief I adopt in this case I will surely take to be about the very man that I take you to have the same belief about. And as this is exactly what you expect me to do, you will form the belief that I now have the belief you expressed, etc. This, it seems, is the general way with names. It is a default assumption that the recipient of a name will take the content of the utterance to be directly about the name's referent; consequently, if there is nothing to overrule this assumption, both speaker and recipient will adopt it and sharing is the result.

The power to produce sharing of discourse referents contributes importantly to the "social stability" of meaning. Thus the use of a proper name will produce among its users a shared presumption that they all use it to denote the same referent. Each time the name is used and gives rise to a shared discourse referent this presumption is extended or reinforced.

But it is not only proper names that exercise this stabilizing influence. Much the same appears to be true of common nouns. Indeed, traditional terminology ("proper name"–"common name"; "proper noun"–"common noun") has a point which the modern logical distinction between individual and predicate tends to obscure. Common nouns behave in many respects like proper names, and there are a variety of reasons for treating them as introducing discourse referents, representing the kind or concept that the noun denotes, just as proper names do. These discourse referents (which a more sophisticated version of DRT than I have sketched here would incorporate) are subject to sharing in much the same way as those which derive from proper names: A common noun too is used with the presumption that all use it to denote the same concept.

In fact, the sharing phenomenon may well be even more general and extend also to other concept words besides nouns, for instance to verbs or adjectives. For all such words sharing appears to be instrumental in maintaining an intersubjective uniformity of meaning; and for many a word, I suspect, this uniformity is about all the meaning it has.

6 Semantics, Attitude Reports and Self-reflection[50]

6.1 The content of Attitudinal States

One of the obligations of a theory of propositional attitudes is to account for their intentionality. I acknowledged this obligation in the introduction, and the proposals I made in the earlier parts of the paper do discharge it, inasmuch as the DRS's they involve come with an explicit truth definition (which I did not spell out in detail here, but which can be found

---

[50] For reasons of time as much as of space this and the next section have been kept much shorter than they ought to be. Properly expanded versions of these sections will be included in a sequel to the present paper.

in other work on DRT). The increasingly complex representations of attitudinal states, however, to which we were led as we went along, contain notational devices for which no standard truth-conditional treatment yet exists. This is one of the gaps that need filling.

I will not try to do this here, but limit myself to pointing out what appear to be the two main problems that make filling that gap non-trivial. The first of these has to do with the fact that connected components of complex attitudinal states often differ from each other in mode. Thus, as we saw in Section 3, desires are often connected with beliefs and with intentions. I have urged that when attitudes are connected, i.e., when they share one or more discourse referents, we cannot assess their truth conditions in isolation, but only those for the entire connected cluster of which they are part. I did not say, however, how that was to be done. I may have implied that it could be done along the lines of what was said in Section 2 about the truth conditions of the two-sentence discourse (1). But this really makes sense only when all the attitudes in the cluster are all of the same mode, e.g., if all of them are beliefs. Where we have, say, a connected pair consisting of a belief and a desire, truth conditions for their combined content, which treat them as if they were two beliefs—makes little intuitive sense.

As a matter of fact this is not just a problem for an attitudinal theory like the one I have outlined. It is a problem that will have to be faced by any theory of practical reasoning which wants to base its logic on a plausible semantics. Where only belief and desire are involved, a sensible semantic analysis appears to be that according to which according to which the beliefs single out a certain set of possibilities, or possible worlds—those compatible with the beliefs, while the desires select from that set a certain subset, those that are compatible with the desires as well. But it is not obvious how such an analysis could be extended to incorporate further modes. To my knowledge this problem is for all its importance still very far from being solved.

The second obstacle relates to higher order attitudes. These we have been representing by means of the discourse referents $p, q, \ldots$ constrained by conditions such as $Bel(b, p)$ and $p:K$. The first problem here has to do with the discourse referents $p, q, \ldots$ These stand, I said, for parts of attitudinal states (I haven't been very careful in my use of the term "part"; but let us for definiteness' sake agree that a part of state is either a single component or a collection of components). So, it is attitudinal states that should be correlated with p, q, etc., in the evaluation of the DRS's containing them.

So we are committed to the existence of attitudinal states. I do not mind this. That people and other conscious creatures are in complex and ever changing attitudinal states—I would not know what it would mean to deny this. But even if we accept attitudinal states and their parts as real, and also accept that these states are structured in the way I have suggested, there still remains a problem, which is connected with the conditions of the form $p:K$. There are infinitely many such conditions for each of the discourse referents $p, q, \ldots$, one for each K. And for most of the conditions $p:K$, K will be complex. Suppose now that we want to evaluate some such condition $p:K'$ and that we have correlated with p the actual attitudinal state s. What is it for s to satisfy $p:K'$? The naive answer here is of course: "s satisfies the condition if and only if s in fact has the structure identified by K'." But this seems unsatisfactory; for in case K' is complex, one would like to reduce the claim that s has the structure it specifies to simpler structural claims; what one would like is a *compositional* account of the satisfaction of such state predicates.

How could such a reduction be accomplished? I do not know. If we were entitled to think of attitudinal states as literally put together from their structural constituents, just as a sentence is put together from its grammatical constituents, the reduction would therewith be given. But, as I said in the introduction, this is an assumption to which I do not think one is entitled. If on the other hand the justification for ascribing structure to states is strictly functional, then I do not see how a plausible, non-circular compositional account for the satisfaction of these predicates might be given.

6.2 Attitude Reports

Up to this point I have refrained from saying anything about an aspect of the theory of the attitudes that is often seen as the central part of such a theory, and that many see as the only feasible part. This is the semantics of attitude reports. As I explained earlier, I see the matter differently: Only when a sufficiently detailed theory of the attitudes is in place, can we tackle the theory of attitude reports with any hope of success. The practical consequence of this conviction for the present essay is that the treatment of attitude reports too must be relegated to its sequel. For now that the necessary foundations have been laid time and space are up! All I want to do in this subsection is (i) indicate in the briefest outline how the theory of attitude reports builds on what has been discussed here, and (ii) devote a few words to the notion of an attitude report de re.

On the first point I will be very brief indeed. The general strategy is to see an attitude reporting sentence, in the spirit of DRT, as a set of instructions to the recipient for constructing a representation of the reported attitude. Thus an attitude report will produce in the recipient an attitudinal state with the same kind of structure that we used, in Section 5, to represent beliefs which a recipient forms about the beliefs of the speaker. The details of the strategy concern the contributions which the grammatical constituents of the report make to the construction of this structure. Much of the interest of this enterprise derives from the possibility of showing that, as a rule, constituents make the same contributions when they occur inside attitude reports (more precisely, in the complement clauses of attitudinal predicates) as they do when occurring outside such contexts.

Particularly revealing in this connection are the construction rules for different types of NP's. These rules have a special importance within the analysis of attitude reports because they relate directly to the distinction between de re and de dicto. As this distinction has played such an important part in the philosophical literature on the attitudes, and since I have been using the term de re here in a somewhat different context, I want to make a couple of remarks to clarify the connection. Roughly speaking an attitude report de re is the report of a de re attitude. However, our analysis of the notion of an attitude de re showed that it is necessary to draw a number of distinctions which other approaches have overlooked. Since the attitude reported by a given attitude report can be de re in either of the senses we distinguished (i.e., truly de re or only formally de re) the same distinction is applicable to attitude reports. Moreover, we saw that besides the structural features that render attitudes de re, i.e., their anchors, there are related features, linking and sharing. These two can be transferred from the attitudes themselves to the sentences which report them. Thus we find ourselves with a much richer repertoire of distinctions than the comparatively simple opposition between de dicto and de re. The resolution of many of the puzzles about belief that have bemused and amused the philosophical community during the past two decades turns on these finer distinctions. Another important ingredient in the treatment of those puzzles are the construction rules for the different kinds of NPs, which determine what kinds of attitudes (anchored, linked, shared) can be reported by a sentence whose complement contains that kind of noun phrase.

6.3 Self-Reflection

At long last we come to the second part of our proposal, back in Section 3, for representing the factors that partition attitudinal states into their components. Let us focus on an example we already considered in Section 3, that of someone, let us call him Bill, who believes that Dali is dead, and also that he got this belief through reading the New York Times.

It may well seem that all we need to represent these two beliefs in a form which agrees with the suggestions made in Section 3 is now in place: We have discourse referents for attitudes, DRS-conditions characterizing the structure and content of those attitudes and conditions to express the relation in which an attitude stands to the one whose attitude it is. With the help of these notational devices the relevant part of Bill's belief state may be represented as shown in (25).

I do not think, however, that this is quite the right representation. The problem with (25) is that it fails to convey the direct connection that I want to suggest exists between Bill's primary belief (that Dali is dead) and the second order belief about it. The connection is recoverable insofar as the structural specification of p matches that of the primary belief. It also seems reasonable to assume that even in the total belief state of Bill's the primary belief displayed in (25) will be the only one that matches the specified structure of p. And for all I can imagine it may well be a general feature of attitudinal states that they never contain more than one attitude with the same content. If this is indeed so, then representations like (25) will be adequate to the extent that they will always permit the unique identification of the primary attitude that the second order attitude is about.

(25)

$$\langle Bel, \begin{array}{|ccc|} \hline x \;\; y \;\; p & Anch[x] \\[4pt] dead(x) & Dali(x) \\ & V_1(x) \\ & \vdots \\ & V_n(x) \\ \hline \end{array} \rangle$$

$$\langle x, x' \rangle$$

$$\langle Bel, \begin{array}{|lccc|} \hline p: & \begin{array}{|ccc|} \hline x' & Anch[x'] & Anch[y] \\[4pt] dead(x) & Dali(x) & N.Y.T.(y) \\ & V_1(x) & W_1(y) \\ & \vdots & \vdots \\ & V_n(x) & W_m(y) \\ \hline \end{array} \\[30pt] Bel(i, p) \\ Source\ of\ p(y) \\ \hline \end{array} \rangle$$

Nonetheless, I can't help feeling that this would be a case of getting the right results by the wrong means. For I can't help feeling that the link between the second order belief and the primary attitude it is about has the same kind of directness that is distinctive of, for instance, the relation in which we stand to the present time—that relationship which informs our beliefs about what is happening now. In neither case is the connection between the believer and the relevant element that enters into the content of the belief secured descriptively.

A representation of second order attitudes which does justice to the directness of the connection should treat them as pointing directly to the primary attitudes they concern, as if one part of the complex attitudinal state of which both the primary and the second order attitude belong could "directly see" the other part. The simplest formal realization of this idea takes the form of a function which maps each attitude discourse referent that acts as an argument of a secondary attitude onto that component of the state which the secondary attitude is about. (This function fixes once and for all the attitude that might be correlated with the discourse referent in evaluation.) Thus we come to the final proposal of this paper.

First an auxiliary definition. Let AS be a complex attitudinal state, as characterized in (A5). By the *set of self-reflecting discourse referents of* AS we understand the set of those attitude discourse referents p such that (i) p occurs in the universe of a component of AS and (ii) p occurs in a condition of the form $\mathbf{M}(i, p)$ (where $\mathbf{M}$ is a mode indicator and i is as always the special discourse referent for the self.)

Our final proposal for the structural characterization then comes to this:

(A7) A complex attitudinal state can be represented as a pair consisting of (i) a structure AS as described in (A5) and (ii) a function from the set of self-reflecting discourse referents to components of AS.

As before, there is no reason why attitudinal states of this new, extended type could not be the subject of attribution (by one person to another). To do justice to this intuition we would have to characterize the structure of attitudinal states recursively, using (A7) as one of the clauses in that definition. It is intuitively clear, however, how such a definition would go and carrying out the formal details would not reveal anything of interest.

3

A Study in Comparative Semantics

ERNEST LEPORE AND BARRY LOEWER

TWO OF THE most influential philosophers of language, Gottlob Frege and
Donald Davidson, share a conception of the goals of a theory of meaning
for a natural language. Both think that such a theory should encapsulate
knowledge centrally involved in understanding a language and both think
that knowledge of the *truth conditions* of indicative sentences is central to
that understanding. Both think that for an adequate account of understanding, a theory of meaning must be compositional in order to explain
how complex expressions can be understood in terms of an understanding
of their components. Both think that an account of compositional structure
will systematize logical relations among sentences. And both emphasize the
importance of paraphrase into quantificational languages for constructing
semantic theories which systematize the truth conditions and logical relations of sentences.[1] They differ of course as to how those goals can best be
accomplished and in particular as to the ontology and ideology required to
achieve them. Frege freely employs "intensional" entities—sinne—and the
central notion of his theory of meaning is that of an expression *expressing*
a sense. The core of a Fregean theory of meaning for L is a finitely axiomatizable theory which assigns a sense to every expression of L. Davidson, on
the other hand, is an extensionalist. He thinks that the employment of intensional entities in semantic theories actually frustrates the goals sketched
above. For him the central notions of a theory of meaning are drawn from
the theory of reference and the core of a Davidsonian theory of meaning
for L is a finitely axiomatizable truth theory for L.

---

[1] See Davidson [39]; Dummett [46], pp. 92–93; Dummett [47], p. 122. Under
Dummett's influential interpretation, we are emphasizing one aspect of Frege's
philosophy of language. Of course, there are also important differences in the
ways in which Frege and Davidson conceive of the theory of meaning. Frege
thought that the proper objects of the theory are meanings—sinne—and that
there are laws governing these objects to be discovered, while for Davidson the
object is the linguistic activity of speakers.

The differences between Fregean and Davidsonian approaches to the theory of meaning are especially clear when one comes to their accounts of the semantics of indirect discourse and other propositional attitude attributing locutions. Consider, as an example:

(1)   Galileo said that the earth moves.

According to Frege, 'said' in (1) expresses a relation between Galileo and an intensional entity—the proposition expressed by 'the earth moves'. This proposition, like other intensional entities, is *abstract, independent of any particular language*, and *possesses its semantic properties* (its truth conditions) *essentially*. (Most contemporary philosophers of language would agree with this characterization of a proposition, though they might differ with Frege concerning other matters, for example, whether logically equivalent sentences express the same proposition and whether concrete individuals are constituents of some propositions.[2]) The Fregean account links the meaning of 'the earth moves' with the semantics of (1) in a natural way. For (1) to be true Galileo must have uttered something which expresses the same proposition as expressed by 'the earth moves'.

Davidson agrees with Frege that 'says' expresses a relation. But there the agreement ends. His paratactic account proposes that an utterance of (1) relates Galileo, not to a proposition, but to the utterance of 'the earth moves' that is a part of the utterance of (1). This relatum is *concrete, is in a particular language*, and *possesses its semantic properties contingently*. Davidson's account differs from Frege's in a second and more radical way. Frege viewed the complement 'that the earth moves' as a *complex name* of the proposition expressed by 'the earth moves'. Its reference is a function of the references of its constituent expressions. On the other hand, according to Davidson, from a logical point of view, an utterance of (1) consists of utterances of two sentences, one of 'Galileo said that' and the other of 'the earth moves', where the latter utterance is *demonstrated* by the former. These differences result in the assignment of different truth conditions to, and different logical relations among, propositional attitude ascriptions. The two theories also differ in their implications for ontological and epistemological issues concerning propositional attitudes. Given these differences the question naturally arises of how to evaluate the two accounts. Which, if cither, is closer to being an adequate semantics for attitude attributing English sentences? We will address this question below.

Before discussing Frege's and Davidson's accounts it will be useful to discuss briefly a proposal which rejects the assumption common to them that (1) is relational. According to Quine [141], and more recently Schiffer [165], 'says that the earth moves' is a semantically unstructured monadic predicate. To say that the predicate is semantically unstructured is not to

---

[2] See, for example, Kaplan's "On the Logic of Demonstratives" [92], and Stalnaker's *Inquiry* [178].

say that expressions that occur in it do not possess meanings or references,[3] but it is to say that these meanings and references are irrelevant to the semantic value of the predicate.[4]

There are however two well known objections to this idea. One is that since there are infinitely many indicative sentences in English there will be infinitely many atomic monadic says-that predicates. This means that a truth theory for a language containing 'says that' requires a distinct satisfaction axiom for each such predicate and is not finitely axiomatizable. Whether one considers this an objection depends on whether one thinks that an adequate semantic theory for a natural language must be finitely axiomatizable. Davidson [32] has argued that the semantics of any language which can be learned and understood by human beings must be finitely axiomatizable. The basic idea is that knowing a language involves knowing the truth conditions of its sentences and we can represent this knowledge only finitely. Davidson's arguments have not gone unchallenged and we do not want to place much reliance on them here. It does, however, appear that one understands (1) in virtue of understanding its component expressions and it is hard to see how the Quine-Schiffer account can explain this. Note that if someone failed to understand 'moves' he would not understand (1). Why should this be so if the semantic value of 'moves' is irrelevant to the semantic value of (1)?[5]

The second objection against the Quine-Schiffer strategy is that certain valid inferences seem to require treating 'says' (and other attitudinal verbs) as relational. For example, (1) implies:

(2)   There is something which Galileo said.

---

[3] In *Word and Object* ([141], Chapter 6), Quine suggests that we treat sentences like 'Galileo says that the earth moves' as consisting of a subject and a one-place predicate, 'says-that-the-earth-moves', true of persons. The dashes between the words indicate that the expression is semantically simple. He draws an analogy with 'cat' in 'cattle'. The *word* 'cat', which refers to cats, does not even occur in the word 'cattle'. It is just an orthographic accident that the string of letters 'cat' occurs in 'cattle'. Similarly, Quine seems to be suggesting that it is just an orthographic accident that the words 'the earth' occur in 'says that the earth moves'. He need not have held such a severe view. It would suit his purposes as well to hold that 'the earth' occurs in 'says that the earth moves', while denying that any of its semantic features contribute to the semantic value of the sentence. This move has the advantage of allowing one to say that 'the earth' in sentence (1) refers to the earth while blocking unwanted inferences.

[4] Notice that Davidson agrees that the meaning of 'the earth moves' does not compositionally contribute to the semantic value of 'says that the earth moves' since 'the earth moves' is not a semantic component of an assertive utterance of (1).

[5] Schiffer [165] describes a model in which a person "knows" the infinitely many truth conditions, even though they are not finitely axiomatizable. It would be worth exploring Schiffer's view, but that is not our present purpose.

This inference seems to be an instance of the argument form $[R(g,t)$. Therefore, $(\exists x)R(g,x)]$. Schiffer ([165], pp. 234–239) replies to this point by suggesting that the inference from (1) to (2) can be accommodated by the non-relational account as long as the quantifier in (2) is understood substitutionally. In that case, (2) is true just in case there is a true substitution instance of 'Galileo said x'—and there is one if (1) is true. The substitution term need possess no reference and 'say' need not be relational.

Schiffer's suggestion is not plausible. On his substitutional interpretation, the truth of '$(\exists x)R(g,x)$' requires the truth of some sentence of the form '$R(g, \text{that } p)$'. But (2) can be true even though there is no way in English of expressing what Galileo said. In fact, the following sentence seems logically consistent: 'Galileo said something on his thirtieth birthday which we cannot express in our language'. On Schiffer's substitutional account, this sentence is logically false. In any case, the truth value of a substitutionally interpreted quantified sentence of L is subject to the vicissitudes of the supply of substitution instances of L, but the truth value of (2) does not seem so subject.[6] While neither of these objections to the monadic theory of propositional attitude attributions is conclusive, we think they show that this theory is *prima facie* less plausible than the relational account.

A Fregean Theory

According to Frege, the referent of:

(3)   The earth moves.

—which is a truth value—is the result of applying the referent of 'moves' (a function) to the referent of 'the earth'. (The reference of a whole is a function of the references of parts.) The referent of (3) is also determined by (3)'s sense—the proposition that the earth moves—which is in turn composed of the senses of 'moves' and 'the earth'. (The sense of the whole is a function of the senses of the parts.)

As is quite well known, Frege's theory runs into difficulty with attitude attributing sentences. The problem is that on his theory co-referential

---

[6] Schiffer considers this problem and remarks that 'it is difficult to see how [(2) could be true without there being some way of reporting what Galileo said] when we appreciate that substitutions may contain demonstratives and roundabout descriptions ([165], p. 289). His suggestion is that the substitution term 'that p' may include demonstratives. But then he owes us an explanation for how substitutional quantification can be made sense of once we have substitution instances with demonstratives in them. It will no longer suffice to say that a sentence '$(\exists x)Fx$' is true only if there is a substitution instance of 'Fx' which is true since sentences with demonstratives are only true relative to a context. In any case, even if we allow demonstratives and roundabout descriptions, it is not so difficult for us to see how (2) can be true without there being any way of reporting what Galileo said in our language.

terms are substitutable *salva veritate*. For example, since 'the earth' and 'the third planet from the sun' are co-referential, (1) should have the same truth value as:

(4)   Galileo said that the third planet from the sun moves.

But it is easy to imagine that (1) is true, while (4) is false.[7] Frege's immensely clever way around this difficulty is to postulate that terms that occur in certain 'oblique' contexts, for example, 'says that ___', do not possess their usual references, but instead refer to their usual senses. Since 'the earth' and 'the third planet from the sun' express different senses, the substitution principle is not violated. Also, since the usual sense of 'the earth moves' is a proposition, it follows that (1) asserts a relation between Galileo and a proposition.

The Fregean account invalidates the inference from (1) and 'the earth = the third planet from the sun' to (4); but which substitution principles, if any, does it validate? Let's use '$S(a, b)$' to mean that 'a' and 'b' express the same sense. Then on the Fregean account this inference form is valid:

(I) $Said(g,$ that $Fa)$, $S(a, b) \vdash Said(g,$ that $Fb)$

Are the English counterparts of this inference form intuitively valid? The answer depends on when '$S(a, b)$' is true. As is often remarked, Frege did not provide a clear and precise account of when words express the same sense. So, it is not clear which inferences of form (I) are sound. In the Fregean theory, furthermore, it is not all that clear which substitution principles are intuitively valid. Does 'Galileo said that Dobbins is a steed' follow from 'Galileo said that Dobbins is a horse'? So, it is doubly difficult to check Frege's theory by comparing its validities with intuitively valid inferences. In any case, there are two well known proposals for identity of sense of atomic terms. One is that '$S(a, b)$' is true just in case 'a' and 'b' are synonymous in an ordinary dictionary sense of synonymy (whatever that is). The other is that '$S(a, b)$' is true just in case 'a' and 'b' have the same reference. Each proposal is problematic. A well-known worry concerning the first is the vagueness of dictionary synonymy and the fear that there may be no principles which underlie judgments of dictionary synonymy. In any case, according to the OED, 'fortnight' and 'two week period' are synonymous. But the inference from this synonymy and 'Galileo said that a fortnight is a two week period' to 'Galileo said that a fortnight is a fortnight' seems invalid. The second proposal is clearer—or as clear as sameness of reference is—but it also seems to license invalid inferences; for example, from 'Galileo said that Hesperus = Phosphorus' to 'Galileo

---

[7] The sense of (1) determines the True while the sense of (4) determines the False. On the other hand, it follows from reference compositionality and the co-referentiality of 'the earth' and 'the third planet from the sun', that the references of (1) and (4) are the same.

said that Hesperus = Hesperus'. A counterexample immune proposal is that '$S(a, b)$' is true iff 'a' and 'b' are substitutable *salva veritate* in all contexts, including indirect discourse and propositional attitude contexts. This proposal not only greatly diminishes the explanatory value of (I) but also its scope, since distinct expressions may never be substitutable *salva veritate* in all contexts.

The Fregean account can fairly straightforwardly handle quantifications into propositional attitude contexts. Consider:

(5)   There is someone whom Galileo believes to be a spy,

which is naturally paraphrased as:

(6) $(\exists x)B(g, Spy(x))$

If, as Frege thought, propositions are composed only of senses, then (6) cannot be the correct paraphrase of (5) since its quantifier must range over senses. There are various proposals in the literature for remedying this. The nicest is Kaplan's [90], who suggests that (5) be paraphrased by (6*):

(6*) $(\exists x)(\exists \$)(D(\$, x) \ \& \ Q(\$) \ \& \ B(g, Spy(\$)))$

This account says that there is an individual *and* there is a sense which determines that individual ($D(\$, x)$) and which satisfies certain other conditions Q (is vivid, etc.) such that Galileo believes the proposition formed from $\$$ and the sense of 'is a spy'. (7) receives the paraphrase (7*):

(7)   Everyone is believed by Galileo to be a spy.
(7*) $(x)(\exists \$)(D(\$, x) \ \& \ Q(\$) \ \& \ B(g, Spy(\$)))$

While there is a great deal more to be said about the Fregean treatment of quantifying in, we will not say it here. The important point for comparing the Fregean and Davidsonian accounts, as we will see, is that the Fregean account of the semantics of quantified-into sentences is completely compositional. The reference (and sense) of (6*) is completely determined by the references (senses) of its constituent expressions.

The Fregean account has certain other consequences for the logic of propositional attitude attributions that are worth noting. First, of course, (1) implies (2), and (1) and (8) imply (9):

(8)   Davidson said that the earth moves.
(9)   There is something both Galileo and Davidson said.

This seems correct. Further, (1) does not imply the existence of English sentences or utterances (though it may imply the existence of an utterance of Galileo's). This also seems right.

Some especially important inferences involve semantic concepts. Consider the following inferences:

(II)   (1), The earth moves $\vdash$ Galileo said something true.

(III) (1), Everything Galileo said is true $\vdash$ The earth moves.

Both these inferences seem intuitively valid. For them to be validated by Frege's account, a connection must be made between expressions of the forms 'S' and 'that S is true'. Specifically, we need premises of the form:

(10) T(that S) iff S,

where '$T(x)$' is the predicate 'x is true'. The following paraphrases of the two inferences above are valid in first-order logic:

> Said(g, that the earth moves), The earth moves, T(that the earth moves) iff the earth moves $\vdash$ $(\exists x)(Said(g,x)$ & $T(x))$
>
> Said(g, that the earth moves), $(x)(Said(g,x) \rightarrow T(x))$, T(that the earth moves) iff the earth moves $\vdash$ The earth moves.

According to the Fregean theory, instances of (10) express logical truths—though of course they are not first-order logical truths. The relevant instances of (10) can be systematized by a Tarski-like truth theory run not over linguistic expressions but over senses. We can think of such a theory as logical axioms added to a Fregean theory.[8]

At first pass the Fregean account of propositional attitude sentences looks pretty good. It assigns truth conditions to propositional attitude sentences which seem correct; it is compositional; and it more or less systematizes the intuitively valid inferences involving propositional attitude sentences.

The Paratactic Account

Despite its initial plausibility, Davidson rejects the Fregean account and proposes his own in its place. We will discuss his reasons for rejecting Frege's proposal later. In this section we describe Davidson's paratactic account. According to it, the logical form of sentence (1) is:

(11) Said(g, that)

If u is an utterance of (1), then the demonstrative in its logical paraphrase (11) refers to the utterance of 'the earth moves' contained in u. Davidson further suggests that the predicate '$Said(x,y)$' be *analyzed* as '$(\exists u)(U(x,u)$ & $SS(u,y))$', where '$U(x,u)$' holds when x utters u and '$SS(u,y)$' holds when utterance y *samesays* utterance u. (Davidson usually uses samesaying to express a relation between speakers, while we use it to express a relation between *utterances* and other content possessing items.) We will discuss this relation presently.

---

[8] '$(x)(x$ satisfies S iff x is wise)' and '$(x)(x$ satisfies &(A,B) iff x satisfies A and x satisfies $B)$' are examples of axioms of such a theory.

In a language which contains demonstratives, truth conditions are generalized over utterances of sentences (LePore and Loewer [101]). For example, the generalized truth condition of 'Sam likes that' is: $(x)(u)$(if u is an utterance of 'Sam likes that' and the utterance of 'that' demonstrates x, then u is true iff Sam likes x). The truth condition for (1) is:

(12) $(u)(x)$(if u is an utterance or inscription of (1) and the occurrence of 'that' in u demonstrates x, then u is true iff
$(\exists y)(U(g, y)\ \&\ SS(x, y)))$,[9]

It is a convention that this referent is the portion of u following the occurrence of 'that'. But this connection, we claim, is not part of the semantics of u.

According to the paratactic account, a typical utterance of (1) relates Galileo to an English utterance which is referred to demonstratively. But this does not preclude there being true instances of $Said(g, x)$ which relate Galileo to things other than English utterances. In fact, if (1) is true, then on Davidson's account $Said(g, x)$ relates Galileo to an utterance which samesays the utterance of 'the earth moves' and to anything else which samesays Galileo's utterance. Indeed, if there are propositions and one of them samesays Galileo's utterance, then Galileo is $Said$-related to this proposition. Although the term which refers to the complement of (1) is a demonstrative, there is no reason why reference to content bearing items cannot be made non-demonstratively. Thus, 'Galileo said the Lord's Prayer' is paraphrased by '$Said(g, l)$', where 'l' is a name of the Lord's Prayer. This referent is an abstract entity, the Lord's Prayer. The only restriction on true instances of $Said(g, x)$ is that they relate Galileo to a content bearing item. It follows that '$(\exists x)Said(g, x)$' can be true even if there is no name, description, or demonstrative in English which refers to what Galileo said. Its being true requires only that there is an utterance of Galileo's to which he is related by $Said$. In contrast to Schiffer's account, the paratactic account provides no reason to interpret the quantifier substitutionally.

---

[9] Above we are following Davidson in interpreting 'that' in (1) as a demonstrative. A number of philosophers have objected to the paratactic account by arguing that 'that' in (1) does not have the syntactic and/or phonological features of a genuine demonstrative. (See, for a recent example, Segal [173], pp. 79–80.) But these objections, even if correct, are not fatal to the paratactic account. Even if 'that' is not a demonstrative in (1), (11) may be its logical form. In that case, although no demonstrative *word* occurs in (1), utterances of it still involve demonstrations. The paratactic account is committed to there being a demonstrative in (1)'s logical form but need make no commitment as to how it is expressed in (1). That a demonstrative does not appear, for example, in French and Italian propositional attitude sentences does not show that the paratactic account is wrong for these languages.

The question has been raised concerning whether the paratactic account can be extended to other propositional attitude attributions.[10] But the extension is straightforward. An utterance of:

(13) Galileo believed that the earth moves.

possesses the logical form $B(g, \text{that})$, where the demonstrative refers to the portion of the utterance following 'that'.

One worry is that Galileo, unlike his sayings, may have a belief which goes unexpressed by him or anyone else. Thus 'There is something Galileo believes' may be true even though no utterance of the sentence 'Galileo believes that' (where 'that' demonstrates an utterance) is true. This shows that the extension of 'believes' must include items other than utterances. Someone might conclude from this (Schiffer [165], p. 128, seems to) that it follows that utterances *cannot* be in the extension of 'believes'. This would be fatal to our version of the paratactic account since according to it the demonstrative in an utterance of (13) refers to an utterance. But, as we noted in our discussion of 'says', there is nothing wrong with supposing that the extension of propositional attitude relations includes utterances and other *content* bearing items. It is plausible to suppose that there are belief states which possess content and that whenever it is true to say of someone that he believes that p he is in a belief state with the content that p. No commitment need be made to the nature of these belief states, whether they are physical or involve a language of thought, etc. On this supposition 'There is something Galileo believes' may come out true even though there is no utterance ever made which expresses his belief. The suggestion also yields the following analysis of (13) which parallels Davidson's analysis of (1):

$$(\exists \alpha)(R(g, \alpha) \ \& \ SS(\alpha, that)) : [\text{The earth moves}]$$

where α is a belief state and R is the relation Galileo bears to his belief states. On this account, although an utterance of a propositional attitude sentence always involves a demonstration of the complement utterances, 'believes' can have any content bearing item in its extension.

One feature of the paratactic account is that it does not validate any of the substitution principles discussed in the previous section. Even if utterances of p and q express the same proposition and Galileo assertively produced an utterance which samesays p, there is no *logical* guarantee that this utterance samesays q and so no license to infer 'Galileo said that:[q]' from 'Galileo said that:[p]'.[11] The failure of substitution principles is even

---

[10] See, for example, Blackburn [7], Burge [17], Higginbotham [80], and Schiffer [165].

[11] Of course, to speak of inference within the paratactic account involves developing a logic for languages with indexicals and demonstratives and constructing an inference relation between utterances. The basic idea is that an utterance of

more extreme. Consider two utterances u and u^* of (1). As Burge [17] (and others) have pointed out, on the paratactic account it is logically possible for u and u^* to differ in truth value. The reason is that the occurrences of 'that' in u and u^* have distinct demonstrata. In view of the controversy concerning substitution principles we think it is a good feature of the paratactic account that it does not validate them. We can introduce substitutivity principles by adding principles governing the samesay relation. Two plausible proposals are:

> $(u)(u')$(if u and u' are utterances of sentences of the form 'G said that p' and 'G said that p'' and v and v' are the component utterances of p and p' of u and u' and $SS(v, v')$, then u is true iff u' is true)

and

> $(v)(v')$(if v and v' are utterances of the same sentence, then $SS(v, v')$)

These principles need to be restricted to utterances whose complements do not contain demonstratives, indexicals, and other context-sensitive features. (Two utterances of 'G said that I am rich' if uttered by different people may differ in truth value.) There are further principles concerning the samesay relation we might consider. For example, if p' results from p by substituting co-referential proper names and u and u' are utterances of p and p', then $SS(u, u')$. But, as we mentioned, this has counter-intuitive results.

Some of the other inferences discussed in Section 1 which are intuitively valid are not validated by the paratactic account. Specifically, inference (II) is not valid: [The earth moves, G said that the earth moves $\vdash$ G said something true.] This is remedied by treating the inference as an enthymeme as follows:

> The earth moves, (u)(if u is an utterance of 'the earth moves', then $T(u)$) iff the earth moves, $Said(g, \text{that})$ & that is an utterance of 'the earth moves' $\vdash$ Galileo said something true.

This inference is valid on the assumption that the demonstratives in the third premise are co-referential. The additional premises required to turn (II) into a valid inference all express truths which a competent (and attentive) speaker of English who reads or hears (II) knows. It thus seems to us not unreasonable for the paratactician to treat (II) as enthymematic. Notice that the Fregean theory is in a similar boat with regards to (II). He needs to add a premise stating the truth conditions of the proposition expressed by 'the earth moves' to make (II) a valid inference. Of course, the important difference is that the additional premise on the paratactic account is contingent.

---

u of S follows from an utterance of u' of S' just in case every model in which S is true relative to the contextual features of u is one in which S' is true relative to the contextual features of u'.

At a first pass the paratactic account seems to come close to satisfying our adequacy conditions on an account of utterances of indirect discourse sentences. It assigns truth conditions to utterances of (1); it is compositional; and, with some massaging, it seems capable of accounting for intuitively valid inferences (and rejecting those not valid). However, in a first pass comparison with the Fregean account it must seem overly complicated and syntactically bizarre. So, we next want to look at Davidson's reasons for rejecting the Fregean account.

Davidson's Objections to Frege

Davidson rejects not just Frege's account of propositional attitude sentences, but his whole theory of senses. His objection to Frege's theory of senses as a theory of meaning and to the Fregean account of propositional attitude sentences stem from a conviction that senses frustrate the construction of a Tarski truth-definition. Since a Fregean (or in any case the philosopher's-of-language Frege) agrees with Davidson in holding that knowledge of truth conditions is central to language understanding, he should take these objections seriously. In "Truth and Meaning" [33], Davidson argued that *senses* are useless to a theory of understanding. He remarks (p. 20) that:

> the switch from reference to meaning leads to no useful account of how the meanings of sentences depend upon the meanings of words (or other structural features) that compose them. Ask, for example, for the meaning of 'Theatetus flies'. A Fregean answer might go something like this: given the meaning of 'Theatetus' as argument, the meaning of 'flies' yields the meaning of 'Theatetus flies' as value. The vacuity of this answer is obvious. We wanted to know what the meaning of 'Theatetus flies' is; it is no progress to be told that it is the meaning of 'Theatetus flies'. This much we knew before any theory was in sight. In the bogus account just given, talk of the structure of the sentence and of the meanings of words was idle, for it played no role in producing the given description of the meaning of the sentence.

At first sight Davidson's objection seems to be that a Fregean theory does not explain how the meaning of—the sense expressed by—a complex expression depends on the senses expressed by its constituents. But this cannot be right. A Fregean theory of meaning will, for example, yield (as Davidson says) the theorem:

(14) The sense expressed by 'Theatetus flies' = the sense expressed by 'flies' applied to the sense expressed by 'Theatetus'.

This bit of information does specify how the meaning of the complex depends on the meanings of its parts. Davidson's real complaint seems to be that this information does not yield understanding of an utterance of 'Theatetus flies'. In particular, one can know that (14) is the case without knowing that 'Theatetus flies' is true iff Theatetus flies. Further, Davidson suggests that senses are a road block on the way to truth conditions.

Frege should grant Davidson's point that knowledge that (14) is the case is not knowledge of truth conditions, but should deny that (14) is an obstacle to systematizing truth conditions. A sense theory by itself will not logically entail (in first-order logic) a truth theory. But, as we have mentioned, senses have the special and peculiar feature of possessing their semantic properties essentially. And Frege thought that someone who *grasps* a sense will (in virtue of this grasping) know its semantic properties. For example, someone who grasps the sense of 'is red' will know that that sense is satisfied by something iff it is red. This knowledge can be made explicit by a truth theory *on* senses (rather than linguistic expressions). Such a theory will entail a theorem of the form:

> The sense of 'flies' applied to the sense of 'Theatetus' is true iff Theatetus flies.

This and the theory of senses will imply that 'Theatetus flies' is true iff Theatetus flies.

In view of this, we see that senses do not prevent the assignment of truth conditions to sentences, but they seem to be unnecessary. Why not, as Davidson does, run a theory of truth directly on the natural language without a detour through senses? His remark that intensional entities do not "oil the wheels" of interpretation seems justified if one means by this that they are not required by a theory of truth for a language containing sentences like 'Theatetus flies'. But Frege could make two points in response. One is that senses come into play in specifying the truth conditions of propositional attitude sentences. The other is that a truth theory is only part of a theory of understanding. To understand a sentence one needs to know not only conditions under which it is true but also what proposition it expresses. We will discuss both points.

Frege claimed that (1)'s truth conditions are that Galileo is *Said*-related to the proposition that the earth moves. If this is correct, then if any indirect discourse sentence is true, there are propositions. But Davidson has developed two arguments that seem designed to show that Fregean semantics for propositional attitude discourse fails to produce a theory of truth which is serviceable in an account of language understanding.

The first argument attempts to show that a Fregean semantical theory capable of handling expressions with iterated propositional attitude operators is not finitely axiomatizable. Here is what Davidson ([33], p. 99) says:

> Neither the languages Frege suggests as models for natural languages nor the languages described by Church are amenable to theory in the sense of a truth definition meeting Tarski's standards. What stands in the way in Frege's case is that every referring expression has an infinite number of entities it may refer to, depending on the context, and there is no rule that gives the reference in more complex contexts on the basis of the reference in simpler ones. In Church's languages, there is an infinite number of primitive expressions; this directly blocks the possibility of recursively characterizing a truth predicate satisfying Tarski's requirements.

Davidson's thought seems to be that on the Fregean theory the reference of 'the earth' in each of the sentences 'A says that the earth moves', 'B says that A says that the earth moves', ..., 'C says that B says that A says that the earth moves', and so on, is different, where each subsequent occurrence of 'the earth' refers to the sense expressed by the previous occurrence. Given that there is no rule which gives the reference of 'the earth' in a context with n iterations from its reference in a context with $n - 1$ iterations—as Russell says, there is no backward road from reference to sense—it follows that there is no finite truth theory for a language which allows iterations of 'says that'. But why does Davidson think that each iteration of 'says that' requires a new reference? His reference to Church does not help. Church [28] argued that there is an infinite hierarchy of senses by supposing that any sense can be referred to. If a_1 refers to sense s_1, then a_1 itself expresses a sense s_2 which in turn can be referred to by a_2 which expresses s_3 and so on. This argument is completely independent of the semantics of indirect discourse and so cannot show that a Fregean semantics for indirect discourse requires an infinity of senses.

In fact, it seems easy for Frege to block Davidson's argument. We can suppose that if 'the earth' occurs within the scope of one or many attitude verbs, then it refers to its ordinary sense. That is, there are only two distinct levels of sense. It would appear that to refute this supposition, say, for a context involving two attitude verbs, one would have to find an example which satisfies the following conditions: (i) expressions 'a' and 'b' express the same ordinary (that is, first level) sense and so are substitutable in 'Says that Fx' but (ii) 'a' and 'b' are not substitutable in 'Says that says that Fx'. This would show that their references in the doubly iterated contexts must be different and so the expressions cannot both refer to their ordinary senses. If one can find some way of generating examples of this sort for n-iterated propositional attitude verbs, then one would have an argument for Davidson's conclusion. We know of no way of generating such examples or even a convincing example for contexts involving iterated propositional attitude verbs.[12] Furthermore, it is hard to see how there could be a persuasive example since it is always open to Frege to take failure of substitutivity in double indirect discourse to show that first level senses differ. We conclude then that Davidson's worry that Frege's theory of the

---

[12] One might think that a Mates-like example of the following sort works: 'fortnight' does not seem substitutable for 'two weeks' *salva veritate* in 'Laplace wondered whether Galileo believed that two weeks is a fortnight'. If these expressions have the same ordinary senses, it follows that they do not both refer to their ordinary senses in this context. But the example shows the need to introduce third level senses (to refer to the second level senses) only on the assumption that 'fortnight' and 'two weeks' express the same first level sense. It is hard to see how one could establish this.

logical form of propositional attitude attributions precludes its formulation as a finite theory of truth is *unproven*.

Another objection Davidson lodges against Frege's account is its failure to preserve "semantic innocence." He says ([34], p. 108):

> Since Frege, philosophers have become hardened to the idea that content-sentences in talk about propositional attitudes may strangely refer to such entities as intensions, propositions, sentences, utterances, and inscriptions. What is strange is not the entities, which are all right in their place (if they have one), but the notion that ordinary words for planets, people, tables, and hippopotami in indirect discourse may give up these pedestrian references for the exotica. If we could recover our pre-Fregean semantic innocence, I think it would seem to us plainly incredible that the words 'The earth moves', uttered after the words 'Galileo said that', mean anything different, or refer to anything else, than is their wont when they come in other environments.

Why does it seem incredible that 'the earth' as it occurs in (1) does not possess its usual reference—the earth? The answer is that it seems that someone who understands English—and specifically the words 'the earth moves'—understands them the same way, whether they occur in or out of propositional attitude contexts. This is supported by the ease with which we can go from, for example, 'the earth moves' and 'Galileo said that the earth moves' to 'Galileo said something true'. If the words that occur after 'said' possess references different and unrelated to their references in 'The earth moves', then why should this and similar inferences be valid? It is this question, we think, that is at the heart of Davidson's charge of semantic "corruption."

A Fregean must grant that the reference of an expression depends on the context in which the expression occurs. It is this which allows him to maintain compositionality of reference while accommodating the failure of substitutivity of identity. But he can mitigate Davidson's objection. We showed how within a Fregean theory (supplemented by a truth theory run on senses) the inferences cited above are valid even though the references of expressions in oblique contexts differ from their ordinary references. So the Fregean theory's failure to be semantically innocent does not provide an impediment to its being a theory of understanding.

As far as we can see, contra Davidson, there is no obstacle in principle to the construction of a theory of sense S for a language L containing propositional attitude verbs which together with a truth theory on propositions entails a truth theory for L. Among the T-sentences S entails will be, for example:

'Galileo said that the earth moves' is true iff $S(g,t)$,

where 'S' is a relation between people and propositions and 't' is a functional name of the proposition that the earth moves.[13] Davidson might

---

[13] The name 't' has the form '$f(e,m)$', where 'e' is a name of the sense of 'the earth' and 'm' is a name of the sense of 'moves'.

still object that these are the *wrong* truth conditions for (1). But that is quite a different objection, one that we will address later.

Fregean Objections to Davidson

From a Fregean perspective, a theory of truth for a language L, while part of a theory of meaning for L, omits information that a theory of meaning for L should supply. In particular, it fails to state what senses sentences express. (See, for example, Foster [58], Loar [113], and LePore and Loewer [102]). This objection should have no force against someone who sees the theory of meaning as the theory of understanding unless it can be shown that information concerning what senses expressions express are involved in understanding sentences. In fact, it seems that such information is involved. Consider Al, for example, who hears Karl utter 'I am hungry'. On this basis and given his understanding of English, Al will be in a position to infer that Karl *said* that he is hungry. A theory of meaning for English should make explicit the information possessed by someone who understands English which justifies this inference. For a Fregean there is a natural way to represent Al's reasoning:

(15) Karl assertively uttered 'I am hungry'.

(16) This utterance expresses the proposition that he [Karl] is hungry.

(17) $(p)(c)(u)$(if c assertively utters u and u expresses p, then c said p)

(18) So, Karl said that he [Karl] is hungry.

The information contained in (16) provides a bridge from the fact that a certain utterance has been made to the speaker having said that he is hungry. But in an account like Davidson's which makes no reference to propositions, it is hard to see how this gap can be bridged. Notice that it will not do to replace (16) with the following T-sentence:

(16') $(u)(x)$(if u is an utterance of 'I am hungry' by x, then u is true iff x is hungry.)

since the inference from (15) and (16') to (18) is invalid. It appears that Al's knowing an adequate truth theory for Karl's language is insufficient to support an inference from the fact that Karl uttered a certain sentence to a conclusion concerning what he said. This objection should be taken seriously by Davidsonians since it apparently shows that a truth theory is inadequate to its appointed task. Further, since knowledge of the propositions expressed by utterances is sufficient, it looks like the Davidsonian's eschewing intensional entities has hamstrung his theory.

However, it turns out that there is a way for Davidson to preserve his extensionalism, while specifying the information involved in inferring (18) from (15). Interestingly, this way presupposes the correctness of the paratactic account of indirect discourse. According to the paratactic account, the correct paraphrase of (18) is:

(19) $(\exists u)(U(\text{Karl}, u) \ \& \ SS(u, \text{that}))$: [he is hungry]

If, as in the story, Al knows that Karl assertively uttered 'I am hungry' and also knows that Karl's utterance samesays the utterance represented by the brackets in (19), then he is in a position to conclude that his utterance of (19) is true. But (19) is the paratactic paraphrase of (18). So, assuming the paratactic account is correct, the Davidsonian has a way of representing the information which underlies a person's ability to learn what speakers of his language say without appealing to intensional entities. This departs from the view Davidson holds in "Truth and Meaning" [33] since we are denying that knowledge of a truth theory alone is sufficient for understanding. Knowledge of, or ability to determine, the extension of the samesay relation is required as well. However, such knowledge already is involved in understanding indirect discourse on Davidson's account, so our suggestion is clearly within the spirit of truth theoretic semantics.

A Fregean is likely to find the above response unsatisfactory for two reasons. One is that it relies on the equivalence between 'Karl said that he is hungry' and Davidson's paratactic account of it, and this is just what he rejects. The second is that he may suspect that Davidson's samesay relation in some way involves covert appeal to intensional entities. So, even if the paratactic account is correct, indirect discourse sentences involve a commitment to an intensionalist ontology.

First, we will briefly discuss a couple of well-known objections that (1) is not equivalent to its paratactic paraphrase (Blackburn [7], and Schiffer [165]). These objections, while they can be lodged without accepting Frege's theory, are natural from a Fregean perspective. Recall that the Fregean account interprets (1) as relating Galileo to a proposition, while the paratactic account interprets (1) as relating him to an utterance of an English sentence. It seems that the Fregean has the advantage here. First, (1) does not seem to be about, or to entail the existence of, English utterances or utterances of any language, expect possibly Galileo's. What (1) says might be true even if English did not exist. Second, it is possible to know that:

$(\exists u)(U(g, u) \ \& \ SS(u, \text{that}))$: [The earth moves]

without knowing that Galileo said something true iff the earth moves. The first problem is due to the fact that the demonstratum is an English utterance, the second is due to the fact that this demonstratum possesses its truth conditions contingently. It seems that propositions—entities not wedded to a particular language and which possess their truth conditions essentially—are better suited to be the objects of *propositional* attitudes than are utterances.

We have discussed both these points in a previous paper (LePore and Loewer [103]) and so will be brief here. The first point can be parried by noting that the paratactic paraphrase of 'It is possible for Galileo to have said that the earth moves even if there were no English utterances' is:

(S)   It is possible that there are no English utterances and *Said*(*g*,that): [the earth moves]

In possible world terms, an utterance *u* of (S) is true just in case there is a world *w* which contains no English utterances but in which Galileo produced an utterance which samesays the utterance demonstrated by 'that' in *u* in the actual world. This is consistent (and true). So, the paratactic account can accommodate the fact that (1) might be true even if there were no English utterances. No doubt more needs to be said but this should go some distance towards deflecting the objection.[14]

We already have indicated the paratactic reply to the second point when we discussed inferences (II) and (III) above. Anyone who knows the truth conditions of an utterance of 'the earth moves' will, if he knows that (1) is the case, also know that Galileo said something which is true iff the earth moves. So, although it is possible for someone to know that Galileo said something which samesays that: [the earth moves] without knowing that Galileo said something which is true iff the earth moves, any competent speaker of English will be in a position to make the inference.

Even if these objections can be successfully answered, a different Fregean objection concerns the way in which reference to an attitude object is made on the paratactic account. Because (according to the paratactic account) the logical form of (1) is '*Said*(*g*,that)', it has the consequence that 'the earth moves' is not a *semantic* component of (1). It might seem that this is of little importance since the truth conditions of 'the earth moves' still figure in determining the truth value of '*Said*(*g*,that)', since they will figure in the account of the samesay relation. Be that as it may, the failure of Davidson's theory to count 'the earth moves' as a semantic component of (1) does give rise to severe problems for sentences which apparently involve quantification into attitude contexts.

Recall that the Fregean paraphrase of (5) is (6*):

(5)   Galileo said of someone that he is a spy.

(6*) $(\exists x)(\exists \$)(D(\$, x) \ \& \ Q(\$) \ \& \ S(g, Spy(\$)))$

In (6*) a quantifier from outside the attitude verb binds a variable that occurs within its scope. Quantification operates compositionally, so the truth value of the whole sentence depends on the semantic value of the open formula in the quantifier's scope. But on the paratactic account a quantifier that occurs outside the demonstrated sentences cannot bind a variable that occurs within since the demonstrated sentence is not a semantic constituent of the whole sentence. In '$(\exists x)Said(g,that)$: [*x* is a spy]' the quantifier is idle.

---

[14] An utterance of '$(\exists u)(U(g, u) \ \& \ SS(u,that))$: [the earth moves]' does not logically entail 'There are English utterances' anymore than 'That is a beauty' uttered pointing at a sloop logically entails 'There are sloops'.

There have been many attempts to extend the paratactic account to sentences which like (5) apparently involve quantifying in.[15] An approach we propose that may work is to paraphrase (5) as (20):

(20) $(\exists x)(\exists u)(U(g,u)$ & $Of(u,x)$ & $SS(u,\text{that}))$: [he is a spy]

The first part of (20) says that Galileo produced an utterance which is *of* (or *about*) something and which samesays that. The second part characterizes the sentence-type of the utterance demonstrated by an utterance of the first part. It contains a pronoun 'he' not bound by the quantifier. The demonstrated utterance of 'he is a spy' bears the samesay relation to certain other utterances; for example, it may bear it to an utterance of 'Bellarmino è una spia'. What qualifies an utterance as being samesaid by this utterance of 'he is a spy'? A perhaps not implausible answer is that an utterance u must be of a sentence which contains a demonstrative or proper name or some other term which rigidly refers to an individual of whom 'is a spy' is predicated. (20) is true iff among Galileo's utterances there is one which rigidly refers to an individual and says that individual is a spy. Consider a different example:

(21) Galileo said of Bellarmine that he is a spy.

This is paraphrased by:

(22) $(\exists u)(U(g,u)$ & $Of(u,b)$ & $SS(u,\text{that}))$: [he is a spy.]

The truth of (22) requires Galileo to have produced an utterance about Bellarmine that samesays the demonstrated utterance u' of 'he is a spy'. Whether this utterance samesays an utterance of Galileo's depends not only on the sentences (or phrases) uttered, but on features of the contexts of the utterances. In particular, for u' it is relevant that it occurs embedded in an utterance of (21). This makes only Galileo's utterances which refer to Bellarmine candidates for samesaying u'. A precise statement of the supposed rules that determine the features of utterances relevant to assessing whether one samesays the other is difficult, but we see no obstacle in principle to their formulation.

This brings us to the objection that the paratactic account's reliance on the samesay relation is in some way cheating. It is clear that a truth theory for a paratactic language makes no explicit reference to senses. The worry is that an adequate explanation of the samesay relation will involve senses. There is an obvious Fregean explanation of samesaying. It is that '$SS(u,u')$' is true iff u and u' express the same proposition. We will argue that this Fregean analysis of samesaying is incorrect and will offer a different way to conceive of the samesay relation which apparently does not involve intensional entities.

---

[15] For example, see Quine [144], Temin [181], Hornsby [81] and Boer and Lycan [8].

Some reasons for why this analysis of samesaying is incorrect were sketched earlier. While Frege does not provide a general account of when two utterances express the same sense, it is usually thought that, whatever the account is, it will turn out that, for example, 'A fortnight is a fortnight' and 'A fortnight is two weeks' express the same sense. If so, then on the suggested analysis of samesaying, utterances of these sentences samesay each other. But this cannot be the relation that serves the paratactic account since someone can say that a fortnight is two weeks without saying that a fortnight is a fortnight. As long as different expressions of the same language can express the same sense, there will be examples of this sort. The suggested analysis also seems too restrictive. We frequently correctly indirectly report what a person says by producing a complement utterance (the utterance demonstrated, if the paratactic account is correct) not synonymous with the reportee's utterance. So, whatever the analysis of the samesay relation may be it does not seem coextensive with the relation of expressing the same Fregean proposition.

Refuting the above Fregean analysis does not show that senses are not somehow involved in the samesay relation. If anything, it makes more urgent the question of when does one utterance samesay another? This question is especially pressing and potentially embarrassing for Davidson since he originally emphasized the importance of a finite representation of semantic knowledge. How do we know when an utterance samesays another?

There are really two issues. One is the conceptual issue of characterizing the samesay relation. The other is the epistemological issue of characterizing the knowledge of the samesay relation involved in language understanding. As for the first question, the beginnings of an answer is to be found in what Davidson [36] [37] and others have called the "theory of interpretation." [16] When one person indirectly reports another she attempts to produce an utterance which in her mouth (language, context, etc.) provides for her audience the gist of what the reportee said. She attempts to *interpret* him. An interpretation manual from his language to hers will map his utterances onto hers. Davidson has emphasized that there are certain constraints on correct interpretation manuals; for example, they must maximize agreement and simplicity. Other writers have emphasized further or different constraints. But whether Davidson or anyone else has succeeded in capturing in a few maxims our interpretive practices, it is clear that these practices, and in particular the practice of indirectly reporting others, is sufficiently robust to establish a distinction between correct

---

[16] One thing is clear. While a theory of samesaying for a language L may be constrained by, and connected to, a truth theory for L, the truth theory will not do the job of specifying the extension of the samesay relation for L by itself. An adequate truth theory for L is certain to yield theorems 'S is true iff p' where S and 'p' do not samesay each other.

and incorrect reporting and even degrees of correctness in reporting. The practice within a linguistic community of indirect discourse reporting, correcting, revising, and so on, fixes the extension of the samesay relation. This characterization of the samesay relation does not, it seems, make any use of Fregean senses.

If we suppose that an account of the samesay relation along the above lines is acceptable, there remains the question of representing a competent speaker's knowledge of the samesay relation. An approach analogous to Davidson's account of truth conditions would be to find a finite set of axioms which imply theorems of the sort:

$(u)(u^*)(S)(S^*)(C)(C^*)$(if u is an utterance of S in context C and u^* is an utterance of S^* in C^*, then $SS(u, u^*)$),

where 'S' and 'S^*' are sentences of the speaker's language. A problem facing the construction of such a theory is that contextual information relevant to the samesay relation is so varied and complex that it is hard to see how to describe it and how to take it into account. A second problem is that it seems reasonable that any such theory one person might devise for another's language should be viewed only as a tentative hypothesis defeasible by applications of the principle of charity or whatever principles our interpretive practices conform to. A way of thinking about knowledge of the samesay relation we think worth exploring is that it be represented in terms of a list of rules of thumb which, while generally applicable, are always subject to being overridden by the general principles of interpretation.

Conclusion

The Fregean account and the paratactic account assign different truth conditions and different logical forms to indirect discourse attributions—so different that one might have thought there would be decisive arguments partisans of one account could deploy against the other. In fact, proponents of each account have thought that they had shown the other account irreparably defective. But the lesson of our investigation is that the accounts appear to have the resources to rebuff these arguments. This is not to say that the accounts are without problems. Fregeans owe an account of sameness of sense which validates the appropriate substitution principles. And paratacticians owe an account of how to extend their treatment to "quantifying in" sentences, and they also owe a more explicit and precise account of the samesay relation.[17] But at this stage of the game it seems to us that neither account has been refuted.

If we are to find reasons for favoring one account over the other, we might have to look beyond the data of truth conditions and logical relations to their underlying metaphysical and epistemological commitments.

---

[17] See our forthcoming "How to Get Out of Quantifying In."

In particular, the Fregean theory is committed to a realm of abstract entities which possess their semantic properties essentially. Knowledge of a language for Frege involves not only knowing what senses expressions of the language express, but also "grasping" these entities. Both these commitments are likely to strike contemporary philosophers as *unnaturalistic*. Davidson's theory also makes metaphysical and epistemological commitments. On his account, sentences possess truth conditions, utterances are related by samesaying, and language speakers finitely represent this knowledge. But these seem more modest and more in keeping with a naturalist temperament. Investigation into whether a Davidsonian theory really is more naturalistic than a Fregean theory—and if so, whether that is a virtue—is another undertaking.[18]

[18] An earlier draft of this paper was presented at Washington University in St. Louis. We would like to thank the members of the philosophy department there and Louise Anthony, Bruce Aune, Andrea Bonomi, Ray Eluguardo, Michael Hand, Paolo Leonardi, James Tomberlin, John Wallace, and especially Johannes Brandl and Donald Davidson for their comments on earlier drafts of this paper. We would also like to thank our students Luca Bonatti, Gary Gates, and Shaun Nichols for their stimulating discussion and helpful comments.

4

Wherein Is Language Social?

TYLER BURGE

IN THIS PAPER I will develop two limited senses in which the study of language, specifically semantics, is the study of a partly social phenomenon. These senses are compatible with the idea that the study of language is a part of individual psychology. I will argue for this standpoint from some obvious facts about human interaction together with elements from a view, which I have supported elsewhere, that the semantics of a language is partly dependent on relations between individual speakers and their physical environments. Most of what I say about language will apply to individual psychology. I begin by discussing two background senses in which language is social.

Language is social in that interaction with other persons is psychologically necessary to learn language. Some philosophers have made the further claim that there is some conceptually necessary relation between learning or having a language and being in a community. I do not accept this view. I assume only that it is a psychologically important fact that we cannot learn language alone.

Language is social in another sense. There is a rough, common-sensical set of languages—English, German, and so on—and dialects of these languages, that are in some vague sense shared by social groups. Of course, problems attend taking common-sense languages to be objects of systematic study. The normal divisions among languages correspond to no significant linguistic distinctions.

But this issue is really quite complex. In studying language or dialect in a systematic way, we commonly do not specify who uses the construction at issue, and we commonly assume that there is common ground among a large number of speakers—even though we are studying matters that are not species-wide. In historical studies, for example, we must abstract from individual usage in order to get any generality at all. We simply do not know enough about the quirks of individual usage to make an interesting subject-matter: one must study such things as the history of a word, understood more or less in the common-sensical, trans-individual way. In semantics, one provides theories of reference or meaning in natural language again in nearly total disregard of individual variations, even for phenomena that are by no means universal or species-wide.

These facts of theoretical usage suggest that there is some theoretical point to taking dialects or other linguistic units as abstractions from some sorts of social patterns. Perhaps the abstractions warrant thinking of individual variation as an interference to be accounted for after the primary theorizing is done. I think that there is something to this point of view. Nothing that I will say contradicts it. But the point of view is limited. It cannot provide anything like a complete picture.

One source of limitation derives from the wide variation among any group of individuals on numerous non-universal aspects of language use. People do not share exactly the same vocabulary, for example. People often use words in idiosyncratic ways that exempt them from evaluation by any socially accepted standard. Such quirks motivate the bromide that one should not invoke majority usage "imperialistically" to fit individual variations into a standardized mold. These two points alone make it likely that no two people speak the same "version" of any natural language or dialect.

There is a general reason for variation among individuals' language use. Languages depend on the experiences, usage, and psychological structures of individuals. Variation in individuals' word meaning, for example, is the natural result of the close relation between meaning and belief. Although the precise character of this relation is controversial and although intuitively meaning does not vary as freely as belief, some variation in meaning with individual belief is inevitable. The interplay between meaning and belief is a special case of the interplay between actual languages and psychology—about which similar points regarding individual variation could be made. It is therefore plausible that in studying language one must study the languages of individuals, idiolects.

These considerations suggest aiming for a science of universal aspects of language and for a study of non-universal aspects of language, both of which are tailored to the usage and psychology of individual speakers. I accept this much. Some have drawn the further inference that such a program's method of kind-individuation is independent of any considerations of social interaction among individuals. I will argue that this inference is unsound.

The inference just cited may be suggested by Chomsky's methodology for studying syntax. Actually, Chomsky is more cautious. What he is firm about is that there is a study of *universal grammar* which can be investigated independently of the diversity among individuals, and that linguistics (at least the sort of linguistics he pursues)—both universal and individual— is a part of individual psychology.[1] I shall argue that social factors may

---

[1] See *Knowledge of Language* [25] (p. 18). Chomsky recognizes the possibility of "other kinds of study of language that incorporate social structure and

enter in complex ways into individual psychology and the semantics of idiolects.

Unlike many philosophers, I do not find Chomsky's methodology misguided. His views that linguistic structures are real, that some of them are universal, and that they are mental structures seem to me substantially more plausible than alternatives.[2] Arguments that we may speak merely in accidental accord with the structures postulated in linguistics, or that there is no scientific way to investigate universality of syntax, or that generative linguistics has no direct place in psychology, seem to me unconvincing and indicative of mistaken methodology. I shall not review these arguments.

The study of universal grammar is informed by certain simplifying idealizations. The idealization most relevant to this discussion attempts to cut through the variation and "noise" associated with usage in a community. The linguist considers an idealized "speech community" that is "uniform"— internally consistent in its linguistic practice (cf. footnote 1). Without denying that individuals are members of a community, and without denying that they could develop into mature language-users only because they are, the idealization attempts to study an individual in complete abstraction from the actual presence of others. Any given individual is taken as a representative having universal linguistic abilities or cognitive structures. The assumption is that underlying the variation among individuals, there is a common initial linguistic capacity that is specific enough to have certain definite structural features and that is capable of further linguistic development in certain delimited and specifiable ways. Variations in individual grammar are taken to be results of a fixing of parameters from a set of delimited alternatives.

For present purposes, I accept this idealization regarding universal grammar. It has received substantial support through its fruitful application both in pure linguistics and in developmental psycholinguistics. (I will conjecture about a qualification on the idealization as applied to individual syntax later; cf. footnote 4.) I believe that the methodology accompanying this idealization has some application to universal and individual aspects of semantics. But here the situation is, I think, more complex. In particular, I think that relations to others do affect the individuation of some semantical kinds. To consider the role of social elements in semantics, I want to start further back.

---

interaction." Chomsky's methodology for studying language goes back to *Aspects of the Theory of Syntax* [22].

[2] This view hinges not only on intuitive linguistic data but on studies of development, learning, psychological simplicity, language deficit, psychological processing, and so on. See, for example, Chapter 1 of Chomsky's *Lectures on Government and Binding* [24].

In recent years I have argued that the natures of many of our thoughts are individuated *non-individualistically*. I will have to presuppose these arguments. But according to their common conclusion, the individuation of many thoughts, of intentional kinds, depends on the nature of the environment with which we interact. What information we process—for example, what perceptions we have—is dependent on the properties in the empirical world that members of our species normally interact with when they are having perceptual experiences. What empirical concepts we think with are fixed partly through relations to the kinds of things we think about.[3]

It is easy to confuse this view with another more obvious one. It is obvious that if we did not interact with the empirical or social worlds, we would not have the thoughts we do. Our thoughts and perceptions are causally dependent on the environment. My view concerns not merely causation; it concerns individuation.

Distinguishing the point about individuation from the point about causation is easiest to do by putting the point about individuation in terms of supervenience. Our thoughts do not supervene on the nature and history of our bodies, considered in isolation from the environment, in the following sense: It is in principle possible for one to have had different thoughts from one's actual thoughts, even though one's body had the same molecular history, specified in isolation from its relations to a broader physical environment. The same chemical effects on our bodies might have been induced by different antecedent conditions (perhaps, but not necessarily, including different causal laws). The point about individuation is not only that actual thoughts (like actual chemical effects) depend on the actual nature of the environment. Even if the effects had been chemically the same, it is possible in some cases for the thoughts, the information about the environment carried in our mental states, to have been different—if the environmental antecedents of those effects had been relevantly different. The kind of thought that one thinks is not supervenient on the physical make-up of one's body, specified in isolation from its relations to the environment. Thought kinds are individuated in a way that depends on relations one bears to kinds in one's physical environment. On this view individual psychology itself is not purely individualistic.

The failure of supervenience in no ways casts doubt on investigations of neural or biological realizations of mental structures. The failure of

---

[3] *Non-individualistic* in this context does not entail *social*. The environment can be either physical surroundings or social surroundings. I begin with physical surroundings alone.

The arguments against individualism that I shall be presupposing may be found in "Individualism and the Mental" [11], "Other Bodies" [12], "Cartesian Error and the Objectivity of Perception" [14], "Individualism and Psychology" [15], and "Intellectual Norms and Foundations of Mind" [16]. Different arguments bring out different environmental interdependencies.

supervenience requires only that the identity of certain mental structures be dependent on relations between the individual and the environment. The identity of a heart depends on its function in the whole body—on its relations to parts of the body outside the heart. In a crudely analogous way, the identities of some mental kinds depend on those kinds' relations to entities beyond the individual's body. They depend on cognitive function, on obtaining information, in an environment in something like the way the kind *heart* depends for its individuation on the function of the heart in the body that contains it.

The failure of supervenience also does not entail that an individual psychology that takes its kinds not to be supervenient on an individual's body must study—or make theoretical reference to—the relations between individual and environment that are presupposed in the individuation of its kinds. It is open to psychology to take such kinds as primitive, leaving their presupposed individuation conditions to some other science or to philosophy. I believe this often to be the right course.

The arguments for anti-individualistic individuation of mental kinds can be extended in relatively obvious ways to show that much of semantics is not purely individualistic.[4]

---

[4] Are syntactical elements and structures individualistically individuated? This question is close to the issue regarding the autonomy of syntax. But one should not identify the two questions. The discussions of the autonomy of syntax concern whether some non-syntactical parameter must be mentioned in stating syntactical generalizations. Our question concerns not the parameters mentioned in stating rules of syntax, but the individuation of the syntactical elements. Syntax could be non-individualistic and yet be autonomous (see the preceding paragraph in the text). Evidence has been suggesting that syntax is much more nearly autonomous than common sense might have realized. My reasons for thinking that individual psychology is non-individualistic in its individuation of some thought kinds have nothing directly to do with syntax. They derive purely from considerations that, within the study of language, would be counted semantic. What is at issue then is whether because of some functional relation to semantics, some syntactical kinds are non-individualistically individuated.

I think it arguable that much of syntax is individualistically individuated, or at least no less individualistically individuated than ordinary neural or biological kinds are. But it seems likely that lexical items are individuated in a content-sensitive way. Words or morphemes with the same phonetic and structural-syntactic properties are distinguished because of etymological or other semantic differences. Even if it turned out that every such lexical difference were accompanied by other syntactic or phonological differences, it would seem plausible that the latter differences were dependent on the former. So it seems plausible that the lexical differences do not supervene (in our specified sense) on other syntactic or phonological differences.

Although most philosophers write as if only word types are ambiguous, it is clear that word tokens are often ambiguous. It is arguable that *only* word tokens,

The claim that semantics is non-individualistic is not merely a claim that the *referents* of an individual's words could in principle vary even though the history of the individual's body, considered in isolation from the environment, were held constant.[5] The claim is more comprehensive. The empirical referents of an individual's word are obviously not themselves part of the individual's psychology, or point of view. Thoughts are the individual's perspective on the world. And meanings or senses are, very roughly speaking, a speaker's way of expressing such perspective in language. They are what an individual understands and thinks in the use of his words. My thesis is that even (many of) those aspects of semantics that would be reflected in meaning or sense, and that would be represented in an individual's thought processes, in his psychology, are non-individualistically individuated. What a word means, even in an individual's idiolect, can depend on environmental factors, beyond an individual's body, considered as a molecular structure.

---

never word types, are ambiguous. I do not find this view plausible: words with different but etymologically and semantically related senses are individuated as the same word type. But the view is a useful antidote to habits in the philosophy of language. In any case, word individuation appears to be semantically dependent.

Assuming this to be true, and assuming that semantics is non-individualistic, it follows that what it is to be a given word sometimes depends (in the way that what it is to be a given meaning or concept depends) on relations between the individual and the objective, empirical world. *Whether* this is true about lexical items, and how far it might extend beyond the individuation of lexical items, is a question I leave open here. The answer will not very much affect the practice of generative grammar, since environmental relations need not be mentioned in syntax. But it will affect our understanding of the place of syntax in our wider theorizing about the world.

Similar issues might be raised about some universal syntactic categories (animate, agent, etc.). And as James Higginbotham has pointed out to me, analogous questions may be raised about the relation between phonology and ordinary perception. Ordinary perceptual kinds are not individualistically individuated (see footnote 6). It may be that this fact should affect our understanding of perception studies in phonology.

[5] This view, though not trivial, is a consequence of a view that is widely accepted. It is a consequence of the work of Donnellan and Kripke, and indeed Wittgenstein, on reference. I will not defend it here. But I will develop a reason for its inevitability below. Numerous examples indicate that an individual's proper names, kind terms, demonstratives, and various other parts of speech have definite referents even though the individual could not, by other means, discriminate the referent from other possible or actual entities that might have been in an appropriate relation to the individual's words—other entities that might have been the referent even though the individual's body could have remained molecularly the same. See Kripke [95], Donnellan [43], Putnam [132] [134], and numerous other works.

I think it plausible that some meanings of words are universal to the species in that if a person has the requisite perceptual experience and acquires language normally, the person will have words with those meanings. A likely source of such universality is perceptual experience itself. It appears that early vision is language-independent and constant for the species. Because of the evolution of our species, we are fashioned in such a way that perceptual experience will automatically trigger the application of perceptual notions associated with innate dispositions. Linguistic expressions for such perceptual notions as edge, surface, shadow, under, curved, physical object, and so on, are likely to be tied to elementary, universal perceptual experience, or to innate states fixed by species-ancestors' perceptual interactions with the world.

Many such notions can be shown to be non-individualistically individuated. It is possible to construct hypothetical cases in which the optical laws of the world are different, and the interactions of one's species with elements of the world are different, so that different perceptual notions, carrying different perceptual information, are innate or universally acquired. But in these same cases, one can coherently conceive an individual whose bodily history is molecularly identical to one whose perceptual notions are like ours. (The optical differences need not prevent, in certain special cases, a given individual from being affected in the same chemical way by different causal antecedents in the empirical world.) So the perceptual content or information of his experience is different—he has different perceptions— even though his body is, individualistically specified, the same. In such a case, it is clear that the meanings or senses of his words for objective, perceptual properties will also be different.[6]

Thus the view that certain concepts and meanings are non-individualistically individuated is compatible with those concepts and meanings being innate. The effect of the environment in determining psychological kinds

---

[6] See Marr's *Vision* [118] for a very explicit statement of the non-individualistic methodology. For a more general review of the point that anti-individualistic individuation is implicit in all scientific theories of perception, see Stillings's "Modularity and Naturalism in Theories of Vision" [180]. For the cited philosophical arguments, see Burge, "Cartesian Error and Objectivity of Perception" [14] and "Individualism and Psychology" [15]. The former article discusses Marr's theory. For perception, the point is really pretty obvious even apart from philosophical argument: perceptual states are individuated by reference to physical properties that bear appropriate relations to subjects' states or those of his species-ancestors.

Although Chomsky does not discuss non-individualistic features of the visual system, he clearly makes a place for psychological states that have a different genesis and different conditions for individuation from those psychological states that constitute the structures of universal grammar. He counts such states part of the "conceptual system," and uses vision as a prime example (see Chomsky's *Rules and Representations* [23]).

may occur in the evolution of the species as well as in the experiential history of the individual.

Whether or not they are universal, virtually all concepts and meanings that are applied to public objects or events that we know about empirically are non-individualistically individuated. Such meanings attributed by semantics, and such concepts attributed by individual psychology, are non-individualistic to the core.

So far I have stated an anti-individualistic view of psychology and semantics that is entirely independent of social considerations. The failure of individualism derives, at this stage, purely from relations between the individual and the empirically known physical world. Now I want to use considerations that underlie this non-social anti-individualism to show how social elements enter the individuation of linguistic and psychological kinds. In a sense I will derive principles underlying social anti-individualistic thought experiments (see "Individualism and the Mental" [11]) from obvious facts, together with some of the principles underlying non-social anti-individualistic thought experiments.

As a means of setting background, I begin with Chomsky's suggestion for incorporating social elements into semantics. Responding to Putnam's "division of linguistic labor," he writes:[7]

> In the language of a given individual, many words are semantically indeterminate in a special sense: The person will defer to "experts" to sharpen or fix their reference. . . . In the lexicon of this person's language, the entries [for the relevant words] will be specified to the extent of his or her knowledge, with an indication that details are to be filled in by others, an idea that can be made precise in various ways but without going beyond the study of the system of knowledge of language of a particular individual. Other social aspects of language can be regarded in a like manner—although this is not to deny the possibility or value of other kinds of study of language that incorporate social structure and interaction.

Chomsky's proposal is certainly part of a correct account of the individual's reliance on others. I do not want to dispute the cases that he specifically discusses. I think, however, that the proposal cannot provide a complete account. My first concern is that it might be read to imply that in all relevant cases, the reference of an individual's own word is semantically indeterminate: determinateness only appears in the idiolects of the "experts." (I am not sure whether Chomsky intends the proposal in this way.) Sometimes the reference of a relevant term is incomplete or vague. But sometimes, even in cases where the individual's substantive *knowledge in explicating* features of the referent is vague, incomplete, or riddled with false belief, the reference is as determinate as anyone else's. The reference of an individual's word is not always dependent on what the individual

---

[7] *Knowledge of Language* [25], p. 18. The relevant articles by Hilary Putnam are "Is Semantics Possible?" [132] and "The Meaning of 'Meaning'"[134].

knows or can specify about the referent. When the individual defers to others, it is not in all cases to sharpen or fix the reference but to sharpen the individual's explicative knowledge of a referent that is already fixed. Our and the individual's own attitudes toward the specification of the reference often make this clear (see footnote 5). For present purposes, brief reflection on various natural-kind terms that we use without expert knowledge should make the point intuitive. One might use 'feldspar', 'tiger', 'helium', 'water', 'oak', or 'spider', with definite referents even though one cannot oneself use one's background knowledge to distinguish the referent from all possible counterfeits. Knowledge obtained from better-informed people—they need not be experts—often tells one more about the standard kinds we all refer to with these words. It does not *in general* change the referents of our words. (This is not to deny that sometimes experts' terms have different, more technical meaning than lay usage of the same word forms.) The referents of such kind terms is simply not fixed entirely by the individual's background knowledge. Individuals often recognize this about their own terms. Although this point could be supported through numerous cases, and through more general considerations, I think that it is fairly evident on reflection. I shall assume it in what follows.

Even granted this qualification, Chomsky's proposal will not provide a complete account of the individual's own language—or even of the individual's knowledge of his or her idiolect. For in some cases, an individual's explicational ability not only does not suffice to fix the referent of the individual's word; it does not exhaust the meaning expressed by a word in the individual's idiolect.

I distinguish between a lexical item and the explication of its meaning that articulates what the individual would give, under some reflection, as his understanding of the word. Call the former "the word" and the latter "the entry for the word." I also distinguish between the concept associated with the word and the concept(s) associated with the entry. Call the former "the concept" and the latter "the conceptual explication." Finally, I distinguish between a type of meaning associated with the word, "translational meaning," and the meaning associated with its entry, "explicational meaning." For our purposes, the explicational meaning is the semantical analog of the conceptual explication. The translational meaning of a word can be articulated through exact translation and sometimes through such trivial thoughts as *my word 'tiger' applies to tigers*, but need not be exhaustively expressible in other terms in an idiolect.

A traditional view in semantics is that a word's explicational meaning and its translational meaning are, for purposes of characterizing the individual's idiolect, always interchangeable; and that the individual's conceptual explication always completely exhausts his or her concept. This view is incorrect. It is incorrect because of the role that the referent plays in individuating the concept and translational meaning, and because of the role that non-explicational abilities play in the individual's application of the word and concept. Accounting for a person's lexical entry or conceptual explication is relevant to determining the nature of a person's meaning or concept. But the two enterprises are not the same. I will try to give some sense for why this is so.

Let us begin by concentrating on the large class of nouns and verbs that apply to everyday, empirically discernible objects, stuffs, properties, and events. I have in mind words like 'tiger', 'water', 'mud', 'stone', 'tree', 'bread', 'knife', 'chair', 'edge', 'shadow', 'baby', 'walk', 'fight', and so on. Except for tense, these words are not and do not contain indexicals in any ordinary sense. Given only that their meaning in the language is fixed, their applications or referents are fixed. They do not depend for their applications on particular contexts of use; nor do they shift their applications systematically with context or with the referential intentions of speakers. Without contextual explication or relativization, we can trivially, but correctly, state their ranges of applications: 'tiger' applies to tigers; 'walk' applies to instances of walking; and so on. Contrast: 'then' applies to then. This latter explication requires a particular context to do its job, a particular, context-dependent application of 'then' to a salient time. The constancy of application of non-indexical words, within particular idiolects, is a feature of their meaning and of the way that they are understood by their users.

Although the reference of these words is not all there is to their semantics, their reference places a constraint on their meaning, or on what concept they express. In particular, any such word w has a different meaning (or expresses a different concept) from a given word w' if their constant referents, or ranges of application, are different. That is part of what it is to be a non-indexical word of this type.[8]

The individual's explicational beliefs about the referents of such words, his conceptual explications, do not always fix such words' referents, even in his idiolect. So, by the considerations of the previous paragraph, they do not always fix such words' meanings or concepts in the individual's idiolect.

The point that explicational beliefs do not always fix reference is substantiated not only through the examples that have dominated the theory of reference for the last forty years (see footnote 5). It is also supported by

---

[8] The ontology of meanings or concepts is unimportant for these purposes. But I assume the standard view that the meaning or concept should not be identified with the word—since different words could express the same meaning or concept, and the same word can express different meanings or concepts. I assume also that the meaning or concept should not be identified with the referent, since a meaning or concept is a way of speaking or thinking about the referent. Of course, sometimes words express meanings or concepts that have no referent. And meanings or concepts normally have vague boundaries of application.

The point about non-indexicality can be established on purely linguistic grounds. I discuss the non-indexicality of the relevant words in more detail in "Other Bodies" [12].

considering the dialectic by which we arrive at conceptual explications, or lexical entries.

Sometimes such explications are meant to produce approximate synonymies (as in the explication of 'knife'). Other times, not ('tiger', 'water'). In the cases we are discussing applications of the words are backed by and learned through perceptual experience. Perceptually fixed examples typically determine the application of the word before conceptual explications do.[9]

Conceptual explications are typically inferences from these perceptual experiences, or general epithets derived from the remarks of others, or both. In attempting to articulate one's conception of one's concept, one's conceptual explication, one naturally alternates between thinking of examples and refining one's conceptual explication in order to accord with examples that one recognizes as legitimate. It is crucial here to note that the legitimacy of examples does not in general derive from one's attempts at conceptual explication. Although sometimes examples are shown to be legitimate or illegitimate by reference to such explications, the normal order—in the class of words that we are discussing—is the other way around. The examples, first arrived at through perception, tend to be the touchstone for evaluating attempts at conceptual explication.

Consider the sort of dialectic in which people try to arrive at an explication of the meanings of their words. First attempts are usually seen to be mistaken. Reflection on examples leads to improvements. The altered characterizations improve on one's characterization of a referent that is assumed to have been fixed. (They are not normally mere sharpenings of reference, or changes in the meanings of one's word.) They are equally improvements in one's conceptual understanding of one's own concept or meaning.

Such dialectic typically adds to one's knowledge. Suppose I explicate my word 'chair' in a way that requires that chairs have legs, and then come to realize that beach chairs, or deck-chairs bolted to a wall, or ski-lift chairs, are counterexamples. Or suppose that I learn more about how to discriminate water from other (possible or actual) colorless, tasteless, potable liquids. In such cases, I learn something about chairs or water that I did not know before. In these cases it is simply not true that the reference of my words 'chair' and 'water' must change. Although it is true that my conception—my explication—changes, it remains possible for me to observe (with univocal use of 'chair'): "I used to think chairs had to have legs, but now know that chairs need not have legs." It remains possible for me to have thoughts about water as water, knowing that there might

---

[9] This point is now common not only in the philosophical literature (see Putnam [132] and [134] and Burge [12]) but also in the psychological literature. See Rosch and Lloyd [151], and Smith and Medin [175]. For excellent philosophical discussion of this literature, with criticism of some of its excesses, see Kobes [94], Chapter 6.

be other liquids that I could not, by means other than use of my concept *water*, discriminate from it. Thus there is a sense in which the concept, and the translational meaning of the word in the idiolect, remain the same despite the changed discriminating ability, or change in explication.

Of course, my ability to come up with better explications by considering examples with which I am already familiar indicates that I have more to go on than my initial explications suggest. Perhaps I have "tacitly cognized" more than what I give as my reflective explication, before I arrive consciously at a better explication.

I think that this view is right. But it would be a mistake to infer that I always already know the correct explication in some suppressed way. It would be an even more serious mistake to infer that our tacit conceptual explications exhaust our concepts. There are several reasons why these moves are unsound.

In the first place, the dialectic involves genuine reasoning—using materials at hand to form a better conception. Granting that we have the materials in our mental repertoires to form a better conception does not amount to granting that we have already put them together. Reflection on the examples seems to play a role in doing this. When I give a mistaken explication of 'chair', I may have failed to hold empirical information in my memory, or failed to put together things that I knew separately. I may have failed to believe at the time of explication that there were legless chairs, even though I had experience and even perhaps knowledge from which I could have derived this belief. Thus the sort of unconscious or tacit cognition that is involved is not just an unconscious analog of having reflective knowledge of the proposition formed by linking the concept and the improved conceptual explication. Attribution of tacit cognition entails only that the mental structures for deriving the recognition of examples are in place and will (ideally) lead to such recognition, when examples are presented.

In the second place, there is substantial evidence that some of the "underlying" materials are stored in our perceptual capacities and are not, properly speaking, conceptualized (see footnote 9). We are often able to project our concept (e.g., *chair*) to new cases never before considered. Often this projection seems to be based on perceptual capacities that are modular and preconceptual. Thus the "materials" that are put together and worked up into conceptual explications through the process of dialectic sometimes do not, before reflection begins, appear to be the right sort to count as criterial knowledge, even unconscious criterial knowledge.

In the third place, even the perceptual abilities need not suffice to discriminate instances of the concept from every possible look-alike—from look-alikes that might have been normal in other environments, and which in that case might have determined other concepts, but which play no role in the formation of concepts in the speaker's actual environment. The explicated concepts are determined to be what they are by the actual nature of objects and events that we can perceptually discriminate from other relevantly similar things in the same environment. Thus even our perceptual abilities and our conceptual explications combined need not provide necessary and sufficient conditions for the correct application of our concepts in all possible environments in which the concepts have a definite application. They therefore need not fully exhaust the content of our concepts.

There is a more general reason why our explicational abilities, including our unconscious ones, do not in general and necessarily suffice to exhaust the concepts that they serve to explicate. One's cognitive relation to the examples that played an initial role in fixing one's concept is perceptual. That relation inherits the fallibility of perceptual experience. Since the concepts under discussion are not merely given by conceptual explications, but are partly fixed through examples in the environment, their conceptual explications must correctly describe the examples. Conceptual explications (and dictionary entries) are not normally true by logic and stipulation. They are true because they capture examples that are fixed partly through perceptual experience. But our cognitive relations to the examples are fallible. So the conceptual explications and dictionary entries that sum up our current discriminative abilities are fallible. The things that we perceive and that fix our concepts may not be just as we see and characterize them. Yet they may be genuine instances of the concepts. And we are subject to misidentifying other things that fit our perceptual schemas and conceptual explications as instances of our concepts, when they are not. So those schemas and explications do not necessarily exhaust the concepts or meanings that they explicate.[10]

Our commitment to getting the examples right is part of our understanding of the relevant class of words and concepts. This commitment is illustrated in, indeed explains, many cases of our *standing corrected* by others in our attempts to explicate our own words and concepts. Such correction, by oneself or by others, is common in the course of the dialectic. One sees oneself as having made a mistake about the meaning of one's own word, in one's explication of one's own concept.

Some philosophers have characterized all cases of standing corrected as pliant shifts of communicative strategy. According to this view, I previously used 'chair' in my idiolect with a meaning that did in fact exclude legless chairs. But on encountering resistance from others, I tacitly shift my meaning so as to surmount practical obstacles to communication or fellowship that would result from maintaining an idiosyncratic usage.[11]

I agree, of course, that such practically motivated changes occur. But they cannot explain all cases of our standing corrected. For such correction is often—I would say, typically—founded on substantive, empirical matters

---

[10] I have discussed other problems with exhaustive conceptual explications in "Other Bodies" [12] and "Intellectual Norms and Foundations of Mind" [16].

[11] See Davidson's "Knowing One's Own Mind" [40].

about which there are cognitive rights and wrongs. We make mistakes, sometimes empirically correctable mistakes, that others catch, and that bear on the proper explication of the meaning of words in our idiolects. In such cases we come to understand our idiolects better.

Others are sometimes better placed than we are to judge the fit between our proposed lexical entries, or our conceptual explications, and the examples to which our words or concepts apply. Thus we may correctly see others as sometimes understanding our own idiolects better than we do. When we defer to someone else's linguistic authority, it is partly because the other person has superior empirical insight, insight that bears on the proper characterization of examples to which our words or concepts apply. The reason for their insight is not that they have made a study of us. It is also not that they are foisting some foreign, socially authorized standard on us. It is that they understand their idiolects better than we understand ours, and they have a right to assume that our idiolects are in relevant respects similar, or the same.

The justification of this assumption, also fallible, has two main sources. One is the publicity of the examples and our shared perceptual and inferential equipment. Given that we have been exposed to substantially similar knives, chairs, water, trees, mud, walkings, and fightings, and have heard these associated with the same words, it is to be expected that we project from actual examples in similar ways. Although our kind-forming abilities may differ in some instances, it is reasonable to expect that they will typically be the same, especially with concepts that apply to entities of common perceptual experience. Normally we will be committed to the legitimacy of the same examples, and will be committed to characterizing those examples, correctly. Given that the examples are public, no one has privileged authority about their characteristics.

A second source of the assumption that others can correct one's explications is that a person's access to the examples—to the applications that help fix the relevant concept—is partly or fully through others. Words are initially acquired from others, who are already applying these words to cases. Word acquisition occurs in conjunction with acquisition of information, information from testimony, or communication with others, about those cases.

Of course, until the learner develops some minimal amount of background knowledge and likeness of application, he or she cannot be said to have acquired the word in the predecessor's sense, or with the predecessor's range of applications. But as we have seen in the preceding paragraphs, possession of an infallible explication is not required—because it is not possible.

The dependence on others for access to examples grows as one's linguistic and cognitive resources widen. In some cases we depend heavily on the perceptual experience of others (as with 'tiger', 'penguin', and 'rain', for those of us in California). In other cases we depend on theoretical background knowledge ('gene', 'cancer') or on more ordinary expertise ('arthritis', 'carburetor'). In many such cases, we intentionally take over the applications that others have made. We rely on their experience to supplement our own. And we accept corrections of our explications from them because they have better access to the examples which partly determine the nature of our concepts. Although the function of explication varies significantly in these various cases, the main points of the argument for social dependence apply equally, indeed even more obviously, to terms that are less closely associated with direct perception.

Since fixing examples—or more broadly, referents—that partly determine an individual's concept or translational meaning is sometimes dependent on the activity of others with whom he interacts, the individuation of an individual's concepts or translational meanings is sometimes dependent on his interaction with others. Even where the individual has epistemic access to the examples independently of others (for example, where he perceives instances directly), others may have superior knowledge of the examples. They may therefore have superior insight into the proper explication of the individual's words and concepts: they may have put together relevant cognitive materials in a way that provides standards for understanding the individual's words and concepts. In such cases, the individual's deference may be cognitively appropriate.

The cases in which the individual does and does not have independent access to the examples might seem to be significantly different. The former case might be seen as showing only that others may know more about the explication of the individual's meanings and concepts than he does, and that it is easier to understand an individual's idiolect by studying idiolects and attitudes of others. One might still insist, relative to this case, that the materials for determining the individual's concepts or meanings do not involve the individual's relations to others.

Though I need not contest this point for the sake of present argument, I doubt that it is correct. It is metaphysically possible for an individual to learn his idiolect in isolation from a community. But it is no accident, and not merely a consequence of a convenient practical strategy, that one obtains insight into an idiolect by considering the usage and attitudes of others. In learning words, individuals normally look to others to help set standards for determining the range of legitimate examples and the sort of background information used in explicating a word or concept. I believe that this is a psychological necessity for human beings.

The second case, where the individual has had limited relevant access to the examples independently of others, provides independent ground for thinking that individuation of an individual's concepts or meanings is sometimes dependent on the social interactions that the individual engages in. If others had provided access to a different range of examples, compatible with one's minimal background information, one would have had different meanings or concepts.

Let me summarize the argument that an individual's idiolect and concepts cannot be fully understood apart from considering the language and concepts of others with whom he interacts. Numerous empirically applicable words are non-indexical. Non-indexical words must have different translational meanings, and express different concepts, if their referents are different. Our explicational abilities, and indeed all our cognitive mastery regarding the referents of such words and concepts, do not necessarily fix the referents. Nor therefore (by the first premise) do they necessarily fix the translational meanings or concepts associated with the words. To be correct, our lexical entries and conceptual explications are subject to correction or confirmation by empirical consideration of the referents. Since such empirical consideration is fallible, our cognitive relations to the referents are fallible. Others are often in a better position to arrive at a correct articulation of our word or concept, because they are in a better position to determine relevant empirical features of the referents. This, for two reasons: the referents are public, so no one has privileged authority regarding their properties; and we are frequently dependent on others for linking our words to the referents and for access to the referents. Since the referents play a necessary role in individuating the person's concept or translational meaning, individuation of an individual's concepts or translational meanings may depend on the activity of others on whom the individual is dependent for acquisition of and access to the referents. If the others by acting differently had put one in touch with different referents, compatibly with one's minimum explicational abilities, one would have had different concepts or translational meanings.[12] Although I have argued only that this conclusion derives from obvious facts of social interaction, I have conjectured that it derives from psychological necessities for human beings.

The argument does not depend on assuming that people ever share the same concepts or translational meanings.[13] However, the argument

---

[12] I think that this argument admits of an important extension. The argument derives non-individualistic variation in an individual's meanings or concepts from variation in empirical referents to which the community provides access. But the variation need not occur in the referents. It may depend on the nature of our cognitive access through the community to the examples. The variation may occur in the way the referents are approached in the community. Thus it may be that the referents are held fixed, but the community's cognitive access to them may vary in such a way as to vary the concept, without varying the effect on the individual's body or rudimentary explicational abilities. This extension is, I think, a corollary of the Fregean observation that referents (or examples) do not determine meanings or concepts. Since my purpose has been to establish a minimal sense in which language is social, I shall not illustrate or develop this extension here.

[13] This is also true of the argument in "Individualism and the Mental" [11]. The conclusion can rest on the mere assumption that the referents of the concepts in the actual and counterfactual communities are different. (Loar [115]

makes it plausible that people in a community do often share concepts and translational meanings, despite differences in their beliefs about the world, and even differences in their explications of the relevant terms. Most empirically applicable concepts are fixed by three factors: by actual referents encountered through experience—one's own, one's fellows', or one's species-ancestors', or indirectly through theory; by some rudimentary conceptualization of the examples—learned or innately possessed by virtually everyone who comes in contact with the terms; and by perceptual information, inferential capacities, and kind-forming abilities, that may be preconceptual. The referents are often shared, because of similarity of experience and because of intentional reliance on others for examples. So the concepts and translational meanings associated with many words will be shared. Shared idiolectal meanings and shared concepts derive from a shared empirical world and shared cognitive goals and procedures in coming to know that world.[14]

---

seems mistakenly and crucially to assume the contrary in his critical discussion of "Individualism and the Mental.") For all that, I know of no persuasive reason for thinking that in every relevant case the person in the actual community cannot share his concept or meaning (e.g., *arthritis*) with his fellows.

[14] So it appears that there is an element of meaning that can remain constant and common across individuals, despite the interdependence of meaning and belief noted at the outset. It is notable that this constancy in no way depends on the assumption of a distinction between sentences that are *true* purely by virtue of their meaning and sentences that depend for their truth on the way the subject-matter is. (Like Quine, I find this distinction empty.) See Burge [16]. Belief in the relevant element of meaning does not even depend on invocation of a distinction between criterial or linguistic truths or other sorts of truths (although like Chomsky and unlike Quine, I think that this latter distinction, commonly conflated with the previous one, is clearly defensible).

Another point about the semantics of word meaning bears emphasizing. There is a relevant semantical distinction between cases in which the individual has sufficient materials in his conceptual repertoire to construct a given lexical entry, maximally faithful to the range of applications or examples that he recognizes as legitimate, and cases in which the individual's dependence on others is such that his repertoire allows only entries that are less full than those of others. In the latter cases it is *not true*, on my view, that the "communal" entry is the "correct" entry within the person's idiolect. I take it that lexical entries sum up an idealized conceptual understanding. If the person lacks resources to arrive at some given entry, the entry is not part of his idiolect.

But it does not *follow* from this difference that the person does not have the same concept, or the same translational meaning, that others have. To think this would be to confuse concept and conceptual explication, or translational meaning and explicational understanding. In not sharing this explication with others, the person will not fully share an understanding of the word (or the conception of the concept) with others. But lexical entries (conceptual explications) do not determine the translational meaning (concepts); they may even be mistaken, and

Traditional philosophy tended to ignore the first and third factors in concept determination, and to expand the second into the requirement of necessary and sufficient conditions that "define" the meaning or concept and that must be believed if one is to have the relevant concept at all. The dissolution of this picture makes possible an appreciation of the dependence of the individuation of our empirical concepts on direct or indirect perceptual relations to our empirical environment.

Drawing on these ideas, together with obvious facts about social interaction, I have tried to show that idiolects are social in two senses. First, in many cases we must, on cognitive grounds, defer to others in the explication of our words. Second, the individuation of our concepts and meanings is sometimes dependent on the activity of others from whom we learn our words and on whom we depend for access to the referents of our words. The second sense grounds the view that individual psychology and the study of the semantics of idiolects are not wholly independent of assumptions of interaction among individuals.

---

only contingently related to it. The person still has his or her perceptual abilities for picking out referents, and the relevant referents may still be partly fixed by the person's reliance on others. Thus as far as present considerations go, the person's concept may be shared with others even though his or her conceptual explication or lexical entry may differ.

5

Narrow Content

ROBERT STALNAKER

THE NARROW CONTENT of a mental state is supposed to be a kind of content that is wholly internal to the mind of the person in the mental state. A number of philosophers have argued that for purposes of the psychological explanation of behavior, and perhaps also for the purpose of explaining the authoritative access that we all seem to have to our own intentional mental states, we need a notion of narrow content. These philosophers acknowledge, in response to arguments and examples presented by Tyler Burge [11], among others, that the ordinary contents referred to in ordinary attributions of occurrent thoughts and propositional attitudes are often not narrow in the required way, but they argue that we must, and we can, factor out the component of content that is internal to the person, that this component is what does the work in intentional explanation of behavior, and that this component is what explains the essential accessibility of our own thoughts and beliefs.

The internalist project—the project of explicating a conception of narrow content and applying it to the explanation of intentionality—is an appealing one since it seems intuitively obvious that our thoughts and beliefs are wholly our own. What we see and know is partly a matter of what we are looking at, and what is true, and we can get it wrong. But we can't be wrong about what we think, or think we think about. When I retreat from saying how things are to saying how they seem—how they are *according to me*—I retreat from a claim about the world to a claim about my own mind, and I can tell that the claim is true by introspection—by observing what is internal to my mind. Burge's anti-individualist arguments seem to conflict with these compelling intuitions; the internalist project tries to defuse these arguments by carving out a different notion of content—one that somehow can reconcile the intentionality of mental states with their apparent internality. But despite its intuitive appeal, I have some doubts about the project; I think it is less clear than is sometimes supposed what narrow content is, and what function it is supposed to play. And I am not convinced that there is a conflict between the conclusions that the anti-individualist reaches about intentional states and the intuitions that motivate the internalist. I will raise a number of questions about narrow content: first, just what kind of object is a narrow content supposed to be, and in what sense is this kind of content narrow or purely internal to the mind? Second, what role is narrow content supposed to play in the description and explanation of mental phenomena? How is the ascription of narrow content related to the ordinary ascription of wide content? Third, do we really need narrow content to explain the role of content in the explanation of behavior, and the access that we have to the contents of our own thoughts?

I will focus in my discussion on two recent papers [114] [115] by Brian Loar in which a concept of narrow content is developed, motivated, and applied. Loar's papers contain some ingenious examples and challenging arguments, and I think they make explicit some of the deeper and more elusive reasons for the attraction of the internalist project, and for the intuitive resistance that most of us feel to the anti-individualist conclusions that Burge argues for. But as I will argue, I don't think his defense of internalism is entirely successful, or entirely clear. I do think that something like Loar's conception of narrow content will play a role in a satisfactory account of intentional explanations, but I will argue that it isn't really narrow content at all.

What Is Narrow Content, and What Is Narrow about It?

We might begin by asking about ordinary wide content. What kind of object is a wide content, and why is it wide, or "not wholly in the head"? There is little agreement about the details of an account of ordinary wide content, but it seems clear and uncontroversial that the content of a speech act, attitude, or thought is an abstract object that has (or perhaps just is) a set of truth conditions. When I believe, hope, or predict that Dukakis will win in November, the content of my belief, hope, or prediction is something that is (or will be) true if and only if Dukakis wins in November. Everyone agrees that truth conditions are essential to propositional content as ordinarily conceived: if there are conditions in which your belief will be true and mine false, that is sufficient to establish that our beliefs have different contents. On some accounts, a difference in truth conditions is also necessary for a difference in content. The content of a belief, hope, or prediction on this kind of account is just the set of truth conditions itself. We may represent content, on this conception, as a set of possible situations or possible worlds, since thoughts true under the same conditions are true in the same possible worlds.

Whether one adopts this simple coarse-grained conception of ordinary content or some more fine-grained notion that determines a content in this sense, it will be common ground that the contents of thoughts are abstract objects and not mental events or states. While there may be disagreements over the identity conditions for propositional contents, it is generally agreed that different people may sometimes believe the same thing, and that it can happen that what I hope is exactly what you fear. So there is a trivial sense in which the contents of thoughts and the meanings of expressions "ain't in the head": as abstract objects, they are not anywhere in space. But Burge [11] and Putnam [134] had more in mind than this when they argued that meaning and content were not wholly internal. What the twin-earth stories purport to establish is that the having of a particular thought or attitude is a non-intrinsic property. What fails to be internal if content is wide is not the content itself, but the property of having a thought with that content. It is not the proposition that copper is cheaper than gold that is external in the relevant sense; it is the property of believing (or thinking, wishing, etc.) that copper is cheaper than gold. The Putnam-Burge thought experiments show such properties to be non-internal by exhibiting cases of thinkers differing with respect to such a property while not differing with respect to any intrinsic property.

So what the internalist needs is not just a new notion of content, but a different account of the way we are related to those contents. Contents, wide or narrow, are abstract objects we use to pick out certain mental states. Narrow content must be a kind of content that can be used, together with a different account of the way we are related to that kind of content, to pick out mental states that are intrinsic. How does it do it? Loar's idea is that the narrow content of a belief should be identified, not with its *truth conditions*, but with what Loar calls its *realization conditions*. Realization conditions, like ordinary truth conditions, determine a set of possible worlds: the worlds associated with the realization conditions for Bert's belief will be, Loar tells us, "those in which Bert's thoughts are or would be true if they are or were not misconceptions." It is not entirely clear what this means, but on a straightforward interpretation, the idea might seem to be this: to see whether a certain belief is realized in a given possible world, we ask whether a certain possibly counterfactual conditional is true in that world. Suppose the belief in question is Bert's belief that copper is less expensive than gold. To see whether a given possible world w satisfies the realization conditions for that belief, we ask not whether it is true in w that copper is less expensive than gold, but rather whether it is true in w that if Bert's conceptions of gold, copper, etc., were not misconceptions then copper would be less expensive than gold. But this can't be what is meant. For whether Bert's conceptions are misconceptions or not in w, it is unlikely that the relative prices of gold and copper will depend on whether his conceptions are correct. Suppose that in w, Bert's conceptions of gold and copper are misconceptions. What will the truth value be, in w, of the counterfactual, 'if Bert's conceptions of gold and copper were correct, copper would be less expensive than gold'? Unless this is a bizarre world in which Bert's mental states have some kind of causal influence on the economic situation, this counterfactual will be true in w if and only if its consequent is. So, ignoring such bizarre worlds, the realization conditions will be the same as the truth conditions on this interpretation, and they will not, in any case, be narrow in the required sense.

I think what was intended is instead something like this: Imagine a set of possible worlds, in all of which Bert exists and is thinking a certain thought. Now we can distinguish the following two questions: first, we may ask what the actual content of Bert's thought is, and then evaluate that content relative to each of the possible worlds in the set. Second, we may ask, for each of the worlds in the set, what the content of Bert's thought is in that world, and whether that content is true in that world. Question one asks, what is the content of Bert's thought in the actual world, and then, for each world w, what is the truth value of that fixed content in w. Question two asks, for each w, what is the truth value, in w, of the content that Bert's thought has in w. Each of these questions will yield a proposition—a set of possible worlds. But if the content of Bert's thought—what he is thinking, when this is understood in the ordinary wide sense—varies from world to world, then the two propositions will be different. And if Burge's thought experiments are to be believed, the content of Bert's thought will vary from world to world, even if Bert's subjective perspective remains the same. But while this wide content—the proposition determined by the answer to the first question—might vary with changes in social and other environmental conditions, the proposition yielded by the second question will be the same no matter which of the possible worlds in which Bert is thinking his thought is the actual world. So this proposition is a plausible candidate for the narrow content. To see more concretely how the procedure goes, consider a familiar twin-earth example. Bert is thinking, "Water is the best drink for quenching thirst." We can evaluate the wide and narrow contents of this thought relative to four possible worlds: a is the actual world (in which, let us assume, water is indeed the best drink for quenching thirst); b is the usual twin-earth counterfactual situation: this world is just like the actual world, except that the stuff called "water" there is XYZ. In b, XYZ is the best drink for quenching thirst. c is a world with water, like the actual world, but in c there is another drink, called gatorade, that quenches thirst better than water. Finally, d is the twin-earth version of c, where twin-gatorade quenches thirst better than XYZ, the stuff they call water there. Bert inhabits all of these possible worlds, and in each of them he is thinking a thought that he would put by saying, "Water is the best drink for quenching thirst." The actual wide content of Bert's thought is the proposition that is true in a and false in b, c and d. The wide content that Bert's thought has in world c is the same, since what they call "water" there is water. But in b and d, the content of Bert's thought is a different proposition, one that is true in b and false in the other three worlds. These facts about the actual and counterfactual wide contents of Bert's thought can be represented in a two dimensional matrix that defines what I have elsewhere called a *propositional concept*—a function from possible worlds into propositions. We can extract from it a proposition—which I have called the *diagonal proposition* determined by the propositional concept: the proposition that is true at w if and only if the proposition that is the value of the function for argument w is true at w. In this example, the diagonal is the proposition that is true in worlds a and b, and false in worlds c and d. I think this is a plausible candidate for the realization conditions, or narrow content, of a thought, in the sense Loar had in mind.

Now I think, and have argued, that propositional concepts and diagonal propositions are useful devices for representing and explaining some facts about the *attribution* of belief, but I am not sure they will yield a notion of narrow content that will do all that the internalist wants such a notion to do. Let me point out a number of facts about it.

First, this explanation makes clear that the determination of narrow content presupposes that we can identify a thought independently of its content. The analogous presupposition about speech acts is unproblematic. If I *say* that water is the best drink for quenching thirst, I do it by uttering certain sounds, and we can describe the utterance event in a way that makes no commitment about its content. So there is no problem asking what the content of *that* utterance event would have been had *it* taken place on twin earth. Perhaps one can also identify occurrent thoughts independently of their contents, but it is not at all clear in the case of beliefs, intentions, and other states and attitudes that one can identify something that is the belief or intention in abstraction from its content, something about which we can ask, what would the content of *that* belief have been if *it* had been a belief I had on twin earth. If we assume that there is a language of thought, and that to have a belief or desire is to have a token of a mental sentence expressing the belief or desire stored in the appropriate place in the brain, then the presupposition would be unproblematic; but if we don't make this assumption, we have no obvious way to individuate the property of believing that P except by using the content, that P.

Even if we could individuate thoughts or beliefs independently of their contents, this would not necessarily suffice to yield a determinate narrow content for them by the procedure I have suggested. Suppose we identify mental thought tokens by their physical or syntactic properties. These properties surely will not be sufficient to determine even the narrow content of the thought token. Presumably, the same particular physical event or state that is a particular thought that water is the best drink for quenching thirst might, if the functional organization of the thinker were different enough, have not only a different wide content, but also a different narrow content. Consider again the analogy with sentences. Suppose that in a counterfactual situation more radically different from ours than twin earth we find the pattern of sounds identical to the one that in fact constitutes an utterance of 'Water is the best drink for quenching thirst'. But suppose that in this counterfactual world, these sounds occur in a language utterly unlike English, both in syntax and semantics. What they mean there might be roughly translated as "what time does the next bus leave for the zoo?" Presumably, the similarity in the acoustical pattern will not be sufficient to give this utterance the same meaning or content that it has in the actual world in any sense, wide or narrow, even though one could define a propositional concept, and a diagonal proposition representing realization conditions, for a sentence token individuated simply by its sound pattern or shape. For this procedure to yield a plausible notion of narrow content for tokens of either a public or a mental language, we need to assume the tokens have the same narrow content in each of the relevant possible worlds. But the procedure itself provides no basis for saying when narrow content differs, or changes, and when it remains the same. We do know that the narrow content of a mental state is an internal property of the person who is in that state, so we know that the narrow contents of the thoughts of internally indiscernible twins are the same. But presumably it is not only wholly indiscernible twins who can think the same thought—thoughts with the same narrow content. In what ways might two thinkers differ in their over all mental states while still remaining capable of thinking thoughts or having beliefs with the same narrow content? Suppose I continue to believe that water is the best drink for quenching thirst, but my other beliefs about water change: I learn that water is H_2O, and not XYZ as I previously thought, that it expands when it freezes, that salt dissolves in it, etc. The wide content of my belief that water is the best drink for quenching thirst remains the same, but what about the narrow content? I'm not sure how this question is supposed to be answered.

Even if these questions receive satisfactory answers, it will remain true that the narrow content or realization conditions of a thought, explained as I have explained them, will be defined only relative to a very limited set of possible worlds: specifically, only for possible worlds containing the thought token. The realization conditions for the thought are satisfied in a given possible world if and only if the proposition expressed by the thought *in that possible world* is true. Suppose the thought I am thinking could be naturally expressed as follows: "There is a hole in the ozone layer." If I focus on the wide content, then I can consider not only whether this thought is true in the actual world, where I am thinking it, but also whether it would be truc if, say, human beings had never existed to pollute the atmosphere. But we can't evaluate the realization conditions for the thought in such a possible world, since the thought won't exist there. We might try to extend the procedure to apply to possible worlds not containing the thought by asking a counterfactual question about such a world: what *would* the content of the thought be if it were thought there. This may work in some cases, but it is likely to leave a large amount of indeterminacy in the narrow content of our thoughts. Consider a version of another one of the familiar stories: Bert, who is a little confused about arthritis, thinks his father has this disease in his thigh. In a counterfactual world, Bert's belief is internally the same, but the social semantic facts in this world are different: 'arthritis' refers there to a wider class of diseases, including the one that Bert's father has in his thigh. The wide content of Bert's belief is false in all worlds, but the narrow content is false in the actual world and true in the counterfactual world. But now consider a possible world in which both the language and the state of medical knowledge are quite different. In this world there is no word like 'arthritis', in Bert's language, and Bert has no thoughts about his father's health. Are the realization conditions for Bert's actual thought satisfied in this counterfactual world? Bert didn't have the belief there, but if he had, would it have been true or false? So far as I can see, there is no way to tell.

The source of all these problems with this procedure for defining narrow content is the fact that according to this account, narrow content is derivative from (actual and possible) wide content. The explanation of realization conditions takes for granted that somehow, the external and internal facts about a mental event or state that we have identified determine a content (in the ordinary sense) for that state. Then from the actual wide content, together with the facts about what the wide content would be under various counterfactual conditions, we extract the narrow content. Narrow content, as defined by this procedure, presupposes rather than explains wide content.

A number of narrow content theorists, including Loar, have pointed to an analogy between narrow content and what in David Kaplan's [92] semantics for demonstratives is called *character*. Character is the kind of meaning that context dependent expressions have. The character of a sentence is a function from context into content. If one thinks of a possible world containing an utterance token as providing a context for that utterance, then a propositional concept will also be a function from contexts into contents. But even if characters and propositional concepts are similar abstract objects, their roles in the explanation of content are reversed. Kaplan's characters are a kind of meaning. They are part of a semantic theory explaining how utterances come to have the contents they have. The semantics for a context sensitive language assigns characters to sentences; then these characters, together with facts about the contexts in which they are used, determine contents. But narrow content, or "context indeterminate realization conditions" are abstracted from the wide contents that mental acts and states acquire, by whatever means, from the way they are embedded in the world.

If narrow contents don't play a role in a semantics for the language of thought, what role do they play? What claim does the internalist want to make about narrow content? Loar appeals to two very different kinds of considerations to motivate his internalist account, two very different roles for narrow content in the explanation of intentionality. The first concerns the role of content in the explanation of behavior; the second concerns the accessibility of thinkers' thoughts to themselves.

Narrow Content and the Explanation of Behavior

In "Social Content and Psychological Content" [115] Loar develops ingenious variations on some of the examples that echo through the literature
on intentionality in order to raise some problems for the externalist about
the role of content in the explanation of behavior. The general point is that
content of the ordinary wide, socially infected kind does not individuate
intentional mental states in the way that is optimal for the explanation of
rational behavior. On the one hand, it fails to distinguish psychologically
distinct intentional states; on the other, it distinguishes cases that are the
same in all relevant respects, and so misses generalizations. Let me sketch
briefly one of Loar's examples, and then look at the conclusions he draws
from this example, and others like it. The story is a variation on both
Kripke's story of Pierre and Burge's arthritis example: Paul, when living
in France, learns of a disease that is called, in French, 'arthrite', and comes
to believe that he has this ailment in both his thigh and his ankle. But
he does not realize that this is the same disease as the one that, in English, he has learned to call 'arthritis'. He knows that arthritis—the disease
he calls 'arthritis'—is a disease of the joints only. Now suppose that Paul
comes to believe that he has two problems with his ankles, one that he calls
'arthrite', and another that he calls 'arthritis'. "It seems," Loar says, "that
'believes that he has arthritis in his ankles' is doubly but univocally true
of Paul, by virtue of beliefs with distinct psychological contents" ([115],
p. 104). It seems intuitively obvious that Paul has two distinct beliefs that
play distinct roles in the explanation of his actions. One of these beliefs
might lead him to call the doctor, while the other motivates him to take
aspirin. He might change his mind about one, while continuing to believe
the other. So we need a kind of content that can distinguish the two beliefs,
as (Loar alleges) ordinary wide content does not.

Loar does not take examples like this one to support a revision of
our common sense psychological explanations; instead, he takes them to
show that commonsense psychological explanations, as they are, appeal to
narrow content even though the 'that'-clauses that occur in such explanations refer to wide or socially infected content. "I shall argue," he says,
"that psychological content is not in general identical with what is captured
by oblique 'that'-clauses, that commonsense constraints on individuation
induce only a loose fit between contents and 'that'-clauses" ([115], p. 102).
Loar identifies two principles relating content to the ascription of content
that he takes the examples to show to be mistaken. First, "sameness of
de dicto or oblique ascription implies sameness of psychological content."
Second, "differences in de dicto or oblique ascription imply differences in
psychological content" ([115], p. 102). Loar suggests that Burge's arguments that the kind of content we appeal to in ordinary explanations of
action is wide content assumes these principles, and we can avoid or defuse
his conclusions if we deny them.

Now I agree that Loar's examples present a puzzle and a challenge, but I am not at all clear what his response to them is. I do not understand the two principles that he questions, and I do not see how one can distinguish the content we appeal to in ordinary belief attributions from the referents of the 'that'-clauses that occur in such attributions.

I see two ways to interpret the principles about the relation between oblique ascription and psychological content, the difference depending on what sameness or difference of oblique ascription is taken to be. On the one hand it might mean that the *expressions* (the 'that'-clauses) that ascribe the content are the same or different; on the other hand, it might mean that the *referents* of the 'that'-clauses are the same or different. But on the first interpretation, neither principle has any plausibility, and neither need be assumed by Burge's arguments. The first principle—that sameness of the ascription clause requires sameness of content—will be false of 'that'-clauses that are context dependent. Loar does restrict this principle so that it does not apply to ascriptions containing indexical pronouns and demonstratives, but if there are general terms that are context-dependent, then the principle will be false even if the contents referred to are ordinary wide contents. The second principle implies, on this interpretation, that there cannot be two different expressions referring to the same content; this can't be what was intended.

On the second interpretation, what the principles say is simply that the referents of the 'that'-clauses in ordinary belief ascriptions are psychological contents. So to deny the principles is to say that the kind of content referred to in the belief ascriptions that occur in commonsense psychological explanations are not psychological contents. But this can't be right, since psychological content is *defined* by Loar as the kind of content referred to in such belief ascriptions: "By *psychological content*," he says, "I shall mean whatever individuates beliefs and other propositional attitudes in commonsense psychological explanations" ([115], p. 99). The *thesis* is that psychological contents, defined this way, are narrow contents. The way the thesis is supposed to be reconciled with Burge's arguments is by denying these principles about the relation between ascription clauses and contents. But interpreted the second way, the principles look to be true by definition—by Loar's definition of psychological content.

At one point Loar puts his point in terms of "a loose fit between contents and 'that'-clauses." We have no reason to think "that psychological states are captured by a neat set of content-specifications." The suggestion seems to be that there is a determinate "way things are from the thinker's point of view," and that the fact that things seem the way they do is a purely internal property of the thinker. But our language, being "shot through with social and causal presuppositions," can capture that internal content only imperfectly. I think this is partly right: I agree that there is a kind of looseness of fit in some cases between states of belief and the words we use to describe them. But I don't think the belief states themselves—the ways the world is according to the thinker—are any less causally and so-cially infected than the language in which beliefs are ascribed. Let's look at some of the examples.

In the world as Paul thinks it is, there are two distinct diseases both of which he suffers from in his ankle. One is called 'arthritis' (in English), and the other is called 'arthrite' (in French). The first is a rheumatoid ailment that is limited to the joints, while the second is one that can reside in one's thigh. Paul (in the world as he believes it to be) has the second disease in his thigh as well as in his ankle. Now the problem of looseness of fit comes when we try to say what belief attributions are made true by these facts about what the world according to Paul is like, and which facts about the world according to Paul are the ones that make certain belief attributions true. As Loar says, our description of the world according to Paul seems to make it true twice over that Paul believes he has arthritis in his ankle. When he says "I have arthritis in my ankle," he is expressing a different belief from the one he expresses when he says "j'ai l'arthrite dans ma cheville." But which of these beliefs are we ascribing when we say "Paul believes that he has arthritis in his ankle"? This is, I agree, a puzzle—about belief *attribution*—but I don't think it supports internalism. Suppose we set aside questions about belief attributions and look directly at the world according to Paul: what facts make it true that the world as Paul takes it to be is the way it is? Are the relevant facts purely internal facts about Paul, or are facts about the environment Paul is embedded in—for example about the way he came to be in the internal state he is in, and the way words are used by people in Paul's linguistic communities—also part of what makes it true that we can describe Paul's mental state in terms of the set of possible worlds conforming to the description I have given? To answer this question we need an account of what makes content attributions true. The strategy for providing such an account that seems to me most promising—the causal-information theoretic strategy—will explain content in terms of counterfactual dependencies that tend to hold, under normal conditions, between thinkers' internal states and their environments. I don't see how an account of this general kind could be an internalist one, and I don't know of any promising alternative.

Suppose an externalist, information-theoretic account of belief were a correct account of what relates a thinker to the kind of situation that is the way the world seems to him. Suppose that what makes it correct that the world according to Paul is as described is that under certain normal conditions Paul would be in the internal state he is in only if, and because, the world were actually that way. This would be a non-internalist account of what Loar calls psychological content, since the correctness of the content description would depend on certain general causal regularities external to Paul. But the same problems about belief ascription that Loar's examples bring out will still arise. So I don't think those problems tend to support an internalist account of psychological content.

According to Loar's picture, there are two dimensions of content associated with a particular mental state, a purely internal content—the way the world seems from the point of view of the thinker—and a social content, which is what content ascriptions refer to. The former kind of content is what really explains behavior. I am not sure what, on Loar's account, the role of the latter kind is supposed to be. But it seems to me that to talk of the way the world seems from the point of view of the believer is just to talk about what the believer believes. If there is a divergence between the way the world seems to the thinker and the way the world must be to make a content clause in a belief ascription true, then the belief ascription is false. What the puzzle cases bring out is that in some situations, when one's picture of the way things are diverges from the way they actually are in certain ways—it is difficult, without some circumlocution, to describe that picture. But when we describe it correctly, psychological content and so-called social content will coincide.

I have been trying to argue that Loar's examples and arguments raise genuine problems for an account of belief and belief attribution, but they don't show that psychological content—the kind of content relevant to psychological explanation—is narrow. But Loar has phenomenological reasons for thinking that the way the world seems from the thinker's point of view, must be an internal property of the thinker. I will conclude by looking at some of these reasons.

Narrow Content and Subjective Intentionality

The basis of Loar's phenomenological argument for internalism is the intuition that we have privileged access to our own thoughts—specifically to their intentional or semantic properties. It seems to be essential to thought that one know what one's thought is about, and this, Loar suggests, is incompatible with the anti-individualist conclusions. "A natural view of one's own thoughts," he says, "stands in sharp contrast with the conclusion of the externalist argument. From a pre-critical perspective, knowledge of the references of my own thoughts is privileged in a certain way, and that perspective involves no apparent conceptions of external reference relations" ([114], p. 96). The idea is that it is essential to having a thought that, in some sense, the thinker knows what the content of the thought is, and what the thought is about. I can't think about my thought about x without at the same time thinking about x, and recognizing that my thought is indeed a thought about x. Loar makes this point with the following example: "I am now attending to my thought that Freud lived in Vienna. I register what the thought is about—Freud, Vienna, the one inhabiting the other. I note the thought's references and truth conditions. I may be wrong about the non-semantic question whether Freud actually exists (timeless). But it is difficult to see how I might be wrong in my purely semantic judgment that this thought is about Freud if Freud exists"

([114], p. 96). Most of this seems right, but why does it contrast or conflict with the externalist's conclusion? Loar's argument for a conflict between externalism and privileged access focuses on a number of externalist analyses of the reference relation. The general form of the argument is like this: in judging that my thought is about x, I do not judge that I stand in relation R to x [where what goes in for 'R' is some possible externalist analysis of reference or aboutness]. Therefore, R cannot be a correct analysis of the aboutness relation to which I have privileged access. For example, Loar says "It is implausible that in judging that my thought is about Freud I judge that it has a given causal-historical relation to Freud—a relation no one has yet managed to characterize" ([114], p. 97). There are two things wrong with this argument: first, a philosophical analysis of some concept might be correct, even if someone competent in using the concept does not know the analysis. In general, one cannot refute an analysis (for example, of knowledge as justified true belief $+\ldots$) simply by noting that a person may judge that he knows something without judging that the various conditions of the analysis hold. There may be a problem explaining how an analysis can be correct if a competent speaker doesn't know it—a paradox of analysis—but this is a general problem. Unless all philosophical analyses are either trivial or false, the argument Loar gives cannot be sound. But second, in any case, the externalist is not committed to the claim that relations of reference and aboutness are analyzable. Burge, in defending an externalist account of intentionality, proposes no analysis of aboutness and does not suggest that there is one to be found. Kripke, in his defense of a causal account of reference, explicitly disclaims any reductive ambitions. One may characterize or categorize aboutness without defining or analyzing it.

Is it right, as Loar claims, that "from a pre-critical perspective," my thought that my thoughts about Freud are about Freud "involves no apparent conceptions of external reference relations"? I don't think so. Even if our pre-critical perspective is committed to no detailed analysis of reference—no *articulated* conception of an external reference relation—I think the intuition that reference and aboutness are causal, external relations lies close to the surface. Look, for instance, at the arguments and examples developed by Saul Kripke [95] in defense of a causal account of reference. The arguments appeal, not to philosophical theory, but to intuitions about our ordinary "pre-critical" conception of reference. It will be readily agreed, independently of philosophical theory, that we could not possibly refer to or think about Freud if the man had no influence or effect at all on our minds. If we had never heard of him, our thoughts could not be about him. *That* is surely not an esoteric philosophical conclusion.

If we set aside questions of the reduction or analysis of intentional relations, is there a conflict between the thesis that we have privileged access to what our thoughts are about and the thesis that the aboutness relation is external? I don't think so. One way to see at least the prima facie compatibility of these theses is to construct a simple model of something with analogues of intentional states about which the analogues of the two theses are uncontroversially true. Suppose we have an electronic device capable of registering some limited information about its environment. Suppose it is equipped with a sensor that observes blocks passing by on a conveyer belt and records their shape (sphere, cube, or pyramid) and color (red, yellow, or blue). It records this information in a simple code: '*Rs*' means red sphere, '*Yp*' means yellow pyramid, etc. As new blocks appear, the old information is passed on through a succession of memories. So at any time, the machine stores information about what the current object is, and what the preceding objects were. A '*Bc*' in the first memory means (or tends to carry the information) that the previous object was a blue cube. The reason this internal state has that content is that under normal conditions, it will be in that state only if the previous object was a blue cube. The "normal conditions" qualification is there because our device is not perfect. If lighting is abnormal, if a non-standard object is put on the conveyor belt, or if a chip is defective, the device's main register might contain the inscription '*Bc*' when there is no blue cube before it. But in this case, the inscription still has the content, *blue cube there* because this is the information that *would* be carried if conditions were normal.

Our device is very simple—it does not have beliefs or other full-blooded intentional states—but it does have states that can be described in terms of propositional content, and it is clear that its contentful states are relational, and not intrinsic, states. Its states have the content they have—they tend to carry the information that they tend to carry—in part because of facts about the environment in which the machine functions.

Now let us add a reflective capacity to our device—the capacity to have second-order informational states, or to carry information about its own representational states. We will do this by giving our device an internal sensor that can observe its own memories. (Maybe this is part of a system for introducing redundancy to correct for errors). If the first memory contains a '*Bc*', the internal sensor, when it observes it, records a '*Bc₁*', registering that its first memory is of a blue cube. This state has this content because under normal conditions the internal sensor's register will be in this state only when the first memory registers a blue cube. Since this is a different sensor, its normal conditions may be different—for example, external lighting conditions will be irrelevant. Its conditions may be normal (correctly observing that the first memory has the content, *blue cube*), even if the content of the memory itself is misinformation.

Now this is about as simple a case of second-order informational states as one could have; it is a long way from self-consciousness or thought, but it is a case in which content can be used to characterize internal states, and in which there are states with content that other states with content are about. And while I don't think such a machine would have a rich inner life—I suspect there isn't much it is like to be it—it does, I think, illustrate the kind of privileged access, or "self-interpretation," that Loar finds in more full-blooded cases of thinkers reflecting on their thoughts. As Loar says, a thought about a Freud thought is itself a Freud thought. In the same way, the registering of a registering of a blue cube is itself a registering of information about blue cubes. This is because the content of the second-order state is derivative from the content of the first. There is nothing very mysterious here, and nothing incompatible with the externalist account I have given of the role of content in the description of the internal states of our device.

Still, there does seem to be a conflict between the intuition that we know what we are thinking about and the externalist's twin-earth stories. The externalist taught us that the content of the thought that Bert would express by saying "water is the best drink for quenching thirst" is different from the content of the thought he has on counterfactual twin earth that he would express there the same way. But nothing internal to Bert distinguishes the two worlds, so he doesn't know which one he is in. But then doesn't it follow that he doesn't know what the content of his belief is? He does know that his statement, "my 'water' thoughts are about water" is true, but it seems that he doesn't know what the content of *that* is.

The first thing to note about this argument is that if it works it will support a much more general conclusion. There is nothing special about reflective thoughts about content here: if Bert does not know which of these two worlds he is in, then he doesn't know that there is water in the bathtub he is sitting in. The twin-earth argument that we don't know the contents of our own thoughts (as the externalist understands content) is just a version of a familiar general skeptical argument.

This is not the place to develop a general response to skepticism, but the strategy that seems to me most promising (defended by Alvin Goldman [66] and Fred Dretske [44], among others) recognizes that claims to knowledge are essentially contrastive and context dependent. Bert knows that there is water in the bathtub because he can distinguish the actual world, in which there is water in the bathtub, from certain relevant alternative worlds, in which water is not there: for example, worlds in which the bathtub is dry, or filled with gasoline, or mashed potatoes. Similarly, Bert knows that his 'water' thoughts are about water because he can distinguish the actual world, where they are about water, from relevant alternative situations in which he is thinking about other things such as gasoline or mashed potatoes.

We do not need narrow or purely internal content to explain privileged access to the content of one's thoughts. The explanation is simpler: the external facts in virtue of which my Freud thoughts are about Freud are the same external facts in virtue of which my thoughts about my Freud thoughts are about Freud. The external environment in which I think my thoughts is the same environment as the one in which I reflect on those thoughts.

I have argued that the externalist can account both for the role of content in psychological explanation and for privileged access and the transparency or self-interpreting character of thought, without invoking a notion of narrow content—content that picks out mental events and states in terms of purely intrinsic properties of the thinker. But Loar's examples and arguments do force us to recognize the context dependence of ascriptions of content, and I think something like Loar's conception of narrow content will help to describe and explain the ways in which our uses of content to characterize the states of mind of ourselves and others are context dependent. I think Loar is right that we can describe psychological content in terms of what he calls realization conditions—conditions that must be satisfied in a thinker's world for that world to answer to the thoughts he has there. But I have argued that he is wrong to think that realization conditions can give us a way to get at purely internal psychological properties of thinkers. Content, whether psychological or social, is a way to connect ourselves to others, and to the environments in which we and they are embedded.

6

Cognitive Access and Semantic Puzzles

JOSEPH OWENS

ONE OF THE more notorious elements in the Cartesian model of mind is the kind of inner access it accords rational subjects: introspection is supposed to provide them with something like incorrigible access to the contents of their consciousnesses. This paper is concerned with a different but related principle, one that has to do with the subject's ability to compare and reidentify mental states, in particular beliefs. Briefly put, the principle of interest is: introspection provides the rational subject with unerring access to sameness and difference in her beliefs. This element in the Cartesian picture, which we label "the Cartesian model of access," has received virtually no attention despite the fact that it figures crucially in a number of paradoxes and puzzles and is implicit in many semantic arguments. My primary goal in this paper is to argue against the Cartesian model of access and to outline some of the benefits that follow on its rejection.

Though this principle has been virtually ignored, it does figure in Nathan Salmon's recent and important book, *Frege's Puzzle* [157], and even though his primary concern is quite different from mine, I will approach the topic by way of his discussion. Salmon's primary project is to defend a Millian or Russellian account of proper names as having no semantic value over and above reference. These Russellian accounts seemingly legitimize the interchange of co-referential names in all contexts. And this, of course, is at odds with the widely-shared Fregean intuition that two sentences, such as those given below could differ in truth value:

(a)   The Babylonian astronomer believed that Hesperus is Hesperus.

(b)   The Babylonian astronomer believed that Hesperus is Phosphorus.

This is where the Cartesian picture of access comes into play. Salmon argues that the Fregean intuition that sentences (a) and (b) could differ in truth value is persuasive only to one who accepts the Cartesian model of access, and he, for one, does not accept it. In Section 1, I will examine in some detail his account of belief, his reasons for rejecting the Cartesian model of access, and the way in which he attempts to undermine the problematic Fregean intuition. While I accept his rejection of the Cartesian model, and concur with his claim that the rejection of this model enables the theorist to offer intuitive resolutions to a number of puzzles, I argue that it does not do everything he claims for it; in particular, it does not undermine the standard Fregean objections to interchanging co-referential proper names in belief contexts. It does not enable the Russellian theorist to avoid the problem posed by (a) and (b) above. In Section 2, I will turn to a more direct examination of the Cartesian picture of access, providing independent reasons for rejecting it, and outlining some of the theoretical benefits that follow on its rejection.

1 Salmon's Treatment of Beliefs Under Guises

Salmon analyzes belief as a three-place relation; this analysis, he claims, allows for the interchange of names in sentences such as (a) and (b), and at the same time explains the widespread rejection of such interchanges. He motivates his theory with a new and interesting "puzzle," a puzzle which seemingly calls out for a tripartite analysis of the kind he espouses. First the puzzle and then the analysis. I will follow his strategy of presenting the puzzle in two installments ([157], pp. 92–98).

Elmer, the famous bounty hunter, is after the notorious jewel thief, Bugsy Wabbit. After examining the F.B.I.'s copious records on Bugsy (photographs and all), Elmer decides, on January 1, that Bugsy is indeed a dangerous individual. On June 1, however, Elmer hears from the F.B.I. that Bugsy has been seen acting very deferentially, that he has been seen walking away from a game after having been accused of cheating. He says to himself: "It seems as though Bugsy may not be dangerous after all. I think I'll just have to wait and see."

We have here the story of an individual who formed the belief that Bugsy was dangerous on January 1, held to that belief until June 1 and, then, apparently, decided to suspend that belief on June 1, to hold off and neither believe nor disbelieve that Bugsy was dangerous. Now to the second installment.

The story is as above, but, unbeknownst to Elmer, Bugsy has heard that the bounty hunter is on his tail, and he disguises himself so as to be unrecognizable; he doesn't bother, however, to change his name, it being so very common. Elmer meets up with Bugsy and befriends him, not recognizing him as the very one he is chasing. On April 1, Elmer overhears an argument between his friend Bugsy and another individual. This stranger is very frightened of Bugsy and Elmer thinks to himself: "It certainly seems as though my new friend Bugsy is a dangerous fellow." He continues to think of his friend in this light even after June 1, the day he decided to suspend his original judgment on the jewel thief.

This is only a fragment of the story, but it is enough to generate genuine puzzlement. What, for example, are we to say of Elmer's apparent "change of heart" on April 1, the day he "came to believe" that Bugsy (his friend) was dangerous? We could simply say that he came to believe that Bugsy was dangerous, and leave it at that. To do so, however, would be very misleading given that Elmer already believed that Bugsy was dangerous, and had ever since January 1. June 1 poses an even more difficult problem. We have already agreed that he suspended his original judgment on that day and that he decided it was better to hold off on the question as to whether Bugsy was dangerous or not. But now it looks as though he also believes, on that very day, that Bugsy, his friend, is dangerous. It seems as though any simple account of belief is not going to do justice to the conflicting intuitions this story generates; in particular, it seems as though we have to allow that one can hold to a belief (e.g., the belief that Bugsy Wabbit is dangerous) in one way and, at the same time, suspend judgment when the belief is considered in another way. This, in effect, is just what Salmon does: he construes the objects of singular belief as Russellian propositions and these objects, he argues, are grasped or accepted under *guises*, or modes of apprehension. More importantly, an individual may assent to a proposition under one guise while rejecting it under another ([157], pp. 103–118).

Salmon thus argues that an ascription of a singular belief, such as that Bugsy Wabbit is dangerous, is best construed as an ascription of a relation between a subject, a Russellian proposition (which, unlike the Fregean, contains the very individual designated by the singular term rather than some conceptual representation of it), and some manner of apprehension of the proposition, i.e., some *guise* under which the proposition is presented and grasped. In the puzzle, Elmer is acquainted with the individual Bugsy in two different ways and knows him under two different guises: as the notorious jewel thief and as his friend. Similarly, the Russellian proposition, which contains the individual Bugsy, is grasped by Elmer in two different ways, corresponding to the two ways in which he is acquainted with single element in the proposition, Bugsy. And just as he need not recognize himself as meeting the same individual when he encounters the jewel thief and his friend, so he need not recognize himself as entertaining the same proposition whenever he entertains the proposition that Bugsy is dangerous. Following Salmon, I will use the term '*BEL*' to designate the ternary relation that is supposed to obtain between a subject A, a Russellian proposition P, and a guise, when A believes that P. *BEL* is something like *assenting* to a proposition *under* a guise. The heart of the analysis, then, is as follows ([157], pp. 109–111):

(1)   'A believes p' may be analyzed as $(\exists x)(A$ grasps p by means of x & $BEL(A, p, x))$;

(2) A may stand in *BEL* to p and some x by means of which A grasps p, without standing in *BEL* to p and all x by means of which A grasps p; and

(3)   'A withholds belief from p', in the sense relevant to Elmer's be-
fuddlement, may be analyzed as $(\exists x)(A$ grasps p by means of x &
$\neg BEL(A,p,x))$.

This analysis provides for a simple, intuitive solution to the problems
posed by Elmer. Following (1), ascriptions of singular belief are analyzed
as existentials; roughly, they assert that there is some guise or other under
which the subject grasps and assents to the relevant proposition.[1]

And now we can account for the obvious. Even though Elmer had
already believed that Bugsy was dangerous, he came to accept that belief
under a new guise on April 1, and thus we account for some of the tension in
our original intuitions. As far as June 1 goes, we can say what we wanted to,
namely, that Elmer both continues to believe that Bugsy is dangerous and
suspends the belief that he is dangerous. This is so because (4) and (5) below are consistent. Indeed, both are true of Elmer on June 1 ([157], p. 112):

(4) $(\exists x)$(Elmer grasps the proposition that Bugsy is dangerous by means
of x, & BEL(Elmer, the proposition that Bugsy is dangerous, x))

(5) $(\exists x)$(Elmer grasps the proposition that Bugsy is dangerous by means
of x, & $\neg BEL$(Elmer, the proposition that Bugsy is dangerous, x))

(4) and (5) are consistent and, given (1) and (3), they justify our characterizations of Elmer as both believing and suspending belief in the proposition
that Bugsy is dangerous.

So much for Salmon's puzzle, but what of Frege's puzzle? The machinery introduced above is *not* in and of itself an adequate explanation of our
different attitudes towards the sentences:

(a)   The Babylonian astronomer believed that Hesperus is Hesperus.

(b)   The Babylonian astronomer believed that Hesperus is Phosphorus.

Since, on this account, the proposition ascribed by (a) and (b) is the
same, they will receive the same analysis. Both will be analyzed as:

> There is a guise x such that the Babylonian Astronomer grasps the
> proposition that Hesperus is Hesperus (i.e., the proposition that Hes-
> perus is Phosphorus) by means of x, and the Astronomer bears the
> BEL relation (assents) to this proposition under this guise x.

Hence we need something more than this analysis if we are to explain (away)
the difference in our attitudes to (a) and (b). This is precisely what Salmon
attempts to do. We can, he claims, take account of this once we realize that
such ascriptions of belief serve not only to assert that the subject stands in a
certain relation (the believing relation) to a Russellian proposition, but also
"suggest" or "indicate" the guise under which the proposition is assented

---

[1] This analysis thus bears some interesting similarities to that advocated by
David Kaplan in [90].

to ([157], pp. 114–118). The ascription does *not assert* that the singular proposition is assented to under a *particular guise*; it is supposed to be more like a Gricean implicature. And just as it is misleading, but not false, to say, "Smith is in the bathroom or the bedroom" when I know he is in the bathroom, so, too, would it be misleading, but not false, to say, "The Babylonian Astronomer believed that Hesperus is Phosphorus." Strictly speaking, this sentence is true; the Astronomer assents to the proposition ascribed. However, it is misleading in that he would *not* assent to it under the guise here *suggested*. Popular opinion, according to Salmon, is incorrect in supposing that (a) and (b) could differ in truth value, but there *is something* to the common prejudice. He writes:

> The ancient astronomer agrees to the proposition about the planet Venus ... when he takes it in the way it is presented to him through the ... sentence 'Hesperus is Hesperus,' but he does not agree to this same proposition when he takes it in the way it is presented to him through the ... sentence 'Hesperus is Phosphorus'. The fact that he agrees to it at all is, strictly speaking, sufficient for the truth of both the sentence 'The astronomer believes that Hesperus is Hesperus' and the sentence 'The astronomer believes that Hesperus is Phosphorus'. Though the sentences are materially equivalent, and even modally equivalent ..., there is a sense in which the first is better than the second, given our normal purpose in attributing belief ... The first sentence also manages to convey *how* the astronomer agrees to the proposition. Indeed, the second sentence, though true, is in some sense inappropriate; it is positively misleading in the way it (correctly) specifies the content of the astronomer's belief. It specifies the content by means of a 'that'-clause that presents the proposition in the "wrong way," a way of taking the proposition with respect to which the astronomer does not assent to it. This does not affect the truth value of the second sentence, for it is no part of the semantic content of the sentence to specify the way the astronomer takes the proposition when he agrees to it. ([157], pp. 116–117)

Once again, this is intuitive: (a) and (b) turn out to have the same truth value but (b) is inappropriate in that the 'that'-clause in (b) presents the proposition under a guise in which it would not have been accepted by the astronomer. Problems begin to surface, however, when we turn to his explicit discussion of the relationship between guises and 'that'-clauses. The solution just presented seems to suppose that each *'that'-clause* somehow suggests a specific guise under which the proposition in question is presented and grasped (*without*, of course, *asserting* that it is grasped under that guise). But in his explicit discussion of how guises and 'that'-clauses are linked, we get a different story:

> It happens in the 'Hesperus'-'Phosphorus' type of case, that the clause used to specify the believed proposition also carries with it a particular way in which the believer takes the proposition ... In these cases, the guise or appearance by means of which a believer would be familiar with a proposition at a particular time *t* were it presented to him or her through a particular sentence is a *function of the believer and the sentence* (my italics). ([157], p. 117)

Details aside, this remark indicates a different picture of belief ascription, one in which the guise suggested is not simply a function of the 'that'-clause; it also depends on who the subject is. We have to decide between the two alternatives. Guises are objectively correlated with and suggested by 'that'-clauses, or they are not. One conception is "quasi-semantic" (even if pragmatic) in character in that the guises are *objectively* linked to 'that'-clauses. Call this the "objective construal." The other conception is much more psychological in character: the guise is something like an *individual's* mode of apprehension of the proposition. In this understanding of guise, ascriptions of the form $\ulcorner x$ believes that $Fa,\urcorner$ $\ulcorner y$ believes that $Fa,\urcorner$ and so on, do not in any way suggest that x and y agree in assenting to the relevant proposition under *one and the same guise*; these various ascriptions may be all true *and none of them misleading*, even though the subjects, x, y, etc., share no common guise. The 'that'-clause is not objectively linked to a guise; it does not suggest any specific guise. Let us call this the "non-objective construal." I submit that neither notion of guise is capable of playing the roles Salmon allocates to guises.[2]

The Non-Objective Reading

Under this interpretation the clauses 'that Hesperus is Hesperus' and 'that Hesperus is Phosphorus' are not objectively correlated with guises. They do not of themselves suggest any specific guises; these come only with the choice of a particular subject. This is an individualistic and psychological construal of the guise's role, in which the guise is the individual's peculiar mode of apprehension of the singular proposition, and this is dictated by the character of his relationship to the individual that "figures" in the proposition, the one denoted by the proper name (in the 'that'-clause). Thus, in this reading, the name itself does not suggest any one guise as opposed to another. Different individuals may associate different guises with the same name; indeed, one and the same individual may associate different guises with one name, and be willing to assent to the relevant proposition only under one of the guises. This, after all, is what is supposed to have happened in the case of Elmer. In resolving that puzzle, Salmon spoke of the different guises under which Elmer grasped the proposition that Bugsy Wabbit is dangerous, and these different guises were suggested not by different names nor by the name 'Bugsy Wabbit'. These guises would not figure in an account of English (not even in one which purported to deliver all the subtleties), nor are they part of what we learn when we learn the language. They are suggested, rather, by what we know of Elmer and of his relations to Bugsy Wabbit. (We used one and the same name,

---

[2] There are other difficulties facing this analysis which I will not attempt to treat of here. Of special note is the fact that, on this analysis, co-referential names are interchangeable even in multiply embedded contexts. Salmon explicitly addresses this issue ([157], p. 84*n*4), but it remains counterintuitive.

'Bugsy Wabbit', when speaking of Elmer's beliefs, despite the differences in guise.) This conception of guise helps to resolve our puzzlement regarding Elmer, but it is a far cry from what we need to resolve the Fregean problem, to explain (away) our reluctance to accept (b). As long as we suppose that the clause 'that Hesperus is Phosphorus' suggests a specific guise, we can understand how such an ascription might be less than appropriate in characterizing the belief of a particular subject (one who assents to the proposition presented by this 'that'-clause, but *only* under a guise other than the specific one suggested by it). But how should we understand the account once we have abandoned the notion that each 'that'-clause suggests a specific, and so possibly a misleading, guise? It is difficult to see how this guise theorist could even begin to explain our different attitudes towards (a) and (b), but it is instructive to see how one might try.

The only plausible response that comes to mind goes something like this: One does not need to suppose that there is some specific guise always associated with, and suggested by, the clause 'that Hesperus is Phosphorus' to recognize the inappropriate character of (b). In a sentence of the form 'S believes that Fa', we read the clause 'that Fa' as suggesting a certain guise, *given* what we know of the *subject*, S. We will, for example, understand the clause 'that Hesperus is Phosphorus' to suggest one guise in the sentence, 'Whipple believes that Hesperus is Phosphorus', and a very different guise in the sentence, 'The Babylonian astronomer believed that Hesperus is Phosphorus'. Given our knowledge of ancient Babylon, its language, its astronomical theory, etc., we would understand the sentence 'The Babylonian astronomer believed that Hesperus is Phosphorus' to suggest at least that the astronomer would have assented to the sentence 'Hesperus is Phosphorus', or, more accurately (since the astronomer did not speak English), to the Babylonian translation of 'Hesperus is Phosphorus'. Suppose, for the sake of this example, that the Babylonian translation of this sentence is 'Ka si Pho', as opposed to 'Ka si Ka', which, we will assume, translates 'Hesperus is Hesperus'. The idea, then, is that the sentence 'The Babylonian Astronomer believed that Hesperus is Phosphorus' is misleading in that it suggests that the astronomer would have assented to 'Ka si Pho'. This is misleading in that we know enough of Babylonian astronomy to know that the astronomer would have rejected the proposition under this guise.[3]

This seems like a fairly mild, non-contentious implicature, but mild or not, it cannot be maintained inside this non-objective guise theory. It can be maintained only if one supposes that a translation from English into Babylonian selects 'Ka si Pho' rather than 'Ka si Ka' as the Babylonian equivalent of 'Hesperus is Phosphorus', and this is something one is not entitled to do under the current construal of the theory. The Babylonian

---

[3] I am considering here only the most plausible of implicatures, but the point is intended to be perfectly general. This is the kind of implicature Salmon seems to have in mind ([157], p. 116).

astronomer, we may allow, would assent to 'Ka si Ka', but not to 'Ka si Pho'. But it is another matter entirely to suppose that this fact in any way serves to *explain our* reluctance to characterize the astronomer as 'believing that Hesperus is Phosphorus'. Clearly we can, in this way, explain our reluctance to accept (b) only if we suppose that a correct translation of the English into Babylonian serves to pair the sentence 'Hesperus is Phosphorus' with the sentence 'Ka si Pho' and the sentence 'Hesperus is Hesperus' with the sentence 'Ka si Ka'. Equally clearly, we have no right to *this* supposition within this theoretical framework. The reason is simply this: under this version of the account, the two English sentences, 'Hesperus is Hesperus' and 'Hesperus is Phosphorus', don't differ semantically *and* they fail to differ in implicatures; they do not suggest different guises. Since, under this construal, 'that'-clauses or the contained sentences are not objectively correlated with specific guises (do not suggest specific guises), we cannot suppose these two English sentences to differ in any of these features. We have then *no reason* for supposing that there is *any* interesting objective difference of a semantic or pragmatic character which would serve to differentiate between these sentences and, hence, no reason for supposing that one of them serves to translate the Babylonian 'Ka si Pho' in a way which the other does not.

One might be tempted to suppose that one could justify the following correlations:

(1) 'Hesperus is Hesperus' *paired with* (c) 'Ka si Ka',

(2) 'Hesperus is Phosphorus' *paired with* (d) 'Ka si Pho',

on grounds that (1), unlike (2), is a logical truth. This difference, one might argue, should be reflected in the translation, and it is so only if we pair (1) with (c) and (2) with (d).[4] This doesn't work, however. It is an easy matter to construct examples which lack such asymmetry. Indeed, just add the name 'Venus' to the pot, and consider the Babylonian, Astro, who, according to legend, apparently believed that Hesperus is Venus, but not that Phosphorus is Venus.

What we now have to explain is our different attitudes to the following sentences:

(e)   Astro believes that Hesperus is Venus.

(f)   Astro believes that Phosphorus is Venus.

This problem is clearly of a kind with the traditional one: (f) is inappropriate in a way in which (e) is not. But here we certainly cannot hope to distinguish between 'Hesperus is Venus' and 'Phosphorus is Venus' on grounds of the special status of one of them as a logical truth; neither one

---

[4] Hilary Putnam [131] employed this kind of strategy in an attempt to justify the interchange of synonyms in embedded belief contexts, and the strategy failed there for similar reasons.

is a logical truth. We can, thus, safely ignore the fact that (1) is a logical truth; this feature does not serve to distinguish between certain pairs of English sentences (e.g., those embedded in (e) and (f)) in such a way as to justify linking one with a specific Babylonian sentence and linking the other with a quite different Babylonian sentence which differ only in having co-referential proper names interchanged.

Under this conception of guise, then, there is no justification for pairing (1) and (2) with (c) and (d) respectively; and consequently *no hope of explaining our different attitudes towards* (a) *and* (b) *as resulting from the fact that* (a) *suggests that the astronomer would have assented to 'Ka si Ka'* (which, we are assuming, he would have), *while* (b) *suggests that he would have assented to 'Ka si Pho'* (and he would not have). The problem, once again, is that the 'that'-clauses embedded in (a) and (b) *do not suggest* different specific translations. Once we concede that (a) and (b) don't differ in even this minimal respect, we have no option but to deny that they suggest different guises of *any* sort. A simple example may serve to illustrate this point. Suppose that the difference between (a) and (b) is meant to be something like this: (a) suggests that the astronomer believed that the Morning Star is the Morning Star (which he did) while (b) suggests that he believed that the Morning Star is the Evening Star (which he did not). The problem is to justify this. Why think that (a) and (b) have these implicatures? Once again, we cannot support this assignment of guises by supposing, for example, that the Babylonian astronomer links the description 'the Morning Star', with the name 'Hesperus' and the description 'the Evening Star' with the name 'Phosphorus'. The Babylonian does not associate anything with the English names 'Hesperus' and 'Phosphorus'. It seems as though any justification for the claim that (a) and (b) have *these* guises will rest on the intuition that the Babylonian would have associated something like these descriptions (or their Babylonian equivalents) with the Babylonian names which correspond to 'Hesperus' and 'Phosphorus'. We can then justify this assignment of guises only if we suppose that the names 'Hesperus' and 'Phosphorus' translate, respectively, two distinct Babylonian names, e.g., 'Ka' and 'Pho'. But we have already seen that this latter supposition is one that cannot be maintained within this theoretical framework. It appears, then, that the nonobjective reading simply does not provide for the desired distinction between (a) and (b). If (b) is to mislead in presenting the proposition in a way in which the Babylonian astronomer would have rejected it, then the clause 'that Hesperus is Phosphorus' must convey a specific guise, i.e., there must be a guise objectively associated with the clause. Let us see, then, how the theory fares when construed in this manner.

The Objective Account

This version of the theory, in which each 'that'-clause is supposed to objectively suggest some specific guise, faces problems of a very different kind. First, this form of the theory does not fit well with the kind of solution

Salmon urges to the puzzle posed by Elmer. Recall that that solution required us to think of *Elmer* as associating *two* different guises with the sentence 'Bugsy Wabbit is dangerous', depending on whether he is thinking of Bugsy Wabbit as the jewel thief or as his friend. He assents to the proposition under the one guise while withholding assent under the other. Intuitive though it is, this simple resolution fits poorly with the objective construal of the theory. Once we suppose that some *one guise is objectively* linked to the sentence 'Bugsy Wabbit is dangerous' (or to the corresponding 'that'-clause), then the sentence 'Elmer believes that Bugsy Wabbit is dangerous' will itself *suggest* the guise under which Elmer is supposed to assent to the proposition. If the sentence 'Elmer believes that Bugsy Wabbit is dangerous' is true, and if it suggests the guise under which the relevant proposition is assented to, then further information about the diverse ways in which Elmer is acquainted with Bugsy Wabbit are irrelevant. This is a very different understanding of guise than that which figures in the resolution of Salmon's puzzle—much more Fregean and less psychological in character (even if such guises are not supposed to figure in the truth-conditions for propositional attitude ascriptions). Second, there is, on this approach, a problem with sentences which attribute the same belief to many individuals. For instance, in sentences such as 'The Romans and Babylonians both believed that Hesperus is not Phosphorus' are we to suppose that they *all* apprehended and assented to the proposition under the same guise (the one objectively suggested by the 'that'-clause)? Again, to suppose this is the case is to cast the notion of guise in a very Fregean mold, very different than that which it appears to play in the resolution of Salmon's puzzle.

    This brings me to the underlying problem: the theorist who supposes that guises (implicatures) are objectively correlated with 'that'-clauses is confronted with the problem which has long haunted Fregeans, i.e., specifying the guises, or Fregean senses, that correspond to the various singular sentences or 'that'-clauses. Suppose that a and b are co-referential proper names. This theorist, then, should be able to say something about the different guises associated with the two clauses, 'that Fa' and 'that Fb'. In demanding this of the guise theorist we are demanding no more than is standardly demanded of the Fregeans. For simplicity, let us suppose that the guises are specified by assigning different implicatures to the two sentences:

(1) S believes that Fa (e.g., S believes that Hesperus is Phosphorus)

(2) S believes that Fb (e.g., S believes that Hesperus is Hesperus)

The prospects for characterizing these implicatures are bleak. In the first place, these implicatures cannot be very substantial. It won't do, for example, to suppose that a sentence of the form 'S believes that Hesperus is Phosphorus' has as an implicature, suggests in *any* way, that S believes that the Morning Star is the Evening Star. The kind of considerations that Kripke urges against the descriptional theory of names tell equally against this kind of account. Just as you cannot interchange a name and a definite description and be assured of preserving truth value, so you cannot suppose *in general* that a belief sentence of the form 'S believes that Fa', supports an implicature of the form

(3)   'S believes that $F(\imath x)\phi x$.'

We have to concede that these 'that'-clauses do not have implicatures of this strong kind. I.e., *they do not objectively suggest a description under which the believer apprehends the individual denoted by the name.*[5] The fact that they are implicatures rather than entailments (and so defeasible) is not of any great consequence in this regard. It is simply not true that a sentence of form (1) *suggests* that some specific sentence of form (3) is true.

On the other hand, if we weaken the implicatures to make them plausible, they no longer meet the needs of the theory. The most plausible line is to suppose that (1) and (2) differ in that (1) *objectively* suggests that S would assent to some translation of 'Fa' while (2) objectively suggests that S would assent to some translation of 'Fb'. (Once again we must speak of translation, since we have to allow that the language of the ascriptions (1) and (2) might not be one the subject S speaks). These are objective features of the belief ascriptions (1) and (2). The translations are different, and hence one of these belief ascriptions may be inappropriate, even though the other is perfectly acceptable.

But this strategy is clearly a shell game. The strategy, once again, presupposes that 'Fa' and 'Fb' have different translations, and it is this that poses the problem. Given that they don't differ semantically they will have different translations only if they differ in some other respect, e.g., in implicature or something of that sort. But now we are confronted with the circle: We started out trying to characterize the difference in implicature in terms of difference in translation. (1) suggests that S would assent to a translation of 'Fa' while (2) suggests that S would assent to a translation of 'Fb', and these are different. But now, when pressed as to why one should suppose that they have different translations, we attempt to justify that claim by appealing to their different implicatures. If our only reason for supposing that (1) and (2) differ in implicature or guise is the intuition that 'Fa' and 'Fb' have different translations, then we need independent reasons for saying that they have different translations. This cannot, in turn, be defended by *supposing* that they have different implicatures.

It is difficult to see how to characterize the different implicatures objectively assigned (1) and (2) without running foul of Kripke-style objections. It may be possible to do this. That is, it *may* be possible to specify guises

---

[5] Remember that on this objective construal we have to pair a 'that'-clause of the form ⌜that Fa⌝ with one of the form ⌜that $F(\imath x)\phi x$.⌝ Here you don't get to select the replacement in the light of what you know of the subject. And this is highly implausible.

in such a way as to make it plausible that the guises so specified are objectively correlated with 'that'-clauses which contain proper names. But the important point is this: the possibility of doing so is simply the very possibility Fregeans have insisted on in their appeal to individual concepts, and the problems facing the guise theorist are the familiar ones that have long confronted Fregeans. In short, guises do not provide for any easy solution to Frege's puzzle. The theorist who uses them to explain our different attitudes towards (a) and (b) must give us some account of the different guises objectively correlated with the different singular terms.

2 Cognitive Access to Sameness and Difference in Belief

In the previous section I have argued that guise theory fails in its primary task, that of undermining the Fregean intuitions against interchange of proper names in belief contexts. It leaves intact the Fregean burden of providing characterizations of the sentences embedded in (a) and (b) which do justice to our initial intuitions. However, this account contains an important epistemological insight that sets it apart from traditional, Cartesian accounts. In the traditional understanding, rational introspection is supposed to provide subjects with all they need to determine sameness and difference in belief.[6] Nothing more than introspection is needed to determine whether or not the belief they entertain, express, or reject today is the same or different from the belief they entertained, expressed, or rejected yesterday. True, we find in the literature little or no explicit discussion of how subjects are supposed to determine such sameness and difference in beliefs, but it is quite clear that rational introspection was implicitly assigned this task. To mention just one pertinent example, consider the alleged incompatibility between being fully rational and subscribing to explicitly contradictory beliefs. A fully rational subject, it was supposed, would not subscribe to contradictory beliefs for the simple reason that such contradictions were assumed to be introspectively detectable. Clearly, in assigning this capacity to the rational subject we are presuming it to have the more primitive ability to introspectively determine sameness and difference in belief. To introspectively detect contradiction one needs to be able to recognize, introspectively, that *this belief* is the negation of *that belief*. Such guaranteed introspective access to sameness and difference in one's own beliefs is explicitly rejected by the guise theorist, who conceives of propositions (thoughts, beliefs, belief-contents) as being entertained, accepted, and rejected under guises, guises which can serve to blind a subject to

---

[6] We will eventually dispense with talk of introspection in favor of a more negative requirement of the following sort: a subject's ability to recognize sameness and difference in belief is not supposed to be contingent on knowledge of empirical features of the world.

the fact that the propositions she is now entertaining is the very one she rejected yesterday.

I heartily endorse this rejection of the Cartesian model of cognitive access, and the remainder of this paper will be an elaboration on and defense of a non-Cartesian model. I will first distinguish a couple of components in the Cartesian model, and then offer some reasons for rejecting this general picture. My reasons are different from Salmon's, and in particular, they have nothing to do with any allegiance to Russellian propositions.

The Cartesian Conception of Cognitive Access

The Cartesian model that is of concern to us in this paper contains two essential components.

(1) There is the characteristic epistemic element: the fully rational subject is supposedly able to determine sameness and difference in belief content by rational introspection alone. The force of this point is best appreciated from a negative perspective: in the Cartesian model, the subject's ability to determine sameness and difference in belief contents is supposed to be free of any essential reliance on the subject's knowledge of factors which are not accessible to rational introspection, i.e., free of any essential reliance on the subject's knowledge of contingent features of the world or of the subtleties of linguistic practice. So, for example, subjects' abilities to recognize explicit contradictions in their beliefs is not supposed to be contingent upon their knowledge of the external world, upon knowledge such as that it contains XYZ rather than H_2O, nor is it supposed to be contingent on their knowledge of the rules of interchange.

Belief content is, in this regard, sharply distinguished from linguistic content, the content a speaker's sentence has *as* a sentence of a public language. Such linguistic content is, of course, a function of the relevant public conventions, and, since these public conventions are not accessible to introspection alone, introspection is not assigned the task of determining sameness and difference in such conventional content. The question as to whether two strings of a public language agree or differ in linguistic content cannot be decided by introspection, no matter how penetrating the inner vision. Belief contents are, however, supposed to be things of a different kind; such contents supposedly parade naked before the inner introspective eye, which is in a position to make judgments of sameness and difference with unrivaled certainty.

(2) In addition to the epistemic element, the traditional picture incorporates a semantic component. By this I mean that the belief contents, which are stipulated to satisfy the epistemic requirement, are intended to be semantically relevant, that is, relevant in evaluating sentences of the form ⌜S believes that P.⌝ In characterizing a subject as believing that P, we are attributing a particular belief content, a content which supposedly satisfies the epistemic requirement (1). In imposing the epistemic requirement on belief contents, the proponent of the Cartesian model intends to

speak of *ordinary* belief contents, those things ascribed and talked about in our everyday belief ascriptions. The epistemic requirement is not merely being imposed on some esoteric kinds of psychological contents, far removed from and irrelevant to the evaluation of our ordinary talk of belief, desire, etc. The Cartesian claim is not simply that there exists *some* level of representation which satisfies the epistemic requirement. It would not, for example, be satisfied by the discovery that the subject has unconscious access of this kind to the representations that figure at primitive levels of visual processing. For our purposes we can ignore talk of different levels of representation and their contents unless they are relevant to the evaluation of ordinary belief ascriptions. Our concern is with puzzles and paradoxes that plague our ordinary understanding of belief talk. How can we really say of Elmer that he believes that Bugsy is dangerous and that Bugsy is not dangerous, while at the same time holding him to be perfectly rational? Can it be true that the Babylonian astronomer did not believe that Hesperus is Phosphorus, given that he believed that Hesperus is Hesperus? Given the nature of the problems at hand, we are concerned only with those contents that are relevant to evaluating ordinary belief characterizations. The all-important question is: *Do such contents satisfy the epistemic requirement?* The assumption has been that they do and this plays a crucial role in generating the puzzlement in many of the problems cited. Salmon rightly rejects it. This characterization of the belief content as semantically relevant is, of course, extremely vague. Later we examine two ways in which such contents can be semantically relevant, but this will do for the moment.

In the next section I offer reasons for rejecting the traditional conception of cognitive access, and I emphasize once again that in rejecting the claim that belief contents satisfy the epistemic requirement I am *not* claiming that no psychological contents satisfy this requirement, but only that the kinds of contents that figure in the evaluation of belief ascriptions do not satisfy it.

Reasons for Rejecting the Cartesian Model of Access

First, a brief statement, or restatement, of some of the positive advantages that result from abandoning the Cartesian model of access, and then a look at some serious internal difficulties in the model.

Rejecting the Cartesian picture provides for intuitive resolutions to a number of genuine paradoxes.

We find in the recent literature a number of genuine and deep puzzles which seem to threaten the very coherence of basic intuitions. They suggest that the intuitions which figure in our ordinary practice of ascribing psychological attitudes verge on being inconsistent. Salmon's own puzzle is an example of this. The story he tells seems to reveal deep tensions in our intuitions. Given the first segment of the story, we are strongly disposed to believe that Elmer, on June 1, abandons the belief that Bugsy Wabbit is dangerous. But the second installment, then, equally disposes us towards maintaining that he continues to believe that Bugsy Wabbit is dangerous well beyond June 1 without giving us any reason for thinking that our initial characterization was mistaken. Here primitive intuitions generate conflict and *something* has to give. We can resolve this conflict only by abandoning one of the pretheoretic intuitions that created the difficulty in the first place. Rejecting the Cartesian model of access enables us to do just that: it justifies us in rejecting the claim that Elmer *simply abandons* the belief that Bugsy is dangerous on June 1. On June 1 he withholds assent to that belief under one guise, but he continues to assent to it under another guise; he simply is not in a position to recognize that the belief content he assents to under one guise is the same content he rejects under another guise. The core of this resolution, then, lies in its rejection of the Cartesian model of access, not in any explicit appeal to Russellian propositions. Any account, incorporating any plausible metaphysics, which motivates the abandonment of the Cartesian model of access—thereby allowing rational subjects to take different attitudes toward one and the same content—will underwrite a resolution of this sort.

Further, as Salmon himself observes ([157], pp. 129–132) abandoning the Cartesian model provides the wherewithal to resolve Kripke's famous puzzle about belief [96]. In this puzzle the primary actor is Pierre, a fully competent, monolingual French speaker, who, we are told, is also a model of rationality. Pierre has seen all kinds of photographs depicting the charms of London (though the captions, of course, speak of 'Londres'), and he is led to exclaim, "Londres est jolie," thereby expressing his belief that London is pretty. He is then transported to a poor quarter of London, where he learns English from his new acquaintances. He learns that the city he now lives in is called 'London', without ever learning that it is the city he also refers to as 'Londres'. Aware of the grime around him, he sincerely asserts: "London is not pretty." It certainly seems as though he now believes that London is not pretty, and does so without ever abandoning the belief that London is pretty. (Remember that he is still disposed to assent to 'Londres est jolie'.) This is problematical in that Pierre is, by hypothesis, a paradigm of rationality; he is, Kripke stipulates, "one who would never let contradictory beliefs pass." What are we to say of Pierre? To deny him either of the contradictory beliefs seems to violate clear criteria of belief attribution, or at least the received view of that practice, but, Kripke argues, neither can we ascribe both beliefs to him; to do so would violate his assumed rationality. Kripke writes:

> Does Pierre, or does he not, believe that London is pretty? It is clear that
> our normal criteria for the attribution of belief lead, when applied to this
> question, to paradoxes and contradictions ... As in the case of the logical
> paradoxes, the present puzzle presents us with a problem for customarily
> accepted principles. ([96], p. 259)

It should be clear that this is a problem only for one who accepts the Cartesian model of cognitive access. The puzzle simply dissipates once one abandons the supposition that rational introspection provides Pierre (or anyone) with the ability to recognize the same thought whenever and however he entertains it. Having abandoned this supposition, we can no longer stipulate, as Kripke does, that Pierre's rationality requires us to suppose he never lets contradiction pass ([96], p. 257). Having granted that something more than rationality may be required if Pierre is to recognize himself as expressing the same thought on different occasions, one must also recognize that something more may be needed to detect contradictions. The role of the Cartesian principle in this puzzle is even more evident when the puzzle is cast in a metalinguistic fashion. The story Kripke tells seems to suggest that the following three sentences are all true:

(1)   Pierre believes that London is pretty,

(2)   Pierre believes that London is not pretty,

(3)   Pierre is perfectly rational.[7]

It is this that Kripke finds so puzzling. How is it possible for (1), (2), and (3) to be jointly true? We can now offer a simple and intuitive response: *the belief contents which are relevant to the semantic evaluation of* (1) *and* (2) (the contents Pierre expresses with the aid of French and English sentences) *do not satisfy the Cartesian epistemic requirement*. Hence, Pierre's subscription to contradictory beliefs does not undermine his presumed rationality.

"Frege's Puzzle," however, is a very different matter. We have already noted that this puzzle is not resolved by any simple abandonment of the Cartesian model of access; this will not explain away our different attitudes towards the following sentences:

(a)   The ancient Babylonian astronomer believed that Hesperus is Hesperus,

(b)   The ancient Babylonian astronomer believed that Hesperus is Phosphorus.

But this, of course, just raises the further question of why we should expect an adequate theory to do this. We have as yet been given no good reason

---

[7] David Lewis reads Kripke's story as suggesting something very different. In "What Puzzling Pierre does not Believe" [108], Lewis argues that the story suggests that the following three propositions are all true: (1) Pierre believes that London is pretty. (2) Pierre believes that London is not pretty. (3) Pierre is not inconsistent. Lewis argues that the puzzle thus calls out for an account that explains how (1), (2) and (3) might all be true, and he offers some suggestions in this direction. I am inclined to think that Lewis is here setting himself an impossible task; if (1) and (2) are true, Pierre *is* thereby guilty of inconsistency. The closing pages of this paper bear on Lewis' argument, and I discuss it in some more detail in "Contradictory Belief and Cognitive Access" [126].

to think that the problems posed by Hesperus/Phosphorus cases are of the same kind as those posed by the Kripke and Salmon stories. The latter stories are puzzling in that they reveal tensions in our pretheoretic intuitions, which clearly need to be alleviated. The Fregean examples reveal no such conflict. They are offered as illustrations of the failure of interchange in belief contexts, and, as such, they are a source of genuine puzzlement and tension only to one already committed to such interchange. For Frege, as for the vast majority of subsequent theorists, the apparent failure of interchange constituted a datum rather than a puzzle. True, an adequate account of belief should do justice to this phenomenon, but there is no reason to think that an account succeeds in this venture only if it explains away the apparent failure of interchange, thereby revealing it to be *merely* apparent.

Some internal problems in the Cartesian model of access.

As I emphasized above, my concern here is only with semantically relevant belief contents, only with such contents as are intended to contribute to the truth conditions (or assertibility conditions) of sentences of the form, ⌜S believes that P.⌝ In what follows I shall speak only of truth conditions, but the argument applies without any essential modification to alternative accounts in which truth is replaced by some weaker requirement, such as warranted assertibility. Contents may plausibly be viewed as contributing to the truth conditions of belief sentences in either of two ways: (A) On the traditional Fregean schema, the truth value of the sentence is a function of the subject, the believing relation, and the proposition (thought) assigned P. (B) "Narrow Content" theorists, on the other hand, see the truth value of such sentences as a function of the subject, the belief relation, the belief content, *and* relevant contextual factors, i.e., such theorists view propositional content as derivative, determined by narrow content plus context.[8] It is possible, no doubt, to construct accounts in which belief contents play more indirect and complex roles in the evaluation of belief ascriptions. These, however, are the obvious alternatives. In any case, I take them to be representative, and I will content myself with arguing that contents which are semantically relevant in either of these ways do not satisfy the epistemic requirement.

(A) *Belief content as propositional content.* In the Fregean model, belief contents (Fregean thoughts) play a direct and intuitive semantic role: each sentence P is assigned a thought or belief content as one of its semantic values, and a sentence of the form ⌜S believes that P⌝ is said to be true if and only if S stands in the belief relation to the belief content assigned P. In this model, the sentences ⌜S believes that P⌝ and ⌜S believes that P^*⌝ differ in truth value only if P and P^* are assigned different belief contents. This intuitive semantics is, of course, motivated by the pretheoretic conception of belief sentences as vehicles for ascribing belief contents or

---

[8] For a sampling of such accounts see: Fodor [55]; Lewis [110]; McGinn [122].

thoughts to the believing subject. It is a relatively simple matter to show that such content—propositional content—does not satisfy the Cartesian epistemic requirement. This is one of the lessons to be drawn from a series of now familiar examples: Kripke's tale of Pierre, Twin-Earth examples of the kind first discussed by Putnam, and Burge-style examples, which focus on the way in which the psychological interpretation of individuals is sensitive to their linguistic context.[9] Though these examples differ in emphasis, they all illustrate ways in which propositional content is, in part, a function of contextual factors. Consequently, sameness and difference in propositional content is, in part, a function of these same external, contextual factors. The subject's ability to detect such sameness and difference is contingent upon his knowledge of these external factors, and this undermines introspective access to sameness and difference.

Consider first a variation on the Pierre story. Once again, given what he has heard and seen, Pierre, a monolingual French speaker, is inclined, at t_1, to assent to 'Londres est jolie'. Pierre, it seems, believes that London is pretty, and expresses that very content when he says 'Londres est jolie'. Suppose that the rest of the story is as Kripke tells it, except that Pierre is transported to one of the finer neighborhoods of London. At t_2, having acquired English, he comes to assent to 'London is pretty' without ever learning the 'London' and 'Londres' are co-referential. It seems clear that Pierre expresses the same propositional content by these two sentences, the same belief, but no amount of introspection will reveal this to him. This point may be reinforced by comparing this story with the following one.

Our subject once again is Pierre. He hears the same sounds, has the same phenomenological life, is disposed to utter the same sounds, and so on. Indeed, we may assume that Pierre is physically just as he was in the story just told, down to the last molecule. In particular, assume that he has the same visual experiences (characterized non-intentionally), and that he is disposed to assent to 'Londres est jolie' and to 'London is pretty', exactly as in the previous example. The one difference is this: the photographs Pierre sees, and the stories he hears in his native France are, in this example, all of Liverpool rather than London. Liverpool in this world is called 'Londres' by Pierre and his colinguists (who speak a language *very* like French, indeed, indistinguishable from French, with the exception of these two place names). Here there is *no* inclination to say that Pierre expresses the same proposition or thought by the sentences 'Londres est jolie' and 'London is pretty' (to which he assents upon arriving in London). In contrast to the first story, Pierre apparently gives vent to different beliefs at t_1 and at t_2, and all of this without any relevant internal, nonintentional difference in Pierre. The different interpretations are, of course, supported by relevant contextual differences, but these differences are not reflected in Pierre or in his proximate environment when characterized nonintentionally. The

---

[9] See Kripke [96]; Putnam [134]; Burge [11].

name 'Londres' is "linked" to London in the first example and to Liverpool in the second; this difference is not accessible to introspection. Such examples clearly illustrate that sameness and difference in propositional content is contingent upon external factors, and so not detectable by introspection alone.[10] Were Pierre's physical history just as we have described it, and were we to present Pierre with the question, "Which story is true of you?", he would not be able to determine introspectively which of the two stories was true of him. No amount of internal introspection will enable him to decide whether the belief(s) he expresses with the sentence 'Londres est jolie' and 'London is pretty' are the same or different. In stating this we are not, of course, claiming that he does not know what he believes. He can accurately characterize the contents of his own beliefs, but in doing so he uses the very terms (concepts) that figure in the object-level beliefs ('Londres' and 'London').

The Pierre examples focus on proper names and the role of context in determining coreference and translation, but the point is perfectly general. The original Twin Earth examples illustrate the context sensitivity of belief ascriptions containing natural kind terms, and it is a simple matter to construct variations on these examples in which a subject's inability to introspectively determine sameness and difference in belief is linked to the interplay of such general terms. Consider first an example of the original kind. Alf has acquired the term 'cilantro' in a perfectly ordinary way: he knows it is an herb that figures prominently in Mexican cooking, he is familiar with its characteristic aroma, and so on. He says to himself, "A salsa is not a salsa without a liberal dose of cilantro," thereby expressing the belief that a salsa is not a salsa without a liberal dose of cilantro. Alf has the usual counterpart on Twin-Earth, Alf*, who is a particle for particle replica of Alf; he hears the same sounds, is disposed to utter the same sounds, etc. Like Alf, A* has acquired the Twin-Earthian term 'cilantro' and he, too, says to himself, "A salsa is not a salsa without a liberal dose of cilantro." But unlike Alf, he does not thereby express the belief that a salsa is not a salsa without a liberal dose of cilantro. There simply is no cilantro on Twin Earth; there a very different herb has many of the superficial properties of cilantro, and Twin-Earthians use their term 'cilantro' to designate this herb rather than cilantro. In characterizing Alf*'s belief, which he expresses with the aid of the Twin-Earthian term 'cilantro', we should at least use a term that is extensionally equivalent to theirs, and this rules out our term 'cilantro'. In assigning propositional attitudes and propositional contents to these individuals, we take account of the relevant differences in their environments and we assign them different propositional contents, even though they are

---

[10] Lewis [108] and Stalnaker [178] use examples of this kind to very different ends. They construe Pierre's inability to tell which story is true of him as undermining the claim that Pierre believes that London is pretty. I discuss this strategy in "Contradictory Belief and Cognitive Access" [126].

physical replicas. Once we take this lesson to heart and recognize that the identity of propositional contents is a function of such contextual factors, we are left with no inclination to suppose that mere introspection enables one to determine sameness and difference in such contents.

Once again this point can be emphasized by considering variations on the original example. We assume, again, that Alf has acquired the term 'cilantro' in some ordinary fashion; he is familiar with the herb, uses it frequently, and enjoys its very distinctive flavor. He readily assents to 'I relish the flavor of cilantro'. In addition, he has, among his dried herbs, a bottle of ground coriander, which does not look, smell, or taste like the familiar cilantro. He is fond of coriander, too (though he uses it for very different dishes), and is ready to assent to 'I relish the flavor of coriander'. He is surprised then when told that 'coriander' is just another name for cilantro—that the two names are synonymous. He thinks again of the belief(s) he expressed using 'cilantro' and 'coriander', and he wonders if they were the same or different. Given that the terms are synonymous, we have good reason to think that he expressed the same belief on these two occasions. But *he* is certainly in no position to ascertain this by introspection, nor is he in a position to distinguish, again by introspection, between the world he is actually in and a world in which he and his proximate environment are physically replicated, but which differs from the actual world in that in it 'cilantro' and 'coriander' are used to designate two different herbs. Once again, sameness and difference in propositional content need not be detectable by introspection alone.[11] And this is not due to the occurrence of physical items in the object of thought, or to the special status of singular terms of a Russellian sort; it is due simply to the way in which attitude *ascriptions* are sensitive to a variety of contextual factors. In the Russellian model, in which the object denoted by the singular term is a constituent of the thought, sameness of object guarantees sameness of thought. In accounts which appeal to the context sensitivity of belief ascriptions, difference in physical object may indeed justify different belief ascriptions, thereby revealing propositional content as violating the Cartesian epistemic requirement, but they do not support the further and more questionable intuition that sameness in object somehow guarantees sameness of thought.

(B) *Belief content as narrow content.* It is now widely conceded that examples of this kind demonstrate the context sensitivity of belief *ascriptions*,

---

[11] The point of these examples is emphasized in the following variation: Consider the alternative world in which 'coriander' and 'cilantro' are not synonymous. Alf* says to himself: "I relish the flavor of cilantro," and then "I don't relish the flavor of coriander." Jean overhears and accuses him of holding contradictory beliefs. Not quite sure of himself, Alf* consults a reliable dictionary and learns that 'cilantro' and 'coriander' are not even coextensive. It certainly seems as though this information should be relevant to Alf*'s quandary, to resolving his doubts. But this is difficult to accommodate on the Cartesian model.

thereby illustrating ways in which contextual variation can justify attributing different *propositional contents* to subjects in the absence of any relevant nonintentional difference. And it seems to me that we have little or no option, then, but to admit that propositional content does not satisfy the Cartesian epistemic requirement.

When put in this fashion, however, it invites an obvious response: the Twin-Earth examples expose the inadequacy of Fregean semantics rather than some new and peculiar feature of belief content. Fregean advocates of propositional content start from the naive assumption that ascriptions of the form ⌜S believes that P⌝ are true just in case S bears the believing relationship to the propositional content expressed by P. In operating with this simple semantics, it is *they* who ignore the ways in which such ascriptions are sensitive to contextual factors. No wonder, then, that they subsequently find themselves saddled with a notion of psychological *content* that is context sensitive. The lesson to be drawn from Twin-Earth examples is not that psychological content is context sensitive, but that *our initial semantics was overly simple*; and one responds to this, not by opting for some strange notion of belief content which is contextually sensitive in this bizarre way, but by developing a more adequate semantics, one in which the contextual factors have an explicit role. This strategy appears to enable the theorist to respect the context sensitivity of belief *ascriptions* without supposing that the contents they attribute are themselves context sensitive in the way the examples have been interpreted. The suggestion is that we replace the simple Fregean formula with one of the form:

> ⌜S believes that P⌝ is true if and only if S stands in the believing relation to the belief content (call this "narrow content") ascribed by P, *and* S's context is of a certain sort C (e.g., contains H_2O rather than XYZ).

Thus, an ascription true of Alf can be false of Alf* even though Alf and Alf* don't differ in psychological content. This puts the Twin-Earth examples in a very different light. It is the difference in *context*, not content, that accounts for the fact that the ascription 'Alf believes that a salsa is not a salsa unless it contains a liberal dose of cilantro', is true of Alf but not of his Twin-Earth counterpart. The English sentence is used to ascribe a specific narrow content to Alf, and *this narrow content is shared by his doppelganger even though the same English sentence is not true of him.* This kind of account seems to satisfy all of our initial intuitions: we get to *say* different things of the doppelgangers without thereby supposing that they somehow differ in psychological content.

Moreover, our objector urges, this appeal to "narrow content," which remains constant despite variations in propositional content, is no *ad hoc* move born of desperation. The Twin-Earth examples do reveal something striking about our practice: they illustrate ways in which ascriptions of content (not content itself) are sensitive to contextual factors. And in attempting to address the issue by appealing to narrow content, the theorist is merely following a familiar and accepted strategy: he is treating these context sensitive sentences as one treats paradigmatic context sensitive sentences, those containing indexicals. It is commonplace to recognize that even though you and I express different propositions by our respective tokenings of 'I am ill', there is also a clear sense in which we say exactly the same thing. In Kaplan's terminology [92], these different utterances agree in *character*. Propositional content which varies from one context of utterance to the next is not viewed as a semantic or psychological primitive, but is construed as a function of this more primitive character and the relevant contextual factors. The lesson is clear: in treating sentences which are sensitive to various contextual features, construe propositional content and truth value as a function of a content which is invariant across these contexts *and* the relevant contextual features.

The Twin-Earth examples appear to pose no special problem for the advocates of narrow content. They can grant all of the following: (1) the doppelgangers express different propositions by their respective utterances of the sentence, 'A salsa is not a salsa without a liberal dose of cilantro', (2) the English ascription 'Alf believes that a salsa is not a salsa without a liberal dose of cilantro' is true of the Alf but not his doppelganger, and (3) such *propositional* content does not satisfy the Cartesian epistemic requirement. But it is a mistake to think that any of this tells against the original claim that *belief content* satisfies the Cartesian epistemic requirement. Alf and Alf* bear the believing relation to the same narrow content. Even though the open sentence '—believes that a salsa is not a salsa without a liberal dose of cilantro' is true of one and not the other, this simply reflects differences in context and does not imply that they differ in psychological content. Finally, since these narrow contents are not context sensitive, there is absolutely no reason whatsoever to suppose that *they* fail the Cartesian epistemic requirement. This simple strategy of incorporating the relevant contextual features within the truth conditions *seems* to enable defenders of the Cartesian model of access to do justice to the context sensitivity of belief ascriptions without relinquishing their epistemic intuitions.

What are we to say in response to this? First, it is important to note that the alleged similarity between sentences which ascribe beliefs and indexical sentences rests on an ambiguity. Sentences containing indexicals are context sensitive in that *one and the same sentence* (e.g., *the English sentence*, 'I am ill') may be used to express different propositions in different contexts of utterance. It is this that leads the theorist to postulate two kinds of "content" (one that varies from context to context and one that is constant) and to accord the contextual features an explicit semantic role. Twin-Earth stories, and others of this kind, do not demonstrate *this kind* of contextual sensitivity, i.e., they do not illustrate ways in which one and the same sentence (say, a particular sentence of *English*) expresses different propositions in different contexts of utterance. There is no reason to think that Alf and Alf* utter two tokens of the *same sentence*, in the usual sense of this notion. Rather they utter strings from two *different* languages that happen to be *physically* indistinguishable. Alf and Alf* are examples of individuals who don't differ when characterized nonintentionally, but who satisfy different intentional characterizations, including sentential characterizations. They reveal ways in which we take account of a subject's environment in characterizing that subject's beliefs, not ways in which the proposition expressed by a single sentence varies from context to context. The surface similarity between sentences which ascribe beliefs and indexical sentences, and the subsequent modeling of narrow content on character, is thus highly misleading.

I turn now to some difficulties of a more intrinsic nature. I will focus here on two: First, once we grant that propositional content fails to satisfy the epistemic requirement, there is simply no point in imposing this requirement on some further kind of content; and second, there *is* good reason to think that *any* notion of content that is semantically relevant (narrow or not) will fail to satisfy the epistemic requirement.

First, we are supposing that our imaginary objectors have conceded the wayward character of propositional content, that they recognize that it does not satisfy the epistemic requirement; hence, that a fully rational subject may be truly said to believe that P and that not-P. Having conceded this much, they introduce narrow content on the scene, and this content, they claim, satisfies the epistemic requirement. It is certainly fair to ask at this point: Why bother? What role is this content intended to play? What problems or needs is it intended to meet? The question of interest is not, "Why want contents that are such as to satisfy the epistemic requirement?", but the slightly more complex question, "What rationale is there for imposing this requirement on narrow content once one has conceded that propositional content does not satisfy it?" So far as I can tell there is simply no rationale; no apparent goal is served by imposing this requirement on narrow content. Let us approach this issue by way of the simpler question: Why want contents of any sort to satisfy the epistemic requirement? Though reams have been written on the ability of subjects to introspectively determine the contents of their own consciousness, their beliefs and desires, virtually nothing has been written on the subject's ability to determine sameness and difference in beliefs. Consequently, even though the traditional picture of mind clearly presupposes that we are able to introspectively determine sameness and difference in content, we look in vain for any argument in favor of this claim or for any detailed account of the goals supposedly served by it.

As soon as we stop presupposing some unarticulated notion of immediate access to sameness and difference in belief and attempt to justify or motivate this conception, we encounter severe difficulties. I suspect that there is some tendency to suppose that access to sameness and difference of content is guaranteed by subjects' immediate and reliable access to the contents of their beliefs. Hence, it is enough to argue for the latter claim. If fully rational subjects know the content of the belief entertained at time t_1, and know the content of the belief entertained at t_j, then, putting aside worries about memory lapses and the like for the moment, surely they are thereby in a position to determine, immediately, whether these are the same or different. This inference is to be avoided. It clearly fails when one is concerned with the *beliefs* of subjects such as Kripke's Pierre, and the analogous inference fails in the case of reference. Pierre certainly knows what it is he *believes* (the proposition) when he assents to the sentences 'Londres est jolie', and he knows what it is he believes when he assents to 'London is pretty'. His awareness of the propositional contents of his beliefs simply does not enable him to recognize them as the same. The same is true with regard to reference: given two names, one can certainly know who it is one uses each name to refer to without thereby knowing whether or not one uses them to refer to the same or different individuals. In both cases the inference fails for similar reasons: the subject's second order beliefs about his object-level beliefs (or about objects referred to) are themselves fashioned with the aid of concepts (or terms) used in the object-level beliefs. A subject who has acquired the terms 'London' and 'Londres' can *use* these terms (concepts) in fashioning beliefs about his object-level beliefs, which are themselves fashioned with the aid of these very terms (concepts). Indeed, this may well be the subject's only accurate way to characterize his object-level beliefs. One cannot simply assume then that subjects are in a position to determine whether or not the beliefs they entertain at t_1 and t_2 are the same or different simply because they know what it is they believe at t_1 and t_2.

Nor am I aware of any convincing linguistic or phenomenological arguments in favor of such access. The linguistic data has already been garnered by the anti-individualists in their campaign against the Cartesian model, and the phenomenological data is again sullied by the fact that second-level judgments of content are themselves fashioned with the aid of notions that figure in the object-level beliefs. In fact, there appears to be no interesting positive argument for the supposition that belief contents should be individuated in such a way as to satisfy the Cartesian epistemic requirement. So far as I can tell the *only* reason for retaining this picture of cognitive access is the role it plays in the Cartesian model of the *rational* subject as the one who would never subscribe to contradictory beliefs. This conception of rationality is certainly popular and initially intuitive, and it does presuppose that the fully rational subject can introspectively determine sameness and difference in belief. This, I suggest, is the *only* reason we have for wanting a notion of content that is such as to satisfy the epistemic requirement. This is of no help to the proponents of narrow content, however. *They* cannot employ this notion of rationality in their efforts to motivate the Cartesian picture of cognitive access, for they have already abandoned it. Proponents of narrow content concede that belief ascriptions are context sensitive and that propositional contents do not satisfy the epistemic requirement. In doing so they concede that rationality is compatible with holding contradictory beliefs. Pierre, they allow, is fully rational despite the fact that he both believes that London is pretty and that London is not pretty. In granting this, they abandon the original motivation for the Cartesian epistemic requirement, and, to put it mildly, it is difficult to see what, if anything, is to be gained by supposing that there is some other form of content which satisfies the Cartesian requirement. The subject's ability to determine sameness and difference in this other form of content is not going to enable him to detect sameness and difference in his *beliefs*. Introspective access to sameness and difference in *propositional* content served a fairly well-defined epistemic goal in that it placed limits on what *beliefs* one could ascribe to a rational subject; but once one grants that the rational subject does not have this kind of access, there is no remaining goal to be served by supposing the subject does have this kind of access to another kind of content.

I turn now to the second difficulty. There are strong reasons for thinking that semantically relevant contents of any kind—narrow or otherwise— will fail to satisfy the epistemic requirement. If narrow contents are to be semantically relevant, they must figure in the evaluation of belief sentences; the acceptability of such sentences must rest partly on the question of whether or not the subject assents to this or that specific narrow content. (This, however, is not to say that we must be able to specify the content in a natural language). Given the way in which the paradigmatically semantic propositional content failed the epistemic requirement, the proponents of narrow content cannot appeal to narrow content and leave it at that; they owe us some account of how such contents are meant to succeed where propositional contents failed, an account of how these contents are meant to figure in the semantic evaluation of belief sentences while satisfying the epistemic requirement. Narrow content was introduced as that content which remains invariant across Twin-Earth contexts, and its intuitive semantic role is as follows:

Each sentence, P, is assigned a specific narrow content, N, as one of its semantic values, and a sentence of the form $\ulcorner S$ believes that $P\urcorner$ is deemed true if and only if S bears the believing relation to the narrow content N and, in addition, the context satisfies some specific conditions C.

These contents, explicitly designed to remain invariant across Twin-Earth contexts, seem to be just what we need to satisfy the epistemic requirement. It was, after all, the context dependency of propositional content that proved so problematic. But appearances are misleading. Contents assigned this kind of role fail the epistemic requirement. In this model each sentence P is assigned one specific narrow content as one of its semantic values, and the open sentence $\ulcorner$ ___ believes that $P\urcorner$ will be true of a subject x at times t_1 and t_2 if and only if x bears the believing relation to this same narrow content at t_1 and t_2 and the context is of the requisite kind. In particular, the open sentence '___ believes that London is pretty' will be true of Pierre at t_1 and t_2 if and only if Pierre bears, at t_1 and t_2, the believing relation to the narrow content associated with 'London is pretty'. Consider again the example sketched above, the one in which Pierre finds himself in one of the finer parts of London. At t_1 he assents to 'Londres est jolie', expressing his belief that London is pretty, thereby satisfying the open sentence '___ believes that London is pretty'. At t_2 he assents to 'London is pretty', and seems, once again, to satisfy the open sentence, '___ believes that London is pretty'. Hence, we must suppose that he assents to the same narrow content on these two occasions, and, being fully rational, introspection should provide him with all he needs to recognize this. But it is quite clear that introspection is not up to this task. It is not just that he does not recognize sameness in *propositional* content. The London which Pierre experiences at t_2 may in fact bear little resemblance to the city depicted in the photographs Pierre peruses at t_1; and there is no reason to think that there is *any* notion of content such that it is true to say of Pierre that he can introspectively recognize himself as entertaining the *same* content on these two occasions. Narrow contents which are assigned this kind of straightforward semantic role violate the epistemic requirement.

If narrow contents are to be semantically relevant, sentences must be allocated specific narrow contents. An account, for example, which maintains that a sentence of the form $\ulcorner S$ believes that $P\urcorner$ is true if S bears the believing relation to *any* narrow content (and the context is of a certain kind) would be grossly inadequate; it would fail to provide different narrow contents with any selective role in the evaluation of different belief ascriptions. An adequate model must link particular belief ascriptions to specific narrow contents. In the previous example we considered only the most obvious type of assignment, one in which each sentence is paired with a single narrow content, and we have seen that such contents will not satisfy the epistemic requirement. It is, of course, not necessary that the assignments be of this simple kind; one might, for various reasons, assign a number of narrow contents, N_1, N_2, N_3, to a sentence P, and construe the sentence $\ulcorner S$ believes that $P\urcorner$ as true if S bears the believing relation to any one of these narrow contents. This less rigid account may seem to provide the proponent of narrow content the wherewithal to escape the difficulty just scouted. He can grant that Pierre believes that London is pretty, at t_1 and t_2, and that introspection does not enable him to recognize himself as entertaining the same narrow content on these two occasions. But, he can now argue, this does not show narrow content to violate the epistemic requirement, for we have been given no reason to think he was entertaining the same narrow content on the two occasions. Pierre can entertain the belief that London is pretty by entertaining any one of a number of narrow contents, N_1, N_2, etc. (again assuming that the context is of the right kind); and in the case at hand, we may suppose that he assented to one of these narrow contents at t_1 and to a different one at t_2. Here we have the same belief, different narrow contents, and no violation of the epistemic requirement. But in reality, this move simply postpones the inevitable. Suppose that, in our efforts to respond to the problem posed by Pierre, we claim that there are *two* different kinds of narrow content associated with 'London is pretty', and that Pierre does not recognize himself as entertaining the same narrow content when he says "London is pretty" and when he says 'Londres est jolie' for the very simple reason that he entertains one of these contents on one occasion, and the other on the other. A simple variation on the Pierre examples exposes the inadequacies of this move. Assume that Pierre spends some time in Germany before going to England. He learns German as a first language, and once again is acquainted with photographs of London, much different from those he saw in France, and from the London he is eventually transported to. The city depicted is a pretty one, and he says as much; he asserts, "London ist schön." Pierre, it appears, believes that London is pretty. Indeed he has and expresses the same belief in three different contexts, using three different sentences in doing so, and without recognizing the French, German, and English names as co-referential. This is enough to dispose of the modified account now before us. This account would have Pierre assenting to the same narrow content on at least two of these occasions, and hence in a position to introspectively recognize himself as doing so. It is clear that Pierre is no more able to recognize any sameness in content across these contexts that he was in the original example. Further multiplication of narrow contents just adds complexity without any obvious gain. Narrow content, to the extent that it is semantically relevant, does not satisfy the epistemic requirement.

I think it fair to conclude that semantically relevant contents will not satisfy the epistemic requirement. So far as I can tell there are only two plausible ways in which contents are supposed to be semantically relevant; as propositional content or as narrow content. Propositional contents clearly fail in this regard, and narrow contents, while initially appearing to offer hope of being truly Cartesian, violate the requirement as soon as one attempts to spell out their semantic role. They, too, fail the epistemic requirement. Contents which figure in the evaluation of belief ascriptions do not satisfy the Cartesian picture of access. This important feature of psychological content undermines a variety of semantic arguments and it resolves some puzzling examples, but it does not enable the Russellian theorist to sidestep the Fregean puzzle.[12]

---

[12] I have received help from many, including C. A. Anderson, K. Falvey, W. Hanson, H. E. Mason, and J. Wallace.

7

On Some Thought Experiments about Mind and Meaning

JOHN WALLACE AND H. E. MASON

> No two of us learn our language alike, nor, in a sense, does any finish learning
> it while he lives.   W. V. Quine, *Word and Object*
>
> Seldom, very seldom, does complete truth belong to any human disclosure;
> seldom can it happen that something is not a little disguised, or a little
> mistaken ...   Jane Austen, *Emma*

RECENT DISCUSSIONS OF the nature and standing of mind have tended to
focus on propositional attitudes. That is perhaps not surprising. Diverse
as they may be, propositional attitudes appear to take objects, contents as
they have come to be called, not easily accounted for by the most prominent
theories of mentality. In a widely discussed series of papers Tyler Burge
has attempted to specify the critical failing: a widely shared predisposition
to favor individualistic accounts of mental phenomena.[1] Mental states attributed with the ascription of a belief or a desire, or, for that matter, a
guess or a hunch or a wish, are not properly conceived as states of an individual considered in isolation: specification of the states they are requires
reference to an appropriate social context. In Burge's view such questions
as the question whether it is possible for persons' propositional attitudes
to be different while their internal physiological states are the same take
on a very different cast once it is recognized that in virtue of their content
propositional attitudes are socially constituted and socially individuated.
Among currently prominent theories, both functionalist theories and physicalistic theories supposing that mental states supervene on physical states
fall prey to this objection.

---

[1] Burge's papers in which the arguments are presented or summarized or characterized include "Individualism and the Mental" [11], "Other Bodies" [12], "Two
Thought Experiments Reviewed" [13], "Individualism and Psychology" [15], "Intellectual Norms and the Foundations of Mind" [16], and "Individualism and
Self-knowledge" [18].

Burge attempts to establish the social constitution of specific propositional attitudes with a series of arguments proposing in each case to show
that a specific propositional attitude is constituted by its social context.
He offers, in fact, a kind of template for producing arguments to that effect. Taking as a base cases in which a propositional attitude is attributed
to a person despite his misunderstanding of the 'that'-clause which gives
content to the attitude, Burge asks us to consider counterfactual cases in
which the social and linguistic context is altered, making an honest attitude of the propositional attitude in question. Where the content was
misunderstood in the actual case, it is in the changed social and linguistic
context a well-understood content, the belief in question now true in its
altered context. Thus, words taken in the original situation to exhibit a
false belief are taken in the counterfactual cases to exhibit a true belief.
Adding the stipulation that the only difference between the actual and the
counterfactual case is the difference in the social and linguistic context, and
that there are in particular no physical differences in the person subject
to the changed attitudes, Burge is able to conclude that the difference of
social context and only that makes for the difference in resulting propositional attitude. In that respect the propositional attitudes expressed by
words understood in terms of the linguistic conventions prevailing in the
circumstances in which they are uttered are said to be socially constituted
or socially individuated.

Arguments to this effect can be constructed, Burge suggests, in any of
a myriad of cases in which the content of an avowed belief is only partially
understood. The altered social and linguistic conditions postulated in a
counterfactual circumstance in the construction of such arguments facili-
tates the conclusion that content is socially constituted. In later papers
Burge offers an argument of a slightly different form to a somewhat more
negative conclusion. That argument, offered to show that propositional attitudes are not well-conceived as inner states of an individual, turns on the
question of what alteration in the contents of a person's beliefs could be expected where certain of the physical conditions immediately relevant to the
belief were fundamentally altered. Where aluminum took on the characteristics of molybdenum and molybdenum those of aluminum, Burge argues,
a person's belief that his canoe was made of aluminum would necessarily
come to have an altered content. Any attendant social discontinuities are
not taken up in the construction of the argument, but its rejection of individualism is supposed to work in tandem with arguments of the earlier form.

Burge's idea that minds are socially constituted is both suggestive and
provocative, but it cannot be said that it is developed in much detail beyond what is provided in the thought experiments he offers. What content
is given to the distinction between individualistic and social theories of the
mind must thus be sought primarily in Burge's treatment of the thought
experiments, and the basis he finds in those thought experiments for rejecting individualistic theories. It is puzzling that the thought experiments

as sketched by Burge should be thought to bear that weight of consideration. It is, indeed, hard to believe that such important questions could rest
on what are bound to strike many readers as fanciful arguments. In this
paper we will develop those doubts, giving some attention to both types of
thought experiments Burge offers. We will also raise some doubts about
the notion of the content of propositional attitudes which Burge appears
to assume in the specification and use of the thought experiments.

As already noted, the thought experiments have two parts: the description of an "actual situation" and the description of a "counterfactual
situation." The central idea is that differences between the two situations
leave unchanged the protagonist's physiological states but change the evidence on which ascription of propositional attitudes is based in such a
way that the protagonist's propositional attitude psychological states must
differ. So conceived, the experiments raise two sets of questions. First,
any counterfactually contemplated change would bring with it a cascade of
other changes: how confident can we be that the changes would leave the
protagonist's internal physiological states unchanged? Second, everyday
ascription of propositional attitudes presupposes a background of normal-
ity: how confident can we be that counterfactually induced changes do not
render the background so bizarre that not clear conclusions can be drawn
about sameness and difference of propositional attitudes?

1 Arthritis in the Thigh

Burge ("Individualism and the Mental" [11], pp. 77–78) describes the actual
situation of the "arthritis in the thigh" case as follows:

> A given person has a large number of attitudes commonly attributed with
> content clauses containing "arthritis" in oblique occurrence. For example,
> he thinks (correctly) that he has had arthritis for years, that his arthritis in
> his wrists and fingers is more painful than his arthritis in his ankles, that
> it is better to have arthritis than cancer of the liver, that stiffening joints
> is a symptom of arthritis, that certain sorts of aches are characteristic of
> arthritis, that there are various kinds of arthritis, etc. In addition to these
> unsurprising attitudes, he thinks falsely that he has arthritis in his thigh.

The description of the counterfactual situation runs as follows:

> The second step of the thought experiment consists of a counterfactual sup-
> position. We are to conceive of a situation in which the patient proceeds
> from birth through the same course of physical events that he actually does,
> right up to and including the time at which he first reports his fear to his
> doctor. Precisely the same things (non-intentionally described) happen to
> him. He has the same physiological history, the same diseases, the same in-
> ternal physical occurrences. He goes through the same motions, engages in
> the same behavior, has the same sensory intake (physiologically described).
> His dispositions to respond to stimuli are explained in physical theory as
> the effects of the same physical causes. All of this extends to his interaction
> with linguistic expressions. He says and hears the same words (word forms)

at the same times he actually does. He develops the disposition to 'Arthritis can occur in the thigh' and 'I have arthritis in the thigh' as a result of the same physically described proximate causes. ... in both the actual and the counterfactual situations, he acquires the word 'arthritis' from casual conversation or reading, and never hearing anything to prejudice him for or against applying it in the way he does, he applies the word to an ailment in his thigh (or to ailments in the limbs of others) which seem to have roughly similar pains or other symptoms to the disease in his hands and ankles. In both actual and counterfactual cases, the disposition is never reinforced or extinguished up until the time he expresses himself to his doctor. We further imagine that the patient's nonintentional, phenomenal experience is the same. He has the same pains, visual Fields, images, and internal verbal rehearsals. The *counterfactuality* in the supposition touches only the patient's social environment. In actual fact, 'arthritis', as it is used in his community, does not apply to ailments outside the joints. Indeed, it fails to do so by a standard, nontechnical dictionary definition. But in our imagined case, physicians, lexicographers, and informed laymen apply 'arthritis' not only to arthritis but to various other rheumatoid ailments. The standard use of the term is to be conceived to encompass the patient's actual use. We could imagine either that arthritis had not been singled out as a family of diseases, or that some other term besides 'arthritis' were applied, though not commonly by laymen, to arthritis. We may also suppose that this difference and those necessarily associated with it are the only differences between the counterfactual situation and the actual one. (Other people besides the patient will, of course, behave differently.)

To appraise this argument is to appraise two claims. First, there is a complex counterfactual, the key elements of which can be summarized as follows: If the social usage of the word 'arthritis' had been different in the way described and this difference had in no way impinged on the experience of the protagonist, then the correct description of the protagonist would shift from 'He believes that he has arthritis in his thigh' (a correct description in the actual situation) to 'He believes that he has tharthritis in his thigh' (a correct description in the counterfactual situation, 'tharthritis' being a term introduced just in order to allow formulation of such a description).

In short, selected changes in external circumstances would shift the protagonist's belief contents.

Second, there is a claim connecting the shift in correct descriptions with identity and difference of belief: If correct description of the protagonist's beliefs shifts in this way from the actual to the counterfactual situation, then his beliefs in the actual situation are different from his beliefs in the counterfactual situation.

In short, shifts in the protagonist's belief contents imply that he has different beliefs.

Burge believes that it can be concluded from these two claims, taken as premises, that propositional attitude psychological states are *not* individualistically constituted. Several comments about the argument are in order.

The upshot will be, not that the premises are *false* (though if one had to choose between saying that they are true and saying that they are false, false would be closest), but that they do not rise to the level of falsehood.

The complex counterfactual needs to be firmly distinguished from a simpler counterfactual which is naturally associated with it: If the social usage of the word 'arthritis' had been different in the way described, then the belief that would normally be expressed by a member of the society saying 'I have arthritis in my thigh' would be a belief that the person has tharthritis in his or her thigh.

This counterfactual is a truism. But it is not the counterfactual we have to appraise. The additional condition in the antecedent, that the difference in social usage had never impinged on the protagonist, had made no difference to his experience and no difference to his learning of language, creates a compound counterfactual assumption that, on its face, is quite puzzling. Social practices in the counterfactual situation are substantially different from what they are in the actual situation, but these differences have made no difference to the experience of the protagonist. With respect to the changes in social practices the protagonist is a kind of Crusoe; as far as they are concerned, he is out of it. It is odd, to say the least, that the case of such an isolate should be thought to reveal that individual psychology is socially constituted. Odd or not, how could it be that someone is enough in the society to learn its use of the word 'arthritis' sufficiently to have attributed to him belief contents containing the word, but too much out of the society to be touched by changes in fundamental social practices involving the word?

A standard way of taking a counterfactual assumption of a change in word meaning is that it is accompanied by a recoding of messages, so that the original meanings are transmitted. If '2' and '4' trade denotations, we promulgate to first-graders an old truth in the rearranged terms, '4 + 4 = 2.' Applied to the present case, this convention would lead to the systematic replacement of the word 'arthritis' in linguistic exchanges in the counterfactual situation by some other word or phrase which, in the counterfactual situation, means arthritis. Such a phrase is readily available, namely 'arthritis in the joints'. If, however, in imagining this case the standard convention were followed and the replacement of 'arthritis' by 'arthritis in the joints' were made systematically, the protagonist's sensory experience, and thus his physiological states, would be different in the counterfactual situation; for on the occasions in the past when he had heard or read 'arthritis', and at least several such occasions were involved in his learning of the word, he would now hear or read 'arthritis in the joints'. It is clear that Burge is imagining the case in some other way, with the standard convention not in force. So how is Burge imagining the case? He offers us some help when he says, in the quoted passage, that the people in the counterfactual situation possibly have not singled out arthritis as a family of diseases. In a later paper ("Two Thought Experiments Reviewed" [13],

180 John Wallace and H. E. Mason

p. 286), he writes that "No one in the counterfactual community thinks of any disease as arthritis." This still leaves the situation vague on a point that may be crucial to the argument. The problem is this: in the actual situation the protagonist learned the word 'arthritis' by hearing it used on, say, 50 to 100 occasions in which speakers, communicating with normal amounts of care and of clarity of purpose, saw fit to use 'arthritis'. On the counterpart 50 to 100 occasions in the counterfactual situation, these speakers still persist in using 'arthritis', even though it now has a different meaning for them. In order to evaluate Burge's argument it is important for us to know in as much detail as possible how this came about. For depending on how the case is imagined, two things could go wrong with the argument. The factors that explain these speakers' persistence in using the term in spite of its changed meaning might themselves be systematic social (or even physical) forces which would impinge directly on the protagonist in ways that affect his physiological states. Alternatively, the explanation might reveal something bizarre in the circumstances under which the protagonist learned the word. Suppose, for example, that the occasions on which the protagonist had heard or read the word 'arthritis' were all ones in which the speaker or writer was using the word only as a step to mentioning it, perhaps to comment on its spelling, or to make a rhyme. With no change in intention, these speakers and writers would have continued to use, and mention, the same word in the counterfactual situation. It was from encountering the word on these occasions that the protagonist had learned his use of it. If this were the situation, the protagonist would not have had sufficient understanding of the word to have any beliefs about arthritis. The important point, however, is that the thought experiment is not described in enough detail for us to know how it happened that the protagonist was totally insulated from the changes that would naturally flow from the difference in the social usage of 'arthritis'. The antecedent of the counterfactual we have to appraise is baffling.

Let us turn to the consequent of the conditional and to the question of the correct descriptions of the protagonist's beliefs. Is it correct to say that, in the actual situation, the protagonist believes that he has arthritis in his thigh? Burge insists that it is. He writes ([13], p. 88):

> I have presented the experiment as appealing to ordinary intuition. I believe that common practice in the attribution of propositional attitudes is fairly represented by the various stages. This point is not really open to dispute.

Surely the correct thing to say, given the way Burge has described the case, is not that the point is not open to dispute, but that it is not open to appraisal. Attributions of propositional attitudes are based on what people see, what they do, what words they exchange. Of all this Burge gives us nothing. In his comment, as in the original presentation of the example, Burge simply tells us, *ex cathedra*, what the person believes. It is fundamental to the argument, however, that the protagonist in the actual situation suffers from a serious misunderstanding of, or confusion about, the meaning of 'arthritis'. This misunderstanding is itself strong ground for denying that the simple 'He believes that he has arthritis in his thigh' is a correct description of what the protagonist believes.

One way of seeing this is to notice a tension that arises from Burge's presentation of the thought experiment. Burge's description of the case makes it natural to suppose that the protagonist's basic mistake was to attach a meaning, different from that reflected in the surrounding society's usage but a coherent meaning nevertheless, to 'arthritis'. This comes out in two ways. A natural picture of the learning of general terms is that the learner makes a projection from the cases on which he or she learned the term to applications in new cases. Burge's description of the case invokes this picture and makes it clear that the protagonist made a projection that overlaps with, but differs from, the social usage of the term. Thus it is natural to suppose that he attached a meaning, but not society's meaning, to the term. A second reason for thinking that the protagonist succeeded in attaching a meaning to 'arthritis' is that Burge, in describing what 'arthritis' means in the counterfactual situation, can specify its meaning there by saying that society's usage in the counterfactual situation "encompasses" the protagonist's usage in the actual situation. If the protagonist did not attach a coherent meaning to the term in the actual situation, this way of describing the counterfactual situation would not work. In assessing someone's evolving mastery of a term there are roughly two kinds of cases. In one kind of case, the person's use of a term has a large element of randomness; it might be, for example, that outside a core of simple cases, in which the person consistently applies the term in society's way, his uses of it are scattered and appear to follow, not a deviant pattern, but no pattern. In the other kind of case, the person's use of the term is patterned in a discernible and stable way, but a way that deviates from society's usage. Burge pretty clearly describes his arthritis case as being of this second kind. For if the protagonist uses the term with a large element of randomness, how could one be confident that his usage was encompassed by society's usage in the counterfactual situation? Given this understanding of the case, intuitions come to bear which say that in ascribing beliefs to the protagonist we should use words which reflect the ways in which he is categorizing the world. Thus we are tempted to say that the protagonist in the actual situation, like the protagonist in the counterfactual situation, believes that he has tharthritis in his thigh. To be sure, we are also tempted to say that he believes that he has arthritis in his thigh. We are pulled in two directions.

What are we to make of this tension? Is it necessarily resolvable by somehow deciding or determining either that he believes that he has arthritis in his thigh or that he believes that he has tharthritis in his thigh? Why should it be? It is worth reminding ourselves that frequently, when we report someone's beliefs, we do so in response to a question about the person's views on a *topic*, and not in response to a question of the form, "Does the person believe that p, or not?" That is, frequently, the question to which we are responding is focused on the person's stance toward a topic and not toward a specific sentence. When this is so, our response frequently takes the form of a narrative in which belief sentences—in the philosopher's sense, sentences of the form 'x believes that p'—are embedded with other sentences, some of which may not even be explicitly psychological in character, but which set a scene, describe a context, or provide relevant background. Judging from the surface of our practice, the narrative surrounding belief sentences frequently is not mere embellishment but is integral to conveying what we wish to convey about the person's outlook. For if someone were to press us, saying, "That long story is all very well, but what I want to know is: does x believe that p or not: yes or no," we often would reject the question. Philosophical discussion of conceptual change provides many examples of this phenomenon. Did Priestly believe that oxygen is the active agent in respiration and combustion?[2] Did this or that one of Harvey's precursors, who believed that the heart acted to move the blood but through a mechanism like boiling and at a pace like the tides, believe that the heart circulates the blood?[3] Did George III, who said positive things about the embryonic political parties of his day, believe that political parties make a constructive contribution to government?[4] Did Jefferson and Madison believe that citizens of the United States in the 20th century should have a right to private ownership of hand guns? Conceptual differences across cultures are another source of examples. There are also many examples close to home, among ourselves, our friends, our students, in which, when we seek to characterize someone's view, we find in the relevant evidence a mixture of confusion, misunderstanding, or error. The "arthritis in the thigh" thought experiment presents a situation of this kind.

In such situations the complexity of the evidence requires us, if we are to be true to it, to characterize the person's views with belief sentences embedded in a complex narrative and to reject the demand for an answer to simple questions of the form, "Does x believe that p: yes or no?" In common practice, the general form of answers to questions about someone's view is not:

x believes that p.

It is rather:

Gloss. x believes that p. Gloss.

---

[2] See Kuhn, *The Structure of Scientific Revolutions* [98], Chapter 6.

[3] See Bylebyl, *Cardiovascular Physiology in the Sixteenth and Early Seventeenth Centuries* [19].

[4] "There were no proper party organizations in 1760, though party names and cant were current; the names and the cant have since supplied the materials for an imaginary superstructure." (Namier, *The Structure of Politics at the Accession of George III* [124] (p. x).)

The glosses may contain other belief sentences, sentences of other propositional attitudes, sentences describing the subject's uses of words, sentences about the subject's learning of terms, and sentences about relevant circumstances and conditions.

The situation is even more complicated than this. Many cases fit the pattern just sketched. One might naturally say, "Yes, it is correct to say that x believes that p, provided you keep in mind the information provided by the glosses in the surrounding narrative." But there are also many cases in which, still keeping to the topic and responding to the question about someone's views, we cast our answer as a narrative that makes no explicit belief attributions, but describes instead, in indirect discourse terms, what the person said. In effect, one says, "In the complex circumstances I am not sure what to say about x's beliefs *per se*, but it is correct to say that x said that p, provided that you keep in mind such-and-such aspects of the circumstances." In yet other cases even indirect discourse may commit us further than the evidence supports and we may retreat to describing, in the context of a narrative, what he said in direct discourse terms. All of these may be good, and in the circumstances the best available, responses to our interlocutor's interest in the person's views.

For example, among the ways we might describe the protagonist are the following:

He applies 'arthritis' in the normal way to ailments of the joints but also to similar-seeming ailments in other parts of the body. He believes that he has arthritis (perhaps with underlining intonation) in his thigh.

He applies 'arthritis' in the normal way to ailments of the joints but also to similar-seeming ailments in other parts of the body. He says that he has arthritis in his thigh.

He applies 'arthritis' in the normal way to ailments of the joints but also to similar-seeming ailments in other parts of the body. He says, "I have arthritis in my thigh."

Recall that some considerations pulled us toward describing the protagonist in the actual situation as believing that he has arthritis in his thigh; other considerations pulled us toward believing that he has tharthritis in his thigh. What we are seeing now is that both sets of considerations can receive their appropriate weight and reflection in an appropriately complex response to questions about a person's views on a topic.

How does Burge's counterfactual claim, that selected changes in external circumstances would shift the protagonist's belief contents, stand in the light of these observations? We might say that the observations show the claim to be false: because of the lack of detail in the description of the thought experiment we do not know what gloss would best figure in a correct description of the protagonist's belief in the actual situation, but because of the protagonist's misunderstanding, we can see that some gloss would be needed; the simple 'He believes that he has arthritis in his thigh' *can't* be a correct description of the protagonist's views. Such a criticism, however, gives the claim too much credit and underestimates the difficulty in which the strategy of the argument is embogged. A counterfactual cannot be understood unless one knows what in the actual situation to hold constant when imagining the counterfactual premiss true. Burge's argument leaves this crucial issue dark. Light on this matter, when it comes, will illuminate a scene in which all of the the protagonist's conversations in which others have used the word 'arthritis' is curiously buffered from social practice—buffered, in that people continue to use the same word in the same sentences, even though their meanings are significantly changed. A proposed description of a person's beliefs cannot be appraised unless one knows something about the social and physical environment—what kinds of occasions that invite application of the term is the environment likely to present?—and something about the protagonist's past behavior, including especially his past applications of relevant terms. Burge's argument leaves these crucial issues dark, also. About all one can say is that the social environment seems certain to be fairly bizarre, in ways that one would want to remark on in attributing beliefs to the protagonist. So much that is crucial is obscure, so much does it seem that clarifying one aspect of the situation would confound others, that it is best to say, not that the claim is false, but that it does not rise to the level of falsehood.

Let us turn to Burge's second claim, that shifts in the protagonist's belief contents imply that he has different beliefs. Once it is recognized that description of a person's beliefs may in general require a gloss, it is obvious that the question whether two persons, or a person and his or her counterfactual counterpart, believe the same thing becomes more complicated. To raise, out of the blue, this latter question invites the response, "what are you getting at?" It is easy to forget this so long as one thinks of belief ascriptions as always having the simple unglossed form '*x* believes that *p*.' For then one easily falls into thinking that the question of sameness or difference of belief reduces to the question of sameness or difference of meaning in the content sentence. But this is far from the truth. Consider George III and Franklin D. Roosevelt on the topic of political parties. With appropriate glosses, each believed that political parties make a constructive contribution to government. But did they believe the same thing, or have the same belief, about the role of political parties? One might naturally say, "No, they had such different experience of political parties and in such different circumstances, that we do not want to say that they had the same belief in this case." Or one might say, "Yes, they had the same belief, if you like to say so, but relative to the surrounding narrative that puts matters in their proper light." The question of identity here seems quite special, it has to be given a point, and we are not prepared in advance with criteria which enable us to address it.

Burge suggests a line along which he would respond to these criticisms. He notices the everyday practice of providing glosses on belief attributions. He mentions the following cases ([11], p. 91):

> Suppose I am advising you about your legal liabilities in a situation where you have entered into what may be an unwritten contract. You ask me what Al would think. It would be misleading for me to reply that Al would think that you do not have a contract ..., if I know that Al thinks a contract must be based on a formal document. Your evaluation of Al's thought would be crucially affected by his inadequate understanding. In such cases, it is incumbent on us to cite the subject's eccentricity: "(He would think that you do not have a contract, but then) he thinks that there is no such thing as a verbally based contract."

> ... the same sort of example can be constructed using attitudes that are abnormal, but do not hinge on misunderstanding of any one notion. If Al had thought that only traffic laws and laws against violent crimes are ever prosecuted, it would be misleading for me to tell you that Al would think that you have no legal problems.

He proceeds to the following general observations:

> Both sorts of cases illustrate that in reporting a single attitude content, we typically suggest (implicate, perhaps) that the subject has a range of other attitudes normally associated with it. ... it is usually important to keep track of, and often to make explicit, the nature and extent of the subject's deviance. Otherwise, predictions and evaluations of his thought and action, based on normal background assumptions, will go awry. When the deviance is huge, attributions demand reinterpretation of the subject's words. Radical misunderstanding and mental instability are cases in point. But frequently, common practice seems to allow us to cancel the misleading suggestions by making explicit the subject's deviance, retaining literal interpretations of his words in our mentalistic attributions all the while.

It is a long-standing philosophical project to distinguish literal falsity from other kinds of inappropriateness. There are in the literature a number of approaches, more or less completely worked out, to carrying out the project, the best known developed by Paul Grice.[5] Burge's remark that "common practice seems to allow us to cancel the misleading suggestions by making explicit the subject's deviance," and his parenthetical use earlier in the passage of the word 'implicate', suggest that he might defend his assumption that in the sorts of cases he is considering unglossed belief ascriptions can stand alone by appealing to the apparatus developed by Grice and others to sort our various kinds of implication and presupposition. Perhaps this line of defense can be made to work. There are, however, strong disanalogies between the present case of belief attribution and cases to which Grice's apparatus seems to apply most naturally and successfully.

---

[5] *Studies in the Ways of Words* [68], especially Chs. 2 ("Logic and Conversation"), 3 ("Further Notes on Logic and Conversation"), and 15 ("The Causal Theory of Perception").

In the cases of statements like 'the pillar box looks red' and 'my wife is either in the kitchen or in the bedroom' there are specific further propositions which are plausibly claimed to be implied, i.e., 'there is some reason to doubt or deny that the pillar box is red' and 'I do not know which room my wife is in'. There is then a question, which Grice's ideas are supposed to help us answer, of what impact failures of the implied conditions have on the possibility of truth or falsity of the original statements. By contrast, in the case of belief attribution, e.g., 'Al believes that you do not have a contract', there is no further specific statement that is implied; what is implied is rather some sweeping statement like, as Burge suggests, 'Al has a range of other attitudes that are normally associated with believing that you do not have a contract', or, in addition or alternatively, 'Al's understanding of the notion of contract conforms to ours in relevant respects' or 'generally speaking, Al would go on in new instances to apply his notion of contract in the same way we would apply ours'. This contrast is important in considering the applicability of Grice's notion of cancellability. The implication of 'the pillar box looks red' is cancellable in that one can withdraw the implication by saying, 'the pillar box looks red and in saying so I do not mean to imply that there is ground for doubting or denying that it is red'. In the case of 'my wife is either in the kitchen or in the bedroom' the implication that the speaker does not know which room she is in is cancellable by adding, 'and I am not saying that I don't know which'. It would be self-defeating, on the other hand, to say 'Al thinks that you do not have a contract, and I am not saying that his notion of contract conforms to ours in relevant respects'. This canceling clause goes too far in pulling the rug of meaning from under the initial statement. It is too close to saying, 'Al thinks you do not have a contract, and I am not saying he knows what a contract is'. These remarks do not show that Grice's framework, or something like it, cannot be deployed to defend Burge's arguments. They tend to show, however, that work remains to be done to so deploy it.

It is worth remembering that the point of Grice's distinctions and conversational principles is to give us tools for analyzing conversational oddity, to help us distinguish oddity that springs from violating norms concerning relevance, amount of information, and level of detail of information from oddity that springs from violating the norm that requires us to speak in a way that fits the facts. There is a strong intuition that, when the evidence on which attribution of attitudes is based contains relevant error and misunderstanding, or contains patterns and knowledge and ignorance and ways of understanding different from those our audience would normally expect, unglossed attributions of attitudes go wrong by failing to fit the facts.

Burge devotes a section of "Individualism and the Mental" ([11], pp. 92–99) to a long and sensitive discussion of how English speakers handle belief attributions in contexts where there are or have been relevant misunderstandings. He distinguishes "four ways of reinterpreting the thought experiment," i.e., four ways of weighing and registering the protagonist's misunderstanding of 'arthritis' in the actual situation so as to deny that he believes that he has arthritis in his thigh. The four ways are: treat the occurrence of 'arthritis' as *de re* ('He believes *of* arthritis that he has it in his thigh'); declare that the "subject's attitude or content is indefinite," i.e., so indefinite that no belief can be attributed; introduce a new term which exactly captures the subject's meaning (e.g., 'tharthritis') and use it in place of 'arthritis' in attributing the belief; or count the subject's error as purely metalinguistic ("the subject believes that 'arthritis' applies in English to the ailment in his thigh"). It is surprising that Burge does not discuss, in this important section of his paper, the most common way of giving misunderstandings their proper reflection in belief attributions, namely, qualifying the attribution with a gloss. This strategy is not only very common, it is infinitely subtle. In formulating a gloss we have all the resources of language at our disposal. Burge misleads himself by supposing that there are four discrete boxes into which reflections of deviance in the subject's use of words must fall. The truth is that there are an infinite number.

2 Contracts

Another of Burge's thought experiments of the first type, turning on a misunderstanding, involves a case in which someone, let's call him Daniel, is under the misconception that agreements are not legally binding, and therefore not contracts, unless they are written and signed by the parties. Thus we may imagine that Daniel assents to the following sentences:

> A contract must be written.

> It is part of the nature of current law and legal practice that unwritten agreements have no force in law.

It would presumably be a sympathetic extension of the case for Daniel to say of Edward, to whom he admits he has made a verbal promise:

> Edward can't sue me, because we don't have a contract.

As in the 'arthritis in the thigh' case, Daniel's usage of the term 'contract', while at variance with the surrounding society's, is imagined to be stable and consistent. In the counterfactual situation, the community meaning of 'contract' is the same as the meaning Daniel attaches to it in the actual situation, i.e., 'legally binding agreement based on a written document'. This change in usage, however, has left unchanged the underlying practice in the ways in which legally binding agreements can be reached. Verbal agreements may be legally binding. The counterfactual community may have another word for 'legally binding agreement not based on a written document'. Daniel's use of 'contract' in the counterfactual situation is the same as his use in the actual situation; thus in the counterfactual situation his usage conforms to the community's. In the counterfactual situation, however, Daniel is out of touch with the community in another way. He is not aware that legally binding agreements can be reached without being put in writing and is under the misconception that legally binding agreements can only be reached by being written down.

In Burge's view, the correct thing to say of Daniel in the actual situation is that he believes that contracts must be written. This is so because he affirms 'A contract must be written' and in attributing beliefs to him we must hold him accountable to social usage in the actual situation (i.e., to normal English usage). In Burge's view, the correct thing to say of Daniel in the counterfactual situation is that he does not believe that contracts must be written. This is so because, though he affirms 'A contract must be written', he is accountable to social usage in the counterfactual situation, where correct application of 'contract' is limited to written agreements; the content he expresses by his affirmation might be approximated: that a written contract must be written. Presumably Burge would say also that Daniel in the actual situation believes that he does not have a contract with Edward, while Daniel in the counterfactual does not believe this.

As in earlier cases, we have to ask two questions. Is it plausible that the cascade of changes flowing from the basic change will leave Daniel and his counterpart physiologically the same? And is it true that the beliefs of Daniel and his counterpart are correctly described in the way Burge claims?

It is important to keep in mind, in understanding this example, that the basic legal and economic practices are supposed to be the same in the actual and counterfactual situations; people in the two situations have the same resources for binding their future behavior toward each other with the force of law. And in both situations Daniel's grasp of the basic practices is the same; in both situations he is laboring under the misconception that legally binding agreements must be based on written documents. (It is clear that this is how Burge intends the case, for he says that Daniel is disposed to assent to 'It is part of the nature of the law and legal practice that unwritten agreements have no force'. Daniel's counterpart in the counterfactual situation must have the same disposition. Burge also says of the protagonist in the counterfactual situation, "the lawyer might have to point out [to him] that there are other legally binding agreements that do not require written documents.") With so much that is basic to law and economy the same, it does seem plausible that the change in society's usage of words might have occurred without changing Daniel's experience and physiological make-up. But this has to be said quite tentatively, for three reasons. Our use of the word 'contract' is no accident. The evolution of this use over the past four centuries is inseparable from the social changes associated with the rise of capitalism.[6] What other differences

---

[6] See, for example, Gabel and Feinman, "Contract Law as Ideology" [65] (pp. 172–184).

might have come in train with a more restricted application of the term, we hardly know. On the detailed level of Daniel's interactions with his peers, whether these interactions remain unchanged in the counterfactual situation depends on how we imagine the case. If Daniel in the actual situation had said, "Edward can't sue me," and had given as reason, "we don't have a contract," then Daniel in the counterfactual situation would have had to make the same utterances, otherwise the experience, and physiological make-up, of Daniel and his counterpart would have been different. If Daniel had said this in the counterfactual situation, his audience is likely to have responded, "That is not enough of a reason for thinking he can't sue you; there are other kinds of legally binding agreements besides contracts." In the actual situation the reasoning Daniel articulated was plausible to the audience; the misunderstanding which afflicted his thinking and his conclusions was, so far, hidden. The very same words, in the mouth of Daniel's counterpart, made error manifest. If the audience had responded by challenging his reasoning, then his experience would have been different from Daniel's in the actual situation. Finally, the earlier point that a standard way of taking a counterfactual assumption of a change in word meaning is that it is accompanied by a recoding of messages applies also in this case. As Burge is imagining the case, this convention is not in force. But then Daniel and his counterpart learned the word "contract" under circumstances in which the persons speaking to them were amazingly indifferent to what they were saying; somehow it didn't matter whether they put in the sentences Daniel heard a word that meant "contract" or one that meant "written contract." How could this be?

How would we describe the beliefs of Daniel and his counterpart? There is certainly some plausibility in saying, contrary to Burge, that Daniel's counterpart believes that contracts must be written. For there is some plausibility in saying that Daniel's counterpart believes that legally binding agreements must be written and, in the language in which the belief is being reported (our language), 'contract' and 'legally binding agreement' are somewhat like synonyms. The fact that Daniel in the actual situation learned 'contract' under circumstances in which his interlocutors were indifferent between using 'contract' and using 'written contract' gives some plausibility to saying that Daniel in the actual situation does not believe that contracts must be written, despite his assenting to a sentence that would normally express this content. There are pulls in the opposite directions as well. Normal practice gives expression to both pulls by accompanying the belief ascription with a gloss that makes explicit the misunderstandings present in the evidence. The more telling point, however, is that this confused situation provides a clear case in which the question, "Do they believe the same thing or not?" has to be *given* a point before we have any idea how to answer it. Again, the argument does not get off the ground.

3 Aluminum and Molybdenum

Another of Burge's thought experiments involves the replacement, in the counterfactual situation, of aluminum by molybdenum. In the counterfactual situation aluminum is as rare on Earth as molybdenum is in the actual situation, and molybdenum is as plentiful. In the counterfactual situation pots and pans are made of molybdenum; the inhabitants use molybdenum foil in food preparation and preservation; molybdenum paddles are used to propel molybdenum canoes. There is also an accompanying semantic shift; in the counterfactual situation "aluminum" is used to refer to molybdenum. The protagonist, let us call him Al, uses aluminum utensils and products in his daily life and has normal, but not specialist, knowledge of aluminum and molybdenum. Burge wants to say that in this case (i) Al and his counterpart in the counterfactual situation have the same physical history and physiological states and (ii) Al believes that *his* canoe is made of aluminum while his counterpart does not believe that his canoe is made of aluminum, but believes instead that it is made of molybdenum.[7]

This argument seems substantially different from the arthritis argument because there the major change was a change in the social usage of a term, whereas here the major change is a change in the physical environment. Also, the present argument appears not to turn essentially on a situation which involves a misunderstanding or confusion. As before, to appraise the argument is to appraise two claims.

First, there is a complex counterfactual the key elements of which can be summarized as follows: If aluminum and molybdenum had been interchanged in the way described and this difference had in no way impinged on the experience of the protagonist, then the correct description of the protagonist would shift from 'She believes that her canoe is made of aluminum' (the correct description in the actual situation) to 'She believes that her canoe is made of molybdenum' (the correct description in the counterfactual situation).

Second, there is a claim connecting the shift in correct descriptions with identity and difference of belief: If the correct description of the protagonist's beliefs shifts in this way from the actual to the counterfactual situation, then her beliefs in the actual situation are different from her beliefs in the counterfactual situation.

Some of the points made in assessing the arthritis argument transpose in obvious ways to apply to the present argument. The question of the intelligibility of the antecedent of the complex conditional deserves special treatment.

---

[7] This case is adapted from Putnam, "The Meaning of 'Meaning' " [134]. Burge endorses the argument, but deploys a slightly different version of it which we take up in due course.

In the actual situation, on earth, aluminum is the most plentiful metallic element, the third most common of all elements, and composes 8 percent of the crust by weight. Molybdenum is a trace element in plant and animal metabolism; it has a specific gravity slightly smaller than that of lead, significantly greater than that of iron, and about four times that of aluminum; it has an extremely high melting point (aluminum, 660 degrees centigrade; molybdenum, 2620 degrees centigrade). What else would be different in a counterfactual situation in which molybdenum is as plentiful as aluminum is in the actual situation, and is used in ways similar to the ways in which aluminum is used? Consider that the distributions of elements in the earth is no accident; it is an empirical question whether it could have been as radically different as we are asked to imagine it in this case without Al's being physically different. To take one tack, for example, the inner planets in our solar system, and the Earth's moon, all have a similar composition; the outer planets, on the other hand, have a composition quite different from that of the inner planets and are significantly less dense. Is this the sort of empirical regularity we are supposed to take into account in deciding whether Al and his counterpart would be physically identical? Or another tack: plant and animal metabolic systems might have evolved differently in an environment in which molybdenum was plentiful; plant and animal bodies, including that of Al's counterpart, might be physically different; again, it is an empirical question. Another tack: using molybdenum pots, pans, and canoes would be like wearing lead tennis shoes and paddling lead canoes; wouldn't our muscles, and the bones the muscles move, and the nervous system serving the muscles, be different if we regularly placed the them under greater loads? Another tack: the problems of refining, forming into household products, and transporting large quantities of a substance as recalcitrant as molybdenum are such that a society which found it economical to do this must be very different from our own, perhaps in placing an extremely high value on heavy, silvery pans, say for religious reasons, or perhaps in having much cheaper sources of energy. It is also noteworthy that on Earth aluminum, being so plentiful, is ingested almost continuously by most human beings and that it can play a role in the etiology of diseases of the nervous system, including Alzheimer's disease (Brody [9]). What are the counterparts to these effects with molybdenum in the counterfactual situation? Given all these ways in which the basic change on which the thought experiment turns might have changed the physical constitution of the protagonist, how are we supposed to assure ourselves that Al and his counterpart are physically identical? How does that environment work?

The implications of the difference in specific gravity between aluminum and molybdenum can be seen in another way. Burge implies that Al and his counterpart have the same non-intentionally described dispositions. This claim can be probed by the following test. The experimenter will present to each subject an aluminum pan and a molybdenum pan made of the same volume of material and having the same shape, size, and thickness; the molybdenum pan will weigh about four times as much as the aluminum pan. The experimenter will say to the subjects: "Here are two pans, one made of aluminum and the other made of a rare metal called 'molybdenum'. We would like you to handle the pans, lift them, do what you like with them, then tell us whether the aluminum pan is heavier, lighter, or about the same weight as the molybdenum pan." This is the stimulus, the same for both protagonists. It seems plausible that Al in the actual situation will respond by saying, "the aluminum pan is lighter," and that his counterpart will respond by saying, "the aluminum pan is heavier." Al and his counterpart, presented with the same stimulus, have given different responses; they have different non-intentionally described dispositions. What makes this story plausible is that, given the way the case is presented, we assume that each protagonist is familiar with the pans in her world and knows what heft to expect of a pan of which 'aluminum' is true. The difference in weight between the pans is so obvious and striking that each quickly identifies "the aluminum pan," each identifying a different pan, because of the different meanings they attach to "aluminum." Having identified "the aluminum pan," the judgment of comparative weights is easily and immediately made. Al reports, correctly, that the aluminum pan is lighter; his counterpart reports, correctly, that the molybdenum pan is heavier.

It might be replied to this objection that, of course, if the subjects have had experiences of lifting pans in their environments, learning experiences which enable them to make the discriminations the objector assumes they will make in the stimulus-response test, then the subjects have already had different experiences, having lifted pans of different weights, developed muscles with different strengths, and so on. This reply makes a correct point: for the difference in disposition to have developed there must have been a prior difference in experience. But it brings to light an oddity in the example. If the example is to have any chance of establishing the intended point, Al and his counterpart must have had only the most distant inter-actions with aluminum and molybdenum objects. Al has not used utensils made of aluminum, lest Al and his counterpart have different experiences of heft; Al has not ridden in, much less lifted, an aluminum canoe, because the canoes of Al and his counterpart, with their different mass, would sit, and move, differently in the water.

Let us turn to the belief ascriptions in the consequent of the complex counterfactual conditional. How inclined will we be to say, point blank, that Al believes that his canoe is made of aluminum while Al's counterpart believes that his canoe is made of molybdenum? As the previous discus-sion brings out, much is obscure in how we are supposed to imagine the situation. It seems clear, however, that if the antecedent of the conditional is to have a chance of being true, then Al's interactions with aluminum in the actual situation, and his counterpart's interactions with molybdenum in the counterfactual situation, will have to be bizarrely distant and tenu-ous. The bizarre circumstances will be the material for glosses in describing the subjects' beliefs about the metals. What about sameness and difference of belief? As in the arthritis case, this question has to be given a point. Given that Al and his counterpart have been shielded from the differences in weight, metabolic role, and so forth which molybdenum has with aluminum, then, having qualified our attributions of attitudes with appropriate glosses ("He can't tell, from the heft, the difference between an aluminum canoe and a lead one. Of course, a lead canoe is much heavier, but he doesn't actually paddle her aluminum canoe, or help lift it. Etc."), we might say that they have the same belief, using this as a way of pointing up their obliviousness to, and immunity from, striking differences that are all about in the environment.

In another paper Burge gives a version of the aluminum/molybdenum argument in which molybdenum drops out and is replaced, not by a specific metal, but by "a similar looking metal" ([15], p. 5). This alteration in the argument may have been designed to avoid difficulties like those we have just seen with molybdenum, though Burge does not say this. In the story Burge tells, the protagonist in the actual situation "thinks that aluminum is a light metal used in sailboat masts," "can pick out instances of aluminum," and knows "many general facts about aluminum." The counterfactual environment "lacks aluminum and has in its places a similar-looking light metal." It is fair to ask Burge: what is this metal? A glance at the periodic table shows that there is no metallic element which fits the needs of the argument any better than molybdenum. So presumably it is an alloy? But what alloy? How do we know that the existence of such an alloy is consistent with the laws of nature, or that its widespread distribution in masts, pots, and foil is consistent with the laws of economics without there being other systematic differences in the environment which would impinge causally on members of the society, including the counterpart of the protagonist? And what differences would these differences make to the glosses we would use in describing the beliefs of the protagonist and his or her counterpart?

In setting out these aluminum examples Burge is careful to emphasize the limits of the protagonist's knowledge of aluminum, that she is "ignorant of aluminum's chemical structure (sic) and microproperties." This limitation on knowledge is needed to help make it plausible that the counterfactual change is compatible with the protagonist's remaining physically the same. For suppose that Alice is a metallurgist who has done detailed experimental studies of aluminum. Then it is natural to construe the counterfactual situation so that Alice does the same studies, but of the metal that replaces aluminum. When she does this, of course, she will get different results, see different meter readings, have different experiences. We do not object to the crafting of the example to try to avoid this kind of objection. It is a mistake, however, to slip from this into the view that aluminum's unknown properties have not been crucial in allowing it to play the role it does in nature, in our form of life, and in the experiences of individuals.

That aluminum has a low melting point may be unknown to most of us;
the pervasive presence of aluminum utensils in our environment, which has
partly determined the experiences we have had, nevertheless depends on it.

So we confront again what is becoming a familiar pattern: we don't really know how we are supposed to imagine the situation. If aluminum and
its counterpart metal are diabolically clever look-alike, feel-alike, weigh-
alike, and, generally, phenomenologically-alike, but physically different,
metals, which the protagonists somehow avoid ingesting and of the physics
of which they are ignorant, then there will be pressures to construe the term
'aluminum' as expressing for both a concept whose extension includes both
metals and to describe them as having the same beliefs about the composition of their masts and canoes. There will be pressures in the opposite
direction as well. The normal way of ascribing beliefs to give appropriate
weight to these pressures is to use glosses which make explicit the remarkable circumstances.

4 Review and Diagnosis

Having examined in some detail several arguments which use the same general strategy, it may be useful to step back and reflect on their methods.
The arguments make extensive use of and, as it were, put in center stage
two practices from everyday life which, in everyday life, are heavily context
dependent. These are, first, propositional attitudes and, second, counterfactual conditionals. The arguments run off the rails by misconstruing
these context dependencies.

In the case of propositional attitudes, the culprit is the myth of sharp
content. This is the view that the *normal expectation* is that a question
of the form 'Does x believe that p?'—where 'p' holds a place to be filled
by a declarative sentence—is a genuine question and should have a definite
answer, yes or no. The expectation of a definite answer, on this view, can
be defeated only by vagueness or ambiguity in the content sentence in the
subordinate 'that'-clause. But matters are not this simple. The truth is
that when we confront a belief sentence with the relevant evidence we may
find that we can give a direct answer, yes or no; we may find that we do not
know what to say, because the evidence contains so many signs of confusion
and mixed messages; and there is an infinite range of cases in between where
we can say something useful, to the point and to the topic, but not a simple
yes or no. The sources of this complexity lie deep in the nature of language.
The language user mobilizes past learning to go on, to talk and to listen,
in the present communication situation. If we think of the terms in the
language, a simple picture of this phenomenon is that the speaker learned
to apply and withhold the term in a range of representative cases, then
went on to apply the term in new circumstances, sometimes successfully,
sometimes not, always learning from both the successes and the failures. It
is this background, nothing less and nothing more, which the speaker brings

to the present communication situation. Each participant in the present communication situation brings this kind of background. The task of the participants in communicating is to coordinate the backgrounds so as to understand and be understood. When they use belief sentences, the circle of coordination expands to include the subject of belief attributions. The complexity of communication is well-captured by Ramsey (in *Foundations of Mathematics and Other Logical Essays* [146], pp. 263–264):

> I used to worry myself about the nature of philosophy through excessive scholasticism. I could not see how we could understood a word and not be able to recognize whether a proposed definition of it was or was not correct. I did not realize the vagueness of the whole idea of understanding, the reference it makes to a multitude of performances any of which may fail and require to be restored.

The everyday practice of attribution of belief has the complexity Ramsey attributes to philosophy. Of course there will be many cases in which the coordination of backgrounds is firmly established and running smoothly and where no gloss on belief sentences is needed. Of course there will be cases in which the task of appropriate coordination of backgrounds around a particular content sentence defeats the communicators. And of course there will be cases in which coordination sufficient to advance the discussion can be achieved, but only by bringing into the foreground, as a gloss, features of the background that surprise normal expectations.

Burge uses repeatedly the metaphor of "partial" or "incomplete" understanding in characterizing and defending his arguments. He says, for example, that in constructing arguments which turn essentially on a misunderstanding, "one may pick a case in which the subject only partially understands the expression" ([11], p. 82). These metaphors set up an illusory ideal. "Partial understanding" suggests that we have a usable notion of complete understanding and perhaps also that we may use with some security metaphors of closeness to and distance from complete understanding. Such a picture misconstrues the complex task of coordination that is communication. If one reviews the way we use 'understand', one finds a prodigious variety of glosses, i.e., of ways of not understanding, which seem to fall in a number of different dimensions. They occur in the discussions which specialists have about their subject as well as in the discussions among novices and in mixed groups of novices and specialists. Complete understanding has not more application to our experience of communication than does complete knowledge to our experience of learning. If we learn a little more, we will understand a little differently. The temptation to deny this is of a piece with the myth of sharp content.

The myth of sharp content is tempting and curiously difficult to put out of one's mind. Davidson has questioned the myth in a recent paper ("Knowing One's Own Mind" [40], p. 449), giving an example involving misunderstanding, and concluding:

... the contents of one belief necessarily depend on the contents of others. Thoughts are not independent atoms, and so there can be no simple, rigid, rule for the correct attribution of a single thought.

A few pages later, however (pp. 454–455), Davidson seems to slip back into the myth, for he writes:

We will always need an infinite supply of objects to help describe and identify attitudes like belief; I am not suggesting for a moment that belief sentences, and sentences that attribute other attitudes, are not relational in nature. What I am suggesting is that the objects to which we relate people in order to describe their attitudes need not in any sense be *psychological* objects, objects to be grasped, known, or entertained by the person whose attitudes are described.

In saying that the relata need not be psychological objects, Davidson perhaps has in mind his paratactic account of the logical form of sentences of indirect discourse, according to which the relata are speech acts. Whatever the relata, the view that belief, and other attitude, sentences are relational seems to require that thoughts *are* independent atoms, for the view leads us to expect that, in the vast range of normal cases, once the argument places of the relational term are filled with expressions of the appropriate kind, the question whether the resulting sentence is true or false will have a definite answer. But this is the expectation that Davidson seemed to reject in saying that thoughts are not independent atoms and that there can be no simple, rigid rule for the correct attribution of a single thought. A juxtaposition of analogous claims for 'heavier than'—it's a relation, but the things it relates are not independent atoms and there can be no simple, rigid rule for saying whether one thing is heavier than another—would be plainly absurd.

The myth of sharp content might be called Frege's grin. Frege gave us a picture of the logical form of belief sentences, and an ontology to match the form, in which belief sentences are relational in the strictest possible sense: the expressions on either side of 'believes' in a belief sentence are singular terms which refer to objects. Frege's ontology of thoughts was needed to provide referents for 'that'-clauses. Davidson and Quine reject Fregean thoughts in their philosophies of language and mind. Many of the reasons Quine has given for questioning the identity conditions of thoughts, or propositions, are of course reasons for rejecting the myth of sharp content. It is puzzling, given all this, that both Davidson and Quine retain the project of giving an account of the logical form of belief sentences, that is, the project of saying generally how the truth conditions of a belief sentence depend on the semantical functions of its parts. Quine's flight from intension, and Davidson's paratactic account, abandon Frege's thoughts, but keep Frege's grin.[8]

---

[8] See Quine's *Word and Object* [141], Chapter 6.

The counterfactual conditional is the other context-dependent device which Burge's arguments misconstrue. The basic difficulty is that we are sometimes uncertain, or completely in the dark, about what to hold constant in the light of the counterfactual assumption. A question whether such-and-such could happen, or what would happen if such-and-such were the case, invites the response: compatibly with what? Ramsey [145] gives examples which illustrate this point. Sometimes we have to discard, temporarily, some background information (but which?) before drawing consequences from a counterfactual assumption: "If he was there, he must have voted for it (or it was passed unanimously), but if he had been there he would have voted against it (such being his nature)" (p. 249), illustrates that syntactical variations sometimes indicate what background information to discard. In other cases we suffer from a dearth of background information: "If he had shuffled the cards, he would have dealt himself the ace" (p. 253). Ramsey "has no clear sense true or false," presumably because of lack of sufficiently determinate background information. Consider the role of background information in the following sequence:

If match m had been scratched, then it would have lighted.

m could have been scratched without lighting.

If m had been scratched without lighting, then it would have been the case that either m was wet or m was not well-made or insufficient oxygen was present.

m could have been scratched without lighting even though m was dry, well-made, and oxygen was present in normal concentration.

If m was dry, well-made, in the presence of a normal concentration oxygen, and was scratched without lighting, then ...?

This sequence reminds us that we have some capacity, in dealing with 'could' statements and counterfactuals, to call on different sets of background information and to shift intelligibly from one set to another. It also suggests that as normal expectations are withdrawn, we fairly quickly reach a point where we do not know what to say. It is true that we frequently use counterfactual statements with confidence, point, and success in everyday communication. In these successful uses, subtle and mutually understood contextual factors appear to fix what is to be held constant. In philosophical discussion and argument, the context which in everyday communication helps determine the sense of counterfactual statements is likely to be lacking; when this is so, explicit declaration of what is to be held fixed is necessary. With counterfactuals, we are always on the verge of being at sea. Counterfactuals like, 'If aluminum were replaced all over the Earth by a similar-looking light metal, then ...', put us at sea. This would be disturbing enough if all we had to judge was whether or not the protagonist would remain physiologically unchanged in the counterfactual situation. But in this special setting of argument, which depends both on counterfactuals and propositional attitudes, it is especially problematic. For the attribution of attitudes takes place against a background of normally expected challenges to going on correctly, in the application of terms and in the use of language generally, in new cases. If we are at sea with regard to the argument's key counterfactual, we are at sea with regard to the background of challenges on which correct attribution of attitudes depends. We might put the matter as follows. Counterfactuals, when they are figuring smoothly in communication, rest on our having a grasp of what is held constant under the counterfactual assumption. Propositional attitudes, when they are figuring smoothly in communication, rest on our grasp of a background of normally expected challenges to the correct use of language. Thought experiments of the kind we have been considering loosen our grasp on both of these backgrounds simultaneously. This is why they tend to run into the sand.

5 Is the Mind Socially Constituted?

An intuition that the individual self is socially constituted has moved poets and philosophers to some of their most haunting expressions. Thinking itself is compellingly modeled as talking to oneself. And it can seem that we possess our mental and moral qualities only when others acknowledge them and reflect them back to us.

> ... man, how dearly ever parted,
> How much in having, or without or in,
> Cannot make boast to have that which he hath,
> Nor feels not what he owes but by reflection;
> As when his virtues aiming upon others
> Heat them, and they retort that heat again
> To the first giver.   *Troilus and Cressida*, III iii 96ff.

> No man is the lord of anything ...
> Till he communicate his parts to others.
> Nor doth he of himself know them for aught
> Till he behold them formed in th' applause
> Where they're extended; who [which] like an arch reverb'rate
> The voice again.   *Troilus and Cressida*, III iii 115ff.

> What went forth to the ends of the world to traverse not itself, God, the sun, Shakespeare, a commercial traveller, having itself traversed in reality itself becomes that self. Wait a moment. Wait a second. Damn that fellow's noise in the street. Self which it was ineluctably preconditioned to become.   *Ulysses* (Gabler ed.), p. 412.

It is plausible that a style of philosophy which pursues clarity through patient drawing of distinctions and analysis of arguments could make an important contribution to the discussion of these ideas and issues. Burge deserves credit for tackling issues about the self and its place in society. It has to be said, however, that the tools he brings to the task are utterly unsuited for it. The thought experiments ignore the daunting complexities of counterfactual reasoning and take for granted the myth of sharp content. In doing so they hide fundamental facts about the social character of language and communication. A more fruitful approach will begin with these facts.[9]

---

[9] We are grateful to C. A. Anderson, Joseph Owens, Michael Root, and Naomi Scheman for their helpful comments on earlier versions of this paper.

8

Belief and the Identity of Reference

KEITH DONNELLAN

WHAT HAS SOMETIMES been called the "new theory of reference," although it isn't that new anymore, faced from the beginning a couple of embarrassing problems. One has to do with existence, which I won't address here. The other has to do with propositional attitudes, or, more precisely, reports of propositional attitudes, reports about beliefs, desires, and other mental states which involve propositions. Saul Kripke, in his paper "A Puzzle About Belief" [96], has proposed a radical way of dealing with this second problem.

I believe Kripke's paper may be a breakthrough for anyone who thinks, as I do, that the new theory of reference is essentially correct. I think, however, that the paper does not quite justify the title. Kripke makes use of a nest of principles having to do with our treatment of the believer's linguistic avowals of belief. I am inclined to protest that the puzzle really is a puzzle about *belief*, about the psychological state itself, which at best manifests itself in one guise as a derivable consequence of such principles. My protest, however, is in no way a rejection of Kripke's general strategy for dealing with the problem posed for the new theory of reference; indeed it is in its unveiling of the strategy that his paper represents, for me at least, a breakthrough.

I

The details of the new theory of reference are well known by now. But let me emphasize a few general points which will concern us here. The theory can be divided into a negative and a positive aspect (with the latter having variations which won't concern us).

The negative aspect is that classical theories about how singular terms must function are wrong. Indexicals, such as 'I', 'here', 'now', and proper names, 'Paris', 'John Stuart Mill', are paradigms of singular terms. Definite descriptions, such as 'the capital of France', 'the most famous utilitarian', etc., are also singular terms. On the classical theory there is no great difference between the two. On the new theory of reference there is a big gulf. But here let's just look at proper names.

Classical theories about the reference of proper names hold that the users of a name must in some way have access to criteria, in the end necessary and sufficient conditions, for the correct application of the name—else, they might say, how could the name really refer to anything?

The new theory of reference by various examples and arguments has shown, I believe, that the classical theory is mistaken. I can, to use my own example, succeed in referring to Thales when I say, "Thales held that all is water," even though the stock of properties I could come up which someone would have to have to be Thales would be either insufficient to pick out any particular person or, worse, might just happen to fit some wanderer in the agora. And similar sorts of objections can be made, I believe, to any variants on the classical view, even current sophisticated ones using modal techniques.

The positive side of the theory can be simply stated: proper names have no semantic function other than to refer to their bearers. In this the theory echoes Bertrand Russell's account of what he called "names" in "the proper strict logical sense of the word." [1] The vital difference, of course, is that the kind of names for which Russell suggested this account form such a restricted set—names of items in immediate experience and possibly of universals—that many have doubted that such names even exist. The new theory of reference holds, on the other hand, that mundane everyday proper names directly refer to their bearers without the mediation of sense, meaning or anything of the kind.

It is perhaps possible to hold that the new theory of reference is correct on the negative side, that it succeeds in its attack on classical reference theory, while not embracing the positive side, that is, while denying that ordinary proper names directly refer in this unadorned manner. For this reason I will call the positive side, following current usage, the "direct reference theory." [2]

The problem facing the direct reference theory is by now well-known. If proper names have no other semantic role but to refer, then it appears that if two proper names refer to the same individual then a principle of substitution is warranted, a principle that says that substitution of one name for the other will not only preserve truth value but also the proposition expressed. And this gives rise to apparently fatal difficulties when the substitutions are made in propositional attitude contexts. In the well-worn example, the ancient Babylonians had two names for what in fact is a single planet. As it appeared as the last heavenly body before dawn they called it "Phosphorus" and as it appeared as the first in the evening they

---

[1] The expression is used in Lecture II of "The Philosophy of Logical Atomism" [153], p. 201. The doctrine, of course, occurs in many places in Russell's writings.

[2] I believe the expression is due to David Kaplan.

called it "Hesperus," not realizing that a single object was involved. It seems straightforward to imagine that they believed that Phosphorus was the god of light, while not believing this about Hesperus. But since the two names in fact refer to the same object, the direct reference theory seems, via substitution, to give the unpalatable result that the ancient Babylonians both believed Phosphorus to be the god of light and did not believe that Phosphorus is the god of light.

To make matters worse, theories about proper names such as that of Russell seem to have no problems dealing with these cases. The names 'Hesperus' and 'Phosphorus', it would be said, abbreviate different definite descriptions and so different propositions are expressed by 'Phosphorus is the god of light' and 'Hesperus is the god of light'. The Babylonians in the imagined example believe the first and do not believe the second and there is no contradiction.

II

Philosophers who are persuaded by the attack on the classical view of reference and who then move to a direct reference theory have sometimes attempted to get out of their difficulties with propositional attitudes, such as believing, by attempting some new analysis of reports of these attitudes.

It is tempting to try to find something which doesn't amount to a Fregean sense or to meaning which nevertheless does the job of distinguishing when it is true that, e.g., an ancient astronomer believed that Hesperus is Hesperus from when it is true that the same astronomer believed that Phosphorus is Hesperus.

With indexicals, as opposed to proper names, this strategy may have a hope of succeeding. David Kaplan's notion of the character of an indexical such as 'I' or 'here' or 'tomorrow' associates with the indexical a semantical rule for assigning to it a referent which is nevertheless not to be equated with a sense or meaning as in classical theories.[3] Suppose someone thinks "I am handsome" while merely ruminating on his virtues, and the same person while gazing at himself in a mirror without realizing that the image is of himself thinks "He is not handsome." On the view of demonstratives and indexicals which makes them directly referential, the proposition involved seems identical in the two episodes. But the threatened paradox of a person both believing a proposition and believing its negation at the same time may be forestalled by the fact that in the one case the person expresses the proposition to himself employing the indexical 'I' which makes its contribution to the expression of the proposition via its "character," a character which, of course, is not functioning when he expresses the same proposition using the demonstrative 'he'. The notion of "character" may have the potential for short-circuiting the paradoxes which constitute the problem for the direct reference theory. But, unfortunately, proper names

---

[3] I am not attributing this "resolution" of the problem to Kaplan.

have nothing associated with them which plays the role of "character" for indexicals. So that when we are dealing with the possible contradictory beliefs one may have when they are expressed by two *names* for the same thing, we cannot look to this sort of remedy.

The attempt to disarm the paradoxes in the case of proper names by an analysis of statements ascribing beliefs which seems to me to come closest to succeeding is that made by Nathan Salmon in his book *Frege's Puzzle* [157]. Belief is treated as a three-termed relation among a believer, a proposition and a "guise" under which the proposition is believed. The guise plays the role of the mode of presentation under which the proposition is believed, but it is no part of the content of the proposition believed. The upshot of Salmon's analysis is that in the Hesperus/Phosphorus story, the ancient Babylonians believed that Phosphorus was the first star of the morning, but under a certain guise. One can say without contradiction that they also did not believe that Hesperus was the first star of the morning, if that means that there is a guise under which they did not believe the proposition. But if it means that it is simply false that they believed the proposition, that under no guise do they believe it, a contradiction, of course, would result. In the story, as we have it, however, it simply is not true that the Babylonians were in this situation. They do believe that Hesperus is the first star of the morning, however much they may deny this when it is put to them using the name 'Hesperus'.

Salmon is willing to admit that our raw intuitions do not go along with this, that we are inclined to say that in the story, it is simply false that the ancient Babylonians believed that Hesperus is the first star of the morning. These intuitions and others (e.g., that contrary to the Salmon analysis, it is simply false that the ancient Babylonians believed that Hesperus is Phosphorus and certainly false that they believed that Hesperus is not Hesperus) Salmon needs to explain away. I find the necessity for this sort of explanation a somewhat heavy burden for the theory to bear, given that intuitions are usually the bottom line in philosophical argumentation.[4] Still, if the analysis is correct, the problem raised by Hesperus/Phosphorus-like cases for the direct reference view would be gotten over.

---

[4] And there is another consideration which bothers me, namely what to say about the beliefs of the ancient Babylonians when expressed using our name for the heavenly body involved, 'Venus'. It seems that on Salmon's view the answers are clear cut in the end: They believed, for example, that Venus is not identical to Phosphorus (because they believed that Hesperus [= Venus] is not identical to Phosphorus) and they believed that Venus is identical to Phosphorus (because they believed that Phosphorus [= Venus] is identical to Phosphorus). But I find it very dubious that any such beliefs expressed by using the name 'Venus' can be attributed to the ancient Babylonians. I am not satisfied, then, that Salmon's analysis is correct, although my reasons for feeling this are less than absolutely conclusive.

III

In "A Puzzle About Belief" [96], Kripke's remedy is radically different. He proposes no new analysis of sentences ascribing beliefs or other propositional attitudes, nor novel ways in which we might enjoy something like Frege's "modes of presentation" without erecting them into senses.

Instead the problem is to be, as the title of his paper suggests, a puzzle about *belief* (and other propositional attitudes). A puzzle, thus, that all theories of reference are saddled with. Or so one might conclude.

I think that Kripke may have shown us, we who want to defend the new theory of reference, the way to go. But I am more dubious that he has shown us that there is a puzzle about belief.

Let's first see what Kripke's argument is, because there can be some misconceptions about it.

In developing the puzzle about belief, Kripke uses three principles (pp. 248–250): the *disquotational principle*, the *reverse disquotational principle*, as I shall call it, and the *principle of translation*:

Disquotation:
If a normal speaker of L, on reflection, sincerely assents to 'p', then he believes that p.

(There are a number of qualifications, as Kripke points out, which would need to be made if the principle is to be made fully acceptable.)

Reverse Disquotation:
If a normal speaker of L believes that p, then he will be disposed to "sincere reflective assent to 'p'."

(Kripke proposes a "strengthened 'biconditional' form of the disquotational principle" which I have here separated into its two directions.)

Translation:
If a sentence of one language expresses a truth in that language, then any translation of it into any other language also expresses a truth (in that other language).

All three principles have some initial plausibility, especially the principle of translation. (The first, the principle of disquotation, however, which purports to connect the propositional attitude, belief, with verbal behavior would certainly give some philosophers some pause.)

By developing a couple of ingenious examples of what could happen in the ordinary way of things, Kripke appeals to our intuitions about when we would say that someone believed, disbelieved, or had no belief, to argue that with these three principles at hand we can develop the very same paradoxical results which the direct theory of reference is supposed to founder upon. From just the principle of disquotation and translation and some not extraordinary background circumstances, and without any theory of reference involved at all, one can, Kripke argues, arrive at the same paradoxical result that the new theory of reference has been charged with.

A fast reading of Kripke's paper might give one the impression that the argument is that there are some very plausible principles about language which do not involve a principle of substitution nor any theory of reference and which together can yield the same paradoxical result which opponents charge the direct reference theory with. So, it's a sort of standoff.

I believe that that isn't Kripke's argument and there is good reason why it shouldn't be. If that were the argument, a lot would depend upon how plausible his two principles are as compared to the argument that the new theory of reference forces on us the validity of substitution with its apparently paradoxical consequences.

Instead, what Kripke argues is that opponents of direct reference presuppose, in their argument, at least the disquotational principle and, in applying their argument to particular examples, the other two principles as well.

But where in their argument do the presuppositions come in? They come in at the very point where, using any particular example, the argument appeals to our intuitions about belief states. The problem for the direct reference theory comes to this: On the direct reference theory proper names such as 'Cicero' and 'Tully' seem to make the same semantic contribution; they both do no more than to pick out a referent and in this case the same referent. So, as Kripke asks, on behalf of the opponents, "How, then, can anyone believe that Cicero was bald, yet doubt or disbelieve that Tully was" if the direct reference theory is correct? But *of course we all know*, it seems, that someone certainly can be in just such a state.

It is just here—in the seemingly innocuous appeal to what we all know to be possible—that the ancient Babylonians, to shift the example, might well have believed that Hesperus was on certain dates the first star of the evening while doubting that Phosphorus was—that the presupposition of Kripke's principles is supposed to enter.

The problem posed for the direct reference theory appeals to our intuitions that a certain psychological state, a certain belief state, is possible—a state which the direct reference view seems to rule out. "Why," Kripke asks (p. 248), "do we think that anyone *can* [emphasis mine] believe that Cicero was bald, but fail to believe that Tully was?" "Well," he says, "a normal English speaker, Jones, can sincerely assent to 'Cicero was bald' but not to 'Tully was bald'."

Kripke then says, "Let us make explicit the *disquotational principle* presupposed here, connecting sincere assent and belief." He then gives the principle: "If a normal English speaker, on reflection, sincerely assents to 'p', then he believes that p."

Kripke's argument, then, seems to be this. The opponents of the direct reference theory maintain that it licenses a principle of substitution in ascriptions of believe that would make it seem impossible for it to be true that someone, e.g., believes Cicero to be bald but fails to believe that Tully is bald, given their identity. The opponents make this out to be an objectionable result by appealing to our intuitions that someone can be in just such a state. But these intuitions of ours depends upon our acceptance of the three principles, the two disquotation principles and the translation principle. These principles are principles of our practice in ascribing belief states and our intuitions about what belief states are possible depends upon accepting them. So in appealing to our intuitions, the opponents of the direct reference view are tacitly accepting these principles.

But, and this is the kicker, the same paradox upon which the direct reference theory is supposed to founder, can be derived from just those principles alone, without any theory of reference being assumed at all.

In other words, quite independently of any theory of reference we might adopt, there is a paradox which can be derived from principles we use in ascribing beliefs to people. And those who pose the objection to the direct reference theory must implicitly rely upon these principles. (That is why Kripke's argument does more than simply claim to be able to derive the paradox from another source.) The principles, of course, result in paradox only in certain cases—the very cases which are used to attack the direct reference view. This, if I am correct, is why Kripke thinks we are dealing with a puzzle about belief, not a problem with the direct reference theory itself.

IV

This is an ingenious solution to what seemed at times to be an intractable problem for the theory of reference some of us hold near and dear. As I have said, I think Kripke's approach may well be a breakthrough. But I have some worries about the actual argument.

If I am correct about the structure of Kripke's argument, everything depends upon whether we *do* presuppose his three principles in our intuitions about puzzle cases—the Cicero/Tully and Phosphorus/Hesperus sort of examples. If our intuitions aren't necessarily based on these principles, then the fact that one can derive the same paradox from the principles that critics of the direct reference theory purport to derive from it will give us only the weaker conclusion that the paradox is not the peculiar burden of the direct reference view.

So, my worry about Kripke's reliance on these principles comes down to questioning whether our intuitions which the critics of direct reference theory trade upon do in fact involve a use of the principles.

Well, let's take one of the two well-known cases. In the Hesperus/Phosphorus case we are, for example, asked to agree that of course the ancient Babylonians might have believed that Phosphorus is the first star of the morning and also disbelieved that Hesperus is—even though their names in fact referred to the same star. Let's suppose that our intuitions are in entire agreement with this. In what way do our intuitions involve Kripke's three principles?

Let's look at the disquotational principle. To paraphrase Kripke, "Why do we think that an ancient Babylonian can believe that Phosphorus is the first star of the morning, but fail to believe that Hesperus is?" Is it really that we are assuming some such principle as that "If a normal Babylonian speaker, on reflection, sincerely assents to, in Babylonian, let's say, 'The first star of the morning is Phosphorus,' then he believes that the first star of the morning is Phosphorus?" Are we also assuming the principle, "If a Babylonian assents to 'The first star of the morning is not Hesperus' then he believes that the first star in the evening is not Hesperus?"

Insofar as we have the intuition that the ancient Babylonians could have believed that Phosphorus is the first star of the morning and at the same time believed that Hesperus is not, although the same star is the object of both beliefs, I very much doubt that we make use of the principle of disquotation.

It is no doubt very plausible that in our ascriptions of beliefs to each other we often make use of the disquotation principle or something like it. Perhaps we do assume that what we take to be sincere assenting to a sentence is *prima facie*, at least, proof that the assenter believes what the sentence expresses.

In fact if the principle is hedged around enough, disquotation may have the status of a truism. If it is in the end a truism, then, of course, it is entailed by anything whatsoever and so entailed by our intuition about the ancient Babylonians. But the question, I believe, is whether our intuition depends upon the principle of disquotation. And I hesitate to say that it does. It certainly is not that I have known some ancient Babylonians who have confided in me their assents and dissents in these matters. That is, I don't think that insofar as I have an intuition about the possible belief states of the ancient Babylonians that it involves making use of the principle of disquotation.

I think rather that the source of our intuition lies in reflections about belief itself, not about a principle about assent. I think we suppose that a person, an ancient Babylonian, for example, might confront an object, a planet for example, in two sets of circumstances, sets of circumstances that for one reason or another do not allow the person to recognize that one and the same object is involved. And in such a hypothetical case we can see that a person may believe about that object that it has a certain property, say, of being the first star in the evening, when he is in certain circumstances, say gazing at a familiar sight in early evening, while at the same time believing that another familiar object viewed in the morning is never the first star in the evening, even though the two objects are in fact the same.

This sort of explanation of our intuitions, has nothing to do with *expressions* of belief, it has to do with the psychological state of belief itself. It seems, then, to make no use of the disquotational principle (nor of the other two principles.)

Look at the reverse disquotational principle: (paraphrasing) If a normal Babylonian speaker who is not reticent believes that Hesperus is the first star of the evening, then he will be disposed to sincere reflective assent to (here we have to substitute something in the Babylonian language) 'Hesperus is the first star of the evening'.

Surely, I would like to say, our intuitions about what could have been the case about Babylonian beliefs doesn't depend upon our assuming this principle.[5]

The principle of translation, that if a sentence of one language expresses a truth in that language, then any translation of it into any other language also expresses a truth, seems to me to be also susceptible of degenerating into a truism. But in any case the explanation I have given of our intuitions about the Babylonians makes no use of it as far as I can see. I can understand and appreciate the appeal to intuitions about the Babylonians beliefs without having any knowledge about what the Babylonian sentences mean.

Let me sum up. Insofar as we have intuitions about a hypothetical case such as that of the ancient Babylonians, they are based upon judgments about what it is possible for someone to believe or disbelieve in such a situation and not upon Kripke's principles about sentences which *express* beliefs or upon a principle about translation from one language to another. The intuition, that is, has nothing to do with language.

We must be careful here. We have not shown yet that an intractable paradox or puzzle results from our judgments about what it is possible to believe or not believe. We have at best shown that the critics of direct reference theory in appealing to our intuitions need not be making any use of certain principles from which a paradox or puzzle can be derived.

It may be also that the only reasons we have for ascribing beliefs or other propositional attitudes to people have to do in the end with their assent or dissent from propositions expressed in language. But that is another matter, another theory to be assessed. I am willing, for example, to ascribe long term beliefs to animals who lack language altogether and to find it possible to imagine one of them in a Hesperus/Phosphorus like situation. Perhaps my dog, who has always, I would avow, believed me to be trustworthy, when seeing me one day dressed in some outlandish costume begins to shake and growl showing that she does not believe me trustworthy. If I dress up this way often enough with similar consequences, I am inclined to ascribe the belief in my trustworthiness still—she has no fear of me dressed in my usual garb—as well as the disbelief and to explain this for a start by assuming that she does not realize that she is dealing with the same person. Perhaps for theoretical reasons I should stop anthropomorphizing animals in this blatant way. But my intuitions about

---

[5] Again, hedging around with qualifications, the principle may be a truism. But that does not mean that the principle is used in generating our intuition. Once again, of course, a truism, being a truism, is entailed by anything at all, and so is entailed by our intuitions, whatever they may be.

the possibility of such a belief situation depends upon no assumptions about linguistic expressions of belief.

V

We can, however, begin to generate a puzzle or paradox merely from our intuitions about what it is possible to believe. In the by now well-known example, Kripke imagines a French speaking person, Pierre, who while in Paris, speaking French, comes to believe what he would express in French as "Londres est jolie." Later he moves to London, lives in a pretty awful neighborhood, learns English, and then sincerely expresses a belief in English by saying "London is not pretty." But in his French moments, as we might put it, he still assents to 'Londres est jolie'. Pierre doesn't connect the city he heard about and longed for in France and the city he knows from living in it.

Here is Kripke's first conclusion about the Pierre example (p. 258):

> Now (using the *strengthened* disquotational principle), we can derive a contradiction, not merely in Pierre's judgments, but in our own. For on the basis of his behavior as an English speaker, we concluded that he does *not* believe that London is pretty ... But on the basis of his behavior as a *French* speaker, we must conclude that he *does* believe that London is pretty.

I might put my worry about the argument by saying that the puzzle we feel really has nothing to do with *language* or with languages at all. We can, it seems, construct the paradox without appealing to principles about expressions of belief. Let us tell the story in this way: Pierre, whatever language he may speak, has heard of a city which he believes to be pretty. His thoughts are about that city—how can he get there, for instance. Then he lands up in the very city his thoughts have been about, not knowing it, of course. He hates that city and believes it to be as ugly as a city can be, not realizing that it is in fact the city he has often thought about. Suppose this city in fact to be London.

I surely want to say that at one time Pierre believed London to be pretty. And, in fact, if the last part of the little story were omitted, the part about his visit to London, I would suppose it quite appropriate to say that unless something changes his mind, he continues to believe this. On the other hand if only the last part of the story were given, only the part about his reaction to the squalor of the city he visits, I would want to say that he does not believe London to be pretty. And, unless this represents a change of mind, I would be happy to say that he never believed this.

But the story has two parts and one can make them seem, at least, to clash in a puzzling and even paradoxical way. Kripke, I think, pinpoints one source of paradox when he says (p. 256), "It seems undeniable that Pierre *once* believed that London is pretty—at least before he learned English ... [I]f any Frenchman who was both ignorant of English and never visited London believed that London is pretty, Pierre did." "Should we say," he argues, "that Pierre, now that he lives in London and speaks English, no longer believes that London is pretty? Well, unquestionably Pierre once believed that London is pretty. So we would be forced to say that Pierre has *changed his mind*, has *given up his previous belief*." And he rightly points out that nothing shows that such an event has taken place

The paradox arises because each part of the story of Pierre, taken separately and as exhausting what is relevant, would warrant opposing contradictory conclusions. In an important sense the two parts of the story are independent of each other—Pierre might never have visited London while retaining his treasured thoughts about the pretty English city; Pierre might never have had those thoughts while being unfortunate enough to make his sojourn in London's nasty precincts. And this independence of the two makes it seem impossible that the presence of one part of the story should have any effect on the consequences normally to be drawn from the other by itself. Kripke, I think, illustrates this stance when he says (p. 256):

> Nor does it have any plausibility to suppose, because of his latter situation after he learns English, that Pierre should *retroactively* be judged *never* to have believed that London is pretty. To allow such ex post facto legislation would, as long as the future is uncertain, endanger our attribution of belief to all monolingual Frenchmen. We would be forced to say that Marie, a monolingual who firmly and sincerely asserts, "Londres est jolie," may or may not believe that London is pretty depending upon the *later* vicissitudes of her career ...

Kripke makes his point with several allusions to the linguistic situation. But it could have been made about my version of Pierre's plight which is silent about those matters. If Pierre never made the journey to London we should be happy to attribute a certain belief to him. How can we deny it to him after he later made the journey? To do so, it would seem, would put in doubt the ascription of the belief to anyone now whose future perambulations and attitudes are uncertain. Yet Pierre's journey to London and his reaction to his stay there *by itself* would seem to license our saying that he does not believe London to be pretty. And so a puzzling—indeed seemingly paradoxical—situation is created by reflections on the state of belief itself.

VI

I have tried to generate the paradox about belief in way which should give it a familiar ring. In fact it begins to look very much like certain puzzles about identity. The ship of Theseus paradox or the more recent puzzles about split brain and brain transfer cases come to mind.

Perhaps we can see this if we characterize these puzzles in general terms and interpolate the Pierre situation as an illustration.

We have, in the general case, two states of affairs, call them A and B, which are independent of each other in the way just illustrated in the Pierre example. We are then invited to agree that if one state of affairs, say A, had existed alone without B then a certain proposition P would have been true. (In the main example, If Pierre had stayed in Paris, never learned English, then it would have been true—given the assumptions of the example—that he believed that London is beautiful.

Next we are challenged to say how the existence of the second state of affairs, B, could have any bearing on the truth value of P. How could Pierre's sojourn in London affect the truth value of the proposition that he believes London to be beautiful? After all, it is a quite independent state of affairs.

Nevertheless, in the general case the existence of B does cast doubt on the truth of P. (One of the things puzzles and paradoxes about identity should teach us is that the existence of the seemingly utterly independent event *can* make a difference.) We are left with a puzzle, a paradox.[6]

VII

I have tried to argue that a puzzle about belief can be generated without presupposing the principles given us in Kripke's paper. And I suggest that the puzzle is of a kind with the hoary ship of Theseus puzzle and the newer ones involving personal identity. In doing this I have in a way absolved the critics of the direct reference theory of necessarily assuming these principles. But the puzzle seems to me to be reinstated at the level of the concept of belief itself. If so, then Kripke's strategy in defense of the direct reference theory can be once again followed. The puzzle is a puzzle no matter what theory of the reference of proper names one has and it cannot be in and of itself a devastating objection that a particular theory seems to generate the puzzle in contexts of ascriptions of belief.

---

[6] In many instance, the troubling second state of affairs admits of degrees along the dimensions of quantity or duration. And when it does, whether we find the situation puzzling or paradoxical can depend upon the answer to the question, how much or how long?

Replacing only a few planks of the ship of Theseus and, with these and a lot of new material, building a duplicate will probably not generate a puzzle about whether the repaired boat or its duplicate is identical to the original ship of Theseus. But replacing 90% of the planks and constructing the duplicate from these and only a small number of additional planks lands us in apparent paradox.

Imagine that Pierre, instead of residing in London for some time, as in Kripke's example, merely passes through. Perhaps his plane on a flight to Marseilles is diverted because of weather to Heathrow. The bus, we can suppose, which busses the passengers to a hotel, passes through the worst quarters of London. Pierre is told that this is London but fails to make the connection with his beloved Londres. The next morning he remarks to fellow passengers as they return to the airport, "London is certainly not beautiful." (Most of the passengers are English-speaking, and Pierre has some command of the language.)

I think this little episode in Pierre's life would not call into question the belief he expresses by saying "Londres est jolie" nor should we hesitate to report his belief in English by saying that Pierre believes London to be pretty.

If what I have said is correct the puzzle about belief is a part of our very concept of belief in much the same way as the puzzle about split brains and the puzzle about the ship of Theseus is a very part of our concept of identity. Of course, there may be ways of defusing the puzzle, just as there have been attempts to do this with the puzzles about identity. So, for example, arguing that belief essentially involves a mode of presentation may remove what would then be only an apparent conflict between the two parts to the story of Pierre. But this will be a theory about the nature of belief. How it would be mirrored in ascriptions of belief will then be a question; and there is no reason, I think, to suppose that the direct reference theory could not accommodate such a theory nor reason to suppose that its main alternative, a Russell-Frege view, has a better shot. Indeed, on the first score, Salmon's analysis is at least very plausible, and on the second, Kripke in the paper we have been concerned with shows that the Russell-Frege view at least has grave difficulties with the puzzle about belief.[7]

There is, however, an important objection which might be raised about the attempt to locate the puzzle in the very concept of belief. A central strategy of mine has been to describe the puzzle cases in general terms, in particular to describe them without the use of names for the object in question. But, it might be said, if we *do* describe the cases with names, our intuitions do not, in fact, lead to a puzzle or paradox. If we imagine the Babylonians, without realizing it, to have named the same heavenly body 'Hesperus' and, at another time, 'Phosphorus', we have no conflict, no obvious paradox in holding that, for example, they believed that Phosphorus was the first star of the morning, that they disbelieved or even that it is false that they believed Hesperus to have this property. In a similar fashion, if we allow ourselves a Marriage of French and English, we find no conflict in holding that Pierre believes Londres is pretty but does not believe that London is pretty. This seems to me to be true and it is a raw datum that must be accounted for in the end. But to say that there is no puzzle lurking here is, I think, wrong.

Kripke says (p. 259), "This is the puzzle: Does Pierre or does he not believe that London is pretty?", adding "I know of no answer to *this* question." And this *is* the puzzle which remains. Kripke's question is couched in English and uses the English name for London. But if one translates his article into another language, other than French, one should use here the name for London associated with that language, a name with which, we can add to the story, Pierre is utterly unfamiliar. There is a way of hearing the question, "Does Pierre believe London to be pretty?", in the context of Kripke's story about Pierre to which I think we may want to say "No he does not." But whatever the analysis is of that reading of the question, that is not the reading to give to Kripke's challenging question. This becomes

---

[7] Kripke [96], pp. 260ff.

clearer if we use the Hesperus/Phosphorus story. Those names are supposedly Babylonian names and bound to the story. But we, of course, have a name for the heavenly body central to that story, the name 'Venus'. And we get the analogue, I think, of Kripke's question if we ask, for example, "Did the Babylonians believe or did they not believe that *Venus* is the first star of the morning?" And I want to say, echoing Kripke, "I know of no answer to *this* question."[8]

---

[8] Does the Frege-Russell view give us a solution to this problem? No. Kripke argues this persuasively as I have mentioned. In the context of the present discussion, another strong reason for believing this is that on the Frege-Russell view we *ought* to be able to answer questions about whether the Babylonians believe that Venus has certain properties. To stick to Russell's version of the view, our name 'Venus' is really a concealed definite description, and we can surely have reason to suppose that the Babylonians did or did not believe that something satisfying that description possesses this or that property. But in fact we do not really know what to say in the cases where the Babylonians believe, e.g., Phosphorus to have a property but have no such belief about whether Hesperus does. Even worse, given that if 'Venus' were for us a concealed definite description then the description would probably make use of concepts the Babylonians lack or concepts that they would not think applied to either Hesperus or Phosphorus, the answer we might well be forced to give on the Russell-Frege view would seem clearly wrong. We would probably be forced to say that they do not believe that Venus is the first star in the morning. Or even that they believed Venus definitely not to be the first star of the morning.

9

A Millian Heir Rejects the Wages of *Sinn*
Nathan Salmon[1]

It is argued, in sharp contrast to established opinion, that the linguistic evidence arising out of propositional-attitude attributions strongly supports Millianism (the doctrine that the entire contribution to the proposition content of a sentence made by a proper name is simply the name's referent) without providing the slightest counter-evidence. This claim is supported through a semantic analysis of such *de re* attributions as 'Jones believes of Venus that it is a star'. The apparent failure of substitutivity of co-referential names in propositional-attitude attributions is shown to be evidentially irrelevant through consideration of analogous phenomena involving straightforward synonyms.

I

In *Frege's Puzzle* [157] I defended a Millian theory of the information contents of sentences involving proper names or other simple (noncompound) singular terms. The central thesis is that ordinary proper names, demonstratives, other single-word indexicals or pronouns (such as 'he'), and other simple singular terms are, in a given possible context of use, Russellian "genuine names in the strict logical sense." [2] Put more fully, I maintain the following anti-Fregean doctrine: that the contribution made by an ordinary proper name or other simple singular term to securing the information content of, or the proposition expressed by, declarative sentences (with respect

---

[1] The present essay has benefitted from discussions with Mark Richard and Stephen Schiffer, from comments by Graeme Forbes and Timothy Williamson, and from discussions at Birkbeck College, London and Oxford University (where portions of the essay were presented as talks in May 1988), and at the University of Minnesota conference on *Propositional Attitudes: the Role of Content in Logic, Language, and Mind*, October 1988.

[2] See Russell's "Knowledge by Acquaintance and Knowledge by Description" [152] and "The Philosophy of Logical Atomism" [153].

to a given possible context of use) in which the term occurs (outside of the scope of nonextensional operators, such as quotation marks) is just the referent of the term, or the bearer of the name (with respect to that context of use). In the terminology of *Frege's Puzzle* [157], I maintain that the *information value* of an ordinary proper name is just its referent.[3]

Another thesis that I maintain in *Frege's Puzzle* [157]—and which both Frege and Russell more or less accepted—is that the proposition that is the information content of a declarative sentence (with respect to a given context) is structured in a certain way, and that its structure and constituents mirror, and are in some way readable from, the structure and constituents of the sentence containing that proposition.[4] By and large, a simple (noncompound) expression contributes a single entity, taken as a simple (noncomplex) unit, to the information content of a sentence in which the expression occurs, whereas the contribution of a compound expression

---

[3] Throughout this essay, I use the term 'Millian' broadly to cover any theory that includes this doctrine. (The term derives from Kripke, "A Puzzle About Belief" [96].) I do not use the term in the more restricted sense of a theory that includes the (apparently stronger) thesis that the reference of a simple singular term completely exhausts the "linguistic function" of the term (whatever that means). John Stuart Mill himself was almost certainly not a Millian, strictly speaking, but his philosophical view of proper names is very much in the spirit of Millianism—enough so for genuine Millians, such as myself, to be counted his heirs.

[4] This separates the theory of *Frege's Puzzle*, together with the theories of Frege, Russell, and their followers, from contemporary theories that assimilate the information contents of declarative sentences with such things as sets of possible worlds, or sets of situations, or functions from possible worlds to truth values, etc.

Both Frege and Russell would regard declarative sentences as typically reflecting only *part of* the structure of their content, since they would insist that many (perhaps even most) grammatically simple (noncompound) expressions occurring in a sentence may (especially if introduced into the language by abbreviation or by some other type of explicit "definition") contribute complex proposition-constituents that would have been more perspicuously contributed by compound expressions. In short, Frege and Russell regarded the prospect of expressions that are grammatically simple yet semantically compound (at the level of content) as not only possible but ubiquitous. Furthermore, according to Russell's Theory of Descriptions, definite and indefinite descriptions ('the author of *Waverley*', 'an author', etc.), behave grammatically but not semantically (at the level of content) as a self-contained unit, so that a sentence containing such an expression is at best only a rough guide to the structure of its content. Russell extends this idea further to ordinary proper names and most uses of pronouns and demonstratives. This makes the structure of nearly any sentence only a very rough guide to the structure of the sentence's content. The theory advanced in *Frege's Puzzle* sticks much more closely to the grammatical structure of the sentence.

(such as a phrase or sentential component) is a complex entity composed of the contributions of the simple components.[5] Hence, the contents of beliefs formulatable using ordinary proper names, demonstratives, or other simple singular terms, are on my view so-called *singular propositions* (David Kaplan), i.e., structured propositions directly about some individual, which occurs directly as a constituent of the proposition. This thesis (together with certain relatively uncontroversial assumptions) yields the consequence that *de re* belief (or *belief of*) is simply a special case of *de dicto* belief (*belief that*). To believe *of* an individual x, *de re*, that it (he, she) is F is to believe *de dicto* the singular proposition about (containing) x that it (he, she) is F, a proposition that can be expressed using an ordinary proper name for x. Similarly for the other propositional attitudes.

Here I will elaborate and expand on certain aspects of my earlier defense of Millian theory, and present some new arguments favoring Millianism. It is commonly held that Millianism runs afoul of common-sense belief attributions, and other propositional-attitude attributions, in declaring intuitively false attributions true. Ironically, the main argument I shall propose here essentially relies on common-sense belief attributions and the semantics of the English phrase 'believes that'. I shall argue, in sharp contrast to established opinion, that the seemingly decisive evidence against Millianism from the realm of propositional-attitude attributions is no evidence at all, and is in fact evidentially irrelevant and immaterial. If I am correct, common-sense propositional-attitude attributions, insofar as they provide any evidence at all, strongly support Millianism without providing even the slightest counter-evidence (in the way that is commonly supposed).

Historically, the most influential objection to the sort of theory I advocate derives from Frege's notorious 'Hesperus'-'Phosphorus' puzzle. The sentence 'Hesperus is Phosphorus' is informative; its information content apparently extends knowledge. The sentence 'Hesperus is Hesperus' is uninformative; its information content is a "given." According to my theory, the information content of 'Hesperus is Hesperus' consists of the planet Venus, taken twice, and the relation of identity (more accurately, the relation of identity-at-t, where t is the time of utterance). Yet the information content of 'Hesperus is Phosphorus', according to this theory, is made

---

[5] There are well-known exceptions to the general rule—hence the phrase 'by and large'. Certain nonextensional operators, such as quotation marks, create contexts in which compound expressions contribute themselves as units to the information content of sentences in which the expression occurs. Less widely recognized is the fact that even ordinary temporal operators (e.g., 'on April 1, 1986' + past tense) create contexts in which some compound expressions (most notably, open and closed sentences) contribute complexes other than their customary contribution to information content. See "Tense and Singular Propositions" [159]. In addition, compound predicates are treated in *Frege's Puzzle* as contributing attributes, as single units, to the information contents of sentences.

of precisely the same components, and apparently in precisely the same way.[6] Assuming a plausible principle of compositionality for propositions, or pieces of information—according to which if p and q are propositions that involve the very same constituents arranged in the very same way, then p and q are the very same proposition—the theory ascribes precisely the same information content to both sentences. This seems to fly in the face of the fact that the two sentences differ dramatically in their informativeness.

This puzzle is easily transformed into an argument against Millian theory, by turning its implicit assumptions into explicit premises. The major premise, which I call *Frege's Law*, connects the concept of informativeness (or that, in Frege's words, of "containing a very valuable extension of our knowledge") with that of cognitive information content (what Frege called "*Erkenntniswerte*," or "cognitive value"):

> If a declarative sentence S has the very same cognitive information content as a declarative sentence S', then S is informative if and only if S' is.

A second premise is the compositionality principle for propositions. A third critical premise consists in the simple observation that whereas 'Hesperus is Phosphorus' is informative, 'Hesperus is Hesperus' is not. Assuming that the information contents of 'Hesperus is Phosphorus' and 'Hesperus is Hesperus' do not differ at all in structure or mode of composition, it follows that they differ in their constituents.[7] This points to a difference in information value between the names 'Hesperus' and 'Phosphorus'. Since these names are co-referential, it cannot be that the information value of each is simply its referent.

As I pointed out in *Frege's Puzzle* [157] (pp. 73–76), there is a very general difficulty with this Fregean argument: an exactly similar argument can be mounted against any of a wide variety of theories of information value, including Frege's own theory that the information value of a term consists in an associated purely conceptual representation. It happens that I, like Hilary Putnam, do not have the slightest idea what characteristics differentiate beech trees from elm trees, other than the fact that the English

---

[6] It has been argued, however, that the information content of a sentence is a function not only of the information-values and the sequential order of the information-valued parts but also of the very logical structure of the sentence as a whole, and that therefore, since the two identity sentences differ in logical structure, the modes of composition of the information values of their parts are different from one another. See Putnam [131], especially note 8 (also in [160], pp. 157n10). For response, see Church [29]; Scheffler [162] (pp. 42n7); Soames [177]; and Salmon [157] (pp. 164–165n4).

[7] See the previous note. There is considerable conflict, however, between Putnam's stance described therein and his more recent concession in his "Comments" on Kripke's "A Puzzle about Belief" [135] (p. 285), that "certainly Frege's argument shows meaning cannot just *be* reference."

term for beeches is 'beech' and the English term for elms is 'elm'.[8] The purely conceptual content that I attach to the term 'beech' is the same that I attach to the term 'elm', and it is a pretty meager one at that. My concept of elm wood is no different from my concept of beech wood. Nevertheless, an utterance of the sentence 'Elm wood is beech wood' would (under the right circumstances) be highly informative for me. In fact, I know that elm wood is not beech wood. At the same time, of course, I know that elm wood is elm wood. By an argument exactly analogous to the one constructed from Frege's puzzle about the informativeness of 'Hesperus is Phosphorus' we should conclude that the information value of 'elm' or 'beech' is not the conceptual content.[9]

---

[8] This particular example is due to Putnam, whose botanical ignorance cannot possibly exceed my own. See "Meaning and Reference" [133] (p. 704).

[9] I had made this same general point earlier in a review of Leonard Linsky's *Names and Descriptions* [154] (p. 451). There, however, I labored under the illusion that the original Fregean argument is sound.

It may be objected that my concept of elm trees includes the concept of being called 'elms' in English, and perhaps even the concept of being a different genus from the things called 'beeches' in English, making the purely conceptual contents different after all. Even setting aside the question of whether such differences can show up in a purely conceptual representation, this objection is mistaken. In the relevant sense of "conceptual content," such concepts as that of being called 'elm' in English are not part of the conceptual content I attach to the term 'elm'. Not everything one believes about elms can be part of the information value of the term 'elm', or of the conceptual representation attached to the term 'elm', as the notion of conceptual representation is intended in Fregean theory. Otherwise, every sentence S that is sincerely uttered by someone and that involves the word 'elm' (not in the scope of quotation marks or other such devices) would be such that the conditional ⌜If there are any elms, then S⌝ is analytically true for the speaker. One could not acquire new beliefs expressed by means of the term 'elm', and hence one could not change one's mind about anything expressed in terms of 'elm' (e.g., that Jones is standing by an elm tree), without literally changing the subject. In particular, there are compelling reasons for denying that any concept like that of being called such-and-such in English can be part of the information value of terms like 'elm' and 'beech'. It is not analytic, for example, that elms are called 'elm' in English. (That 'elm' applies to elms in English is a nontrivial piece of information about English. Things might have been otherwise, and it is not "given" or known *a priori* what the expression 'elm' applies to in English.) Whatever the information value of 'elm' is, there are terms in other languages that have the same information value—e.g., the German words '*Ulme*' and '*Rüster*'. The information value of these German terms does not include any concept of what things of that kind are called in English. A German speaker may know what an elm is—may have a concept of an elm tree—without having the foggiest idea what elms are called in English. Also, for most terms, such as 'tree', 'table', 'anthropologist', 'green', etc., it is distinctly implausible to suppose that the information value of the term includes the concept of being so-called in

This argument employs the same general strategy, and mostly the very same premises (including Frege's Law and the compositionality principle for propositions), as the original Fregean argument in connection with 'Hesperus' and 'Phosphorus'. This generalized Fregean strategy may be applied against virtually any minimally plausible and substantive theory of information value. In this particular application of the generalized strategy, the relevant informative identity statement is not even true, but that does not matter to the general strategy. The truth of an informative identity statement is required only in the application of the general argument against theories that locate information value, at least in part, in reference. In the general case, only informativeness is required. False identity statements are always informative—so informative, in fact, as to be misinformative. Thus, virtually any substantive theory of information value imaginable reintroduces a variant of Frege's puzzle (or else it is untenable on independent grounds, such as Kripke's modal arguments against orthodox Fregean theory).

The sheer scope of the generalized Fregean strategy—the fact that, if sound, it is applicable to virtually any substantive theory of information value—would seem to indicate that the strategy involves some error. That the generalized strategy does indeed involve some error can be demonstrated through an application of the generalized strategy to a situation involving straightforward (strict) synonyms for which it is uncontroversial that information value is exactly preserved. Suppose that foreign-born Sasha learns the words 'ketchup' and 'catsup' not by being taught that they are perfect synonyms, but by actually consuming the condiment and reading the labels on the bottles. Suppose further that, in Sasha's idiosyncratic experience, people typically have the condiment called 'catsup' with their eggs and hash browns at breakfast, whereas they routinely have the condiment called 'ketchup' with their hamburgers at lunch. This naturally leads Sasha to conclude, erroneously, that ketchup and catsup are different condiments that happen to share a similar taste, color, consistency, and name. He thinks to himself, "Ketchup is a sandwich condiment, but no one in his right mind would eat a sandwich condiment with eggs at breakfast; so catsup is not a sandwich condiment." Whereas the sentence 'Ketchup is ketchup' is uninformative for Sasha, the sentence 'Catsup is ketchup' is every bit as informative as 'Hesperus is Phosphorus'. Applying the generalized Fregean strategy, we would conclude that the terms 'catsup' and 'ketchup' differ in information value for Sasha. But this is

---

English. Each is perfectly translatable into any number of languages. The typical German speaker knows what a tree is—has the concept of a tree—even if he or she does not have any opinion as to the English term for a tree. There is no reason why 'elm' should be different from 'tree' in this respect. See Kripke, *Naming and Necessity* [95] (pp. 68–70) and "A Puzzle about Belief" [96] (note 12), and my *Frege's Puzzle* [157] (pp. 163–164n2).

clearly wrong. The terms 'ketchup' and 'catsup' are perfect synonyms in English. Some would argue that they are merely two different spellings of the very same English word.[10] Most of us who have learned these words (or these spellings of the single word) probably learned one of them in an ostensive definition of some sort, and the other as a strict synonym (or as an alternative spelling) of the first. Some of us learned 'ketchup' first and 'catsup' second; for others the order was the reverse. Obviously, it does not matter which is learned first and which second. Either word (spelling) may be learned by ostensive definition. If either may be learned by ostensive definition, then both may be. Indeed, Sasha has learned both words (spellings) in much the same way that nearly everyone else has learned at least one of them: by means of a sort of ostensive definition. This manner of acquiring the two words (spellings) is unusual, but not impossible. Sasha's acquisition of these words (spellings) prevented him from learning at the outset that they are perfect synonyms, but the claim that he therefore has not learned both is highly implausible. Each word (spelling) was learned by Sasha in much the same way that some of us learned it. Even in Sasha's idiolect, then, the two words (spellings) are perfectly synonymous, and therefore share the same information value. Since this contradicts the finding generated by the generalized Fregean strategy, the generalized Fregean strategy must involve some error. This discredits the original Fregean argument.[11]

What is the error? It is tempting to place the blame on Frege's Law. In Sasha's case, the sentences 'Catsup is ketchup' and 'Ketchup is ketchup'

---

[10] Indeed, a similar example could be constructed using the American and British spellings of 'color', or even differing *pronunciations* of 'tomato'.

[11] The argument given here involving the terms 'ketchup' and 'catsup' is related to Kripke's "proof" of substitutivity using two Hebrew words for Germany, and to his argument involving 'furze' and 'gorse', in the conclusion section of "A Puzzle about Belief" [96]. All of these arguments are closely related to Church's famous arguments from translation. (See especially "Intensional Isomorphism and Identity of Belief" [29].) For further discussion of the relation between the position taken in Kripke's article on belief and the position defended here see *Frege's Puzzle* [157] (pp. 129–132), and "Illogical Belief" [158].

The example of Sasha, like the 'beech'-'elm' example, demonstrates that the difficulty involved in Frege's puzzle is more general than it appears, arising not only on my own theory of information value but equally on a very wide range of theories, including various Fregean theories. This is not peculiar to Frege's puzzle. Although I will not argue the case here, a great many criticisms that have been levelled against the sort of account I advocate—perhaps most—are based on some difficulty or other that is more general in nature than it first appears, and that equally arises on virtually any substantive theory of information value in connection with the example of Sasha's understanding of the synonyms 'ketchup' and 'catsup'. (Cf. "Illogical Belief" [158].) Perhaps I will elaborate on this matter in later work.

have the very same information content, yet it seems that the first is informative and the second is not. This would be a mistake. A sentence is *informative* in the sense invoked in Frege's Law only insofar as its information content is a "valuable extension of our knowledge," or is knowable only *a posteriori*, or is not already "given," or is nontrivial, etc. There is some such property P of propositions such that a declarative sentence S is informative in the only sense relevant to Frege's Law if and only if its information content has P. Once the informativeness or uninformativeness of a sentence is properly seen as a derivative semantic property of the sentence, one that the sentence has only in virtue of encoding the information that it does, Frege's Law may be seen as a special instance of Leibniz's Law, the doctrine that things that are the same have the same properties: if the information content of S is the information content of S', then the information content of S has the informative-making property P if and only if the information content of S' does. Since Frege's Law is a logical truth, it is unassailable.

By the same token, the sentence 'Catsup is ketchup' is definitely not informative *in this sense*. The proposition it semantically contains is just the information that ketchup is ketchup, a proposition that clearly lacks the relevant informative-making property P. The sentence 'Catsup is ketchup', unlike the sentences 'Ketchup is ketchup' and 'Catsup is catsup', is "informative" in various other senses. If uttered under the right circumstances, the former can convey to someone like Sasha that the sentence itself is true, and hence that the words (or spellings) 'ketchup' and 'catsup' are English synonyms, or at least co-referential. To someone who already understands 'ketchup' but not 'catsup', an utterance of the sentence can convey what 'catsup' means. These pieces of linguistic information about English do have the informative-making property P, but in order for a sentence to be informative in the relevant sense its very information content itself must have the informative-making property P. It is not sufficient that utterances of the sentence typically impart information that has P, if that imparted information is not included in the semantic information content of the sentence. The question of information value concerns semantically contained information, not pragmatically imparted information.

Exactly analogously, once the word 'informative' is taken in the relevant sense, thereby rendering Frege's Law a truth of logic, one of the other crucial premises of the original Fregean argument against Millian theory is rendered moot. Specifically, with the word 'informative' so understood, and with a sharp distinction between semantically contained information and pragmatically imparted information kept in mind, the assumption that the sentence 'Hesperus is Phosphorus' is informative *in the relevant sense* requires special justification. To be sure, an utterance of the sentence typically imparts information that is more valuable than that typically imparted by an utterance of 'Hesperus is Hesperus'. For example, it may impart the nontrivial linguistic information about the sentence 'Hesperus is

Phosphorus' itself that it is true, and hence that the names 'Hesperus' and 'Phosphorus' are co-referential. But presumably this is not semantically contained information. The observation that 'Hesperus is Phosphorus' can be used to convey information that has the informative-making property *P* does nothing to show that the sentence's semantic content itself has the property *P*. It is by no means obvious that this sentence, stripped naked of its pragmatic impartations and with only its properly semantic information content left, is any more informative in the relevant sense than 'Hesperus is Hesperus'. I claim that the information content of 'Hesperus is Phosphorus' is the trivial proposition about the planet Venus that it is it—a piece of information that clearly lacks the informative-making property *P*. It is by no means certain, as the original Fregean argument maintains, that the difference in "cognitive value" we seem to hear between 'Hesperus is Hesperus' and 'Hesperus is Phosphorus' is not due entirely to a difference in pragmatically imparted information. Yet, until we can be certain of this, Frege's Law cannot be applied and the argument does not get off the ground. In effect, then, the original Fregean argument begs the question, by assuming that the typical impartations of 'Hesperus is Phosphorus' that have the informative-making property *P* are included in the very information content. Of course, if one fails to draw the distinction between semantically contained and pragmatically imparted information (as so many philosophers have), it is small wonder that information pragmatically imparted by 'Hesperus is Phosphorus' may be mistaken for semantically contained information. If the strategy of the original Fregean argument is ultimately to succeed, however, a further argument must be given to show that the information imparted by 'Hesperus is Phosphorus' that makes it seem informative is, in fact, semantically contained. In the meantime, Frege's 'Hesperus'-'Phosphorus' puzzle is certainly not the conclusive refutation of Millian theory that it has been taken to be. For all that the Fregean strategy achieves, some version of Millianism may be the best and most plausible theory available concerning the information value of proper names.

II

What evidence is there in favor of the Millian theory? One extremely important consideration comes by way of the paradigms of nondescriptional singular terms: individual variables. A related consideration involves pronouns. Consider the following so-called *de re* (as opposed to *de dicto*), or *relational* (as opposed to *notional*), propositional-attitude attribution, expressed in the formal mode by way of quantification into the nonextensional context created by the nonextensional operator 'that':

(1) $(\exists x)[x = $ the planet Venus & Jones believes that x is a star].

Such a *de re* locution might be expressed less formally in colloquial English as:

(1′) Jones believes of the planet Venus that it is a star.

What is characteristic of these *de re* locutions is that they do not specify how Jones conceives of the planet Venus in believing it to be a star. It is left open whether he is thinking of Venus as the first heavenly body visible at dusk, or as the last heavenly body visible at dawn, or instead as the heavenly body he sees at time t, or none of the above. The Fregean (or "neo-Fregean") theorist contends that this lack of specificity is precisely a result of the fact that the (allegedly sense-bearing) name 'Venus' is positioned outside of the scope of the oblique context created by the nonextensional operator 'believes that', where it is open to substitution of co-referential singular terms and to existential generalization. What is more significant, however, is that another, non-sense-bearing singular term is positioned within the scope of the nonextensional context: the last bound occurrence of the variable 'x' in (1), the pronoun 'it' in (1′). Consider first the quasi-formal sentence (1). It follows by the principles of conventional formal semantics that (1) is true if and only if its component open sentence

(2) Jones believes that x is a star

is true under the assignment of the planet Venus as value for the variable 'x'—or in the terminology of Tarski, if and only if Venus *satisfies* (2). The open sentence (2) is true under the assignment of Venus as value of 'x' if and only if Jones believes the proposition that is the information content of the complement open sentence

(3) x is a star

under the same assignment of Venus as the value of 'x'.

A parallel derivation proceeds from the colloquial *de re* attribution (1′). Sentence (1′) is true if and only if its component sentence

(2′) Jones believes that it is a star

is true under the anaphoric assignment of Venus as referent for the pronoun 'it'. As with the open sentence (2), sentence (2′) is true under the assignment of Venus as the referent of 'it' if and only if Jones believes the information content of

(3′) It is a star

under this same assignment.

Now, the fundamental semantic characteristic of a variable with an assigned value, or of a pronoun with a particular referent, is precisely that its information value is just its referent. The referent-assignment provides nothing else for the term to contribute to the information content of sentences like (3) or (3′) in which it figures. In fact, this is precisely the point of using a variable or a pronoun rather than a definite description (like 'the first heavenly body visible at dusk') within the scope of an attitude verb in a *de re* attribution. A variable with an assigned value, or a pronoun with a particular referent, does not have in addition to its referent a Fregean sense—a conceptual representation that it contributes to semantic content. If it had, (3) and (3′) would semantically contain specific general propositions, under the relevant referent-assignments, and (2) and (2′) would thus be notional rather than relational. If (2) and (2′), used with reference to Venus, are to be relational—if they are to fail to specify how Jones conceives of Venus—the contents of (3) and (3′) under the assignments of Venus to 'x' and 'it' can only be the singular proposition about Venus that it is a star, the sort of proposition postulated by the Millian theory. This means that the information value of the variable or the pronoun must be its referent.

What is good for the variable or the pronoun, under an assigned referent, is good for the individual constant. Indeed, the only difference between a variable and a constant is that the variable varies where the constant stands fast. The semantics for a given language fixes the reference of its individual constants. It happens that some particularly useful operators, included in the usual mathematical languages, operate simultaneously on a certain kind of simple singular term and a formula, by surveying the various truth values that the operand formula takes on when the operand singular term is assigned different referents (and the rest of the sentence remains fixed), and then assigning an appropriate extensional value to the whole formed from the operator and its two operands. (Technically, the extension of such an operator is a function from the extension of its operand formula with respect to its operand term to an appropriate extension for the compound formed by attaching the operator to an appropriate term and a formula—where the extension of a formula S_v *with respect to* a term v is a function that assigns to any assignment of a referent to v the corresponding truth value of S_v under that referent-assignment.) If a given language includes operators of this sort, it is natural for it to include also special singular terms that are not coupled with a particular referent to which they remain faithful, and that are instead allowed to take on any value from a particular domain of discourse as temporary referent. These special singular terms are the individual variables, and the operators that induce their presence are the variable-binding operators. Individual variables are singular terms that would be individual constants but for their promiscuity. Conversely, then, individual constants are singular terms that would be variables but for their monogamy. The variability of a variable has nothing whatsoever to do with the separate feature that the variable's information value, under an assignment of a referent, is just the assigned referent. It is the simplicity of the variable that gives it the latter feature; the variability only guarantees that the information value also varies. Once the variable is assigned a particular value, the variable becomes, for all intents and purposes pertaining to that assignment, a constant. Hence, if the open sentence (3), under the assignment of Venus as the value of 'x', semantically contains the singular proposition about Venus that it is a star, then the closed sentence

   a is a star,

where 'a' is an individual constant that refers to Venus, semantically contains this same proposition. Assuming that the individual constants of natural language are the proper names, single-word indexical singular terms, and other (closed) simple singular terms, the considerations raised here support the Millian theory.[12]

There is an alternative way of looking at the same result. All of us are accustomed to using special variables or pronouns that have a restricted domain over which they range. In ordinary English, the pronoun 'he' often ranges only over males, the pronoun 'she' only over females. Among special-purpose technical languages, some variables range only over numbers, some only over sets, some only over times. The domain over which a variable ranges (at least typically) must be non-empty, but it can be quite small in size. In standard extensional second-order logic, for example, the range of the second-order variables 'p', 'q', and 'r' is the pair set consisting of (representatives of) the two truth values. Could there be variables whose range is a unit set? Of course there could. Why not? Except that it would be odd to call such terms "variables." Their range is too restrictive to allow for genuine *variation*, in an ordinary sense; they are maximally restricted. Let us not call them "variables," then. What should we call them? We could call them "invariable variables." (This has the advantage that it emphasizes the exact analogy with the less restrictive variables.) Alternatively, we could call them "constants." In fact, we do. The proper names and demonstratives of ordinary language might be seen as nothing other than the hypothesized "invariable variables." Proper

---

[12] The foregoing argument is closely related to a somewhat different argument advanced in *Frege's Puzzle* [157] (pp. 3–7) for the conclusion that so-called *de re* propositional-attitude attributions, such as (1) and (1'), attribute attitudes toward singular propositions. (This is not a premise of the argument; it is a conclusion.) The latter argument was derived from a similar argument of David Kaplan's involving modality in place of propositional attitudes. The new argument is an argument by analogy: Individual constants are relevantly analogous to individual variables and pronouns, differing only in their constancy; hence, so-called *de dicto* propositional-attitude attributions involving proper names also attribute attitudes toward singular propositions. This argument by analogy to variables and pronouns occurred to me sometime in late 1980, and although it is not proffered in *Frege's Puzzle*, it was this argument more than any other that actually convinced me of the highly contentious thesis that the information value of a proper name, or any other closed simple singular term, is simply its referent and nothing more. The argument of the following section occurred to me immediately thereafter. (Cf. *Frege's Puzzle* [157], p ix.) A version of the latter of these is proffered in *Frege's Puzzle* (pp. 84–85, 114–118, and *passim*).

names and unrestricted variables are but the opposite limiting cases of a single phenomenon.[13]

III

This sort of consideration favoring the sort of account I advocate is complemented by a new application of a general form of argument that has been suggested, and usefully exploited, by Saul Kripke.[14]

What compelling evidence is there that the proper names of ordinary language are not simply the hypothesized invariable variables? We have seen that the original Fregean argument from the alleged informativeness of 'Hesperus is Phosphorus' is illegitimate, or at least seriously incomplete. What other evidence is there? An alternative argument against Millian theory derives from the apparent failures of substitutivity in propositional-attitude attributions. Consider the familiar story of Jones and his ignorance concerning the planet Venus. Jones sees a bright star in the dusk sky, before any other heavenly body is visible, and is told that its name is 'Hesperus'. Subsequently he sees another bright star in the dawn sky, later than any other heavenly body is visible, and is told that its name is 'Phosphorus'. What Jones is not told is that these are one and the very same heavenly body, the planet Venus. Although Jones believes the proposition that

---

[13] I know of no convincing evidence that proper names (and natural-language simple singular terms generally, other than pronouns) are not invariable pronominals. The fact that proper names do not seem to be grammatically bindable by quantifier (or other) antecedents cannot be taken as conclusive refutation of the thesis that names are maximally restricted variables. Since quantification employing such variables would not differ in truth value from the unquantified open sentence, binding such variables would serve no useful purpose; the natural evolution of language would have little reason to introduce a device for binding these special invariable pronominals. In any event, the general argument in the text does not require the premise that proper names are variables of a special sort (maximally restricted); it requires only the premise that names are sufficiently *analogous* to (unrestricted) variables—together with the usual semantics governing existential quantification, conjunction, and identity (or the natural semantics governing anaphora in English locutions of the form $\ulcorner$Of a, ... it ...$\urcorner$), and the further premise that a (closed or open) sentence of the form $\ulcorner a$ believes that $S\urcorner$ is true (under an assignment of values to variables) if and only if the referent of a believes the information content of S. See the previous note.

[14] Cf. Kripke, *Naming and Necessity* [95] (pp. 108). Kripke's general methodological observation is given in more detail in "Speaker's Reference and Semantic Reference" [97] (especially p. 16). Kripke does not explicitly consider applying the general strategy specifically to substitutivity-failure objections to Millianism. Whereas he clearly regards such objections as inconclusive at best (see his "A Puzzle about Belief" [96]), I am not certain that he would endorse this particular application of the "schmidentity" strategy to showing the substitutivity phenomena evidentially irrelevant. (I hope that he would.)

Hesperus is Hesperus, he seems not to believe (and indeed to disbelieve) the proposition that Hesperus is Phosphorus. That is, upon substitution of 'Phosphorus' for the second occurrence of 'Hesperus' in the true sentence

(4)   Jones believes that Hesperus is Hesperus

we obtain the evidently false sentence

(5)   Jones believes that Hesperus is Phosphorus.

   The apparent failure of substitutivity in propositional-attitude attributions is generally taken by philosophers to constitute a decisive refutation of the sort of account I advocate. But the very phenomena that appear to show that substitutivity fails would arise even if the Millian theory were absolutely correct (for standard English) and substitutivity of co-referential proper names in propositional-attitude attributions were uniformly valid. In particular, the same feeling of invalidity in connection with substitution in such attributions as (4) would arise even in a language for which it was stipulated—say, by an authoritative linguistic committee that legislates the grammar and semantics of the language, and to which all speakers of the language give their cooperation and consent—that the theory of *Frege's Puzzle* is correct. Suppose, for example, that such a committee decreed that there are to be two new individual constants, 'Schmesperus' and 'Schmosphorus'. (I am deliberately following the genius as closely as possible.) It is decreed that these two words are to function exactly like the mathematician's variables 'x', 'y', and 'z' as regards information value, except that they are to remain constant (with whatever other differences this key difference requires)—the constant value of the first being the first heavenly body visible at dusk and the constant value of the second being the last heavenly body visible at dawn. Suppose further that some English speakers—for example, the astronomers—are aware that these two new constants are co-referential, and hence synonymous. Nevertheless, even if our character Jones were fully aware of the legislative decree in connection with 'Schmesperus' and 'Schmosphorus', he would remain ignorant of their co-reference. Jones would dissent from such queries as 'Is Schmesperus the same heavenly body as Schmosphorus?' Would those who are in the know—the astronomers—automatically regard the new constants as completely interchangeable, even in propositional-attitude attributions? Almost certainly not. English speakers who use 'ketchup' and 'catsup' as exact synonyms but who do not reflect philosophically on the matter—and even some who do reflect philosophically—may be inclined to assent to the sentence 'Sasha believes that ketchup is a sandwich condiment, but he does not believe that catsup is'.[15] On reflection, however, it emerges that this

---

[15] For similar claims, see for example Burge's "Belief and Synonymy" [10]. Burge explicitly disagrees with my contention that such claims express logical impossibilities.

sentence expresses a logical impossibility, since the proposition that catsup is a sandwich condiment just is the proposition that ketchup is a sandwich condiment. Similarly, speakers who agree to abide by the legislative committee's decree about 'Schmesperus' and 'Schmosphorus' and who recognize that these two terms are co-referential—especially if these speakers do not reflect philosophically on the implications of the decree in connection with such *de re* constructions as (1)—might for independent pragmatic reasons be led to utter or to assent to such sentences as 'Jones believes that Schmesperus appears in the evening, but he does not believe that Schmosphorus does' and 'Jones believes that Schmesperus is Schmesperus, but he does not believe that Schmesperus is Schmosphorus'. The astronomers may be led to utter the latter sentence, for example, in order to convey (without knowing it) the complex fact about Jones that he agrees to the proposition about Venus that it is it, taking it in the way he would were it presented to him by the sentence 'Schmesperus is Schmesperus' but not taking it in the way he would were it presented to him by the sentence 'Schmesperus is Schmosphorus'. The astronomers would thus unknowingly speak in a way that conflicts with the usage to which they have agreed. This, in turn, would lead to their judging such belief attributions as 'Jones believes that Schmesperus is Schmosphorus' not only inappropriate but literally false, and to the unmistakable feeling that substitution of 'Schmosphorus' for (some occurrences of) 'Schmesperus' in such attributions as 'Jones believes that Schmesperus is Schmesperus' is logically invalid. Insofar as the same phenomena that give rise to Frege's puzzle about identity sentences and to the appearance of substitutivity failure would arise even in a language for which the theory advanced in *Frege's Puzzle* was true by fiat and unanimous consent (and do in fact arise with respect to such straightforward strict synonyms as 'ketchup' and 'catsup'), these phenomena cannot be taken to refute the theory.

IV

The anti-Millian argument deriving from the apparent failure of substitutivity is closely related to the original Fregean argument about the informativeness of 'Hesperus is Phosphorus'. The analogue of the questionable premise that 'Hesperus is Phosphorus' is informative is the assertion that (5) is false (or that 'Hesperus is Phosphorus' does not correctly give the content of one of Jones's beliefs, etc.). This premise too, I claim, is incorrect.[16]

---

[16] I do not deny the initial intuitive force of the premises that 'Hesperus is Phosphorus' is informative and that (5) is false; I argue that they are nevertheless erroneous, and I propose an explanation for their initial pull. My rejection of these premises is by no means a standard position among Millians. A more common Millian reaction is to concede these premises, and to challenge instead the relevant analogue of Frege's Law—for example, the common and extremely plausible assumption that if 'Hesperus' has the same information value as 'Phosphorus' (as Millianism requires), then (4) is true if and only if (5) is. (The

However, this premise, unlike its analogue in the original Fregean argument, does not simply beg the question. The intuition that (5) is false (according to the story) is strong and universal. We have seen that this intuition cannot be regarded as decisive—or even evidentially relevant—regarding the question of the actual truth value of (5), since (for some reason) the intuition of falsity would arise in any case. But there are forceful reasons for deeming (5) false, and the intuition of falsity must be addressed and explained. A full reply to the objection from the apparent failure of substitutivity involves greater complexities.[17]

In *Frege's Puzzle*, I propose the sketch of an analysis of the binary relation of belief between believers and propositions (sometimes Russellian singular propositions). I take the belief relation to be, in effect, the existential generalization of a ternary relation, *BEL*, among believers, propositions, and some third type of entity. To believe a proposition *p* is to adopt an appropriate favorable attitude toward *p* when taking *p* in some relevant *way*. It is to agree to *p*, or to assent mentally to *p*, or to approve of *p*, or some such thing, when taking *p* a certain way. This is the *BEL* relation. The third relata for the *BEL* relation are perhaps something like *modes* of acquaintance or familiarity with propositions, or *ways* in which a believer may take a given proposition. The important thing is that, by definition, they are such that if a fully rational believer adopts conflicting attitudes (such as belief and disbelief, or belief and suspension of judgment) toward propositions *p* and *q*, then the believer must take *p* and *q* in different ways, by means of different modes of acquaintance, in harboring the conflicting attitudes towards them—even if *p* and *q* are in fact the same proposition. More generally, if a fully rational agent construes objects *x* and *y* as distinct

---

assumption has been challenged merely on the grounds that Millianism is not committed to it. Such a reaction misjudges the force of the Fregean argument: the assumption is independently compelling, and taken in conjunction with the other premises, it precludes Millianism. The Millian is under the gun to reject either this premise or one of the others as untrue, and to motivate his or her rejection of the offending premise.) It has been argued, for example, that whereas (5) attributes belief of a proposition, it does not attribute belief of the very content of 'Hesperus is Phosphorus' (i.e., the singular proposition about Venus that it is it). This merely evades the general problem. Consider instead the parallel assumption that if 'Hesperus is Phosphorus' has the same information (proposition) content as 'Hesperus is Hesperus', then the former correctly gives the content of one of Jones's beliefs if and only if the latter does. This assumption is virtually as certain as Frege's Law. Yet common sense dictates that 'Hesperus is Hesperus' does, and 'Hesperus is Phosphorus' does not, correctly give the content of one of Jones's beliefs (since Jones sincerely and reflectively assents to the first while dissenting from the second, etc.). Cf. *Frege's Puzzle* [157] (pp. 5–6, 87–92, and *passim*).

[17] I provide only an outline of my reply here. See *Frege's Puzzle* [157] (especially pp. 80–118) for the details.

(or even merely withholds construing them as one and the very same—as might be evidenced, for example, by the agent's adopting conflicting beliefs or attitudes concerning x and y), then for some appropriate notion of a *way* of taking an object, the agent takes x and y in different ways, even if in fact $x = y$.[18] Of course, to use a distinction of Kripke's, this formulation is far too vague to constitute a fully developed *theory* of ways-of-taking-objects and their role in belief formation, but it does provide a *picture* of belief that differs significantly from the sort of picture of propositional attitudes advanced by Frege or Russell, and enough can be said concerning the *BEL* relation to allow for at least the sketch of a solution to certain philosophical problems, puzzles, and paradoxes involving belief.[19]

In particular, the *BEL* relation satisfies the following three conditions:

(a) *A* believes p if and only if there is some x such that *A* is familiar with p by means of x and $BEL(A, p, x)$;[20]

(b) *A* may believe p by standing in *BEL* to p and some x by means of which *A* is familiar with p without standing in *BEL* to p and all x by means of which *A* is familiar with p;

---

[18] An appropriate notion of a way of taking an object is such that if an agent encounters a single object several times and each time construes it as a different object from the objects in the previous encounters, or even as a different object *for all he or she knows*, then each time he or she takes the object in a new and different way. This is required in order to accommodate the fact that an agent in such circumstances may (perhaps *inevitably will*) adopt several conflicting attitudes toward what is in fact a single object. One cannot require, however, that these ways-of-taking-objects are rich enough by themselves to determine the object so taken, without the assistance of extra-mental, contextual factors. Presumably, twin agents who are molecule-for-molecule duplicates, and whose brains are in exactly the same configuration down to the finest detail, may encounter different (though duplicate) objects, taking them in the very same way. Likewise, a single agent might be artificially induced through brain manipulations into taking different objects the same way. Cf. *Frege's Puzzle* (p. 173n1).

[19] The *BEL* relation is applied to additional puzzles in "Reflexivity" [156].

[20] I do not claim that a sentence of the form ⌜*A* believes p⌝ is exactly synonymous with the existential formula on the right-hand side of the 'if and only if' in condition (a). I do claim that condition (a) is a (metaphysically) necessary, conceptually a priori truth. (See note 5 above concerning the contents of predicates. It may be helpful to think of the English verb 'believe' as a *name* for the binary relation described by the right-hand side of (a), i.e., for the existential generalization on the third argument-place of the *BEL* relation.) My claim in [157] (p. 111) that belief may be so "analyzed" is meant to entail that condition (a) is a necessary a priori truth, not that the two sides of the biconditional are synonymous. (My own view is that something along these lines is all that can be plausibly claimed for such purported philosophical "analyses" as have been offered for ⌜*A* knows p⌝, ⌜*A* perceives B⌝, ⌜*A* (nonnaturally) means p in uttering S⌝, etc.)

(c) In one sense of 'withhold belief', A withholds belief concerning p (either by disbelieving or by suspending judgment) if and only if there is some x by means of which A is familiar with p and not-$BEL(A, p, x)$.

These conditions generate a philosophically important distinction between withholding belief and failure to believe (i.e., not believing). In particular, one may both withhold belief from and believe the very same proposition simultaneously. (Neither withholding belief nor failure to believe is to be identified with the related notions of disbelief and suspension of judgment—which are two different ways of withholding belief, in this sense, and which may occur simultaneously with belief of the very same proposition in a single believer.)

It happens in most cases (though not all) that when a believer believes some particular proposition p, the relevant third relatum for the BEL relation is a function of the believer and some particular *sentence* of the believer's language. There is, for example, the binary function f that assigns to any believer A and sentence S of A's language, the *way A takes* the proposition contained in S (in A's language with respect to A's context at some particular time t) were it presented to A (at t) through the very sentence S, if there is exactly one such way of taking the proposition in question. (In some cases, there are too many such ways of taking the proposition in question.)

According to this account, (5) is true in the story of Jones and the planet Venus, since Jones agrees to the proposition that Hesperus is Phosphorus when taking it in a certain way—for example, if one points to Venus at dusk and says (peculiarly enough) "That is that," or when the proposition is presented to him by such sentences as 'Hesperus is Hesperus' or 'Phosphorus is Phosphorus'. That is,

BEL[Jones, that Hesperus is Phosphorus, f(Jones, 'Hesperus is Hesperus')].

Jones also withholds belief concerning whether Hesperus is Hesperus. In fact, according to my account, he believes that Hesperus is not Hesperus! For he agrees to the proposition that Hesperus is not Hesperus, taking it in the way he would were it presented to him by the sentence 'Hesperus is not Phosphorus'. That is,

BEL[Jones, that Hesperus is not Hesperus, f(Jones, 'Hesperus is not Phosphorus')],

and hence, assuming Jones is fully rational, it is not the case that

BEL[Jones, that Hesperus is Hesperus, f(Jones, 'Hesperus is Phosphorus')].

As noted above, these consequences of my account do not conform with the way we actually speak. Instead it is customary when discussing Jones's predicament to say such things as "Jones does not realize that Hesperus is Phosphorus; in fact, he believes that Hesperus is *not* Phosphorus." It is partly for this reason that the anti-Millian's premise that (5) is false does not simply beg the question. Yet, according to my account, what we say when we deny such things as (5) is literally false. In fact, (5)'s literal truth conditions are, according to the view I advocate, conditions that are plainly fulfilled (in the context of the Jones story). Why, then, do we not say such things, and instead say just the opposite? Why is it that substitution of 'Phosphorus' for 'Hesperus'—or even of 'Schmosphorus' for 'Schmesperus'—*feels* invalid in propositional-attitude attributions? Some explanation of our speech patterns and intuitions of invalidity in these sorts of cases is called for. The explanation I offer in *Frege's Puzzle* is somewhat complex, consisting of three main parts. The first part of the explanation for the common disposition to deny or to dissent from (5) is that speakers may have a tendency to confuse the content of (5) with that of

(5′)   Jones believes that 'Hesperus is Phosphorus' is true (in English).

Since sentence (5′) is obviously false, this confusion naturally leads to a similarly unfavorable disposition toward (5). This part of the explanation cannot be the whole story, however, since even speakers who know enough about semantics to know that the fact that Hesperus is Phosphorus is logically independent of the fact that the sentence 'Hesperus is Phosphorus' is true, and who are careful to distinguish the content of (5) from that of (5′), are nevertheless unfavorably disposed toward (5) itself—because of the fact that Jones demurs whenever the query 'Is Hesperus the same heavenly body as Phosphorus?' is put to him.

The second part of my explanation for (5)'s appearance of falsity is that its denial is the product of a plausible but mistaken inference from the fact that Jones sincerely dissents (or at least does not sincerely assent) when queried 'Is Hesperus Phosphorus?', while fully understanding the question and grasping its content, or (as Keith Donnellan has pointed out) even from his expressions of preference for the Evening Star over the Morning Star. More accurately, ordinary speakers (and even most nonordinary speakers) are disposed to regard the fact that Jones does not agree to the proposition that Hesperus is Phosphorus, when taking it in a certain way (the way it might be presented to him by the very sentence 'Hesperus is Phosphorus'), as sufficient to warrant the denial of sentence (5). In the special sense explained in the preceding section, Jones withholds belief from the proposition that Hesperus is Phosphorus, actively failing to agree with it whenever it is put to him in so many words, and this fact misleads ordinary speakers, including Jones himself, into concluding that Jones harbors no favorable attitude of agreement whatsoever toward the proposition in question, and hence does not believe it.

The third part of the explanation is that, where someone under discussion has conflicting attitudes toward a single proposition that he or she takes to be two independent propositions (i.e., in the troublesome 'Hesperus'-'Phosphorus', 'Superman'-'Clark Kent' type cases), there is an established practice of using belief attributions to convey not only the proposition agreed to (which is specified by the belief attribution) but also the way the subject of the attribution takes the proposition in agreeing to it (which is no part of the semantic content of the belief attribution). Specifically, there is an established practice of using such a sentence as (5), which contains the uninteresting proposition that Jones believes the singular proposition about Venus that it is it, to convey furthermore that Jones agrees to this proposition *taking it in the way he would were it presented to him by the very sentence 'Hesperus is Phosphorus' (assuming he understands this sentence)*. That is, there is an established practice of using (5) to convey the false proposition that

BEL[Jones, that Hesperus is Phosphorus, f(Jones, 'Hesperus is Phosphorus')].

V

An unconventional objection has been raised by some self-proclaimed neo-Fregeans against versions of Millianism of the sort advanced in *Frege's Puzzle*. It is charged that such theories are, at bottom, versions of a neo-Fregean theory.[21] Ironically, this unorthodox criticism is invariably coupled with the further, standard criticism that such versions of Millianism are problematic in some way or other that neo-Fregean theory is not (for example, in counting sentence (5) true). The fact that this more familiar criticism is directly contrary to the newer criticism is all but completely ignored. More importantly, this more recent criticism betrays a serious misunderstanding of the gulf that separates Frege's theory from that of Mill or Russell.

It should be said that the theory of *Frege's Puzzle* does indeed follow Frege's theoretical views in a number of significant respects. First and foremost, the theory sees the information value (contribution to proposition-content) of such compound expressions as definite descriptions as complexes whose constituents are contributed by the component expressions and whose structure parallels the syntactic structure of the compound itself. Although my theory has been called "neo-Russellian," it departs radically from the theory of Russell in treating definite descriptions as genuine singular terms, and not as contextually defined "incomplete symbols" or quantificational locutions. In addition to this, a semantic distinction is observed, following Frege's distinction of *Bedeutung* and *Sinn*, between a definite description's referent and the description's information value.

---

[21] The charge has been made both in oral discussion and in print. See Forbes [57] (pp. 456–457), Smith [174], and Wagner [184] (p. 446). A very similar charge was apparently first made by Gareth Evans, in Section VI of his "Understanding Demonstratives" [49] (pp. 298–300). Although Evans's criticism was aimed at John Perry's views on demonstratives, a great deal of my reply to my own critics extends to Evans's criticism of Perry.

A similar distinction is maintained for predicates, sentential connectives, quantifiers, other operators, and even for whole sentences. The referent of a predicate is taken to be its semantic characteristic function from (sequences of) objects to truth values; the information value is taken to be something intensional, like an attribute or concept. Sentences are viewed entirely on the model of a definite description that refers (typically nonrigidly) to a truth value. The content ("information value") of a sentence is taken to be a proposition—the sort of thing that is asserted or denied, believed or disbelieved (or about which judgment is suspended), etc., something that is never-changing in truth value. The account of predicates, sentences and the rest as referring to their extensions is defended by means of the principle of extensionality (the principle that the referent of a compound expression is typically a function solely of the referents of the component expressions and their manner of composition). In all of these respects, the theory advanced in [157] self-consciously follows Frege.

There remains one crucial difference, however: the information value of a simple singular term is identified with its referent. This major plank makes the theory Millian (or "neo-Russellian"), and hence severely and deeply anti-Fregean.

Although a great deal of attention has been paid to the differences between Russell and Frege over the question of whether it is false that the present king of France is bald, their disagreement on this question is dwarfed in significance by their disagreement over the information values of simple proper names. This primary bone of contention emerged in correspondence in 1904, even before Russell came to herald his Theory of Descriptions, which later supplemented his Millianism.[22] Russell answered Frege's protest that Mont Blanc with its snowfields cannot be a constituent of the "thought," or information, that Mont Blanc is more than 4000 meters high, arguing that unless we admit that Mont Blanc is indeed a constituent of the content of the sentence 'Mont Blanc is over 4000 meters high' we obtain the absurd conclusion that we know nothing at all concerning Mont Blanc. Although Frege apparently made no attempt at a response (Russell did not seem to be fully apprehending Frege's remarks), one can be certain that he did not regard Russell's vision of the proposition that Mont Blanc is over 4000 meters high as merely a minor departure from his own sense-reference theory. There can be no real doubt that Frege would have vigorously denounced all versions of Millianism as completely inimical to his theoretical point of view.[23]

---

[22] In Frege's *Philosophical and Mathematical Correspondence* [62] (pp. 163, 169–170; also in [160], pp. 56–57).

[23] The (allegedly) neo-Fregean charge that my account is ultimately Fregean is sometimes coupled with (and perhaps predicated on) an extraordinary interpretation of Frege, advanced by Evans (in "Understanding Demonstratives" [49], and in *The Varieties of Reference* [50] (pp. 22–30 and *passim*), on which Frege

What, then, is the rationale for the charge that my version of Millianism is, at bottom, a neo-Fregean theory? My critics have not been absolutely clear on this point. The charge appears to stem from my acknowledgment of something like *ways of taking objects*, and my reliance

---

is supposed to have held that typical nonreferring proper names have no Fregean sense and that declarative sentences involving such names (in ordinary extensional contexts, or in "purely referential position"), while they appear to express thoughts, do not really do so. This highly unorthodox interpretation is based heavily on what seems a tendentious reading of an ambiguous passage in Frege's *Posthumous Writings* [61] (p. 30). Evans and his followers may have been misled by Frege's unfortunate term 'mock thought' (the translators' rendering of Frege's '*Scheingedanke*', which might also be translated as 'sham thought' or 'pseudo-thought'), and by his habitual use of the term 'fiction' in an artificially broad sense—roughly, as a term for any piece of discourse or line of thought (whether of fiction, in the ordinary sense, or otherwise) in which senses occur without *Bedeutungen* and/or in which sentences or their thought contents occur that are either without truth value or not put forward as true. (This use of 'fiction' is not especially remarkable for a mathematician/logician/philosopher keenly interested in truth and its properties.) Evans evidently thought that Frege regarded any such discourse on the model of genuine fiction, and as only seeming to have cognitive content.

In the same work by Frege appear numerous passages that unambiguously preclude Evans's unconventional interpretation. Cf., for example, pp. 118, 122, 194, and especially 191–192, 225. Similar remarks occur in "*Über Sinn und Bedeutung*," in English in [63], pp. 162–163. Curiously, Evans dismisses these passages as "dubiously consistent with the fundamentals" of Frege's post-1890 philosophy of semantics, although Evans fails to cite any passage which is uncontroversially post-1890 and in which Frege unambiguously asserts something straightforwardly inconsistent with these passages (something that uncontroversially entails that the sense of an ordinary proper name depends for its existence on the object it determines). This interpretive stance makes it difficult to imagine what Evans and his followers would accept as convincing evidence that Frege did not hold the theory they attribute to him. (In fact, Frege's use of the phrase 'mock proper name' or 'pseudo proper name'—for nonreferring but nevertheless real singular terms—in the central passage cited by Evans would, even by itself, tend to indicate that Evans's reading of this very passage is not faithful to Frege's intent. Cf. also Frege's "Thoughts" [60] (p. 38), where Frege speaks of "mock assertions" made either by actors on the stage—"it is only acting, only fiction"—or in poetry, where "we have the case of thoughts being expressed without being actually put forward as true," not for lack of the thoughts themselves but for lack of "the requisite seriousness" on the speaker's part.) In any event, Frege unambiguously denied (*Posthumous Writings* [61], pp. 187, 225) that the referent of a proper name like 'Mont Blanc' or 'Etna' is involved in any way in the name's information value; Frege's *explicit* theory (whether internally consistent or not, and whether compatible with any secret doctrines or not) is therefore diametrically opposed to Millianism. (Cf. Salmon, *Reference and Essence* [155] (pp. 9–23), and *Frege's Puzzle* [157] (pp. 46–50, 63–65, 78). John McDowell,

on them to explain away the appearance of falsity in connection with such propositional-attitude attributions as (5). To this somewhat vague and general criticism, a specific and detailed response was offered in [157].[24] To begin with, my ways-of-taking-objects do not have all of the features that characterize Fregean senses. (See below.) Even if they had, however, they play a significantly different role in my theory. My analogy to the philosophy of perception (pp. 122–125) illustrates the anti-Fregean nature of my view (despite its acknowledgment of sense-like entities): Whereas my theory is analogous to the naive theory that we perceive external objects— apples, tables, chairs—Fregean theory is analogous to the sophisticated theory that the only objects of genuine perception are percepts, visual images, auditory images, and so on. The naive theorist of perception sees the 'sees' in 'Jones sees the apple' as expressing a relation between perceivers and external objects, and its grammatical direct object 'the apple' as occurring in purely referential position and referring there to the apple. By contrast, the sophisticated theorist sees the 'sees' as expressing a relation between perceivers and mental objects, and 'the apple' as referring *in that context* to Jones's visual apple image. The two theories disagree fundamentally over *what is perceived*. The naive theorist need not deny that internal sensory images play a role in perception. He or she may even propose an analysis of perceptual relations (like seeing) that involves existential generalization over mental objects. Why not? Perception obviously does involve experience; there need be no quarrel over such trivial and extremely general matters. The fundamental disagreement over the objects of perception remains. This disagreement will manifest itself not only in differing interpretations of such sentences as 'Jones sees the apple', but often even in differing judgments concerning its truth value (for instance when Jones is hallucinating).

Likewise, I do not quarrel with Fregeans over the trivial question of whether belief and disbelief involve such things as conceptualizing. Our fundamental disagreement concerns the more substantial matter of *what is believed*—in particular, the question whether what is believed is actually made up entirely of such things as "ways of conceptualizing." The *ways of taking objects* that I countenance are, according to my view, not even

---

who appears to follow Evans's misreading of Frege, nevertheless disagrees with Evans's notational-variant charge on these, or related, grounds. See McDowell's "Engaging with the Essential" [120] (p. 61), and *"De Re* Senses" [121] (especially p. 104n15).) The important point as far as the present discussion is concerned is that (whatever Frege's real views were) my own view is a form of genuine Millianism.

[24] A number of passages in *Frege's Puzzle* are devoted to pointing out significant advantages of my version of Millianism over Fregean theory (and hence significant differences between them). Cf. pp. 2–7, 66–71 (and *passim*), and Chapter 9, especially pp. 119–126. See also note 18 above.

so much as mentioned in ordinary propositional-attitude attributions. In particular, on my view, a 'that'-clause makes no reference whatsoever to any way of taking the proposition that is its referent, and a 'that'-clause whose only singular terms are simple (such as the one occurring in (5)) makes no reference whatsoever to any way of taking (or conceiving of, etc.) the individuals referred to by those terms. Consequently, ways-of-taking-objects are not mentioned in (an appropriate specification of) the truth conditions of such an attribution. The only way they come into the picture at all is that in some cases, a certain sort of analysis of the propositional attribute designated by the relevant predicate (e.g., belief) involves existential generalization over them—and even this is not true in all cases. There are many propositional locutions that are not attitudinal as such, and that consequently do not involve ways-of-taking-objects in the way that belief does—for example, 'The laboratory test indicates that Mary has contracted the disease' or better still 'It is necessary that Mary is human' (perhaps even 'Jones asserted that Venus is a star'). In short, my ways-of-taking-objects have nothing whatsoever to do with the semantic content of ordinary sentences, and consequently they have nothing whatsoever to do with the semantics of propositional attributions, even attributions of propositional attitude. Ways-of-taking-objects hail from philosophical psychology, not from philosophical semantics.

By contrast, for the Fregean, ways of conceptualizing objects are explicitly referred to in, and pivotal to the truth conditions of, all propositional attributions. I sharply disagree with the Fregean who claims that alethic modality—or even that laboratory tests—involve such things as conceptualizing in just the same way that belief does. (Consider the Fregean account of such valid inferences as 'The physician believes whatever the laboratory test indicates, and the test indicates that Mary has contracted the disease; hence the physician believes that Mary has contracted the disease', or 'It is necessary that Mary is human, and Jones believes that Mary is human; hence Jones believes at least one necessary truth'.)[25] My fundamental disagreement with Fregeans over the objects of propositional attitude is manifested not only in our differing interpretations of propositional-attitude attributions, but often even in different judgments concerning their truth value. (Recall the conflict between the charge that my version of Millianism is neo-Fregean, and the more orthodox Fregean criticisms of Millianism.)

---

[25] Notice also the relative lack of hesitation in substituting for 'Mary' in 'The test indicates that Mary has contracted the disease' any other proper name Mary may have, or even the pronoun 'she' accompanied by ostension to Mary. Where ways-of-taking-objects obviously play no role, they do not matter to what we say in ascribing attitudes. Notice also our reluctance to substitute 'the woman who spent 17 years studying primate behavior in the wild'. Where ways-of-taking-objects obviously do play a role, they do matter to what we say.

Fortunately, Graeme Forbes has provided a somewhat more detailed account of how my view is supposed to "dissolve" into a neo-Fregean theory.[26] It is especially instructive to examine his rationale for this criticism.

Forbes exploits the fact that the neo-Fregean is not shackled by the letter of Frege's specific views, and may preserve the general spirit of Frege's theoretical point of view while departing in various details. Forbes proposes two ways in which a neo-Fregean theory can converge, in certain respects, with my version of Millianism.[27] One thing the neo-Fregean may do is to regard a belief attribution ⌜Jones believes that S⌝, as uttered by a given speaker, as asserting not that Jones stands in the belief relation specifically to P, where P is the "thought" (proposition) that is the sense of S in the speaker's idiolect, but instead that Jones stands in the belief relation to some thought or other that is relevantly *similar* to P. In this way, the neo-Fregean might find his or her way to delivering the same (somewhat liberal) verdicts as I do with respect to various controversial propositional-attitude attributions (presumably, such as (5)).

Forbes's second proposal suggests a particular way of fleshing out the similarity relation involved in the first proposal, one that is designed to ensure that the neo-Fregean's verdicts will always coincide exactly with mine. It is well-known that Fregean theory runs into difficulty with such *de re* constructions as (1) or (1′). Although Frege himself was largely tacit concerning constructions involving *belief of*, a number of neo-Fregeans have proposed various ways of accommodating them within the spirit of Fregean theory. The most famous (and I believe the most compelling) of these neo-Fregean proposals is still David Kaplan's from "Quantifying In" [90].[28] For present purposes, we shall modify Kaplan's proposal slightly. As can be gleaned from the previous section, the Fregean's difficulty with such constructions as (1) arises from a lack of genuine Fregean sense in connection with the open sentence (3), taken under an assignment of a value to x. Kaplan's analysis (as here modified) reconstrues (1) in such a way that (3) is no longer regarded as a proper (i.e., semantic) constituent. Specifically, the open sentence (2) is analyzed into the following:

(6) $(\exists\alpha)[\alpha$ *represents* x to Jones & Jones believes ⌜α is a star⌝],

---

[26] Forbes [57] (p. 457).

[27] Although Forbes does not treat these two proposals as two parts of a single proposal, I shall treat them in unison in this reconstruction of his criticism. Forbes's overall criticism is considerably more effective when his two proposals are united into a single proposal, and I believe that doing so does not necessarily conflict with Forbes's intentions. Either proposal taken alone leaves obvious and significant (not merely notational) differences between the resulting (so-called) neo-Fregean account and my version of Millianism.

[28] Kaplan himself has long since given up on neo-Fregean attempts to accommodate the effects of direct reference.

where the special representation relation designated in the first conjunct is such as to entail that α is an individual concept (a sense appropriate to a singular term) that determines x as its referent, and where the quasi-quotation marks occurring in the second conjunct are sense-quoting marks that function in a manner analogous to standard quasi-quotation marks with respect to (i.e., without attempting to quote the sense of) the sense variable 'α'.[29] (Think of this analysis as resulting from a contextual definition for open 'that'-clauses, analogous to Russell's contextual definition for definite descriptions—complete with scope distinctions, the definiendum's lack of "meaning in isolation," and all the rest.) It is a (fairly) straightforward matter to extend this analysis of such quasi-formal *de re* constructions as (1) to such informal constructions as (1'): The neo-Fregean analysis of (2') is obtained from (6) by substituting the pronoun 'it' for the free variable 'x'.[30] Replacing the bound occurrence of (2) in (1) by its analysis (6) (or the scattered occurrence of (2') in (1') by a nonscattered occurrence of its analysis), we obtain something equivalent to

(7) $(\exists\alpha)[\alpha$ *represents* Venus to Jones & Jones believes $\ulcorner\alpha$ is a star$\urcorner]$,

The neo-Fregean is struck by the fact that this analysis of (1) and (1') is significantly similar to my proposed analysis of

(8)   Jones believes that Venus is a star.

It is a small step to obtain (7) from (8). One need only extend Kaplan's analysis further, to cover all cases in which a simple singular term—whether a variable or pronoun, or even a proper name or demonstrative—occurs free in a propositional-attitude attribution. We thus obtain a special neo-Fregean theory, one according to which (8) asserts that Jones stands in the belief relation to some thought or other to the effect $\ulcorner\alpha$ is a star$\urcorner$, where α is a sense that represents Venus to Jones. Thus (8) is counted true both by this theory and by my version of Millianism. Similarly, (5) is seen on this theory as asserting that Jones stands in the belief relation to some thought or other to the effect $\ulcorner\alpha$ is $\beta\urcorner$, where each of α and β is a sense

---

[29] Strictly speaking, different analyses result from different choices for the representation relation.

[30] Notice that the proposed analyses of such constructions as (2) and (2'), if sound, would effectively block the argument given in Section II above in connection with (1) and (1')—by falsifying the premise that an open sentence of the form $\ulcorner a$ believes that $S\urcorner$ is true under an assignment of values to variables if and only if the referent of a, under the assignment, believes the content of S, under the assignment. (See note 13 above.) The argument takes (2) and (2') at face value, rather than as contextually defined in terms of quantification and quasi-sense-quotation. Kaplan's analysis allows the neo-Fregean to eschew singular propositions altogether, even in the semantics of *de re* constructions. But how plausible is it—independently of the Fregean motivation for the analysis—that (3) is not a (semantic) constituent of (2)?

that represents Venus to Jones. Thus (5) is also counted true, as with my Millianism. Therefore, Forbes argues, my version of Millianism dissolves, for all intents and purposes, into this special neo-Fregean theory—with my talk of "singular propositions" and "ways of taking objects" merely a notational variant of the neo-Fregean's talk of "representation" and "individual concepts." [31]

One significant difficulty with this neo-Fregean proposal is that it does not validate such apparently valid inferences as 'Smith believes that Bush

---

[31] A full development of this (allegedly) neo-Fregean theory would involve David Kaplan's procedure of *articulation*, described in "Opacity" [93] (p. 270).

I have not followed Forbes's proposal in detail. Forbes (on my reconstruction—see note 27) suggests instead that my Millianism be taken to be a notational variant of a neo-Fregean theory according to which (8) asserts that Jones stands in the belief relation to some thought or other to the effect $\ulcorner \alpha$ obtains$\urcorner$, where α represents the entire singular proposition about Venus that it is a star to Jones. This proposal is thwarted, however, in case Jones believes Venus to be a star (so that (8) is, on my view, true), but—perhaps because of Jones's philosophical skepticism concerning singular propositions in general—he does not also believe this singular proposition to obtain (so that Forbes's suggested construal of (8) is false). An analogous difficulty arises if the belief that the singular proposition obtains is replaced with the belief that Venus has the property of being a star. (Suppose Jones is skeptical of properties.)

Forbes's proposed (alleged) version of neo-Fregeanism follows his own in substituting the singular proposition about Venus that it is a star for its truth value as the referent of the sentence 'Venus is a star', and likewise in substituting the property of being a star for (the characteristic function of) its extension as the referent of the predicate 'is a star'. These planks disqualify Forbes's theory as genuinely neo-Fregean. Furthermore (as Alonzo Church and Kurt Gödel independently showed), assuming extensionality, each plank precludes the conjunction of the following two plausible principles: (a) that a definite description refers to the individual that uniquely answers to it, if there is one; (b) that trivially equivalent expressions are, if not strictly synonymous, at least close enough in meaning as to ensure their having the same referent. Forbes apparently rejects both of these principles. In fact, he adopts a Russellian account both of definite descriptions and of modal contexts. These various anti-Fregean elements strongly invite the countercharge that Forbes's so-called neo-Fregean theory collapses into a neo-Russellian theory. (But see below.)

A more literal reading of Forbes's proposal is that my assertion that "(8) is true if and only if there is a way of taking the singular proposition about Venus that it is a star such that Jones agrees to this proposition when taking it that way" is merely a notational variant of the neo-Fregean's thesis that the *de re* attribution 'Jones believes of the state of affairs of Venus's being a star that it obtains' is true if and only if there is some state-of-affairs concept α that represents Venus's being a star to Jones and Jones believes $\ulcorner \alpha$ obtains$\urcorner$. This interpretation construes my assertions ostensibly assigning truth conditions to (8) as really making disguised reference to a different sentence altogether, and as assigning the truth conditions to this other sentence instead of to (8). I find this interpretation

will win the presidency, and so does Jones; hence there is something (some proposition) that both Smith and Jones believe'.[32] This constitutes one fairly dramatic difference between the proposed theory and my version of Millianism. But there are more fundamental differences.

Does the proposed neo-Fregean theory even agree with my version of Millianism on every question of propositional-attitude attribution, without exception, as it is designed to do? On my theory, any propositional attribution involving a proper name within the scope of the 'that'-operator is deemed equivalent to the corresponding *de re* construction in which the name is moved outside the scope of the 'that'-operator. (For instance, (8) is true if and only if (1′) is.) Thus Forbes's proposed neo-Fregean theory succeeds in echoing the verdicts of my version of Millianism only insofar as neo-Fregean analyses along the lines of Kaplan's succeed in capturing the truth conditions of *de re* constructions. Several direct-reference theorists (including Kaplan) have mounted an impressive case that Kaplan-style neo-Fregean analyses fail in this attempt. Hilary Putnam's Twin-Earth argument suffices to demonstrate the point:[33] Oscar believes his friend Wilbur to be stingy, while Oscar's exact doppelganger on Twin Earth, $Oscar_{TE}$, likewise believes his friend $Wilbur_{TE}$ to be stingy. Duplicates in every detail, Oscar and $Oscar_{TE}$ believe the very

---

incredible, and assume it is not what Forbes intends. More likely, he means that my analysis of belief, together with the neo-Fregean analysis of *de re* locutions, make my use of (8) into a notational variant of the neo-Fregean's use of 'Jones believes of the state of affairs of Venus's being a star that it obtains'. (Analogously, Evans (*Varieties of Reference* [50]) seems to propose that Perry's use of such an attribution as (8) is a notational variant "at best" of the neo-Fregean's use of something like (1′).) But this would hardly make my (or Perry's) theory of (8) into a notational variant of the neo-Fregean's theory of *the very same sentence* (8)—we would still disagree concerning its truth conditions—unless the envisaged neo-Fregean goes further and construes (8) as a paraphrase of something like the relevant *de re* attribution. The proposal in the text represents my attempt to construct the strongest possible case for the spirit of Forbes's (and Evans's) criticism while staying as much as possible within the spirit of Fregean theory (and the bounds of plausibility).

[32] Strictly speaking, this depends on the details of Forbes's neo-Fregean proposal. (The proposed theory certainly does not validate the inference 'Smith believes that Bush will win the presidency, and so does Jones; hence there is some proposition to which both Smith and Jones stand in the belief relation'.) Forbes has confirmed, in personal correspondence, that the intended theory does not validate the inference in the text—on the most straightforward reading of its conclusion—and instead allows only the much weaker conclusion that Smith and Jones believe propositions of the same type. (He proposes taking this weaker conclusion as an alternative reading of the conclusion in the text.)

[33] "Meaning and Reference" [133] (pp. 700–704 and *passim*). Cf. *Frege's Puzzle* (pp. 66–67, 70, 176n7).

same Fregean (nonsingular) thoughts. Neither Oscar nor Oscar$_{TE}$ is in possession of any Fregean individual concept (in which only senses occur as constituents) that differentiates between Wilbur and Wilbur$_{TE}$, and consequently neither possesses a Fregean sense that determines the relevant friend as referent independently of context. Assuming that the objects of belief (whether Fregean thoughts or Russellian singular propositions) and their constituents determine their objects (truth values, individuals, etc.) independently of context,[34] each believes something *de re* that the other does not. Oscar's belief concerning Wilbur is therefore irreducible to his beliefs of Fregean (nonsingular) thoughts. The sentence 'Oscar believes that Wilbur is stingy', which is true on my theory, is deemed false by the

---

[34] This assumption is shared by both Frege and myself. As Frege noted, propositions, or "complete thoughts," (unlike indexical sentences or their conventional meanings—or their senses-in-abstraction-from-context) do not change in truth value, or in the objects they concern, when placed in different settings within a single possible world. The alternative would be an account that allows that one subject A may believe one and the very same proposition (complete thought) p as another subject B, yet A's belief of p is correct, or concerns C, while B's belief of p is incorrect, or does not concern C—because of their differing contexts. Any such indexical account of propositions (as opposed to sentences or their meanings) evidently gets things wrong. For suppose p is the alleged "indexical thought" believed by both Oscar and Oscar$_{TE}$ to the effect $\ulcorner \alpha$ is stingy$\urcorner$, where α is the relevant (complete) "indexical individual concept." Notice first that p cannot be the thought that Wilbur is stingy, since Oscar$_{TE}$ does not believe that thought (in his context, whatever that means), or any other thought concerning Wilbur. (The thought that Wilbur is stingy has nothing whatever to do with Wilbur$_{TE}$—on Twin Earth or anywhere else. It is definitely *not* indexical.) Nor is p the thought that *this* person here [pointing to Wilbur] is stingy, for precisely the same reason. Evidently, we do not express p (in our dialect) with the words 'Wilbur is stingy' or 'He [pointing to Wilbur] is stingy'. Nevertheless, barring singular propositions, p is supposed to be the thought that Oscar expresses (in his idiolect) with these words (or with these words-accompanied-by-pointing). Similarly for Oscar$_{TE}$—otherwise, they would not have the same nonsingular thoughts, and consequently would not be exact duplicates. Thus, on most theories (including orthodox Fregean theory and most of its contemporary variations), Oscar should be able to utter the words 'My Twin-Earth counterpart believes with me that Wilbur is stingy' truthfully (thereby attributing to Oscar$_{TE}$ a belief of p). But he cannot. The alleged indexical thought p, therefore, does not exist. (The fact that Oscar cannot truthfully say 'Oscar$_{TE}$ believes that Wilbur is stingy' might be urged as evidence in favor of the theory described in the text! On that theory, coupled with indexical thoughts, Oscar could truthfully say "Oscar$_{TE}$ does not believe that Wilbur is stingy, but the sentence 'Wilbur is stingy' does correctly give the content, in my idiolect, of one of Oscar$_{TE}$'s beliefs." But taking the argument in this way would be perverse. The point of the argument is precisely that the thought that Oscar expresses with the words 'Wilbur is stingy' in his idiolect is no more indexical than the thought that we express in our dialect.)

proposed neo-Fregean theory. The theories are thus diametrically opposed on a key issue.

The Twin-Earth thought experiment illustrates a further, and more central, divergence between my theory and Fregean theory. The way in which Oscar takes Wilbur is presumably exactly the same as the way in which $Oscar_{TE}$ takes $Wilbur_{TE}$—despite the fact that Oscar's thought of Wilbur that he is stingy and $Oscar_{TE}$'s thought of $Wilbur_{TE}$ that he is stingy concern different individuals. By contrast, for the Fregean, each individual concept determines a unique object, or nothing at all. Oscar's thought that Wilbur is stingy and $Oscar_{TE}$'s thought that $Wilbur_{TE}$ is stingy, if they were to have such thoughts concerning different individuals, would have to contain different individual concepts; the sense that Oscar attaches to the name 'Wilbur' would have to be different from the sense that $Oscar_{TE}$ attaches to the same name. This is made impossible by the fact that Oscar and $Oscar_{TE}$ are exact duplicates.[35] This sort of consideration

---

[35] I can find no plausible way out of this problem for the Fregean. A favored response to this difficulty by self-proclaimed neo-Fregeans has been the postulation of special senses the grasping of which leaves no distinctive trace in one's inner (wholly internal, "purely psychological") state of consciousness—so that exact duplicates like Oscar and $Oscar_{TE}$, whose inner states are exactly the same, nevertheless grasp different "individual concepts." This move faces a serious dilemma: Either the postulated "senses" involve nonconceptual objects (presumably the objects they determine, or their surrogates) as constituents—and are thus individuated by their means—or they do not. If the former, the postulation amounts to the adoption of precisely the sort of theory against which Frege (post-1890) rebelled, while misleadingly couching this anti-Fregean theory in Fregean terminology and labelling the theory with the misnomer 'neo-Fregean'. An "object-involving sense"—a Fregean *Sinn* with nonconceptual components— is a *contradiction in adjecto*; the hypothesized theory is the proverbial wolf in sheep's clothing. (See note 23 above. The arguments of the preceding sections apply equally against this anti-Fregean theory. See also *Frege's Puzzle* [157] (p. 67–70).) If the latter, the response seems little more than a desperate attempt to stipulate or hypothesize what is intuitively impossible, or even conceptually incoherent. The very notion of a concept (*qua* graspable content) seems to include as a necessary condition that those concepts actively grasped or apprehended by someone at any given time, if free of constituents not themselves grasped by the mind, are determined by the grasper's inner state of consciousness—in the sense that such a concept is grasped by someone if and only if it is also grasped by anyone in exactly the same inner state. Actively grasping a purely conceptual concept just *is* a matter of (or, at least, supervenes on) being in a particular inner mental state. Cf. the last paragraph of "Thoughts" [60] (p. 54), where Frege says that grasping or believing a thought is "a process in the inner world of a thinker," and that "when a thought is grasped, it ... brings about changes in the inner world of the one who grasps it." See also *Reference and Essence* [155] (pp. 56–58, 65–69). If Oscar's believing ⌜α is stingy⌝ is a "process in Oscar's inner world," where α is a purely conceptual individual concept

points up a crucial difference—in many respects *the* crucial difference—between my ways-of-taking-objects (which are not precluded from determining their objects only contextually) and Fregean senses (which, since they are information values, cannot do so). (See note 18 above.)

The neo-Fregean might attempt to remedy this serious difficulty with his or her attempt to accommodate *de re* constructions, by tinkering with the Kaplan-style analysis (for example, by relaxing the determination requirement on representation). I remain doubtful that this can be successfully accomplished in a plausible manner without resorting to singular propositions, or the like. But suppose I am wrong and the neo-Fregean can find Fregeanistically acceptable necessary-and-sufficient conditions for *de re* belief and other *de re* propositional attributes, including alethic necessity. (Committed neo-Fregeans might suppose that this *must* be possible.) Would this show that my version of Millianism is simply a notational variant of a suitably designed neo-Fregean theory? Certainly not. Even if (1') is true with respect to a possible circumstance if and only if Jones believes some Fregean thought or other of such-and-such a sort in that possible circumstance—so that, on my view, (8) is also true exactly on the same Fregean condition—still (8), according to my account, does not *say* that this Fregean condition is fulfilled. On my view, (8) asserts a certain relationship—the belief relationship—between Jones and the singular proposition about Venus that it is a star. It does not merely *characterize* Jones's belief as being of some Fregean thought *or other* of such-and-such a special sort; it *specifies* a particular belief and attributes it to Jones. In short, even if the neo-Fregean's promise can be kept by adjusting the Kaplan-style analysis (a very big 'if'), the suitably designed neo-Fregean theory ascribes to (8) a very different semantic content from that ascribed by my version of Millianism. The neo-Fregean's semantic truth conditions for (8) are, at best, *a priori* and metaphysically necessarily equivalent to my own. They are not identical.

Finally, we must consider whether the suitably designed theory would be neo-Fregean. It is true, of course, that a neo-Fregean need not follow the master in every detail. (I do not know of any follower of Frege, for instance, who has not shied away from Frege's views concerning the

---

representing Wilbur, and Oscar$_{TE}$ is in exactly the same inner state, how can he fail to believe exactly the same thing? On the other hand, if grasping the postulated individual concepts is not just a matter of being in a particular inner mental state, the entire account becomes quite mysterious. What exactly are these postulated entities—and what is the justification for calling them "senses" or "purely conceptual concepts" that the mind "grasps," when the (alleged) act of grasping them leaves no distinguishing trace in one's inner state? (Contrast our concepts of *blue*, *down*, *left*.) Is there any plausible reason to suppose that there are such concepts that are pure yet traceless? What would *grasping* such an entity amount to, over and above one's inner state? Is there any plausible reason to believe that the mind engages in such activity?

concept *horse*.) But there must be some limit as to how much departure still qualifies as neo-*Fregean*. Certainly the theory of Russell, for example, differs too extensively from that of Frege on central issues to qualify as neo-Fregean. (It is worth noting in this connection that Russell too recognized certain nonsemantic elements from philosophical psychology in his correspondence with Frege over the proposition that Mont Blanc is over 4000 meters high. It is highly doubtful that Frege saw this as simply another way of saying what he himself was saying.) The sort of theory that Forbes envisions (on this reconstruction of his criticism) is a theory that denies that the 'that'-operator occurring in (8) is functioning there merely as a device for sense-quotation, in the same way that it functions in 'Jones believes that the first heavenly body visible at dusk is a star'; specifically, it denies that (8) asserts a relationship between Jones and the sense of the sentence 'Venus is a star'. Furthermore, the theory denies that (8) specifies a particular belief and attributes it to Jones, claiming instead that (8) merely characterizes Jones's belief as being one or another of a particular sort. Most significantly, the theory construes any occurrence of a simple singular term (even of a proper name) within the scope of the 'that'-operator in a propositional attribution (even in an attribution of propositional attitude) as completely open to substitution by any co-referential simple singular term. The theory is specifically designed to have the consequence that Jones believes that Hesperus is Hesperus if and only if he also believes that Hesperus is Phosphorus. It draws no significant distinction at all, in fact, between the ostensibly *de dicto* (8) and the patently *de re* (1′). Otherwise it would be very different from my version of Millianism—obviously so—and hence unsuited to support Forbes's charge of mere notational variance. I submit that there is not enough of Frege's overall theoretical point of view left here for this (would-be) theory to warrant the epithet 'neo-Fregean'.[36] The same would be true of any of its notational variants.

Nor is the envisioned theory a version of Millianism exactly. It is more a curious admixture, a strange brew made up of elements of both Fregeanism and Millianism. I do not claim that one (perhaps even an erstwhile Fregean) could not find reason to adopt this strange theory; I claim only that doing so would involve abandoning too much of the spirit of orthodox Fregean theory for the proponent to qualify as a neo-Fregean.

---

[36] Essentially this same point is made, on similar grounds, by Mark Richard, "Taking the Fregean Seriously" [149] (pp. 221–222). There, and also in "Attitude Ascriptions, Semantic Theory, and Pragmatic Evidence" [148] (pp. 247–248), Richard makes the related criticism of (something like) the envisaged "neo-Fregean" theory that, since it validates substitution of co-referential names, it lacks one of the primary motivations for the original Fregean theory of senses. (Here Richard also recognizes that the envisaged theory and Millianism assign different, even if equivalent, truth conditions to such propositional-attitude attributions as (8).)

Indeed, if (much to my surprise) genuinely Fregean necessary-and-sufficient conditions are eventually found for the *de re*, I would urge any committed anti-Millian to give the envisioned blend of Fregeanism and Millianism serious consideration as a superior alternative to neo-Fregeanism. Given greater flexibility, however, I would strongly advise against its adoption. Some version of genuine Millianism is much to be preferred. (This was the moral of Sections II and III above.)

10

The Mode-of-Presentation Problem

STEPHEN SCHIFFER

THERE ARE WELL-KNOWN reasons, later to be reviewed, for thinking that believing is a relation to things believed. Naturally, this raises the question of what these things believed might be, and among the available answers the one I find most plausible is that they are *propositions*, where by this I mean abstract, mind- and language-independent entities that have essentially the truth conditions they have. Yet there is a problem with the propositional theory of propositional attitudes: it evidently requires "modes of presentation" of the things our beliefs are about, and there is a real question whether anything exists that is capable of playing the propositionalist's mode-of-presentation role. My own feeling is that the mode-of-presentation problem defeats any *nonPickwickian* version of the propositional theory of propositional attitudes, and in closing I'll return to the hint just implied.

Anyway, to begin, consider the sentence

(1)   Ralph believes that Fido is a dog.

The propositionalist for whom I intend to raise a problem holds that 'believes' generally, and so in (1), expresses a dyadic relation between people and propositions, the latter to be construed in the way just glossed.[1] This characterization leaves room, of course, for important differences among propositionalists. They can disagree about the analysis of the belief relation and about the sorts of propositions that make up the range of the belief relation (sets of possible worlds, say, or complex structured entities containing individuals and properties, or things containing modes of presentation of the individuals and properties they are about). They can even disagree about the logical form of (1), some preferring the representation

---

[1] Although I won't trouble to make the connection, I trust it will be clear that the problem I raise for the propositionalist who claims believing is a relation between a person and a proposition is equally a problem for a theorist who holds that believing is a triadic relation among a person, a proposition, and a mode of presentation.

(2) B(Ralph, the proposition that Fido is a dog),

while others prefer something along the lines of

(3) $(\exists m)(\exists m')(m$ is a mode of presentation of Fido & m' is a mode of presentation of doghood & B(Ralph, the proposition that m has m')),

or, mindful of the context sensitivity of sentences like (1), even

(4) $(\exists m)(\exists m')(\Phi m$ & m is a mode of presentation of Fido & $\Phi'm'$ & m' is a mode of presentation of doghood & B(Ralph, the proposition that m has m')),

where Φ and Φ' are contextually determined and implicitly referred to properties of modes of presentation.

Since (1) doesn't really tell us how Ralph conceives either Fido or doghood, the proponent of (2) is apt to take the proposition referred to in (1) to be a singular proposition whose constituents are Fido and doghood, a proposition representable by the ordered pair ⟨Fido, doghood⟩. But even this ostensibly anti-Fregean 'Fido'-Fido theorist, her eye on Frege's Hesperus/Phosphorus puzzle, will not want to suggest that the mere singular proposition exhausts the content of Ralph's belief. She, like the Fregean propositionalist, will also want recourse to modes of presentation. Perhaps she will say that the range of the belief relation contains both singular propositions and propositions containing modes of presentation, and that, necessarily, (2) is true just in case (3) is true. Or—what I think comes to nearly the same thing—perhaps she will join Nathan Salmon [157] and hold that

B(Ralph, ⟨Fido, doghood⟩) iff $(\exists m)BEL$(Ralph, ⟨Fido, doghood⟩, m))

where BEL is that triadic relation among a person, a proposition, and a mode of presentation which obtains when, so to say, the person believes the proposition under the mode of presentation, and where a mode of presentation of a proposition is at least partly a construction of modes of presentation of the individuals and properties contained in the proposition.[2]

What we see, then, is that *all* propositionalists think they need modes of presentation of the individuals and properties our beliefs are about, and this raises the question, What *are* these modes of presentation? It's this question that defines what I call *the mode-of-presentation problem*. It defines a problem because the propositionalist theory of believing—in the form propositionalists want to hold it (I'll get to this qualification

---

[2] In "The 'Fido'-Fido Theory of Belief" [164] I supposed that the mode of presentation of ⟨Fido, doghood⟩, for Salmon, would be a construction *just* of the modes of presentation of Fido and doghood, but in response to a problem I raised, he [158] denies this. The mode of presentation of ⟨Fido, doghood⟩, he holds, contains the mode of presentation of Fido and doghood, but contains, evidently, something else as well, although no account is given of what that something else is.

later)—requires modes of presentation, but one may doubt whether there is anything adequate to play the theory's mode-of-presentation role. At the close of this paper I shall touch on what kind of propositional theory might do without modes of presentation, but since all propositionalists recognize the need for modes of presentation, I shall begin by wondering what these modes of presentation might be.

1 The Notion of a Mode of Presentation

The expression 'mode of presentation', as it occurs in the development of propositionalist theories, is a term of art; to understand it is to appreciate the perceived need for its introduction. Two little stories should help remind us of that need.

The first is the infamous case of the morning dog and the evening dog. There is a certain dog who begs at Ralph's door every morning. Ralph feeds this dog, whom he has named 'Fido', and has grown attached to it. Ralph believes that Fido is male. There is also a certain dog who begs at Ralph's door every evening. Ralph feeds this dog, too, whom he has named 'Fi Fi', and has also grown quite attached to it. Ralph believes that Fi Fi is female, and he thinks that Fido and Fi Fi would make a really cute couple. Unbeknown to Ralph (so to say), Fido is Fi Fi.

The second story is that of the spurious natural kind shmoghood. Ralph came upon a race of creatures which he thought comprised a previously unencountered biological species, and he introduced the word 'shmog' to designate members of that species. "A thing shall be called a 'shmog'," Ralph said, "just in case it belongs to the species of these creatures." Unbeknown to him, however, shmoghood is doghood; Ralph had stumbled not upon a new species but upon a new race of dogs, and thus the property that 'shmog' has been introduced as standing for is none other than doghood.

Given these two stories, any propositionalist would be willing to accept the following as data.

When Ralph says "Fido is male but Fi Fi is female," he isn't being irrational in holding the belief which that utterance expresses. But he couldn't rationally hold the belief that would be expressed by an utterance of 'Fido is and isn't male'. Likewise, Ralph isn't irrational in holding the two beliefs expressed by a morning utterance of 'This dog is male' and an evening utterance of 'This dog is female', even though the same dog is referred to in both utterances. But of course Ralph couldn't rationally hold the belief that would be expressed by a sincere utterance of 'This dog is and isn't male'.

Similarly, when Ralph says "Fido is a dog, not a shmog," and when he says "No dogs are shmogs," he isn't being irrational in holding the beliefs those utterances express. But he would be irrational were he to hold the belief that would be expressed by an utterance of 'No dogs are dogs'.

The propositionalist's appeal to modes of presentation is designed precisely to accommodate these sorts of data. The intuitive idea, definitive of the propositionalist's notion of a mode of presentation, may be called *Frege's Constraint*. Stated informally and in a way that prescinds from the details of any particular propositionalist's account of belief or of belief-ascribing sentences, Frege's Constraint has two parts. First it says that a rational person x may both believe and disbelieve that a certain thing or property y is such and such only if there are distinct modes of presentation m and m' such that x believes y to be such and such under m and disbelieves it to be such and such under m'. Then it says that there are distinct modes of presentation m and m' such that rational person x believes y to be such and such under m and disbelieves y to be such and such under m' only if x fails to realize that m and m' are modes of presentation of one and the same thing. In other words, you can't rationally believe and disbelieve something under one and the same mode of presentation, or under modes of presentation which you realize are modes of presentation of the same thing. The notion of a mode of presentation is thus functionally defined: something is a mode of presentation if it plays the role defined by Frege's Constraint, and nothing can be a mode a presentation unless it plays that role. *To ask what modes of presentation are is just to ask what things play that role.*

It is of course consistent with their acceptance of Frege's Constraint that different propositionalists will utilize modes of presentation in different ways. Thus, as regards the morning-dog/evening-dog story, Nathan Salmon would say that

(5)   Ralph believes that Fido is male

and

(6)   Ralph believes that Fi Fi is male

have the same truth-value, in that both 'that'-clauses refer to the same singular proposition and the two sentences are otherwise the same. Ralph's rationality is acquitted because Salmon's triadic *BEL* relation, in terms of which his dyadic belief relation is analyzed, just is the believing-a-proposition-under-a-mode-of-presentation relation. Salmon would say that

$$(\exists m)(\exists m')(m \neq m' \ \& \ BEL(\text{Ralph}, \langle \text{Fido/Fi Fi}, \text{malehood}\rangle, m)$$
$$\& \ BEL(\text{Ralph}, \langle \text{Fido/Fi Fi}, \text{femalehood}\rangle, m')),$$

where the modes of presentation that make this true are ones which, in the appropriate sense, Ralph fails to realize are modes of presentation of the same thing; perhaps one, which he associates with the name 'Fido', requires thinking of Fido as the morning dog, whereas the other mode of presentation, which he associates with the name 'Fi Fi', requires thinking of the dog with two names as the evening dog.

But the propositionalist who would represent (1) as (4) is free to see appropriate utterances of (5) and (6) as having different truth-values. Ignoring modes of presentation for malehood, this theorist might (to a first approximation) represent the utterance of (5) as

$(\exists m)(m$ represents Fido as the dog who appears in the morning
& B(Ralph, that m is male)),

which is true, and she might represent the utterance of (6) as

$(\exists m)(m$ represents Fi Fi as the dog who appears in the evening
& B(Ralph, that m is male)),

which is false. For this theorist, to believe x to be such and such under mode of presentation m is just to believe the proposition that m is such and such, where the proposition that m is such and such is true in the actual world just in case x is such and such.

I mention these two different propositionalist ways of appealing to modes of presentation not to make invidious comparisons, but merely to illustrate the ways propositionalists may employ the notion. The mode-of-presentation problem I have in mind is a problem for any propositionalist.

Frege's Constraint is, as I said, *definitive* of the propositionalist's use of the notion of a mode of presentation. Another constraint I want to discuss isn't definitive of the notion; it's rather a consequence of the functional definition of the notion of a mode of presentation when that definition is conjoined with certain ancillary assumptions. I shall call this constraint the *Intrinsic-Description Constraint*. To be a mode of presentation for a given theorist is just to play the role defined for that theorist by Frege's Constraint. The Intrinsic-Description Constraint holds that if a thing plays that role—if, that is, it's a mode of presentation—then it must be intrinsically identifiable in a way that doesn't describe it as a mode of presentation or as a possible mode of presentation. In other words, it must be possible to answer the question "What is the mode of presentation of so and so?" in terms of an intrinsic characterization of the mode of presentation whose meaning implies nothing about the thing it applies to being a mode of presentation. If a thing is a mode of presentation, then it must be intrinsically identifiable as some other kind of thing.

Let me try to clarify the meaning and point of this constraint by changing the subject a little. Suppose a theorist were to claim that believing is a relation to *objects believed*, that 'y' in the open sentence 'x believes y' is a genuine *objectual* variable whose values are things believed. Now one might ask, *What are these things believed, these objects of belief?* One asking this question is apt to be asking it with the following thought in mind. "The property of being an object of belief can't be an intrinsic, essential, and individuating property of the things that have it; it's at best a contingent, extrinsic property of them, like the property of being a husband. Consequently, what I need to know—what I'm asking for when I ask what objects of belief are—is an *intrinsic* characterization of those things that happen to be objects of belief, a characterization of them that doesn't characterize them as objects of belief. If I'm told they're functions from possible worlds to truth-values, or sentences, then I'm being offered an answer with the right form, whether or not it's correct." This is the Intrinsic-Description

Constraint applied to objects of belief, to whatever entities make up the range of the belief relation. It holds that being a thing believed is a contingent property of the things having it, and therefore it must be possible to say what "things believed" are in terms other than their being things believed.

Now suppose that the theorist who proposed that believing is a relation to things believed tried to deny the application of the Intrinsic-Description Constraint to objects of belief. He insists that *being a thing believed* is an essential and intrinsic property and that it isn't possible to answer the question "What are things believed?" in other terms. To demand to be told what objects of belief are in terms other than their being objects of belief is, he says, no more legitimate than demanding to be told what sets are in terms of a different intrinsic characterization of sets than their being sets. Just as you can't say what sets are in other and more intrinsic terms, so you can't say what objects of belief are in other and more intrinsic terms (cf. Peacocke [127]).

But this is a very implausible reply. Being a set *is* an essential and individuating property of sets, and that's why it's inappropriate to ask "What are sets?" and expect an answer in *other* intrinsic terms. But it is not at all plausible that *being a thing believed* is an essential and individuating property of things believed. For to say that the property of being a thing believed is an essential property of the things having it evidently implies that these things come into existence only when people believe them, and that seems crazy. Realizing this, our imagined theorist might retreat to the claim that the only intrinsic characterization of objects of belief is that they are *potentially* objects of belief. But this obscurantist reply runs afoul of the correct principle: No potential property without an intrinsic actual property.

Returning to modes of presentation, my point as regards the Intrinsic-Description Constraint is the same as the one just elaborated with respect to objects of belief. The property of being a mode of presentation, like the property of being a thing believed, is a contingent property of whatever things, if any, have it. If there really are things that play the mode-of-presentation role, then it's a contingent fact about them that they play that role. Consequently, if there are modes of presentation, then it must be possible to say what they are in terms that do better than to characterize them as modes of presentation, or as potential modes of presentation.

2 So What Are Modes of Presentation?

If there are things that play the propositionalist's mode-of-presentation role, then it should be possible to say what they are in a way that satisfies Frege's Constraint and the Intrinsic-Description Constraint. Yet I question whether there are such things, for when I survey the list of already-entertained candidate modes of presentation, it seems clear that none of them pans out, and I think it's unlikely that the real modes of presentation have escaped that list.

For consider Ralph's belief that Fido is a dog. The propositionalist will need modes of presentation of Fido, of doghood, and, possibly (see Schiffer [164] and Salmon [158]), of the singular proposition ⟨Fido, doghood⟩, where that mode of presentation isn't determined by those of the proposition's constituents. What, to pare things down, might Ralph's mode of presentation of doghood be?

An individual concept

Every general property Φ determines a unique "individual concept" (Carnap [20]): it's the property of having Φ uniquely; it's the property a thing has just in case it, and it alone, has Φ. The description-theoretic view that modes of presentation are individual concepts has mostly been advanced as a Frege- and Russell-inspired theory about the modes of presentation of ordinary physical objects (see Schiffer [163]), and it has even less plausibility when held as a theory about the modes of presentation of natural-kind properties. In Chapter 3 of my *Remnants of Meaning* [165], I offer several reasons why an individual concept can't be a mode of presentation of doghood, but let me just mention one that I think is particularly devastating. Assume that *THE P* (the property of having the general property P uniquely) is the individual concept that is Ralph's mode of presentation for doghood. How is Ralph able to think about the general property P? Either he is "directly acquainted" with it, and thus can think of it in a way that is unmediated by a mode of presentation, or else he has an individual concept *THE Q* for P. If the latter, then we can ask the same about Q, and it's clear that we shall be stuck with a vicious regress of individual concepts for properties contained in individual concepts unless the chain terminates in an individual concept, *THE X*, whose general property, X, is one that Ralph is "directly acquainted" with. It follows, then, that if Ralph's mode of presentation of doghood is an individual concept, then Ralph must have an individual concept of doghood whose general property, unlike doghood, is one that he can think about without mediation by a mode of presentation. Yet it's clear, I submit, that doghood instantiates no such individual concept.[3]

A "stereotype"

I think the intuitive idea here is that Ralph's mode of presentation of doghood is something like a composite visual image of a dog, something like Locke's abstract general idea of a dog. Of course, it can't *literally* be that, since many people don't think in visual images, but maybe the stereotype

---

[3] The same objection, *mutatis mutandis*, can be made against the proposal that modes of presentation are "nonindividual concepts"—general properties which make no claim to uniqueness. Besides, as I show in [163], the proposal fails to satisfy Frege's Constraint.

proposal can be cashed out in terms of the topical notion of a prototype (see Smith and Medin [175]), if that notion can be made suitably precise and non-question-begging. So one problem with the stereotype proposal is that it's not clear what exactly is being proposed. Two other problems, also canvassed in *Remnants of Meaning* [165] (Section 3.6), are as follows. First, it's difficult to see what the mode-of-presentation relation—the relation that must obtain between two things in order for the one to be a mode of presentation of the other—could be if modes of presentation of natural-kind properties are stereotypes. For suppose that Ralph has only been exposed to German shepherds and Great Danes. He is still able to believe that Fido is a dog, so a relation is needed to link his narrow stereotype to that property of dogs which is constitutive of the entire species, and it's difficult to see what sort of relation this could be. The second problem with the stereotype proposal is a straightforward objection: it seems not to satisfy Frege's Constraint, whose satisfaction is *definitive* of being a mode of presentation. I believe that there are bullfinches and that there are goldfinches, but, being an ornithological ignoramus, I seem to have the same "stereotype" for both natural-kind properties. If that stereotype were my mode of presentation of both bullfinchhood and goldfinchhood, then nothing would prevent my believing and disbelieving bullfinchhood to be instantiated by a certain thing under the stereotype, thus violating Frege's Constraint. As I know that one stereotype does duty for two properties, I could easily believe one property to be such and such under the stereotype and then, under the same stereotype, mistake that property for the other that shares the stereotype and believe it not to be such and such.

A word

Perhaps Ralph's mode of presentation for doghood is the word 'dog', the way then to resolve the shmog story being to say that he has two modes of presentation of doghood, 'dog' and 'shmog'. This idea may appeal to those who hold that one believes a proposition *by accepting a sentence* (see Perry [129] and Soames [176]), which suggests that, as one may believe a proposition by accepting one sentence which expresses it but not by accepting another which also expresses it, the mode of presentation under which one believes the proposition is the sentence by whose acceptance one believes the proposition. And if Ralph's mode of presentation for the proposition that Fido is a dog is the sentence 'Fido is a dog' (by whose acceptance he believes the proposition), then his mode of presentation for doghood in this instance will be the word 'dog'.

The proposal, however, lacks credibility. First, it fails to apply to languageless believers (feral humans, chimps, very young children) and so is insufficiently general. Second, it's hard to see how "accepting a sentence" can be explicated without appeal to propositional attitudes, thereby rendering the account circular. Third, it is easy to conjure up a Paderewski-type counterexample (cf. Kripke [96]) in which Ralph uses the word 'dog' for what he *mistakenly* thinks is two kinds of animal, making him prepared to say 'Fido is a dog', when taking 'dog' in the one way, and 'Fido is not a dog', when taking it in the other way. This is a counterexample to the proposal that Ralph's mode of presentation is 'dog', because the proposal constrains us to say that Ralph only has one mode of presentation, whereas Frege's Constraint requires Ralph to have two distinct modes of presentation of doghood.[4]

A "character"

Kaplan [92] has entertained the proposal that modes of presentation are characters, where the character of a general term like 'dog' is a function from contexts of the word's utterance to the property that is its content. But this, among other problems, can't accommodate the shmog example. For 'dog' and 'shmog' have the same character for Kaplan—that constant function which maps every context onto doghood—but the propositionalist needs to say that Ralph associates distinct modes of presentation with the two words.

A causal chain

Perhaps the belief state Ralph is in when he says 'Fido is a dog' has doghood in its content because of a certain *causal chain* that links Ralph's belief state to doghood. Perhaps, too, the belief state Ralph is in when he says 'Fido isn't a shmog' has doghood in *its* content because of a certain *other* causal chain linking this different belief state to doghood. In this event, why not say that causal chains are modes of presentation of natural-kind properties like doghood? Several problems defeat this proposal, but I shall mention only one (other objections to the proposal may be inferred from the objections presently to be raised against the proposal that modes of presentation are functional roles).

Either these content-determining causal chains are nonintentionally specifiable, in physical or topic-neutral terms, or they aren't. If they aren't, that's because the specifications make irreducible references to the beliefs and intentions of the believer or of others who comprise links in the chain. Now if such irreducible references are required, they will surely be in terms of the contents of those propositional attitudes, in the broad sense that includes the modes of presentations which help to individuate belief states. Then, however, the attempt to identify modes of presentation with

---

[4]Perhaps it will be said that in the appropriate way of individuating words, Ralph really does have two distinct *homonymous* words for doghood. But now we haven't a clue as to what the proposal is until we are given the intended method of word individuation. (Note that the individuation can't appeal to word meanings, because the sort of theorist who appeals to the believing-a-proposition-by-accepting-a-sentence idea will want to say that the meaning of 'dog' is doghood (i.e., the natural kind of dogs) on each of Ralph's uses of the word.)

causal chains is not only circular but also violates the Intrinsic-Description Constraint. This means that the causal chains must be nonintentionally specifiable if they are to be modes of presentation. But the existence of such nonintentionally specifiable content-determining causal chains would constitute a physicalistic or topic-neutral reduction of intentionality, and, alas, the prospects for such a reduction don't look very good (see Schiffer [165], especially chapters 2 and 4).

A functional role

If Ralph believes that Fido is a dog, then he is in a belief state that involves modes of presentation of Fido and doghood. These modes of presentations, by definition, affect the way this belief state can interact with other propositional-attitude states. These modes of presentation, in other words, determine *functional* features of the propositional-attitude states involving them. Why not, then, simply *identify* modes of presentation with the functional characteristics they determine? Let me try to make this idea precise enough to take seriously.[5]

A state *token* has causes and effects, but, being a one shot affair, it doesn't in any nonderivative sense have a causal *role*. Causal, or functional, roles are properties of state *types*, which are in turn properties of state tokens (see Schiffer [165], 2.2). For a state type to have a functional role is just for it to be causally or counterfactually related to sensory inputs, to other state types, or to behavioral outputs. A state type will have indefinitely many distinct functional roles, distinct ways, that is, of being relevantly related to sensory inputs, to other states, or to behavioral outputs. So if Ralph's mode of presentation for doghood is to be identified with some function role, then we need to ask, *which* functional role of *what* state type? Now the mode of presentation of doghood operative in Ralph's present belief that Fido is a dog may also be operative in his belief that dogs bark and in his desire to have a dog. A state type, for our purposes, is simply a property of state tokens. The proposal that the mode of presentation of doghood is a functional role therefore needs a property of propositional-attitude state tokens that can belong both to Ralph's belief that Fido is a dog and to his desire to have a dog.

---

[5] In my [165] I in effect defined the propositionalist position in such a way that modes of presentation had to be propositional constituents that *indexed* functional roles, and thus determined them without being identical to them. No position in logical space was being excluded, I thought, because the view that modes of presentation are functional, or conceptual, roles was covered in my discussion of the two-factor theory of meaning for the language of thought. But I now feel it was a mistake not to have discussed the functional-role proposal directly in terms of the propositionalist theory, and I welcome the opportunity to do so now.

The best way to realize this ambition is to suppose that thinkers are information processors who think—i.e., process information—in a language of thought, the "brain's language of synaptic interconnections and neural spikes" (Lewis [109], p. 346), and to identify Ralph's mode of presentation of doghood with the (relevant) conceptual role of some neural word which expresses doghood. Suppose one had a computational psychology T for Ralph, thinking in the neural code N. T would assign to each "sentence" type of N a complex property whose specification would detail the conditions under which that sentence would be tokened as a belief, a desire, an intention, and so on, and would detail the ways in which those tokenings resulted in bodily movements. Call this complex property of an N sentence its *conceptual role with respect to T*. The conceptual role with respect to T of an N word is its contribution, as determined by T, to the T-determined conceptual roles of every N sentence in which it occurs. I submit that the most plausible version of the view that modes of presentation are functional roles is that they are *the conceptual roles determined for the expressions in a person's language of thought by some correct and comprehensive computational theory of his or her inner processing*. If Ralph thinks in English, then the mode of presentation of doghood that is operative when he says 'Fido is a dog' is the conceptual role, as determined by the most comprehensive correct theory of his inner processing, of the neural variant of 'dog'. The reason Ralph can rationally think that Fido is a dog but not a shmog, while he can't rationally think that Fido is a dog but not a dog, is owed to the different conceptual roles of 'dog' and 'shmog' in his inner code.

The problem with this proposal is that it seems not to cohere with any version of the propositionalist theory worth taking seriously. I shall explain.

The propositionalist, by definition, holds that 'believes' in (1) ('Ralph believes that Fido is a dog') expresses a relation between believers and propositions believed, but we've already noticed that this leaves room for two opposing views about the nature of the 'that'-clause, 'that Fido is a dog'. One view, in fact the classical view, holds that the 'that'-clause is a singular term which refers to the proposition that Fido is a dog. The other view holds that (1)'s 'that'-clause is not a singular term which refers to what, if (1) is true, Ralph believes; rather the 'that'-clause disappears on the correct representation of (1)'s logical form, leaving an existential generalization over modes of presentation, something that gives only an indirect and partial characterization of the proposition Ralph believes. If we ignore now-irrelevant refinements (such as (4)) a first shot at this style of representation was given earlier as

$(\exists m)(\exists m')(m$ is a mode of presentation of Fido & m' is a mode of presentation of doghood & B(Ralph, the proposition that m has m')),

but we'll have to ask what this should look like when modes of presentation are taken to be conceptual roles.

Now if 'that Fido is a dog' refers in (1) to the proposition that Fido is a dog, then that proposition can't be a mode-of-presentation-containing proposition, but must be the mere singular proposition ⟨Fido, doghood⟩. The reason, already noted, is simple: 'believes that Fido is a dog' can be univocally true of people who think of Fido and doghood in very different ways (Helen Keller might be one of them), and one who utters (1) assertively need not be making any implicit, contextually determined reference to a mode-of-presentation-containing proposition, because, even though she is in a position to say that Ralph believes that Fido is a dog, she might not know Ralph's modes of presentation of Fido or doghood. I conclude, then, that

(∗) $B(\text{Ralph}, \langle\text{Fido, doghood}\rangle)$

is the correct representation of (1) if (1)'s 'that'-clause refers to a proposition (and, of course, 'believes' in (1) is dyadic[6]). The next thing to see is that this representation of (∗) can't cohere with the proposal that modes of presentation are conceptual roles of inner expressions.

If (∗) represents (1), then the way to bring in modes of presentation is via Nathan Salmon's proposal that

$B(\text{Ralph}, \langle\text{Fido, doghood}\rangle)$ iff $(\exists m)BEL(\text{Ralph}, \langle\text{Fido, doghood}\rangle, m)$

or something tantamount to it. But we can see in the following way that this can't cohere with the view that modes of presentation are conceptual roles.

Let 'believes∗' express the relation that relates a person to a sentence in his inner code just in case that sentence is tokened in him as a belief (cf. Field [53]). Let $\ulcorner S(a)\urcorner$ be a sentence in x's inner code which contains the name a; let $\ulcorner S(b)\urcorner$ be exactly like $\ulcorner S(a)\urcorner$ except that it contains b where the latter contains a; and let both sentences mean a proposition which contains y, the referent of a and b. Then we may notice that any credible conceptual role psychology must surely countenance the principle that

---

[6] The qualification is needed because one possible representation of (1) involves taking 'believes' to express what Salmon calls the BEL relation, a relation among a person, a proposition, and a mode of presentation of that proposition. One who takes this line may want to represent (1) as, say, '$(\exists x)B(\text{Ralph}, \langle\text{Fido, doghood}\rangle, x)$' (see Schiffer [164]). Although for convenience of exposition I'm limiting myself to propositionalist theories that take believing to be a dyadic relation, I hope it will be clear that obvious extensions of what I say will yield verdicts on all the relevant positions in logical space.

I should also add that the claim that 'Fido is a dog' in (1) refers to ⟨Fido, doghood⟩ if it refers to a proposition must be understood as relative to an implicit background assumption, namely, that if a 'that'-clause is a singular term, then its referent is determined by its syntax and the referents of its semantically relevant parts. In Section 4 I'll mention a way of challenging this assumption.

If x rationally believes* both $\ulcorner S(a) \urcorner$ and $\ulcorner \neg S(b) \urcorner$, then x believes* $\ulcorner a \neq b \urcorner$.

(For example, if Lois Lane rationally believes* 'Superman flies' and 'Clark Kent doesn't fly', then she also believes* 'Clark Kent isn't Superman'.)

If modes of presentation are conceptual roles, then

$BEL(x, p, m)$ iff m is the (relevant) conceptual role of some sentence in x's inner code which "means" p and which x believes*.

But now suppose that the Superman story is fact and that Floyd is in the know about Superman's duplicitous nature (he, unlike Lois Lane, believes* 'Clark Kent is Superman'). Nevertheless, it may still be that, with no loss to his rationality,

Floyd believes that Lois believes that Superman flies

and

Floyd believes that Lois doesn't believe that Clark Kent flies.

Now for the 'Fido'-Fido theory in question—the theory that represents (1) as (∗)—this represents a case of Floyd's rationally believing and disbelieving the same proposition, as the proposition referred to by the second 'that'-clause is the negation of the one referred to by the first 'that'-clause. Letting 'Q' stand for the proposition believed and disbelieved, and supposing that modes of presentation are conceptual roles, we then know that there are distinct sentences $\ulcorner S(a) \urcorner$ and $\ulcorner S(b) \urcorner$ in Floyd's language of thought such that (i) both mean Q, (ii) the second is just like the first except that it has the distinct name b of Superman/Clark Kent where the first has a, and (iii) Floyd rationally believes* both $\ulcorner S(a) \urcorner$ and $\ulcorner \neg S(b) \urcorner$. (If we suppose Floyd thinks in English then the two sentences would be 'Lois believes that Superman flies' and 'Lois doesn't believe that Clark Kent flies'.) But this lands us in the soup, for Floyd doesn't believe* $\ulcorner a \neq b \urcorner$ (he doesn't believe* 'Superman $\neq$ C.K.'), and this is why the 'Fido'-Fido theory doesn't cohere with the proposal that modes of presentation are conceptual roles.

Here is another, but even more succinct, rendering of why the 'Fido'-Fido theory can't cohere with the proposal that modes of presentation are conceptual roles. As the foregoing example shows, the 'Fido'-Fido theory is constrained to have a theory of modes of presentation according to which one can rationally believe and disbelieve a proposition even though one doesn't have distinct modes of presentation of any component of that proposition which one fails to realize are modes of presentation of the same thing (see Schiffer [164] and Salmon [158]). Yet this is not a possibility on the view that modes of presentation are conceptual roles.[7]

---

[7] The careful reader will have noticed that the argument just presented carries with it the further conclusion that the 'Fido'-Fido theory can't cohere with

So much for half of the reason modes of presentation can't be conceptual roles; a summary of the line of argument would be useful before turning to the other half. We were concerned with the question of what Ralph's mode of presentation of doghood might be, but the proposal that it might be a functional role really makes sense only if all modes of presentation are functional roles, and this general thesis allowed us to relax the focus on doghood. Then the rough starting idea, modes of presentation as functional roles, gave way to its most promising refinement: modes of presentation as the conceptual roles (as determined by some comprehensive, correct conceptual-role psychology) of Mentalese expressions. Next, my objection was stated as having the following form: propositionalist theories of belief, which take 'believes' to express a dyadic relation between believers and the propositions they believe, may be divided between those that take the 'that'-clause in (1) to refer to a proposition and those that don't. The most plausible version of the first sort finds the referent of 'that Fido is a dog' to be the mode-of-presentation-less singular proposition ⟨Fido, doghood⟩, modes of presentation coming in as the third term of a triadic relation, the believing-a-proposition-under-a-mode-of-presentation relation (Salmon's *BEL*), in whose terms the dyadic belief relation is to be analyzed. I have just finished arguing that this 'Fido'-Fido theory can't accommodate the proposal that modes of presentation are conceptual roles.

Nor, we shall see, can the other alternative, which denies that the 'that'-clause in (1) is a singular term. Initially, as a first approximation, I had this theorist representing (1) as

$(\exists m)(\exists m')(m$ is a mode of presentation of Fido & m' is a mode of presentation of doghood & B(Ralph, the proposition that m has $m'))$,

but when modes of presentation are taken to be conceptual roles, this can give way to

$(\exists m)(\exists m')B$(Ralph, ⟨⟨Fido, m⟩, ⟨doghood, m'⟩⟩),

where the ordered pair can be our provisional representation of a form of proposition that contains conceptual roles and the things they are modes of presentation of. The theorist will want Fido and doghood in the proposition along with the conceptual roles of words in Ralph's neural code

---

the hypothesis that one thinks in a language of thought. More accurately, it can't cohere with this if we assume that, all else being equal, a rational person can believe* both $\ulcorner S(a) \urcorner$ and $\ulcorner \neg S(b) \urcorner$ only if she believes* $\ulcorner a \neq b \urcorner$. For the 'Fido'-Fido theorist is constrained to hold, first, that Floyd believes* the Mentalese translation of 'Lois believes that Superman flies' and 'Lois doesn't believe that Clark Kent flies' and, second, that Floyd doesn't believe* the Mentalese translation of 'Superman isn't Clark Kent' (just pretend that Floyd thinks in English).

which refer to Fido and doghood, because, as conceptual role can't determine reference (see Field [52] and Schiffer [165], p. 108), Fido and doghood are needed to secure the right truth conditions. There is no need for the representation to mention that m and m' are modes of presentation, because that they are modes of presentation is secured by the way they enter into propositions in the range of the belief relation; and there is no need to mention that modes of presentation are conceptual roles, as that is entailed by the nature of the belief relation.

Let's call the second approach to the logical form of (1) the MP proposal, as it sees (1) as involving a tacit quantification over modes of presentation. The reason I'll mention for doubting that the MP proposal can cohere with the proposal that modes of presentation are conceptual roles is that (a) the marriage implies that 'that'-clauses in belief sentences are *never* singular terms, and (b) that is unacceptable.[8]

If the MP proposal is correct, then that's because believing is a relation that builds in satisfaction of Frege's Constraint: you can't rationally believe and disbelieve the same proposition. It's precisely to secure this that the theorist builds modes of presentation into the propositions comprising the range of the belief relation—or at least into those propositions that wouldn't satisfy Frege's Constraint (in the sense just extended to propositions) without it. But if modes of presentation are conceptual roles, then every proposition (in the range of the belief relation) contains modes of presentation; for whatever object or property is involved in the proposition, there will be some expression in one's language of thought which refers to, or means, that thing, and that expression will have a conceptual role determined by the relevant theory, which is what the proposal says a mode of presentation is. Consequently, on the present assumptions a 'that'-clause in a belief sentence is a singular term only if it refers to a conceptual-role-containing proposition.

It is, however, most implausible that the 'that'-clause in

Ralph believes that the sum of 68 and 57 isn't 5

---

[8] It may well be that the MP theorist's reasons for denying that the 'that'-clause in (1) is a singular term extends to every occurrence of a 'that'-clause in a belief ascription, and if this is so then the conceptual-role proposal will be idle in the argument against the conjunction of it and the MP proposal. But my point as regards (a) is that the MP theorist who also thinks that modes of presentation are conceptual roles has, by that further commitment, no choice but to deny that 'that'-clauses ever refer, in belief sentences, to propositions. It may also be that, as regards (b), the reasons for denying that 'that'-clauses in belief sentences are never singular terms are reasons for denying that the 'that'-clause in (1) isn't a singular term, and this, too, would yield an objection to the MP proposal that was independent of its marriage to the conceptual-role proposal. Needless to say, this sort of overdetermination wouldn't undermine the force of my reason for doubting that the MP proposal can cohere with the conceptual-role proposal.

refers to a proposition which contains the conceptual roles of the relevant words in Ralph's inner code which refer to, or mean, the numbers 68, 57, 5, the plus function, negation, and the identity relation. For a start both Ralph, a brilliant mathematician, and nine-year-old Harold, whose mastery of addition is marginal at best, may believe that the sum of 68 and 57 isn't 5; yet the relevant conceptual roles of the relevant expressions in their respective inner codes could hardly be the same. This means that if the token of the 'that'-clause in the sentence which ascribes to Ralph his belief and the one in

> Harold believes that the sum of 68 and 57 isn't 5

refer to conceptual-role-containing propositions, then they refer to *different* propositions, and, consequently, it can't be that 'that the sum of 68 and 57 isn't 5' has a context-independent reference determined by its syntax and the references of its component parts. If, therefore, the two tokens of the 'that'-clause refer to distinct conceptual-role-containing propositions—one Ralph believes, and one Harold believes—then it must be that one uttering a belief sentence containing the 'that'-clause is making a contextually-determined reference to such a proposition. But it is, I submit, quite impossible to see how a normal speaker in uttering the sentence about Harold could be making an implicit reference to just the right conceptual roles of just the right neural expressions in Harold's *lingua mentis*.[9]

This brings me to (b) and to at least one reason it's unacceptable that 'that'-clauses never function as singular terms in belief sentences. For consider these two inferences:

> Ralph and Harold both believe that the sum of 68 and 57 isn't 5.
>
> So, there is some truth (viz., that the sum of 68 and 57 isn't 5) which they both believe.

> Harold believes that the sum of 68 and 57 isn't 5.
>
> That the sum of 68 and 57 isn't 5 is Saul's theory.
>
> So, Harold believes Saul's theory.

Evidently, both inferences may be sound, and the only way, so far as I can see, that the marriage of the MP and conceptual-role proposals can coherently recognize the soundness of these arguments is to deny that the quantification in the conclusion of the first inference is objectual and to

---

[9] One might try saying that the normal guy's reference to a conceptual role is under a description of the form *the way of thinking of* x *she associates with expression* e. But it's very doubtful, I think, that ordinary people can be relied on to have such sophisticated beliefs, and this is *especially* true once the colloquial notion of a "way of thinking" about something is spelled out so as to secure that the description is uniquely satisfied by just the right Mentalese conceptual role (just suppose that the person who thinks that Harold believes that $68 + 57 \neq 5$ is a nine-year old).

deny that the 'that'-clause in the second premise of the second inference refers to Saul's theory. Now I can imagine how these things might be denied by a theorist who also denied that believing was a relation to things believed and that the logical form of sentences containing 'that'-clauses was representable within a finitely axiomatizable compositional semantics (see Schiffer [165]). But I can't imagine how it could be denied by the present theorist, who believes in propositions, thinks believing is a relation to them, and believes in the need to give a compositional reckoning of sentences like 'That George Bush is a heroin addict is an unfounded rumor'.

3 Should We Keep Looking for Modes of Presentation?

The foregoing six candidates (seven if you count nonindividual concepts—see footnote 3) exhausts all the likely and not so likely candidates I can think of to play the propositionalist's mode-of-presentation role. Needless to say, I may be wrong about the Intrinsic-Description Constraint, and I may have offered bad reasons for dismissing the right candidate for the job; but I can also imagine the following response.

"Look, Schiffer, just because none of the candidates you've considered pans out doesn't mean we won't eventually discover things satisfying the Intrinsic-Description Constraint which do play the mode-of-presentation role. The fact that we can't *now* say what modes of presentation are no more shows there aren't any than the failure to say what genes were before the discovery of DNA showed there weren't any genes. The propositional theory of believing, which requires the existence of modes of presentation, has the status of gene theory before the chemical nature of genes was known, and we should hope that continued research will eventually reveal what modes of presentation are, just as (let's pretend) further research in molecular biology discovered that genes are segments of DNA molecules."

Well, this *isn't* a very good reply, and a propositionalist really ought to be worried if he agrees that none of the candidates so far proposed can play the mode-of-presentation role. The problem can be brought out by noticing a crucial disanalogy between gene theory and mode-of-presentation theory. When biologists wondered what genes were they appreciated that 'gene' was simply an introduced term for whatever plays a certain causal role, and they sought to know what played that role. That required an *empirical* discovery; it took science to discover the role of DNA in the transmission of inheritable characteristics. The situation, however, is different as regards modes of presentation. No one was in a position prior to the relevant research to rule out DNA as that which played the gene role, but what we're stuck for is *merely* a specification of a kind of thing whose members *might* play the mode-of-presentation role. We've gone through the categories that we know about, and I doubt we can make good sense of the idea that some empirical, scientific procedure might reveal to us that modes of presentation are things of some yet undiscovered kind, some category of entity we're not yet even in a position to entertain. If entities of a certain kind really are modes of presentation, then we ought now to be in a position to put them on the list of candidates. It's the fact that we can't see what to add to the preceding section's list that ought to be disturbing to the propositionalist who agrees in dismissing the items already on it.

4 Propositions without Modes of Presentation: a Pickwickian Proposal

Let's notice how a tempting, although not inevitable, line of reasoning can quickly lead a theorist to dilemma. The theorist begins by noticing that the sentence

Reggie believes that eating liver increases sexual potency

has the appearance of saying that Reggie stands in the belief relation to something referred to by the singular term 'that eating liver increases sexual potency'; that is, it refers to *that eating liver increases sexual potency*, the same thing that's the logical subject of the subject-predicate sentence

That eating liver increases sexual potency is untested.

But what, the theorist wonders next, is this thing, *that eating liver increases sexual potency*, that's the referent of the 'that'-clause singular term? Well, he reasons, it's abstract: that eating liver increases sexual potency isn't in space or time; it's mind- and language-independent: that eating liver increases sexual potency would exist and have properties even if there were no thinkers or speakers; and it has a truth condition, which it has essentially: that eating liver increases sexual potency is true in any possible world just in case in that world eating liver increases sexual potency. So, the theorist reasons, the referent of a 'that'-clause, the second term of the belief relation, must be a *proposition*: an abstract, mind- and language-independent entity that has essentially the truth condition it has.

Accepting what he has so far been led to, the theorist wants to stay with common sense and further say that

Ralph believes that Fido is a dog

and

Ralph doesn't believe that Fi Fi is a shmog

may both be true, notwithstanding the identity of Fido and Fi Fi and the identity of doghood and shmoghood (see above, page 251). Thus, the theorist concedes, the 'that'-clauses in these sentences refer to different propositions, and this is where the dilemma enters. For if the 'that'-clauses refer to different propositions, then the occurrences in those 'that'-clauses of the singular and general names must also have different references. 'Fido', 'Fi Fi', 'dog', and 'shmog' must refer not to the dog and the property they refer to in other contexts but to *modes of presentation* of them. Yet the theorist, familiar with the argument of this paper, despairs of finding modes of presentation to be the referents of expressions in 'that'-clauses.

The positions in logical space offering ways out of the dilemma may be divided into those that do and those that don't require denying that the truth condition of a belief sentence has a determination within a finitely axiomatizable compositional truth-theoretic semantics.[10] But those that comport with compositional semantics (e.g., that 'Ralph believes that' is a Hintakkaesque operator or that believing is a relation to linguistic entities) have problems at least as great as the propositionalist's, including mode-of-presentation problems of their own (see Schiffer [165]).

There are two ways out that require denying the possibility of a compositional semantics, and both of course raise the question of the denial's feasibility. Now I think it is feasible. In *Remnants of Meaning* [165] I tried to show that we don't need a compositional truth-theoretic semantics to account for language understanding or for the platitude that the meaning of a sentence is determined by its syntax and the meanings of its component words. So the hypothetical theorist, on my behalf, is willing to take seriously ways out of his dilemma that require denying that natural languages have compositional truth-theoretic semantics.

One of these two ways out is to deny the relational theory of believing and to deny, therefore, that 'that'-clauses are genuinely *referential* singular terms. Syntactically they're singular terms, but they don't have objectual reference to propositions (or to anything else). This solution will appeal to a philosopher who, like the author of [165], finds independent reasons to deny the existence of properties and, therewith, propositions. But there's a price to pay: you've got to make sense of the evident validity of inferences like

Reggie believes that eating liver increases sexual potency.

So there's something Reggie believes.

The only way to do this consistently with the denial that 'that'-clauses really refer is to construe the apparent quantification over propositions (i.e., over referents of 'that'-clauses) as something akin to substitutional quantification. The catch is in the 'something akin to': for reasons we can't now go into, the quantification can't literally be substitutional, and it's not entirely clear in exactly what ways it must be like substitutional quantification. In the end it's not really clear in what clear sense objectual quantification over propositions is being denied. I hasten to add that I don't think that the something-akin-to-substitutional-quantification line can't be made to work; yet I'm sufficiently leery to find the next way out of

---

[10] That is, a finitely axiomatizable theory that entails a truth condition for each sentence of the form 'so and so believes that such and such'.

the theorist's dilemma worth pursuing, especially as it comports well with the spirit, if not quite the letter, of nominalism.

Very well, we now begin by saying, 'that'-clauses refer to propositions, for this is merely to acknowledge that 'that eating liver increases sexual potency' refers to that eating liver increases sexual potency and that that "thing" is abstract, mind- and language-independent (at least in that it exists in worlds in which there are neither thinkers nor speakers), and has its truth condition essentially. So we can accept "objectual" quantification over propositions. What we deny is that the reference of the 'that'-clause is compositionally determined in the standard truth-theoretic way (see Johnston [83] (p. 37), and Schiffer [166] (pp. 59–61)). This doesn't mean that what a 'that'-clause refers to is unaffected by the words it contains; but it does mean that we don't have to see the reference of, say, 'that Fido is a dog' as determined by its syntax and referents independently assigned to 'Fido' and 'dog'. In this way, we're not required to find "modes of presentation" to serve as the referents of 'Fido' and 'dog' when they're ensconced in 'that'-clauses, although we can say that the proposition that Fido is a dog isn't identical to the proposition that Fi Fi is a shmog.

Now taking this line requires that we don't take the existence of propositions very seriously. They exist, but only in a very *deflationary*, or minimalist (Johnston [83]), way. They exist, but only, as it were, in a manner of speaking. Their existence is in some sense a projection of linguistic and cognitive practices that are pragmatically very useful, perhaps indispensable. Whether this Pickwickian version of the thesis that believing is a relation to propositions can be made to work depends on whether we can satisfactorily spell out the deflationary sense in which propositions exist, the sense in which they're merely "projections" of useful practices and owe their existence to a mere "manner of speaking." That must be a project for another day.

11

Consciousness, Unconsciousness and Intentionality

JOHN R. SEARLE

I

ONE OF THE most amazing things about the past half century or so in analytic philosophy of mind is the scarcity of serious work on the nature of consciousness. Even works purportedly about consciousness have very little to say about the general structure of consciousness or about its special features. Thus for example of three recent books containing "Consciousness" in their titles[1] not one contains even an attempt to state a comprehensive account of the structure of conscious states, much less state a general theory that will account for subjectivity, the stream of consciousness, the qualitative character of conscious states, etc. In each case consciousness is regarded not as a primary subject matter in the philosophy of mind but as a "problem," a potential embarrassment to the author's theory, which is, in each case, some version of "functionalism" or "materialism" or "computationalism." What goes for the philosophy of mind also goes for most—not all—mainstream philosophy of language. You can test this for yourself: Which of the many works on meaning by, say Carnap or Quine, has given you the greatest insight into the special features of the relationships between meaning and consciousness?

I think there are many deep reasons for this fear of consciousness in contemporary analytic philosophy. One of the most important of these is that the presuppositions and methods of contemporary philosophy are ill equipped to deal with the *subjectivity* of conscious states. A similar reluctance to accept the consequences of ontological subjectivity also afflicts psychology and cognitive science generally.

In order to account for the mind without consciousness, one must postulate some other sorts of phenomena. The most obvious solution is to

---

[1] Churchland, *Matter and Consciousness: A Contemporary Introduction to the Philosophy of Mind* [30]; Jackendoff, *Consciousness and the Computational Mind* [82]; and Lycan *Consciousness* [117].

postulate *unconscious* mental processes to do the jobs that traditional philosophy, psychology, and common sense ascribed to conscious mental processes. This maneuver takes different forms, but the general tendency in cognitive science has been to drive a wedge between, on the one hand, conscious, subjective mental processes, which are not regarded as a proper subject of scientific investigation; and, on the other hand, those which are regarded as the genuine subject matter of cognitive science, and which, therefore, must be objective. The general theme is always that the unconscious mental processes are more significant than the conscious ones. Perhaps the earliest canonical statement is in Lashley's claim,[2] *"No activity of mind is ever conscious"* (Lashley's italics). Another extreme version of this approach is to be found in Jackendoff's claim[3] that in fact there are two "notions of mind," the "computational mind" and the "phenomenological mind."

I believe that it is a profound mistake to try to describe and explain mental phenomena without reference to consciousness. In this article I will argue that any intentional state is either actually or potentially a conscious intentional state, and for that reason cognitive science cannot avoid studying consciousness. The attribution of any intentional phenomena to a system, whether "computational" or otherwise, is dependent on a prior acceptance of our ordinary notion of the mind, the conscious "phenomenological" mind.

In order to substantiate this claim, I am also going to have to explore the notion of an unconscious mental state. The course of this exploration is rather more complex than I would like, and I need to begin by reminding the reader of the distinctions between ontology, causation, and epistemology. For any phenomenon, but for biological phenomena especially, we need to know:

(1) What is its mode of existence? (ontology)

(2) What does it do? (causation)

(3) How do we find out about it? (epistemology)

So, for example, if we were examining the heart, the answer to our three questions is: the heart is a large piece of muscle tissue located in the chest cavity (ontology); the heart functions to pump blood throughout the body (causation); and we find out about the heart indirectly through such methods as using stethoscopes, cardiograms and taking pulse, and directly by opening up the chest cavity and looking at the heart (epistemology). Now,

---

[2] "Cerebral Organization and Behavior" [99]. I don't think Lashley means this literally. I think he means that the processes by which the various features of conscious states are produced are never conscious. But even that is an overstatement; and the fact that he resorts to this sort of hyperbole is revealing of the theme I am trying to identify.

[3] *Consciousness and the Computational Mind* [82].

these distinctions apply to both conscious and unconscious mental states. The history of the philosophy of mind in recent decades is in large part a series of confusions between these three questions. Thus, behaviorism confuses the epistemology of the mental with the ontology (we find out about mental states by observing behavior, so mental states just consist in behavior and dispositions to behavior). And functionalism consists in confusing the causation with the ontology (mental states have causal relations to input stimuli, other mental states, and output behavior, so mental states just consist in having these causal relations).

Our naive, pre-theoretical notion of an *unconscious* mental state is the idea of a conscious mental state minus the consciousness. But what exactly does that mean? How could we subtract the consciousness from a mental state and still have a *mental* state left over? Since Freud, we have grown so used to talking about unconscious mental states that we have lost sight of the fact that the answer to this question is by no means obvious. Yet it is clear that we do think of the unconscious on the model of the conscious. Our idea of an unconscious state is the idea of a mental state that just happens then and there to be unconscious; but we still understand it on the model of a conscious state in the sense that we think of it as being just like a conscious state and as one which in some sense could have been conscious. This is clearly true, for example, in Freud, whose notions of both what he calls "preconscious" and "unconscious" states are built on a rather simple model of conscious states.[4] Perhaps at its most naive, our picture is something like this: unconscious mental states in the mind are like fish deep in the sea. The fish that we can't see underneath the surface have exactly the same shape they have when they surface. The fish don't lose their shapes by going under water. Another simile: unconscious mental states are like objects stored in the dark attic of the mind. These objects have their shapes all along, even when you can't see them. We are tempted to smile at these simple models, but I think something like these pictures underlies our conception of unconscious mental states; and it is important to try to see what is right and what wrong about that conception.

In recent decades, the connection between consciousness and intentionality is being gradually lost in theoretical writings in linguistics, cognitive science, and philosophy. There has been an effort of varying degrees of explicitness to try to separate the issues concerning intentionality from those concerning consciousness. I think the underlying—and perhaps unconscious—motivation for this urge to separate intentionality from consciousness, even among people who do not share the ideology of the behaviorist-materialist tradition, is that we do not know how to explain consciousness, and we would like to get a theory of intentionality which will not be discredited by the fact that we do not have a theory of consciousness. The idea is to treat intentionality "objectively," to treat it as

---

[4] *Outline of Psycho-Analysis* [64] (pp. 19–25).

if the subjective features of consciousness did not really matter to it. For example, many functionalists will concede that functionalism can't "handle" consciousness (this is called the problem of *qualia*), but they think that this issue doesn't matter to their accounts of belief, desire, etc., since these intentional states have no *quale*, no special conscious qualities. They can be treated as if they were completely independent of consciousness. Similarly, both the idea of some linguists that there are rules of syntax that are psychologically real but totally inaccessible to consciousness and the idea of some psychologists that there are complex inferences in perception that are genuine psychological inferential processes but inaccessible to consciousness, try to separate intentionality from consciousness. The idea in both cases is not that there are mental phenomena which just happen to be unconscious, but somehow in some way they are *in principle* inaccessible to consciousness. They are not the sort of thing that could be or could ever have been conscious.

I think these recent developments are mistaken. There are deep reasons having to do with the nature of mental phenomena whereby our notion of an unconscious mental state is parasitic on our notion of a conscious state. Of course, at any given moment, a person may be unconscious; he or she may be asleep, in a coma, etc.; and of course, many mental states are never brought to consciousness. And no doubt there are many which could not be brought to consciousness for one reason or another—they may be too painful and hence too deeply repressed for us to think of them, for example. Nonetheless, not every state of an agent is a mental state and not even every state of the brain which functions essentially in the *production* of mental phenomena is itself a mental phenomenon. So what makes something mental when it is not conscious? For a state to be a mental state, and *a fortiori* for it to be an intentional mental state, certain conditions must be met: What are they?

To explore these questions let us first consider cases which are clearly mental, though unconscious, and contrast them with cases which are "unconscious" because not mental at all. Think of the difference, for example, between my belief (when I am not thinking about it) that the Eiffel Tower is in Paris, and the myelination of the axons in my central nervous system. There is a sense in which both are unconscious. But there is a big difference in that the structural states of my axons couldn't be themselves conscious states, because there isn't anything mental about them at all. I assume for the sake of this argument that myelination functions essentially in the production of my mental states, but even if myelinated axons were themselves objects of experiences, even if I could feel inwardly the state of the myelin sheaths, still the actual structures are not themselves mental states. Not every unconscious state in my brain which (like myelination) functions essentially in my mental life is itself a mental state. But the belief that the Eiffel Tower is in Paris is a genuine mental state. Even though it happens to be a mental state that most of the time is not present to consciousness.

So here are two states in me, my belief and my axon myelination; both have something to do with my brain; and both are unconscious. But only one is mental, and we need to get clear about what makes it mental and the connection between that feature—whatever it is—and consciousness.

There are at least two constraints on our conception of intentionality which any theory of the unconscious must be able to account for: It must be able to account for the distinction between phenomena which are genuinely intentional and those which in some respects behave as if they were but which are not in fact. This is the distinction I have discussed elsewhere between *intrinsic* and *as-if* forms of intentionality.[5] And second it must be able to account for the fact that intentional states represent their conditions of satisfaction only under certain aspects and those aspects must matter to the agent. My unconscious belief that the Eiffel Tower is in Paris satisfies both of these conditions. My having that belief is a matter of intrinsic intentionality, and not a matter of what anybody else chooses to say about me or how I behave or what sort of stance someone might adopt toward me. And the belief that the Eiffel Tower is in Paris represents its conditions of satisfaction under certain aspects and not others. It is, for example, distinct from the belief that the tallest iron structure built in France before 1900 is located in the French capital, even assuming that the Eiffel Tower is identical with the tallest iron structure built in France before 1900, and Paris is identical with the French capital. We might say that every intentional state has a certain *aspectual shape*; and this aspectual shape is part of its identity, part of what makes it the state that it is.

II

These two features, the fact that an unconscious intentional state must nonetheless be intrinsically mental and the fact that it must have a certain aspectual shape, have important consequences for our conception of the unconscious. Specifically, we understand the notion of an unconscious mental state only as a possible content of consciousness, only as the sort of thing which, though not conscious, and perhaps impossible to bring to consciousness for various reasons, is nonetheless the *sort of thing* that could be or could have been conscious. Someone might have mental states which are impossible to bring to consciousness—because of repression or brain lesions or what have you—but if they are genuine unconscious *mental* states, they can't be the sort of thing which in the nature of the case no one could ever have brought to consciousness. To be mental at all, they must be at least possible candidates for consciousness.

The argument for this thesis is a bit complex, but the central idea behind it can be given a simple formulation: the concept of an intrinsic intentional mental state is the concept of something that has an aspectual

<hr>

[5] "Intrinsic Intentionality" [168]; *Minds, Brains and Science* [171]; and especially "Intentionality and its Place in Nature" [170].

shape. All representation is under aspects. You can see this, if it is not obvious on its face, by reminding yourself that mental contents are possible or actual contents of *thoughts* or *experiences*. What you can believe, you have to be able to think; and what you can perceive, you have to be able to experience perceptually. But the notions of thinking and experiencing are notions which imply the presence of aspectual shapes and that in turn implies accessibility to consciousness. The link, then, between intentionality and consciousness lies in the notion of an aspectual shape. To be intentional, a state or process must be thinkable or experienceable; and to be thinkable or experienceable, it must have an aspectual shape under which it is at least in principle, consciously thinkable or experienceable. It must be the sort of thing that could be the content of a conscious thought or experience.

I will now spell out this argument in more detail. For the sake of clarity I will number the major steps in setting out the argument, though I do not mean to imply that the argument is a simple deduction from axioms. Sometimes, indeed, I will be approaching the same goal from more than one path.

1. The first step is simply to remind ourselves that there is a distinction between *intrinsic* intentionality and *as-if* intentionality; only intrinsic intentionality is genuinely mental.

I have argued at some length for this rather obvious distinction in other writings ([168], [170], [171]), and I will not repeat the arguments here. I believe the distinction is obviously correct, but the price of giving it up would be that everything then becomes mental, because relative to some purpose or other anything can be treated *as if* it were mental. E.g., water flowing downhill behaves *as if* it had intentionality. It *tries* to get to the bottom of the hill by ingeniously *seeking* the line of the least resistance, it does *information processing* in order to *calculate* the size of rocks, the angle of the slope, the pull of gravity, etc. But if water is mental then everything is mental.

2. The second step is to point out that the distinction between the *intrinsic* and the *as-if* lies neither in the behavior of the system in question nor in the fact that there are underlying causal mechanisms which cause the behavior nor in the complexity of the system. These features are not sufficient to account for the distinction, since they can be duplicated equally in both intrinsic and *as-if* systems.

3. The distinction does lie, at least in part, in the fact that the idea of an intentional state is closely connected to the ideas of thinking and experiencing. To be a possible belief something has to be a possible thought content: It is a conceptual truth that anything that can be believed can be thought. Similarly anything that can be a perception can be the content of a perceptual experience. Of course there are plenty of *unconscious* thoughts but even if unconscious they still have to be thoughts.

4. Thoughts and experiences and hence intrinsic intentional states generally, have a certain sort of aspectual shape. They represent their conditions of satisfaction under aspects. For example, the desire for water

can be a different desire from the desire for H_2O, even though there is no way to satisfy the one without satisfying the other. (This aspectual shape of intentional states explains the referential opacity of ascriptions of intentional states. The ascriptions are opaque because the states themselves are aspectual.)[6]

5. This aspectual feature must matter to the agent. It must exist from his/her point of view.

It is, for example, from my point of view that there can be a difference for me between between my wanting water and my wanting H_2O, even though the external behavior that corresponds to these desires may be identical in each case. In the case of conscious thoughts, the way that the aspectual shape matters is that it is constitutive of the way the agent thinks about a subject matter: I can think about my thirst for a drink of water without thinking at all about its chemical composition. I can think of it *as* water without thinking of it *as* H_2O.

Its obvious how it works for conscious thoughts and experiences, but how does it work for unconscious mental states? One way to get at the main question of this discussion is to ask, "What fact about an unconscious intentional state gives it the particular aspectual shape that it has, i.e., what fact about it makes it the mental state that it is?"

6. The aspectual feature cannot be exhaustively or completely characterized solely in terms of third-person, behavioral, or even neurophysiological predicates. None of these is sufficient to give an exhaustive account of *the way it seems to the agent.*

Behavioral evidence concerning the existence of mental states, including even evidence concerning the causation of a person's behavior, no matter how complete, always leaves the aspectual character of intentional states underdetermined. There will always be an inferential gulf between the evidence for the presence of the aspect and the aspect itself. (This is one feature of the other minds problem.)

It is less obvious that a similar condition holds for neurophysiological facts, but it does. Since the neurophysiological facts are always causally sufficient for any set of mental facts,[7] someone with perfect causal knowledge might be able to make the inference from the neurophysiological to the intentional at least in those few cases where there is a law-like connection between the facts specified in neural terms and the facts specified in

---

[6] See *Intentionality: An Essay in the Philosophy of Mind* [169], Chapter 7, for an extended discussion of this issue.

[7] For these purposes I am contrasting "neurophysiological" and "mental," but of course on my view of mind body relations, the mental simply is neurophysiological at a higher level (see *Minds, Brains and Science* [171]). I contrast mental and neurophysiological as one might contrast humans and animals without thereby implying that the first class is not included in the second. There is no dualism implicit in my use of this contrast.

intentional terms. But even in these cases, if there are any, there is still an *inference*. The specification of the neurophysiological in neurophysiological terms is not yet a specification of the intentional, even though the neurophysiological is causally sufficient to fix the mental.

Any account that uses only a third-person objective vocabulary will leave their aspectual character underdetermined; because no third-person objective vocabulary, by itself, will be sufficient to characterize all of the aspectual facts. Thus to take an example of behavioral evidence, the fact that a person consumes H_2O only if it is described to him as 'water' and not if it is described as 'H_2O' would reasonably lead us to conclude that the person desires the substance under the aspect 'water' and does not desire it under the aspect 'H_2O'. But this is still an inductive inference; the behavior still underdetermines the aspect in that it is still in principle possible for the person to exhibit exactly that behavior and yet represent his own desires to himself in ways that are not completely manifested to us in his behavior.

To take the more extreme case of neurophysiological evidence, imagine that we had a perfect science of the brain that enabled us to conclude with empirical certainty from the fact that a man was in state S that he wanted a substance under the aspect 'water' and not under the aspect 'H_2O'. All the same the characterization S is still not yet a characterization of those aspects. S will both cause and realize the aspects but under that description it is still not constitutive of the aspects.

This point is so important that it is worth digressing briefly to explain some of its implications. No amount of purely third-person behavioral evidence is sufficient to entail all of the aspectual features of intentional states. Such third-person evidence always leaves the aspectual features underdetermined. This is one of the weaknesses of behaviorism as a thesis in the philosophy of mind. Behaviorism in the philosophy of mind is now generally regarded as discredited; however, it survives vestigially in the philosophy of language. And you see it in an extreme form in Quine's writings. If you think, as he does, that all of the facts that there are about linguistic meaning are public third-person facts, and if you think, as again he does (and as again I believe is mistaken), that the principle that language is public implies that all the facts that there are about meanings are third-person facts, then you get not merely the underdetermination of aspectual facts by the behavioral facts but you get an *indeterminacy* of aspectual facts. Thus, Quine argues that within certain limits there simply is no fact of the matter about under what aspects a speaker represents a situation when he utters an expression that we are inclined to translate as 'rabbit'. I have argued elsewhere[8] that this view is simply a *reductio ad absurdum* of linguistic behaviorism. Since it is obvious from my own case that there are determinate aspectual facts, if behaviorism leads to a denial of this point that can only show that behaviorism is false.

[8] "Indeterminacy, Empiricism and the First Person" [172].

This is not the place to go into detail, but I believe similar remarks can be made about functionalist analyses of intentional states, at least insofar as they try to give a third-person, objective, account of intentionality. Quine's inadvertent refutation of behaviorism can be applied *mutatis mutandis* to functionalism. Quine's argument shows that any account of purely third-person, objective phenomena given in functional terms will always leave the precise details of aspectual facts underdetermined.[9]

Now, these six considerations lead to our first significant conclusion:

7. There is a sense, then, in which intentional states, conscious or unconscious, are irreducibly *subjective*.

The aspectual character is irreducibly subjective in the sense that no characterization in purely neutral third-person terms will ever be sufficient to express how the aspectual character seems to the agent, but how it seems to the agent is essential to its identity.

So far so good. We seem to have labored heavily to arrive at the common sense conclusion that there is something subjective about mental states even when they are unconscious. But this leads to a very puzzling question: how could unconscious intentional states be subjective if there is no subjective feel to them, no "qualia," no what-it-feels-like-for-me to be in that state? Indeed how could the ontology of the unconscious be anything other than completely objective? To begin to probe this question, let us ask what is the ontology of ordinary mental states, such as my belief that the Eiffel Tower is in Paris, when I am not thinking about such beliefs. And to avoid muddying the waters, let's leave out half-conscious thoughts, peripheral consciousness, nagging but suppressed conscious states and other shadowy phenomena. What is going on, ontologically speaking, when I have a belief that is totally and completely unconscious but nonetheless there? If there are no conscious neurophysiological processes going on in my brain, then the only other processes would be unconscious neurophysiological processes, that is; *the ontology of the unconscious when unconscious is entirely neurophysiological*. The difference, for example, between my unconscious belief about the Eiffel Tower and the unconscious myelinated condition of my axons is not that the one is a feature of my brain in some mental form and the other is purely neurophysiological; they are both purely neurophysiological. You can see this by imagining that the person is totally unconscious, e.g., in a sound dreamless sleep. Now lots of mental attributions are still true of that person, but the only mental *ontology* is neurophysiological. Indeed this point about unconscious states can be put in the form of a general principle:

8. The ontology of unconscious mental states, at the time they are unconscious, can only consist in the existence of purely neurophysiological

---

[9] For this reason functionalism, like the behaviorism that preceded it, remains programmatic. To my knowledge, no functionalist has so far given anything like a plausible analysis of even one intentional state.

phenomena. At the time the states are totally unconscious there simply is nothing else going on except neurophysiological processes.

But now we seem to have a contradiction: the ontology of unconscious intentionality is entirely describable in third-person, objective neurophysiological terms, but all the same the states are irreducibly subjective. How can this be?

I believe there is only one solution to this puzzle. The apparent contradiction is resolved by pointing out that:

9. The notion of an unconscious intentional state is the notion of a state which is a possible conscious thought or experience. There are plenty of unconscious phenomena, but to the extent that they are genuinely *mental* they must in some sense preserve their aspectual shape even when unconscious, but the only sense that we can give to the notion that they preserve their aspectual shape when unconscious is that they are possible contents of consciousness.

This is the main conclusion of this article. But this answer to our first question immediately gives rise to another question: What is meant by 'possible' in the previous sentence? After all, I grant that it might be quite *impossible* for the state to occur consciously, because of brain lesion, repression, or other causes. So, in what sense exactly must it be a possible content of a thought or experience? This question leads to our next conclusion, which is really a further explanation of 9, and is implied by 8 and 9 together:

10. *The ontology of the unconscious consists in objective features of the brain capable of causing subjective conscious thoughts.* Hence when we describe something as an unconscious intentional state we are characterizing an objective *ontology* in virtue of its *causal* capacity to produce subjectivity. But the existence of these causal features is consistent with the fact that in any given case their causal powers may be blocked by some other interfering causes—such as psychological repression or brain damage.

The possibility of interference by various forms of pathology does not alter the fact that any unconscious intentional state is the sort of thing that is in principle accessible to consciousness. It may be unconscious not only in the sense that it does not *happen* to be conscious then and there, but also in the sense that for one reason or another the agent simply *could not* bring it to consciousness, but it must be the *sort of thing* that can be brought to consciousness because it must be the sort of thing that can be the content of a thought or experience.

To summarize: So far I have tried to establish that intentional states, conscious or unconscious, essentially have an aspectual character and this aspectual character is essentially subjective, in the sense that it cannot be exhaustively accounted for in third-person "objective" terms. But since unconscious mental states consist in nothing but objective neurophysiological features of the brain how can they have an intrinsic subjective character? I have suggested that the only explanation for this fact is that unconscious intentional states while not conscious are at least potentially so in the sense that they are the sort of things which could be conscious. When we characterize an unconscious intentional state in terms of its aspectual character, we are characterizing a present brain state in terms of its causal capacity to produce a conscious thought or experience.

Paradoxically, the naive mentalism of my view of the mind leads to a kind of dispositional analysis of unconscious mental phenomena; only it is not a disposition to behavior, but a "disposition"—if that is really the right word—to conscious thoughts.

So the overall picture that emerges is this. There is nothing going on in my brain but neurophysiological processes. Those processes are capable of generating conscious states (which are, of course, higher-level features of the neurophysiological systems and hence neurophysiological themselves). But of the unconscious neurophysiological features, some are mental and some are not. The difference is not in consciousness, for they are both, by hypothesis, unconscious. The difference is that the mental ones are candidates for consciousness. That's all. There isn't any aspectual shape at the level of neurons and synapses.

In my skull, there is just the brain with all its intricacy. All my mental life is lodged in the brain. But what in my brain is my "mental life"? Just two things: conscious states (of course, caused by neurophysiological processes and realized in the structures of the brain) and those neurophysiological states and processes that—given the right attendant circumstances—are capable of generating conscious states. There isn't anything else to the ontology of the unconscious.

III

I want to illustrate these points further by imagining a case in which we would have a use for the notion of "unconscious pain." We don't normally think of unconscious pains, and many people, I believe, would accept the Cartesian notion that in order for something to be a genuine pain, it has to be conscious. But I think it is easy to invoke contrary intuitions. Consider the following: it is a very common occurrence for people who suffer from chronic pains, say, chronic back pains, that sometimes the pain makes it difficult for them to go to sleep. And indeed, once they have fallen asleep, there sometimes are occasions during the night when *their condition causes them to wake up.* Now, how exactly shall we describe these cases? Shall we say that during sleep there really was no pain, but that the pain began when they woke up and that they were awakened by neurophysiological processes which normally would cause pain, but didn't cause pains because at the time they were asleep? Or shall we say, on the other hand, that the pain, i.e., the pain itself, continued both before, during and after their sleep, but that they were not consciously aware of the pain while they were asleep? My intuitions find the second just as natural, indeed probably more natural, than the first. However, the important thing is to see that there is no substantive issue involved. We are simply adopting an alternative vocabulary for describing the same sets of facts. But now consider the second vocabulary: on this vocabulary, we say that the pain was for a while conscious, then it was unconscious, then it was conscious again. Same pain; different states of consciousness of that one and the same pain. We might increase our urge to speak this way if we found that the person, though completely unconscious, made bodily movements during sleep which served to protect the painful portion of his body.

Now what exactly is the ontology of the pain when it is unconscious? Well, the answer seems to me quite obvious. What inclines us to say that the pain continued to exist even though unconscious is that there was an underlying neurophysiological process that was capable of generating a conscious state and capable of generating behavior appropriate to someone who had that conscious state. And in the example as described, that is exactly what happened.

But now if I am right about this then it is hard to see how there could be any factual substance to the old disputes about whether unconscious mental states really exist. If you grant my argument so far, then I am unable to see how it could be other than a purely verbal terminological matter, different only in complexity from the issue about the existence of unconscious pains as I just described it. One side insisted that there really are *unconscious mental* states; the other insisted that if they were really *mental*, why then, they must be *conscious*. But what facts in the world are supposed to correspond to these two different claims?

The evidence that the Freudians adduced involved causal histories, behavior, and conscious admissions by the agent—all of which seemed only interpretable on the assumption of an unconscious mental state, which was just like a conscious state except for being unconscious. Consider a typical sort of case. A man under hypnosis is given a post-hypnotic suggestion to the effect that he must crawl around on the floor after coming out of the hypnotic trance. Later, when conscious, he gives some completely extraneous reason for his behavior. He says, e.g., "I think I may have lost my watch on this floor somewhere," whereupon he proceeds to crawl around on the floor. Now we suppose, with good reason I believe, that he is unconsciously obeying the order, that he unconsciously intends to crawl around on the floor because he was told to by the hypnotist; and that the reason he gives for his behavior is not the real reason at all.

But assuming that he is totally unconscious of his real motives, what is the ontology of the unconscious, right then and there, supposed to be? To repeat our earlier question, what *fact* corresponds to the attribution of the unconscious mental state at the time the agent is acting for a reason of which he is totally unconscious? If the state really is totally unconscious, then the only facts are the existence of neurophysiological states capable of giving rise to conscious thoughts and to the sort of behavior appropriate for someone having those thoughts.

Sometimes there may be several inferential steps between the latent unconscious mental state and the manifest conscious intentionality. Thus, we are told, the adolescent boy who revolts against the authority of the school is unconsciously motivated by hatred of his father. The school symbolizes the father. But again, as in the hypnosis case, we have to ask what is the ontology of the unconscious supposed to be when unconscious? And in this case, as in the hypnosis case, the identification of a specific aspectual shape to the unconscious must imply that there is in the neurophysiology a capacity to produce a conscious thought with that very aspectual shape.

Once you see that the description of a mental state as "unconscious" is the description of a neurophysiological ontology in terms of its causal capacity to produce conscious thoughts and behavior, then it seems there could not be any factual substance to the ontological question: Do unconscious mental states really exist? All that question can mean is: Are there unconscious neurophysiological states of the brain capable of giving rise to conscious thoughts and to the sorts of behavior appropriate for someone having those thoughts? Of course neither side thought of the issue this way, but perhaps part of the intensity of the dispute derived from the fact that what looked like a straight ontological issue—do unconscious states exist?—was really not an ontological issue at all.

I am not sure I am right about this, but it does seem at least *prima facie* that the old Freudian arguments—involving all that evidence from hypnotism, neuroses, etc.—are not so much conclusive or inconclusive as they are factually empty. The issue is not less important for being conceptual or terminological, but it is important to understand that it is not a factual issue about the existence of mental entities which are neither physiological nor conscious.

IV

This account of the unconscious has a useful consequence that I want to call attention to immediately. An old puzzle about intentional states has to do with the absence of any clear principle of individuation, and this problem is especially acute for unconscious beliefs. How many unconscious beliefs do I have? We don't know how to get started answering that question. Earlier, I said glibly that I had a belief that was unconscious most of the time to the effect that the Eiffel Tower is in Paris. But do I also believe the following?

Station wagons are inedible.

Doctors wear underwear.

If someone asked me whether doctors wear underwear or whether station wagons are inedible, I would have no difficulty in answering; but it seems funny to think of them as unconscious beliefs that I have had all along. Whereas it doesn't seem quite as funny to think of the belief about the Eiffel tower as an unconscious belief. Why the difference?

I can so confidently answer questions about doctors, station wagons, and Paris because I have a set of capacities realized in my brain that enable me to generate conscious thoughts and hence generate answers to questions in which I express my conscious thoughts. As long as my thoughts are unconscious they consist only in a neuroanatomy and a neurophysiology that has capacities for generating conscious thoughts and behavior.

The difference between the case of the Eiffel Tower and the other two cases is that I have already had the conscious thought that the Eiffel Tower is in Paris. I learned it at school, I have seen the Eiffel Tower, I climbed to the top, etc. But the other cases are simply manifestations of the capacity of my brain to generate an indefinitely large number of different conscious thoughts. It is hard but not impossible to count speech acts and even to count one's own conscious thoughts insofar as one can individuate them by content. But when it comes to one's unconscious beliefs, the question of counting is of a different sort altogether: I can't count my unconscious beliefs because there isn't anything there to count except in terms of what I have already consciously thought or in terms of what I could consciously think. But the latter class is indefinitely large and does not reflect a fixed preexisting set of mental representations in the brain.

Our ordinary ways of thinking and talking incline us to think of memory as like a big filing cabinet in which we store a whole lot of information in some language or other—as if written on my brain were a whole lot of sentences in English (or in the "language of thought"). And certain researchers in cognitive science have encouraged this conception by postulating that in the brain there are a whole lot of unconscious "mental representations." But as an ontological claim (and how else are we supposed to take it?) that picture is obviously wrong. What we have instead are a whole lot of capacities in the brain for generating conscious thoughts.

V

Let us return to the question that I asked at the beginning of this article: Can we really think of unconscious states as being like submerged fish or like furniture in the dark attic of the mind? I think these pictures are inadequate in principle because they are based on the idea of a reality which appears and then disappears. But in the case of consciousness, the only reality is the appearance. The submerged belief, unlike the submerged fish, can't keep its conscious shape even when unconscious; for the only reality of that shape is the shape of conscious thoughts. To repeat, *the ontology of the unconscious is strictly the ontology of a neurophysiology capable of generating the conscious.*

VI

Now oddly enough, this connection between consciousness and intentionality is lost in discussions of the unconscious mental processes in contemporary linguistics, philosophy, and cognitive science. Many of the phenomena which are cited as explanatory psychological features simply could not have any *psychological* reality because they are not the sort of things that could be mental states.

This is a central feature of much contemporary cognitive science, and it is disguised from us by the vocabulary. Some of the key terms are, in effect, a set of puns: 'information processing', 'intelligent behavior', 'rule following', and 'cognition' are all used in two quite distinct senses, only one of which is genuinely mental. The reason for this is that the authors in question want a third-person objective science but they also want it to be about a mental reality. It is literally impossible to have both of these features, so they disguise their failure by using a vocabulary that looks mental (what could be more mental than engaging in "intelligent behavior"?) but which has been stripped of any mental content. And they can get away with this because they can claim that the mental reality they claim to be discussing is all "unconscious"; but that expression now becomes the biggest pun of all because there are two completely different sorts of phenomena called "unconscious," unconscious *mental* phenomena and unconscious phenomena which have no mental reality at all.

VII

But someone might object: "Well, why does it matter? Why don't we just scrap the old time folk psychological vocabulary once and for all and get on with the genuine science of cognition? Why does it matter whether or not we use a mentalistic vocabulary to describe those brain processes which cause genuine mental phenomena or whether we confine ourselves to a purely neutral physiological vocabulary?" The short answer is that it is crucial to understanding the character of the processes involved that we have a clear distinction between those which are mental (hence also physiological) and those which are only physiological. This can perhaps be illustrated by the example of the famous studies of what the frog's eye tells the frog's brain.[10] The retina in the frog's eye filters out most of the stimulus before transmitting the rest of the signal to the frog's brain. The processes in the retina do not literally involve any rule following, nor cognition, nor intelligence. They are simply brute physiological processes. However, their effect is crucial for the frog's conscious intelligent behavior. By making it possible for the frog to have certain visual experiences and not others, they make it possible for the frog to eat and survive.

I give the example of the frog, because here I take it the facts are obvious. But the same thing should be equally obvious about those neuro-physiological processes in the human brain which enable us to have genuine intelligence, cognition, and rule following, but which are not themselves cases of intelligence, cognition, or rule following. Unless we are clear about

---

[10] Lettvin, Maturana, et al. [104].

this distinction, we have no hope of understanding how the neurophysiology produces its crucial mental consequences; and indeed, many of the disappointments of cognitive science derive from its failure to pose the question in the appropriate terms. We need, in short, to turn Lashley's claim upside down: Roughly speaking, all genuinely *mental* activity is either conscious or potentially so. All of the other activities of the brain are simply non-mental, physiological processes, some of which produce conscious and unconscious mental processes.

12

Consciousness and Intentionality: Robots With and Without the Right Stuff[1]

KEITH GUNDERSON

> ... [T]here are not psychological truths about robots but only about the human makers of robots. Because the way a robot acts (in a specified context) depends primarily on how we programmed it to act. (Paul Ziff, "The Feelings of Robots," 1959.)

> ... I had proposed to Fodor and the other participants that we first discuss a dead simple case of misrepresentation: a coin-slot testing apparatus on a vending machine accepting a slug. "That sort of case is irrelevant," Fodor retorted instantly, "because after all, John Searle is right about one thing; he's right about artifacts like that. They don't have any intrinsic or original—only derived intentionality." (Daniel C. Dennett, "Evolution, Error, and Intentionality," 1987.)

> Type gives body and voice to silent thought. The speaking page carries it through the centuries. (Friedrich Schiller, *Letters on the Aesthetic Education of Man*, 1795.)

CONSCIOUSNESS, I ASSUME, whatever the difficulties in characterizing it, is potently present in our typical intentional activities. I nowhere suppose that its presence in our heads acts as sole arbiter of meaning, but only that it does exist, and plays a typically crucial role in the determination of what the upshot is of what we say or do, subject, of course, to familiar and forceful, notational, social, and environmental constraints.

In order to examine how consciousness functions in our intentional life, and the difficulties it poses for attempts to model the mind (within AI theory or any other), I imagine a world rather like our own except that it contains, along with our commonplace mindless artifactual mimics, robots, created by us, but endowed with real psychological panache. This is not really a thought experiment, but rather an attempt to entertain and maintain

---

[1] Sections of this are slated to become part of a work in progress entitled *Interviews with a Robot*.

a distinction between subjects with genuine (or *original* or *intrinsic*) intentionality, and those without, or with only a derivative sort. Even this turns out to be less simple than pie. Recent arguments by Daniel Dennett[2] purport to undermine the very distinctions being investigated. So Dennett's views are discussed at length, and in the course of their critique an account is offered of the connections (and lack thereof) between the doctrine of original or intrinsic intentionality, privileged access, incorrigibility, and views as to whether certain "deep" (individualistic) facts fix belief states. The two types of imagined robots, thus protected from Dennett's assault on the assumed distinction between them, become vehicles for exploring some salient connections between consciousness and intentionality.

Varieties of derivative intentionality are described and in contrast a tentative parsing of the major elements in conscious original (or intrinsic) intentional behaviors is suggested. It is argued that the very idea of AI models of the mind reside, in part, in the differences between the way in which a programmer typically stands to the computational processes and end results of an executed program, and the way in which a typical speaker/writer stands to the processes and results of speaking or composing within a natural language. Problems that conscious aspects of intentionality create for AI modeling is discussed in connection with the topic of why there could be no real analog to Searle's Chinese Room thought experiment for theories purporting to instantiate pain in a computer or robot.[3] This is linked to reasons why there is no distinction between *original* (or *intrinsic*)

---

[2] In Chapter 8, "Evolution, Error, and Intentionality," of *The Intentional Stance* [42].

[3] See Searle's "Minds, Brains, and Programs" [167]. The argument runs roughly as follows: Searle, who is completely ignorant of Chinese, is incarcerated in a room where he is given two batches of Chinese writing plus some rules in English for correlating them solely on the (formal) basis of their shapes. He is also given a third batch of Chinese inscriptions with further instructions in English for hooking the third batch up with the first two. The latter instructions also tell him how he is "to give back certain Chinese symbols with certain shapes in response to certain sorts of shapes" given him in the third batch. Those providing Searle with all the Chinese writing and the correlation rules in English refer to the first batch as "a script," the second batch as "a story," the third batch as "answers to the question," and the rules in English as "the program." Searle then imagines himself getting so good at following the instructions for manipulating the Chinese inscriptions and the programmers getting so good at concocting sets of instructions that his "answers" to questions cannot be distinguished from native Chinese speakers. Furthermore, he is given stories written in English, about which he is asked questions, which he answers with an alacrity comparable to other native speakers of English. The moral of it all is that although an external observer might view Searle's answers to the Chinese questions about the Chinese stories and his answers to the English questions about the English stories as equally adept, only in the latter case was there any real understanding involved. In the former case Searle claims he simply behaved like a computer. He was, in

and *derived* pain, but only between pain and pain reports (or behavior). To see why this is so helps us to appreciate the range of intentional phenomena where the distinction does make sense. But what is true of pain seems true of non-intentional mental phenomena in general (and what I have previously called program-resistant aspects of the mind[4])—vexingly so, perhaps, for any strong AI theorist or others who might want to incorporate at least some counterparts of such phenomena into their models of the mind through programming.

1 Two Kinds of Robots?

It certainly seems that in some admittedly underdescribed science-fiction type manner we can imagine ourselves as one day designing and building conscious, purposive, intelligent robots—robots which or who, however they do what they do, do it with conscious intent. Maybe they write, maybe they speak, maybe they write and speak, or maybe like cats and dogs they do neither, and are limited to non-verbal yet nevertheless conscious intentional behaviors. What materials we would use, how we might bring off this fantastic feat, and how we would know that we had—not bumping up against an acute "other minds" problem vis-à-vis our own artifacts—are

---

effect, "simply an instantiation of the computer program." Although his inputs and outputs are indistinguishable from those of a native Chinese speaker, he still understands nothing no matter what formal program he is provided with. For the same reason, he argues, various allegedly *strong* AI computers understand nothing.

[4] In *Mentality and Machines* [72]. See especially Chapters Three and Five and pp. 220–230 and 236–247 in the "Unconcluding Philosophic Postscript." (Compare Daniel Dennett's remarks on the topic quoted in Section 7 of this paper.) The distinction between program-receptive and program-resistant aspects of the mind may be in need of a tune-up, however, to protect it from counterexamples purporting to show that various program-resistant features are after all program-receptive via representations in, for example, neural net models (and/or, computational theories of vision such as Marr's, et al.). I am proceeding on the assumption that this can be (easily) done, but I do not try to bring it off here. But for starters, I would distinguish between those aspects of the mind which might be "programmable" *only* in the very *indirect* sense that they could be assigned some representational situs in a computerized neural net model, say, and those which would be directly present in the competencies of a computer: for example, its real capacities for proving theorems, playing chess, etc. It is the inability to imagine what it could be like for the having of a pain, for example, to be instantiated in a machine in this latter direct way which motivated my labelling such aspects of the mind "program-resistant." They were never viewed as being "resistant" to programming in the former much more general sense, and reference to that possibility seems to me entirely beside the point so far as the viability of the distinction is concerned.

questions I believe we need not know how to answer in order to know that nevertheless it is consistent and coherent to imagine ourselves or our heirs as someday designing and building conscious, purposive, intelligent robots. Such robots I will call Utopian *strong* AI robots (or USAI robots).

Certainly, too, and in a non-fictive and much less underdescribed manner, it seems possible to imagine that we might someday design and build non-conscious mimics of our Utopian *strong* AI robots—robots which did various things that our USAI robots intentionally did, but did them without any conscious intent. These mere mimics of USAI robots I shall call MUSAI robots. To imagine a tribe of MUSAIs we need only imagine robots which mimic *some* USAI intentional behaviors. This leaves open what I take to be, in fact, an open question with respect to conscious, intelligent, versatile, subjects (e.g., ourselves): the question of how much of their (our) conscious, intelligent, versatile, behavior could be replicated by non-conscious, non-intelligent means? I won't assume that a MUSAI robot could imitate in a non-conscious non-intelligent way *everything* that a USAI robot might do. For this would be to assume that even the most "souped up" version of Turing's Test[5] for intelligence in a subject or "system" was woefully wrong. Actually, I believe every proposed version of that (teasingly schematic) test to be inadequate in spite of its almost eerie capacity to survive and startle. I even suspect it to be woefully wrong: that there may be no statable limits concerning which conscious intelligent *behaviors* could be prone to non-conscious non-intelligent imitations. (We are always being surprised. Some of what Descartes deemed inconceivable, we feel ho hum about.) This suggests that even if, contrary to certain interpretations of it, passing Turing's Test demanded an extraordinarily versatile display of linguistic and non-linguistic problem-solving competencies, such competencies could not, apriori, be proven safe from an essentially dementalized redescription— a redescription which if proven accurate, would demonstrate the empty victory of passing Turing's Test. But I don't need to hawk that claim here, and content myself with a much more modest proposal: that it makes sense to imagine a tribe of MUSAI robots—mere non-conscious mimics of various actions that USAIs typically perform in conscious intelligent ways.[6]

---

[5] By "souped up" I mean where a machine is imagined as doing virtually *anything* humans can do, so that whatever the purely behavioral epistemic base for ascribing minds to humans amounts to, it is is assumed to be fully replicated in the case of machines. This seems to me a far cry from what A. M. Turing was proposing as a test for intelligence in his famous "Computing Machinery and Intelligence" [183].

[6] Except perhaps to an eliminative materialist (and Dennett, whose views will be discussed in detail), it should seem obvious that we already inhabit a world containing partial counterparts to MUSAIs. For we are conscious intentional beings, and various machines and robots can be used to mimic, imitate, or simulate, a range of our typically conscious intelligent actions by non-conscious

As admittedly underdescribed as our world containing USAIs and MU-SAIs is, what nevertheless *seems* to be part and parcel of it from the start is this: that MUSAIs do not intend anything, for they are incapable of having any conscious concerns. However it is they churn out seeable or hearable inscriptions or utterances in their proxy roles, the symbols employed will never mean anything to *them*. They will not be expressions of any of *their* wants or desires, for they have no wants or desires. Whatever meaning their inscriptions or utterances could possibly come to have, would perforce

---

non-intelligent means. But benign and boring as this claim may seem, there are two closely related and diametrically opposed ways in which even it may become controversial: (1) it is at odds with how what I will call the "piecemeal" version of Turing's Test has been employed from time to time in AI research, and (2) it takes for granted that at *some* interesting level of description machines or robots achieve *the same end results* typically brought about by conscious intentional agents, and do so without any conscious intent. Without focusing on either issue, I shall say something about each in order to protect my seemingly non-contentious initial assumption that we can, without contradiction or incoherence, imagine both USAIs and MUSAIs.

(1) *"Piecemeal" versions of Turing's Test.* However one carps about the actual efficacy of Turing's test for intelligence in a machine, the intent behind it seemed to be to provide a *general* test of intelligence, or a test of intelligence *in general (whatever* that might mean). I think Turing's assessment of his thought-experiment thought-detector was mistaken, and eons ago argued that the computational linguistic competence required for success at the "Imitation Game" is vulnerable to a dementalized redescription. Be that as it may, I think Turing would have been surprised if not amazed at what I will call the "piecemeal" variations on his test utilized in AI research by some of his 20th century boosters. By "piecemeal" variations I mean those (early) studies where a purported computer program model or simulation of human cognitive processes for a highly *specific* task—such as proving a theorem, or playing chess—is evaluated (for "goodness of fit") by whether it passes Turing's Test *for that type of task alone.* Thus if similarities between the computer's theorem proving, say, and a human subject's seem close enough—indistinguishable at the end-results level—the computer is described as instantiating a human-like cognitive process with respect to that task. So on the basis of primarily end-results comparisons together with some assumptions about similarities in inputs, and possibly a few comments about program traces and human protocols thrown in, and all confined within the research context, a machine is more or less viewed as a *strong* AI computer in Searle's sense (not to be confused with my USAIs). The vision (the research program) presumably—though probably never quite articulated this way—would be to build by accumulation, as it were, a psychologically "real" and eventually general computer clone of human cognitive processes: passing Turing's Test task after (seemingly intractable) task. It is rather like Montaigne having argued that animals *simpliciter* were as intelligent as human beings because the fox could do *this* as well or better than a human, the tuna fish could do *that*, the cat could do *this*, etc. (see *Mentality and Machines* [72], pp. 120–121). But even if we ignore this variation on the fallacy of composition, and even if the human mind is viewed

derive from factors external to themselves—complicated factors involving an already existent language and the conscious intentional users thereof. Note: I have stopped just short of actually claiming that MUSAIs are capable of producing anything with any meaning at all. Yet it seems obvious that the mimicking capacities and proxy roles of MUSAIs come within a split hair of guaranteeing that their outputs beg "readings" or interpretations mirroring the "readings" or interpretations of the sorts of *consciously* produced outputs by USAIs (or ourselves) that they (MUSAIs) simulate.

---

as modular in various important respects, there is something wildly absurd about the "piecemeal" employment of Turing's Test. And what's absurd is that it can lead to an insouciant mentalization of just about anything that could replicate a task which, if performed by conscious intentional beings like ourselves, would provide evidence of a mind. This has been noted in different ways by various critics of Turing and functionalism. But I wish to add a new twist.

A bizarre fallout from subscribing to the "piecemeal" Turing's Test, is that were a conscious intelligent human being effectively to assume the role of simulant for various machine-executed tasks which there had never been any prior reason to suppose were evidence of intelligence—say a clock ticking and moving its hands around, or, the dispensing of gumballs (for appropriate coin) down a shoot from inside a giant glass globe—the human simulant would thereby create, in effect, and more or less by *fiat* and retroactively, an example where the obviously mindless machine could now alternatively be viewed as capable of passing Turing's Test with respect to the human simulant of itself and however it was the human decided to do what, for example, the clock did. (Perhaps a slow rotation of arms monitored by slow counting: "1001, 1002, 1003,...") The possibilities for thus strewing *avant garde* mentality throughout the universe by ingenious (and ever mindful) imitations of previously mindless machines together with testing situations which conceal telltale cosmetic clues, should lead us either to celebrate our hitherto unsuspected God-like powers, or to believe that, after all, there was something drastically wrong with the "piecemeal" version of Turing's Test. (See *Mentality and Machines* [72], pp. 174–175, 180–196.)

(2) *Same end results.* The other abovementioned possibly controversial aspect of assuming that we can imagine both a tribe of USAIs and MUSAIs, derives from doubts that a mindless machine could ever *really* bring about the same end results as those typically achieved by conscious intentional agents. Thus airplanes are viewed as not really flying, computers as not really playing chess, etc., or *if* they are, they are said to do so in some unique or what might be called "machine indigenous" *different sense*, or a "scare-quotes" sense (of 'flying,' 'playing chess,' etc.). In spite of the interesting issues involved in figuring out how to nail down similar input and output types across disparate physical systems, I think it is obvious that at some interesting chunky (molar) level of description such similarities do exist. If they didn't, there couldn't even be a Turing's Test, since there would be *nothing* similar enough in the performances of humans and machines to invite comparison. No two different types of physical system would ever really *do* the same thing. The very idea of AI—here with the stress on the 'A' (as it was in the early days of the Field) would be utterly incoherent. There is, of course, a sense in which an electric eye does not do what a doorman used to

(If a MUSAI is used by a USAI to compute a certain sum, we or the USAI might "naturally" say of it, "It came up with such-and-such a sum." That, in other words, is what we regard what it did as having meant, etc.) So should that prove possible, such MUSAI outputs, in whatever form, would (and here I tamper with a quote from John Haugeland ([76], pp. 32–33)[7]):

> ... only have meaning because we give it to them; their intentionality, like that of smoke signals and writing, is essentially borrowed, hence derivative. To put it bluntly: computers (and MUSAIs) don't mean anything by their

---

do in opening doors for people. But there is also a sense in which it does exactly that, and it is because of this that it becomes a useful mimic or substitute for just such previously typically conscious and intentionally executed behaviors. And it is simply a generalization from this type of "aping" or imitative behavior that leads me to suppose that it is both possible and easy to imagine a tribe of USAIs as well as a tribe of MUSAIs.

My comments on the "piecemeal" variation of Turing's Test are designed to protect the tribe of mere MUSAIs from becoming too easily "mentalized." I'll call this *the panpsychism prevention thesis*. My comments on "same end results" are designed to keep intact the "M" aspect of MUSAIs; that although psychologically vacant, they have enough performative oomph to mimic or imitate various conscious intentional actions of USAIs. What they do is not so unique that it fails to match at an end results level various performances of USAIs. I'll call this *the mindless mimicry thesis*. And I shall add to the duo a third thesis: that because of the imitative capacities of MUSAIs, USAIs (as well as ourselves, of course) may find it convenient to use them for their own (USAI) purposes. Thus, MUSAIs can go proxy for USAIs in different social contexts and are capable of performing a range of tasks hitherto brought about by conscious intentional means. (Maybe they answer phones, maybe they pay the bills, maybe they play in a robot rock band, etc.) This possibly redundant thesis I shall refer to as *the proxy thesis*.

[7] The quote I tamper with is this: "The idea is that a semantic engine's tokens only have meaning because we give it to them; their intentionality, like that of smoke signals and writing, is essentially borrowed, hence *derivative*. To put it bluntly: computers themselves don't mean anything by their tokens (any more than books do)—they only mean what we say they do. Genuine understanding, on the other hand, is intentional "in its own right" and not derivatively from something else." Here I quote a sentence more than what I tamper with in order to make a point. The words 'genuine' and 'derivative' tend to suggest something bogus or not quite real. I don't mean by "derivative" intentionality (or meaning) something *without* real meaning when you look at it closely. Smoke signals and writing are paradigms of vehicles of meaning or intentionality, and, I would suggest, contra Haugeland's gloss, bearers of *genuine* intentionality or meaning. It's just that it's bestowed upon them from a source other than themselves. Once such bestowals are entrenched in regularities of use, of course, it would be tedious to call attention to the fact. Consequently, it is natural to talk of their meanings or what they are about—their intentionality—as if it accrued to them on their own, or as if it were self-bestowed. In what follows, whenever I remark on *merely* derivative intentionality, I mean to emphasize the fact that the intentionality is not self-bestowed, but generated from outside the system in question. (Different

tokens (any more than books do)—they only mean what we (or USAIs) say they do.

Their tokens, of course, retain meaning for all the usual reasons; it's just that the MUSAIs don't mean them to mean what they mean. USAIs, on the other hand, blatantly can and do, both individually and collectively, initiate or *originate* meaningful actions linguistic and otherwise. Thus, even though we are the makers of USAIs, this does nothing to cancel the fact that they, in turn, are capable of a wide indeterminate variety of self-generating behaviors. USAIs are not mere puppets; they are more like some population of at-the-end-of-the-story Pinocchios. They possess, I wish to assume, a genuine understanding—*whatever* that may amount to—something which (to shadow Haugeland again) "is intentional 'in its own right' and not, in important ways to be elaborated later, derivatively from something else." Such intentionality I shall, following many others, call *original* or *intrinsic*.

So far our world with presumably two kinds of robots (plus ourselves) is sketchy and uninformative, though, I would have supposed, a coherently imagined one. But are there arguments that might prove or strongly suggest that the alleged distinction between USAIs and MUSAIs is instead highly problematic and that the two differently *labelled* robots are not really two *very* different kinds of robots at all? Incredible as that may appear, I think recent rather complicated objections to the dichotomy between original/derived intentionality by Daniel Dennett in his *The Intentional Stance* obliquely imply that my somewhat sanguine contrasts between USAIs and MUSAIs are not at all what they are cracked up to be. So it seems expedient to take a close look at Dennett's views before trying to analyze what a USAI has that a MUSAI doesn't.

2 Dennett's Two-Bitser, "Survival Machines," or Could USAIs Really Be More or Less MUSAIs?

In a chapter entitled "Evolution, Error, and Intentionality" in the aforementioned book, Dennett, seeks to clobber the doctrine of original (and intrinsic) intentionality. As he puts it:

> The doctrine of original intentionality is the claim that whereas some of our artifacts may have intentionality derived from us, we have original (or intrinsic) intentionality, utterly underived. Aristotle said that God is the Unmoved Mover, and this doctrine announces that we are Unmeant Meaners. I have never believed in it and have often argued against it. As Searle has noted, Dennett ... believes that nothing *literally* has any *intrinsic intentional* mental states. ([42], p. 288)

---

senses of "generated from outside" are discussed in the course of commenting on Dennett's position.) The seductive aspects of this for AI are discussed at length later.

"Evolution, Error, and Intentionality" is an extended defense of this denial, and relies on no single argument. We are instead offered alternative ways of looking at a cluster of presumably intertwined matters—ways which conspicuously preempt any commitment to original or intrinsic intentionality. I shall avoid a detailed appraisal of Dennett's "big picture," however, and limit myself to a look at those pieces of his polemic which impinge on the issue of whether my world of USAIs and MUSAIs is or is not well-imagined. This, by itself, turns out to have scope.

Dennett's Wandering Two-Bitser. Dennett begins by considering the case of a supposedly mindless (i.e., a MUSAI-type) quarter detecting vending machine (a "two-bitser") which, had it been transported to Panama during a certain time, could have been used to detect Panamanian quarter-balboas—coins equivalent to US quarters by standard vending machines. So the machine in the US functions as a two-bitser, and in Panama as a q-balber. But, asks Dennett, what if the two-bitser had a counter (an analog of memory) which recorded the number of times it had detected quarters, and that this had not been reset to zero before being transported to its new niche in Panama? What state would the machine go into upon the occasion of its first receiving a quarter-balboa? Would it go into state Q meaning "US quarter here now"? Or would it go into state QB meaning "Panamanian quarter-balboa here now"? Prior to asking this he assumes that "nothing *intrinsic* about the two-bitser considered narrowly all by itself and independently of its prior history would distinguish it from a genuine q-balber, made to order on commission from the Panamanian government". So the question becomes whether its ancestry as a two-bitser—recorded by its counter—should impinge on our description of its debut state. And Dennett's answer is, that what determines whether the machine is in state Q or QB depends on what it was *selected for* ("literally selected, e.g., by the holder of the Panamanian Pepsi Cola franchise"). If the machine was selected to be a q-balber, then it is in state QB on the first occasion of its use in Panama, and what its counter counted (Q states) prior to that is irrelevant. All this he takes to be non-contentious. Even those (Fodor, Searle, Dretske, Burge, Kripke, et al.) who seem to endorse some version of the doctrine of original or intrinsic intentionality would have no quarrel with Dennett's characterization of the wandering two-bitser, for it has no psychological reality. It is "just a pragmatic matter of how best to talk, when talking metaphorically and anthropomorphically about the states of the device." What gives rise to the scrapping, Dennett feels, is his endorsement of an equivalent pragmatic treatment of human beings. For, he says,

> In the case of human beings (at least), Fodor and company are sure that such deeper facts do exist—even if we cannot always find them. That is, they suppose that independently of any power of any observer or interpreter to discover it, there is always a fact of the matter about what a person (or a person's mental state *really* means. Now we might call their shared

belief a belief in *intrinsic intentionality*, or perhaps even *objective* or *real* intentionality. ([42], p. 294)

It is this that Dennett claims constitutes "the most fundamental disagreement" between himself and Fodor, Searle, et al. He then proceeds to illustrate it with a Twin Earth-type case involving Jones first perceiving horses on Earth, then schmorses on the clone-like planet (schmorses being indistinguishable from horses except to trained biologists with special apparatus, and also being called *horses* by Twin Earthians, but not being horses "any more than dolphins are fish"). The intuition concerning this case that Dennett does not share, and which he attributes to Fodor, Searle, Dretske, Burge, Kripke, Chisholm, Nagel, and Popper and Eccles, is that when Jones confronts that schmorse

> ... either he really is, still, provoked into the state of believing he sees a horse (a mistaken, nonveridical belief) or he is provoked by that schmorse into believing for the first time (and veridically), that he is seeing a schmorse ... (or perhaps he is really in neither, so violently have we assaulted his cognitive system). ([42], p. 295)

Those who, like himself, find this intuition "dubious if not downright dismissible", will keep company with the Churchlands, Davidson, Haugeland, Millikan, Rorty, Stalnaker, Quine, Sellars, Hofstadter, Minsky, "and almost everyone else in AI." Dennett then proceeds to develop a thought experiment "to motivate, if not substantiate, my rival view," and attempts to pin various perplexities on Fodor, Dretske, et al., which derive from clinging to the doctrine of original or intrinsic intentionality.

Dennett's supporting thought experiment runs roughly as follows. For the purposes of experiencing life in the twenty-fifth century he imagines our designing a kind of ambulatory hibernation capsule in which we deeply doze until 2401. This robotic snooze-tank possesses "vision" and "sensory" systems designed to facilitate its general mission to keep us extant until the target time of reawakening. It is highly sophisticated in its self-control system, contrasting with the two-bitser in something like the way, I would guess, Frank Viola's 1988 Cy Young pitching arm contrasts with six year old Willy Wetnose's in Little League ball. It is even capable of "deriving its own subsidiary goals from its assessment of its current state and the import of that state for its ultimate goal (which is to preserve you). And consequently it could end up taking on projects antithetical to your (our) purposes; for example, by being convinced by some other robot "to subordinate its own life mission to some other." In spite of this rich repertoire of adaptive "behaviors," Dennett claims that Fodor and others would refuse to ascribe any real mental life to the system. At most they would credit it with *as if* deciding, seeing, wondering, and planning. He then cautions us that such a robot "would probably perform very creditably in any Turing Test to which we subjected it" and that "it will almost certainly have to be provided with control structures that are rich in self-reflective, self-monitoring power, so that it will have a human-like access to its own internal states" and be capable of assessing them. Thereby it will have "opinions" about what those states mean or "mean," and we should

> ... take those opinions seriously as very good evidence—probably the best evidence we can easily get—about what those states "mean" *metaphorically speaking* (remember: its only an artifact). ([42], p. 298)

The two-bitser, it is emphasized, "was given no such capacity to sway our interpretive judgments by issuing apparently confident "avowals." So ends the thought experiment proper. How, then, to respond to it? The rest of Dennett's lengthy article constitutes his own response. What I want first to focus on is his own initial reaction.

Dennett argues that if one (such as himself) sticks to the view that no products of AI wizardry could have anything but derived intentionality, the "most striking" implication of the intuition is

> ... that our own intentionality is exactly like that of the robot, for the science-fiction tale I have told is not new; it is just a variation on Dawkins's (1976) vision of us (and all other biological species) as "survival machines" designed to prolong the future of our selfish genes. We are artifacts, in effect, designed over the eons as survival machines for genes that cannot act swiftly and informedly in their own interests. ([42], p. 298)

And consequently, it is claimed, "our intentionality" is derived from the intentionality of "selfish" genes! *They* are the Unmeant Meaners, not us!

To allege such an implication is itself quite striking. At first I thought it was intended as a *reductio* of the intuition, and wondered why! But Dennett actually endorses the intuition and seems to welcome the implication, though he quickly assures us that there is a disanalogy between us vis-à-vis our genes and the "survival machine" of his tale vis-à-vis us: genes only have "*as if* intentionality" and do not consciously, deliberately, engineer us in the way we imagine ourselves engineering our protector-to-be robot.

The strategy unfolds as follows. He is only willing to endow his sophisticated "survival machine" with derived intentionality. Taken by itself, this point is one Fodor or Searle could happily agree with. But, of course, the point is not to be taken by itself. It is to be taken in conjunction with another claim; namely, the denial of that other mythic kind of intentionality: original or intrinsic. *Furthermore the non-original derived intentionality of the snooze tank is the same kind of intentionality that we possess; that, and no other.* How should we assess this bold contention?

It is important, I think, to look more closely at how it was arrived at. Recall that Dennett's polemic was triggered by Fodor's claim that Searle was right about one thing—that machines like the two-bitsers, *unlike us*, had only derived intentionality. Searle isn't supposed to be right even about that if we are to believe Dennett. But here it's worth stressing that in his attempt to persuade us of the wrongness of Searle's supposed attitude towards ourselves versus two-bitsers, Dennett does not base his arguments on a direct comparison between them and us, but instead on a mediating comparison between us and his behaviorally much more revved up robots, the "survival machines." But this may be a bit like trying to show that someone's low assessment of tricycles as modes of transportation compared to Cadillacs was wrong by extolling the virtues of a Toyota. It's hard to be clear about this, however. And the reason is that Dennett's "survival machines" are (archly?) ambiguous. (I think, in fact, they epitomize the ambiguity that runs through his accounts of intentionality at least since *Brainstorms* [41] and forces him, with respect to intentional explanation, to juggle a kind of instrumentalism with a "*sort* of realism."—his phrase.[8] This is not a fresh challenge, but what it adds up to here is that we are not sure what we are asked to imagine when we are asked to imagine his snooze tanks toting us hither and yon. Are we to imagine them having some degree of inner psychological reality or not? Dennett anticipates the question when he pauses to consider whether "we have smuggled in some crucial new capacity that vouchsafe the robot our kind of original intentionality" by shifting from the two-bitser to the "survival machines." But that issue is never decisively dealt with. For although those machines are described as "planning," "learning," and "communicating"; they are also rich in scare-quoteless self-reflective self-monitoring powers which include human-like access to their internal states, and make possible their reportings, avowings, and commentaries. And their "opinions" are alternatively treated as opinions to be taken seriously. In short, the ambiguities of Dennett's protector robots seriously blunts the thrust of his thought experiment which was, recall, designed to "motivate, *if not substantiate*" (my italics) his denial of original or intrinsic intentionality. For the question as to when it seems appropriate to hypothesize something like intrinsic intentionality in order to account for complicated behaviors, simply gets recycled in the case of those robots. (And just how human-like is their human-like access to internal states? Etc.) To be shown "that our own intentionality is exactly like that of the robot" could amount to being shown that we as well as certain sorts of robots have original or intrinsic intentionality! Dennett's "survival machines" would thus turn out to be like our USAIs, and not like our MUSAIs.

Apart from these ambiguities, however, we need to assess Dennett's response to his own thought experiment, and his claim that since we, in effect, stand to our genes (or "Mother Nature") in the way that "survival machines" stand to us, our own intentionality is derivative. This suggests that all intentionality should be viewed as derivative. A strange implication of this strategy, however, is that it no longer seems possible to impugn inflated ascriptions of intentionality to a machine by pointing out that the machine is only capable of meaning something in a derivative sense, for a derivative sense of meaning anything is already saturated with the psychological. There is no other kind of intentionality. Ironically it then becomes

---

[8] See his discussion of the issue in "Reflections: Instrumentalism Reconsidered," in *The Intentional Stance* [42], pp. 69–81.

urgent to ask how to keep a lid on the mentalization of machines since reasons to ascribe derivative intentionality seem there for any imaginative asking. So the threat which our *panpsychism prevention thesis* (see footnote 6) was designed to stymie reasserts itself. A spooky fallout from Dennett's approach is that it almost makes you feel that you need to *defend* the thesis that at least some machines which mimic human actions *don't* think!

The general form of the evolution argument is not new. It is a "golden oldie" tune heard long before in philosophical discussions of minds and machines (e.g., in Alan Ross Anderson's anthology *Minds and Machines* [1]). It was in response to Paul Ziff's "The Feelings of Robots" which I quoted at the outset that J. J. C. Smart wrote (in "Professor Ziff on Robots")

> (A) The notion of "living thing" as opposed to "robot" is unclear.
> (1) Let us pretend that the *Genesis* story is literally true. Then Adam and Eve were robots. They were artifacts fashioned by God. If a conflation of ancient theology and modern biology may be allowed, we could even say that God gave Adam and Eve "programs," namely their sets of genes, probably DNA molecules which have the function of recording hereditary information. ([1], p. 104)

And in his "Robots Incorporated" Ninian Smart responds to Ziff's claim that "The way a robot acts (in a specified context) depends primarily on how we programmed it to act" which he (Ziff) employs as an argument against there ever being real feelings in robots, by countering,

> For the sake of simplicity I introduce the notion of Nature to represent the sum of causes going towards the creation of a human being considered as beginning with conception or at any later time in his life. What is wrong, for the determinist, in saying that the way a man acts, in a specified context, depends primarily on how Nature programs him to act? ([1], p. 107)

What the just quoted share with Dennett's thought experiment is the attempt to blunt any sharp distinction in kind between robots and humans through making a case out for us being, in effect, programmed by nature (our genes). In other words, arguments against robot mentality based on a reference to their only doing what they are programmed to do, would undercut the idea of human mentality as well. I once argued [70] against endorsing any *general* form of the argument against machine intelligence based on a simple reference to it being programmed (and against Ziff's position specifically). Nevertheless, I think Ziff's article contains some neglected insights, and I will say something about them in a later section. So too, I think there is something very fishy about the Smarts' and Dennett's we-too-are-programmed-by-nature attempt to zap the gap between us and programmed machines. And what is fishy can be reeled to the surface by considering further the difference between USAIs and MUSAIs.

We are, as it were, the ultimate authors of both USAIs and MUSAIs (though we can, if we like, imagine some MUSAIs being in turn made by MUSAIs). But how, in any interesting way, could reference to the fact of our double authoring serve to support the claim that there isn't a chasm between USAIs and MUSAIs so far as a mental life including intentional activities is concerned? Unless it is incoherent to try to imagine being able to build (1) some kind of conscious intelligent clone of ourselves, and (2) some decidedly non-conscious non-intelligent mentally vacant two-bitser type mechanism which can, however, be used for certain convenient proxy purposes, *nothing* could show the lack of such a gap. But exactly that lack is what Dennett's interpretation of his thought experiment indirectly implies. So there must be something wrong with that interpretation.

Surprisingly, part of what's wrong springs from an equivocal use of *derivative*. The sense, according to Dennett, in which our intentionality is supposed to be derivative, and hence in an important sense like the derivative intentionality of "survival machines" (and even two-bitsers!), is that we are Mother Nature's artifacts. Here *derivative* more or less amounts to "is caused by" and, certainly, our intentionality, whatever the devil it might be, is no doubt caused by *something* and genes seem a pretty firm candidate for the role. (That our genes are characterized as "selfish," following Dawkins, fits in nicely with the "survival machine" conceit. But this is little more than a stylistic flourish. The nub of Dennett's argument is clearly mirrored in the Smarts' articles without that twist.) But this broad sense of *derivative* is not equivalent to the sense of "borrowed" or "derivative" intentionality which, for example, smoke signals (and current computer tokenings) are supposed to have, and which Haugeland discusses. What this latter "borrowed" sense of *derivative* actually adds up to is admittedly interestingly unclear. But it is clearly *not* synonymous with "is caused by something—e.g., our genes." The only way Dennett can make it even remotely seem to be so is to whimsically attribute an ersatz (*as if*) intentionality to Mother Nature (in the section of the article called "Reading Mother Nature's Mind" [42], pp. 298–300). And he is willing, in effect, to anthropomorphize genes in order to make good on the alleged parallel between our being programmed by nature being like our programming a two-bitser (or the psychologically ambiguous "survival machine").

Dennett's anthropomorphizing is not, of course, without its qualifications, and the motivation for it is broader than his desire to do in the doctrine of original intentionality. Nevertheless the move seems desperate, and the (quite necessary) qualifications of the attributions self-defeating. Only if Dennett were really willing to ascribe *conscious* intent to Mother Nature would there seem to be any hope for the proposed parallels being maintained. But even this would not be adequate. We would still need to describe the differences in *proximal causes of performances* across such robots as USAIs and MUSAIs. Although both they and we would have been caused by conscious intentional artificers—us and Mother Nature, respectively—what gets caused is in the one case consciously performing subjects, and in the other case non-conscious devices used for imitation or proxy functions. The MUSAIs are prime candidates for what Searle [167] has called "observer-relative ascriptions of mentality," which is, I think, what many have had in mind when they have talked of machines not really being able to think but only being able to "think" [9] and so on. These ascriptions provide excellent examples of derivative intentionality such as in the case discussed by Haugeland where "computers ... only mean what we say they do."

It is the presumed differences in *proximal causes of performances* that primarily motivates the distinction(s) between original or intrinsic intentionality and derived intentionality. So questions concerning remote origins or derivations (evolutionary or not) of the agents (or "agents") themselves, who (which) *in turn* cause those performances, involve entirely different matters. If use of the term 'original' misleads us into thinking them the same, it is a good reason to ditch the term altogether in favor of 'intrinsic.'

Here it seems useful to digress briefly on observer-relative ascriptions of mentality, e.g., as when we ascribe meaning to indicators on a thermostat, or an empty Clorox bottle used as a walleye fishing buoy. I view these as prime cases of derivative intentionality, though they may seem somewhat different from other examples typically used to introduce or illustrate the term. For example, Searle himself asks:

> How does the mind impose Intentionality on entities that are not intrinsically Intentional, on entities such as sounds and marks that are, construed in one way, just physical phenomena in the world like any other? An utterance can have Intentionality, just as a belief has Intentionality, but whereas the Intentionality of the belief is intrinsic the Intentionality of the utterance is derived. The question then is: How does it derive its Intentionality? ([169], pp. 27–28)

Searle goes on to claim in the course of working out an extended answer to his question,

> So I impose Intentionality on my utterances by intentionally conferring on them certain conditions of satisfaction which are the conditions of satisfaction of certain psychological states. ([169], pp. 27–28)

I am not here concerned with Searle's theory as such. I simply use the quote to display a fairly typical example where something, an utterance (the examples are usually linguistic), is a candidate for derivative intentionality (cf. Haugeland's books and smoke signals). In suggesting that cases of observer-relative ascriptions of mentality involve derivative intentionality, I mean that candidates for those ascriptions such as thermostats, various computers, vending machines—indeed, our entire tribe of MUSAIs—can be seen, if a long enough story is told, as treatable in much the same way (Searle's way, or some other) as utterances, sentences, etc. This is not to say that there are no interesting differences between the way programmers stand to their computers' outputs, and how novelists stand to their novels. Some of these differences, as we shall see, are *quite*

---

[9] See Gunderson [72], pp. 180–196.

interesting. But if we were to fiddle enough with the phrasing of the last quotation we could eventually substitute for "my utterances" something like "performances of these computers (or thermostats) designed and programmed (or produced) by me or others like me with certain functions or purposes in mind" etc. This may all seem transparent, but since cases of observer-relative ascriptions of mentality are not always linguistic (or not just linguistic) and may range over materially diverse media (parking meters, windsocks, sundials, fishing buoys, etc.), and since examples of them obviously tend not to be first-person ones in the way that the linguistic examples of derived intentionality often are, it may be appropriate to assert the similarities. Even given such similarities, however, as we shall emphasize later, derivative intentionality is not a single phenomenon, but more like love, "a many splendoured thing." Before focusing on this, however, I want to offer a contrary assessment to Dennett's of some alleged connections between the idea of original (intrinsic) intentionality and other familiar *dramatis personae* in the philosophy of mind.

3 Original (Intrinsic) Intentionality, Privileged Access, Incorrigibility, and Deep Facts that Fix Meanings of Our Thoughts

Hopefully the foregoing has at least separated the doctrine of original or intrinsic intentionality from the idea of ourselves being "utterly underived" in the sense of somehow not being products of our "selfish" genes, or Mother Nature. No believer in the doctrine need buy in on that. But it is also in some important respects separable from other familiar notions in the philosophy of mind. Dennett believes that Searle, Dretske, Burge, and Kripke resist "rather subliminally" "the idea that we are artifacts designed by natural selection." (I think it would have to be very subliminal. Searle, for one is on non-subliminal record (in "Minds, Brains, and Programs") as having answered the question "Could a machine think?" with "... *only* a machine could think, and indeed only very special kinds of machines, namely brains and machines that had the *same casual powers as brains*" [167], p. 424). Nevertheless, Dennett's hunch as to why the idea is resisted is,

> ... if we are (just) artifacts, then what our innermost thoughts mean—and whether they mean anything at all—is something about which we, the very thinkers of those thoughts, have no special authority. The two-bitser turns into a q-balber without ever changing its inner nature; the state that used to mean one thing now means another. The same thing could in principle happen to us, if we are just artifacts, not only have we no guaranteed privileged access to the deeper facts that fix the meanings of our thoughts, *but there are no such deeper facts.* ([42], p. 300)

He later discusses Kripke on Wittgenstein on rule following ([42], pp. 312–313), and attributes to him (Kripke) a willingness to bring the "outmoded idea" of privileged access (now a mere epistemic skeleton) out its closet. This is seen by Dennett as going hand in creepy hand with the view that although meaning in machines is relative to "the intentions of the designer" ([42], pp. 312–313) our meanings are not. A malfunction in a machine, according to Kripke, "is well defined only in terms of its program, as stipulated by its designer." Kripke's unwillingness to analyze human "malfunction" in the same way, according to Dennett, is because it would suggest our own meaning to be as derivative and inaccessible to us directly, as to any artifact. He then quotes Kripke again (with a two-bitser insert):

> The idea that we lack "direct" access to the facts whether we mean plus or quus [Q or QB, in the two-bitser's case] is bizarre in any case. Do I not know, directly, and with a fair degree of certainty, that I mean plus? ... There may be some facts about me to which my access is indirect, and about which I must form tentative hypotheses: but surely the fact as to what I mean by "plus" is not one of them! ([42], pp. 312–313)

This Dennett takes to be "as powerful and direct an expression as could be of the intuition that lies behind the belief in original intentionality." He then assimilates it to the doctrine that his (frequently cited) ally Ruth Millikan in *Language, Thought, and Other Biological Categories* [123] calls "meaning rationalism" which her book attempts to "topple from its traditional pedestal." According to Dennett, one is forced either to give up the idea that "you are unlike the fledgling cuckoo not only in having access, but also in having privileged access to your meanings" or you have to "abandon the naturalism that insists you are, after all, just a product of natural selection, whose intentionality is thus derivative and hence potentially indeterminate."

By bundling the doctrine of original (intrinsic) intentionality together with Millikan's idea of meaning rationalism it becomes associated with the view that we can a priori know with "Cartesian certainty" what "we are thinking or talking about." She writes,

> The view of my adversary, then, is the view that consciousness is transparently and *infallibly* epistemic. Consciousness is or essentially involves an infallible kind of direct knowing—a knowing that is guaranteed as such from within consciousness itself. Specifically, the claim is that consciousness grasps its own intentionality, or that of its inner representations, with infallibility. Intentionality is a "given," Hence this intentionality cannot consist of mere matter-of-fact, even of naturally necessary, external relations to the world. ([123], p. 91)

The above exhibits a rather extraordinary chain of assumed associations. It is like a variation on Hegel's idea that if we were to explain a rose completely, we would need to explain the whole universe: i.e., if we are to defend the distinction between original (intrinsic) intentionality, we must defend the doctrine of meaning rationalism which includes a defense of infallible privileged access, intentionality as a "given," anti-naturalism, etc. Alas, I would have thought we would have had only to defend the unsubtle suggestion that we can imagine constructing two quite different kinds of robots, USAIs and MUSAIs, where the latter in their proxy roles are on occasion *interpreted* as functioning in certain ways—meaning (*for us* or USAIs) *this*, indicating *that*!

Such a construal, however, involves an admittedly underinterpreted world. For we have simply, by fiat, as it were, declared there to be two different kinds of robots. What need we declare when we declare that the one kind, USAIs, are conscious intentional artifacts? It would go well beyond my present purposes to discuss in detail the evolutionary tack shared by Dennett and Millikan. So I shall simply adumbrate my appraisals of the alleged connections between the idea of a USAI with original (intrinsic) intentionality and the other doctrines cited. More detailed support for them should accumulate, *en passant*, in the sections to come.

Privileged Access. If the denial of this admittedly disputed doctrine implies that there is no typically dramatic *asymmetry* between the way in which I access my own beliefs, thoughts, feelings, desires, plans—as well as my non-intentional sensations, pains, moods, afterimages, hallucinations, etc., *and* the way I am apprised of the supposedly comparable mental states of others, then Kripke should be saluted for "uncloseting" its skeleton and we should try to put some flesh back on its old bones. It is hard to believe that without the asymmetry there would even be phenomena puzzling enough to give rise to the so-called "other minds" problem(s). Tantalizing counter proposals from Wittgenstein and Ryle on up to the present which attempt to softpedal either its existence or its effects, based on theories concerning the socially shared criteria for language use, have not been without their own anomalies. In any case, their canonization seems premature. I have defended this beleagured doctrine and utilized it and kindred asymmetries extensively elsewhere,[10] and hope that examples prominent in the ensuing sections help underscore its plausibility and importance. Note, however, the claim is that the asymmetry *typically* attends our awareness of mental states, processes, and events: direct with respect to our own, indirect with respect to others. (This is not to deny that there are also ranges of examples where either the directness or indirectness may become abrogated to some degree or other.[11]) But more importantly the doctrine as I would defend it involves no commitment whatsoever to the next item on this heading's list.

Incorrigibility. I think that a major reason for the doctrine of privileged access coming into disrepute is that it is frequently treated as an ellipsis for *incorrigible* or *infallible* privileged access. Dennett has done this is in the past, and though it is not blatantly present in "Evolution, Error, and Intentionality," it may be there "subliminally." For it is non-elliptically

---

[10] Most recently in "Leibniz's Walk-In Machine, Perception, and the Perils of Physicalism" [73]; and see "Leibnizian Privacy and Skinnerian Privacy" [71].

[11] See "Leibnizian Privacy and Skinnerian Privacy" [71].

obvious in Millikan's Dennett-endorsed construal of Meaning Rationalism (see quote above). In this connection Kripke's remarks prove instructive. His claim is that we know "directly, and with a fair degree of certainty" and not that we have incorrigible or infallible access to anything. This seems right on the button, and is akin to the doctrine as I interpret it. That direct awareness or privileged access is quite detachable from the notion of incorrigibility or infallibility can be made vivid with the following simple example: I am lying in bed and intentionally twiddle my toes. How do I know that my toes are twiddling? Not, typically, by watching them move, but, directly, by moving them. In doing it, I am aware of doing it, and aware in a way you could never be aware of my doing it. You would, by contrast, need to observe them moving, and then hypothesize that their moving is a result of my intentionally doing something. It might not be. It might be an uncontrollable twitching. So I say to you without looking at them "I'm twiddling my toes" but, sadly, I am not. For I have no toes. My leg has been amputated. A phantom limb phenomenon. No sign of incorrigibility here. Yet the direct awareness remains. For the way in which I was *mistaken* involved a direct though illusory sense of twiddling my toes. In other words, the way I got it wrong is asymmetrical with the way in which you could have gotten it wrong about my toes, or the way in which I could have gotten it wrong about your toes twiddling. *Direct awareness not only attends forms of our knowledge, but attends forms of our mistakes and ignorance.* Once this is made plain, its detachability from the doctrine of incorrigibility or infallibility should be more apparent. And once this separation is made, the role our direct and privileged access may seem to play vis-à-vis "deeper" facts, if there are any, which fix the meanings of our thoughts, deviates from the role it was said to play in the version of the doctrine attacked by Dennett.

With respect to the association between original intentionality and privileged access (*sans* incorrigibility), however, the situation seems something like this: that what we are conscious of is almost always also something to which we have privileged access. So insofar as consciousness is heavily implicated in the exercise of intentionality of any kind, so is or at sometime was, privileged access. Portraying some of the interplay between these notions will be part of the burden of the sections to follow.

Deep Facts that Fix Meanings of Our Thoughts. For Dennett the doctrine of original or intrinsic intentionality seems to carry with it an automatic commitment not only to the idea of a highly authoritative (incorrigible?) privileged access to our meanings or belief states, but also to the idea that there are always deep facts which fix them one way or another. So, for the believer in original intentionality, Jones on Twin Earth confronting that schmorse, will either *really* be in a state of believing (wrongly) that he sees a horse, or he will *really* be in a state of believing (correctly) for the first time that he is seeing a schmorse, or he will *really* be in neither "so violently have we assaulted his cognitive system." In short, there will always be some psychological facts indigenous to the individual alone which could, in principle, at least, prove sufficient for individuating belief states in Twin Earth type cases. I find this contention puzzling.

Even if one were committed to such facts, the more modest version of the doctrine of privileged access (*sans* incorrigibility) means that we would lack any inner infallible *algorithm* for retrieving the beliefs once fixed. But more importantly, commitment to the doctrine of original or intrinsic intentionality seems a much more *general* commitment than Dennett makes it out to be. It is little more than a commitment to there being an important distinction between the way in which the actions of MUSAIs give rise to interpretations of purpose and meaning (in a broad sense) and the way in which we or USAIs do. To claim that it is the conscious intelligent states of the two latter that contribute to the sense and purpose of their interpretable performances—assisted and/or bullied, of course, by various shared social conventions, linguistic and otherwise—falls far short of insisting on the types of belief-fixing facts that Dennett seeks to discredit. If you don't even share the intuition that there are deep qualitative psychological differences between robots like USAIs and robots like MUSAIs, you are, of course, not likely to believe in such facts. But surely to endorse those psychological differences need not commit you to any such finely tuned account of what Jones's belief state really is with respect to horses and schmorses. Nor does it dictate how one should construe the relationship, say, between reference, and the content of belief states, or force one to take any particular stand as to whether meanings could be just in the head, and so on and so forth.

There are no doubt ways of interpreting the doctrine of original intentionality so that it carries a commitment to there *always* being "deeper facts" that somehow "fix the meanings of our thoughts." But here the demeanor of those "deeper facts" that the believer in original intentionality is supposedly saddled with is left unspecified. In any case, I would think that however things at that level (if it is a level) sort out, proponents of original intentionality need only assert that they exercise some conscious (or potentially conscious) creative and revisionary power over what they come to think or believe, and that once fixed (*no matter how!*), those conscious beliefs *in turn* play an important and necessary (not sufficient) role in determining the meanings or readings appropriate to the tokens that express them. So to embrace the doctrine of original intentionality as such, involves no more of a commitment to there being a level of "deeper facts" that fix the content of beliefs, much less any specific account of how that might work, than does embracing the doctrine of privileged access involve a commitment to the doctrine of incorrigibility.

To summarize: we have separated the doctrine of derivative intentionality from Dennett's derived-from-Mother-Nature doctrine, and we have been happy to let it cohabit with the doctrine of privileged access which in turn has been detached from any idea of incorrigibility. And we have distinguished between the general doctrine of original or intrinsic intentionality and any finely tuned interpretation of it involving "deep" facts fixing belief contents. So what was initially assumed about the general differences between USAIs and ourselves and MUSAIs now seems intact and immune, and ready to become a vehicle for exploring some broad connections between consciousness and intentionality.

4 Consciousness and Derivative Intentionalities

What, more precisely, is the difference between our tribe of USAIs (and ourselves) and our tribe of MUSAIs with respect to their intentionality? By definition USAIs are conscious, and MUSAIs are not. But how does their consciousness matter? With respect to that to which we ascribe meanings, the presence of consciousness may or may not make a difference. Consider the following cases in which consciousness is present in a subject, but either has no bearing, or a much diminished bearing, on how what the subject does gets "read" or interpreted. These all strike me as being bona fide examples of derivative intentionality, and taken together give us a glimpse into the rich heterogeneity of the subject.

Parakeets. A sister of mine, when ten, was once awarded a parakeet because over a summer she dragged more kids to Bible School than anyone else. In time it was capable of the following imitations: (1) a rough whistling approximation of the opening phrase of "Yankee Doodle" (he got to the end of "Yankee Doodle came to town"); (2) a quite clearly articulated "Where's the beer, dear?"; and (3) a comparably clear "Hello Joe." ('Joe' was not his name nor the name of anyone in our family nor the name of anyone who ever set foot in our house during that period). None of us were Cartesians, and we all assumed, correctly, I believe, that the parakeet, Joshua, to be precise, was conscious. No doubt, *that* he was conscious, though conscious in a way I shall never fully understand ("What was it like to be Joshua?"), had *something* to do with his three types of human-like tokenings. But it's obvious that however he was conscious had *nothing* to do with the fact that what he emitted sounded more or less like a strain of "Yankee Doodle," or a question, or a greeting. Without knowing it, he was able to produce within a predominantly human context, sound patterns, picked up on mostly as a result of being bombarded with repeated whistlings and phrasings, these all part of an effort "to get the bird to talk."

Alienated Labor, the Hum Drum, the Automatized. As Chaplin's *Modern Times* still poignantly reminds us, there is an unfortunate aptness to the cliche complaint about becoming mere cogs in a machine, being treated like robots, etc. Marx in "Alienated Labor" ([119], pp. 121–131) writes about our relationship to ourselves first being realized or objectified through our relationships with others. He claims that if we end up being related to the products of our labor, our "objectified" labor, "as to an *alien*, hostile, powerful and independent object," we are related in a way that enables someone else "alien, hostile, powerful" and independent of us to be "lord of this object" (i.e., the product of *our* labor). Here we become slaves to that object, for it is an object intended by others, not ourselves. And our very consciousness itself becomes transformed (rather, transmogrified!) through the alienation into a means for producing those objects which we go on churning out just in order to survive. So our consciousness, part of our nature, which would, if in a non-servile role, initiate its own goals and monitor the carrying out of purposes in accord with its wants, desires, etc., becomes itself a mere means to someone else's ends. The worker to whom this happens, according to Marx, "feels himself at home only during his leisure time" and when at work "feels homeless." Such work is viewed as "not voluntary but imposed, *forced labor*." And it becomes "not the satisfaction of a need, but only a means for satisfying other needs."

Apart from ideology, what Marx is pointing to probably strikes a chord in most of us. What underlies the major complaint is that our own conscious wants, desires, and intentions lay idle and count for little in terms of what we do. We simply do "what we're told," do it "because it's a job," do it because "someone has to do it," do it "without thinking about it," etc. Even if we're lucky enough not to feel that our own occupations or professions are that disturbingly sundered from who we feel we are and what we'd like to go on to be and do, most of us have had some experience of alienation from our work. Who, indeed, would choose to do everything their position demands of them? And so we perform various tasks demanded of us in perfunctory or automatic ways. These are, perhaps, part of the hum drum paperwork that we care little and think little about; just long enough to author the minimal response required in order to get it out of our way. Or we are forced into or fit ourselves into some automatized scheme, sticking stamps on dozens of envelopes while thinking of what we will do on our vacation. What we do and what it means is not literally as apart from our own conscious states as the meaning of "Pass the beer, dear" is from the consciousness of Joshua the parakeet. (He's hardly alienated from what he said. He hasn't a clue.) Yet in such cases, though conscious, our own wants and desires, are already on vacation, and the meaning of what we do turns largely on the considerations of someone outside ourselves. Our by nature original or intrinsic intentionality gives way to an interesting extent to a range of performances that derive their meanings largely from the original or intrinsic intentionality of others.

Hypnotized Subjects. Examples of these provide a variation on the general theme of the last sentence, but with their own peculiar physical causes. Consciousness seems present, but subject to outside control, so as not to operate with the the same relevance it has in our ordinary life. (Compare: somnambulism.)

Other Cases: (A) Saying, consciously, exactly what someone wants you to say on pain of torture; (B) uttering the lines of a character in a play; (C) speaking in tongues. (In the standard case the speaker isn't supposed to have a glimmer of what the babbling means, until the interpreter (God-appointed) does an instant *Berlitz* of it all).

The above examples are introduced as a quick exhibit of some situations where although consciousness is present in a subject performing certain tasks, it either contributes nothing to the semantic or pragmatic structuring of those tasks, or operates with respect to them in a minimized or deviant way. The primary interpretation(s) of such "outputs"—their meaning ascriptions—derive, for the most part, from sources outside the agent producing them. In the pure cases, like that of the parakeet, the consciousness cancels out entirely so far as ascriptions of meaning to its three types of outputs are concerned. Imagine yourself being used by aliens to function something like a walleye buoy: you bob around in some lake-like medium, and signal to them an equivalent of "Here's the spot where you usually catch fish." You remain conscious, of course, but your consciousness cancels out so far as being any kind of determinant of how they "read" you. Aspects of some of these these cases map onto some of the points argued by Searle in his "Minds, Brains, and Programs" as well as Ziff's much earlier "The Feelings of Robots."

One way to look at Searle's Chinese Room example is to see it as a case where the consciousness of the subject (Searle) supposedly cancels out so far as the readings and interpretations germane to his inscriptional inputs and outputs are concerned. Searle is conscious in the room, just as the parakeet was conscious in his cage. But Searle no more understands the meanings of what he takes in and puts out, than the parakeet understood the barrage of English it was submitted to and the slender "selection" therefrom that it eventually mimicked. Some of the major disputes generated by the Chinese Room can be viewed as turning on (1) whether being able to do *that* much syntactic stuff, really involves some mastery of Chinese, and drags in semantics, and (2) even if it doesn't, and Searle's own consciousness cancels out, whether the example captures the crucial components of so-called *strong* AI models. There is also, I think, the question as to whether apart from (1), Searle's behavior in following the rules of his instruction manual imports into the situation a certain amount of conscious intentionality which does not cancel out. Be that as it may, I mention his thought experiment at this point in order to add it to the list of examples where the connections between consciousness and meaningful outputs appear, at least, to contrast starkly with those cases where what gets said or done seems under the control in various crucial ways of what an agent consciously means or intends to say or do. (Searle's example is put to a somewhat different use in the final section when I discuss problems which arise when trying to devise an equivalent of it for conscious non-intentional states.)

It should not be surprising, I suppose, that cases where consciousness is present but cancels out should turn out to be the same, so far as ascriptions of intentionality or meaning are concerned, as those where there is no mentality present in the subject at all. Both sorts boil down to cases involving only intentionality of a derivative kind. It was precisely this equivalence that Ziff called attention to when he wrote,

> So Turing posed the question whether automata could think, be conscious, have feelings, etc., in the following naive way: what test would an automaton fail to pass? MacKay has pointed out that any test for mental or any other attributes to be satisfied by the observable activity of a human being can be passed by automata. And so one is invited to say what would be wrong with a robot's performance.
>
> Nothing need by wrong with either the actor's or a robot's performance. What is wrong is that they are performances. ([1], p. 101)

To an interesting degree, I think, the sense that we even need a philosophical distinction between original and derivative intentionality stems (1) from our awareness of the homely but significant contrasts that exist between (a) any of the range of cases mentioned above or others like them, and (b) those more familiar, normal situations, where what we or others say or do is intimately connected with our conscious plans, goals, wants, and desires; and (2) from the suspicion that most AI robots or machines, real or imaginary, which have been treated as examples from (b) really are examples of (a). Ziff's comments above can be seen as showcasing this miscategorization. My critique of Turing a few years later trades on kindred observations, and Searle's Chinese Room objection to *strong* AI, though more elaborate, also has its parallels with Ziff. (As Ziff said of his robots, we might say of Searle: "Nothing need be wrong with either Searle's or an AI computer's performance with Chinese characters. What is wrong is that they are performances.")

Note: when Dennett in "Evolution, Error, and Intentionality" claims that we are not, after all, graced with original or intrinsic intentionality, and that the only intentionality we have is derivative, he is not claiming that our intentionality really turns out to be of a piece with any of the range of examples cited above. It is derivative intentionality only in his highly specialized sense of "being derived from our selfish genes or Mother Nature." One consequence of this is that within the range of subjects who have derivative intentionality in Dennett's specialized sense, there is still the question whether on occasion, or often, or always, they *also* partake of derivative intentionality in any of the more colloquial ways listed above? Hence it would be useful to distinguish between Dennett's sense (DI_1)—should we wish to retain it—and the homely sense (DI_2).

The above provides ample illustrations of cases where although consciousness may be present in a subject, it has either no role or a diminished one in determining the meaning of what is said or done. In these instances, what is said or done derives its meaning almost wholly from outside the agent, and not just in the sense that the usual constraints of acting within a framework involving social and notational conventions are operative. It is outside the agent in its severance from the standard intimate connections between the agents conscious plans, purposes, wants, and desires. These fail to function as its determinants. The obvious next question becomes: What are those standard cases like where the forms that our consciousness assumes retain an intimate and controlling connection with our actions, linguistic and otherwise? Here I must limit myself to a broad sketch of what I think this includes, and hence what any detailed theory of the relationship between consciousness, intentionality, and the many forms of its expression, would have to accommodate.

5 Our Conscious Presence in the Intentional; Some Standard Cases: Writer/Reader and Speaker/Hearer Asymmetries (The Ziff/Sartre Disambiguation Asymmetries)

I refer again to Ziff, and a casual remark he made in the late sixties when we were both involved in linguistics projects at the Systems Development Corporation in Santa Monica. He was fresh from a frustrating seminar on anaphoric analysis with some AI programmers, and said, with an air of disbelief (and with slightly different phrasing), "These guys actually think that a speaker has to disambiguate his *own* remarks in the same way someone else would disambiguate them. They have *no* sense of the asymmetry between how *I* know the meaning of what I say, and how *they* know the meaning of what *I* say."

I shall follow the lead of his simple, rather familiar, yet sometimes disputed, intuition about disambiguation. (Questions concerning how we discern the meanings of others are, after all, like the question of what kind of intentionality to ascribe to robots or machines, a specialized rendition of the other minds problem.) I recalled his remark years later when in thinking about quite different matters (literary criticism) I came upon the following passage of Sartre's "Why Write" [161]:

> Now the operation of writing involves an implicit quasi-reading which makes real reading impossible. When the words form under his pen, the author doubtless sees them, but he does not see them as the reader does, since he knows them before writing them down.

He continues:

> The writer neither foresees nor conjectures; he *projects*. It often happens that he awaits, as they say, the inspiration. But one does not wait for oneself the way one waits for others. If he hesitates, he knows the future is not made, that he himself is going to make it, and if he still does not know what is going to happen to his hero, that simply means that he has not thought about it, that he has not decided upon anything. The future is then a blank page, whereas the future of the reader is two hundred pages filled with words which separate him from the end. Thus, the writer meets everywhere only *his* knowledge, *his* will, *his* plans, in short himself. He touches only his own subjectivity; the object he creates is out of reach; he does not create it for

himself. If he rereads himself, it is already too late. The sentence will never quite be a thing in his eyes.

The speaker/hearer asymmetries that concerned Ziff, seem to me remarkably similar to the writer/reader ones described in a more detailed and metaphorically metaphysical manner by Sartre. I shall first expand on them, and then make suggestions as to how their appreciation contributes to an appreciation of the connections between our conscious plans, wants, and desires, and the expressive behaviors (in these cases linguistic) which they give rise to. (We have to an extent encountered them before in connection with the doctrine of privileged access. But here they are more specifically stated. I shall refer to them as *Ziff/Sartre disambiguation asymmetries*, and provide Ziff with surprising company.)

Suppose, for example, at a party I say "There are some health food nuts for you" and gesture in a general way towards a table which bears a bowl of large organically grown, unsalted, unprocessed cashews, and around which are seated three well known proselytizing promoters of a chain of organic gardening produce outlets. Now someone hearing me and glancing towards the table and recognizing both the type of cashews and the type of people, might wonder, "Did he mean the the cashews? or those guys? or, perhaps, them and the cashews all at once?" But I from my privileged perch as perpetrator of the remark do not in the typical ordinary case have to ask any such thing. And were I to have to ask, it would be a strange thing indeed: "What could I have in mind?" I muse to myself after having had my say, "The cashews?, those guys? or cashews and guys together?" After all it was *my* remark, how could I become so puzzled? But to say I am utterly *un*puzzled is to say I have already settled its meaning for myself in the act of saying it. It comes from me *for* me already disambiguated. Or rather, it comes from me for me to understand as something said to you, either as I wished to say it or not. Even if I then notice that the context has made the remark ambiguous for others, it does not thereby make it ambiguous for me. Should I then wish to help the others out, I clarify my remarks for them by saying more. But in saying more I clarify nothing for myself.

Or, suppose I am writing the first chapter of my novel, and I write down blah de blah blah blah, or whatever. I fret and fuss over it, trying one thing, then another: blah blah de blah blah, blah blah blah blah de blah, but no, blah de blah blah blah, yes, that's it. Etc. Finally I finish it, and hand you a copy. I sit down with my own copy. Is what I do in my act of reading what I just composed similar to what you do in the act of reading what I just composed? Certainly not, although I might find a few blah de blahs that I think should be blah blahs, and you may make similar suggestions. Because what I wrote was largely, though not every comma's worth, determined by what I intended to write, and what I wanted to write was something I was conscious of writing, I became conscious of the content of what I wrote in the act of writing it. What I wrote became an inscriptional embodiment of my wants and intentions, and by being so bears a singular relationship to me. They become a partial representation of me, which is, I think, a slightly different way of putting Sartre's point that the reader in reading his own work "touches only his own subjectivity" and that "The sentence will never quite be a thing in his eyes."

Someone, of course, might respond to all this with "But what if you'd been bonked on the head? or were on drugs? or drunk? or were in the middle of a psychotic episode? or hadn't seen what you'd written in eighty years, it being an old teen-age love letter you find in the attic when you're ninety?" But these are all beside the point. What they show is that there are a myriad of ways in which that singular relationship could be blocked off from the start, or wither away, so that the asymmetry disappears, and the way in which I stand as a reader to what I've written becomes symmetrical with the way others stand as readers to what I've written. But what will never occur is a literal disappearance of the asymmetry from the other direction: namely, through others coming to acquire as direct and immediate a grasp of the already disambiguated (for me) meanings of what I've written as I typically do, so that in reading my sentences, they touch only *their* "own subjectivity." And this is true of the spoken as well as the written word. So there is a sense in which the Ziff/Sartre disambiguation asymmetries seem to constitute an immutable fact about the nature of human communication in general.

Recall, once again, the useful imagery provided by the Chinese Room case. The Ziff/Sartre disambiguation asymmetries do not obtain there. Searle's inscriptional outputs are such that he has no privileged access to their meaning. For he has no access to their meaning whatsoever. There is a sense in which they are his, i.e., he constructs the inscriptional strings. But they are not, following Sartre, part of Searle's subjectivity. He knows no Chinese, so how could they be examples of what he meant to say, and phrased in the way he wanted or was dissatisfied with, and so on? What he is conscious of directly—his own thoughts or intentions—neither monitor nor get expressed in his Chinese inscriptions. Only the Chinese recipients of his responses know how to read them and whether they are ambiguous and so on. If we imagine other English-speaking non-comprehenders of Chinese also receiving Searle's concatenations, they are in the same position vis-à-vis a comprehension of them as is Searle. Those squiggle-squoggles are, indeed, just a thing or object for Searle. They do not, in any way, shape, or form, embody *his* thoughts or beliefs; he has no awareness of what they are about—what they mean. Their compositions were not driven by a conscious monitoring of what he wanted to say, and guided by a selection of the forms of expression best suited to achieve that.

So *if* Ziff/Sartre disambiguation asymmetries are an immutable fact about human communication as they seem to be, and if they are conspicuously absent in the Chinese Room thought experiment, as they certainly seem to be, and *if* the Chinese Room thought experiment maps onto at least some alleged *strong* AIstrong AI models of human cognition as it seems to, that type of model could not be an adequate model of typical speaker/hearer or writer/reader interactions. The importance of Searle's "Minds, Brains, and Programs" is that, if correct, it becomes a *standard* objection to an important (new) alternative way of looking at the mind. As such, it becomes part of a philosophical arsenal. (Compare: the stock of *standard* objections to Cartesian dualism, behaviorism, epiphenomenalism, the identity thesis, eliminative materialism, etc.)

When we reflect further on the above examples of Ziff/Sartre disambiguation asymmetries which are paradigms of situations in which a speaker or writer is in conscious control of his or her medium, certainly the following ingredients seem (typically) co-present and are themselves often directly (asymmetrically) accessible.

(1) Some general sizing up of one's audience—either present or anticipated. (One doesn't talk to babies in the way one talks to graduate students. One doesn't write a letter to one's dog, etc.)

(2) A need, want, desire, or intention to say or write something in general or particular to that audience.

(3) A general awareness of when to initiate the spoken or written discourse in accord with that need, want, desire, or intention.

(4) Along with the requisite anticipatory and retrospective sense of manipulating meanings, an ongoing satisfaction or dissatisfaction with how that is being executed, which in turn Fosters the revising and self-editing of words, phrasings, sentences, and their uses (the speech and writing acts involved).

(5) As fallout from (4) a specific sense of one's *author*ship (or *speaker*-ship): e.g., as at a cocktail party when the conversation is thick yet one retains a sense of which remarks are one's own. (When we feel our sense of that slipping, we know it's time to leave!)

(6) A rough projection of where the initiated or participated-in discourse is going, coupled with moods which fix the extent to which one cares to keep engaged in it and the intensity of involvement (compare (4)): e.g., "I'd better wrap this up or they'll all leave" or "I'm not going to listen to her any longer" or "Tuning in on this gasbag every five minutes or so should suffice" or "This might go on all night" or "I'll rewrite this one paragraph and call it quits for now."

(7) Rather like (6), a sense of when and why to decide on closure. "For better or worse, the poem is finished" or "Tell me about it some other time ... see you." Etc.

(8) A mixed visual, auditory, (and sometimes tactile) sensory awareness of *general* context as well as some of the *specifics* of speech/writing production, auditory inputs, etc., at various levels of linguistic description (although related aspects of some of these—a myriad of syntactic details, for starters—may not be accessible to introspection).

This abbreviated list only points to some of the ways that consciousness informs our intentional behaviors, though it helps remind us of how much is missing in the mimicking accomplishments of MUSAIs and their less versatile ancestors. But if this is all rather obvious, as it seems to be, how should we explain "their" persistent charisma (under one label or another) from at least the seventeenth century to the present, as candidates for modeling the mind? Equivalents of this question have received a broad variety of answers, and John Haugeland's recent *Artificial Intelligence–The Very Idea* [77] strikes me as especially rich in this regard. But I should like to add a novel suggestion of my own to the list which brings into play some of the distinctions of this and previous sections.

6 The "Poulet Effect," Programmers and Their Programs and Computer Machinations, and the Idea of *Strong* AI

Something like the presence of elements (1)–(8) above in USAIs and us, and the absence of them in MUSAIs (and, for the most part, in the Chinese Room) help proscribe their comparative intentional capabilities: the former driven by original or intrinsic intentionality, the latter only capable of a derivative kind. When we are engaged in acts involving the former, we often have, I think, a sense of ourselves being extended into a medium. The medium, as it were, takes on an intimacy with who we are in that we are aware of manipulating it, somewhat in the way a person with an artificial limb has a sense of that limb being part of who they are, something they control, and have a proprioceptive immediate awareness of. The meaning of our words unleashed in conversation or upon a page can take on a kind of prosthetic closeness to who we are, and because of this, though physically detached from us, become as if one with our thoughts and beliefs. We retain an informal sense of the notation becoming mentalized by us insofar as we write what we think. So when we see what we write on the page we see what we think from our point of view, we see our words as in some sense us. But this is no unique achievement. It seems to be a fact of language use in general. And in tacit acknowledgment of our non-uniqueness we may view what others have done by way of manipulating a medium as exhibiting to us *their* thoughts and beliefs, etc. It is this pre-analytic sense of a relationship between ourselves and another's use of an expressive medium which gives rise to the remark by Friedrich Schiller (one much loved by calligraphers) quoted at the beginning of this paper: "Type gives body and voice to silent thought. The speaking page carries it through the centuries." [12] And it was, appropriately, centuries later, as if to to fill in what Schiller's observation

---

[12] I have actually been unable to pinpoint this reference, having only come across it in a calligraphic work. But I think it is altogether likely to be from Schiller's *Letters on the Aesthetic Education of a Man.*

would augur for a reader of such "subjectified" notations, that the French
critic Georges Poulet romantically rounded it all out with,

> This is the remarkable transformation wrought in me through the act of
> reading. Not only does it cause the physical objects around me to disap-
> pear, including the very book I am reading, but it replaces those external
> objects with a congeries of mental objects in close rapport with my own
> consciousness. And yet the very intimacy in which I now live with my ob-
> jects is the following: I am someone who happens to have as objects of his
> own thought, thoughts which are part of a book I am reading, and which
> are therefore the cogitations of another. They are the thoughts of another,
> and yet it is I who am their subject. The situation is even more astonishing
> than the one noted above. I am thinking the thoughts of another. Of course,
> there would be no cause for astonishment if I were thinking it as the thought
> of another. But I think it as my very own. Ordinarily there is the I which
> thinks, which recognizes itself (when it takes its bearings) in thoughts which
> may have come from elsewhere but which it takes upon itself as its own in
> the moment it thinks them. This is how we must take Diderot's declaration
> *"Mes pensées sont mes catins"* ("My thoughts are *my* whores"). That is,
> they sleep with everybody without ceasing to belong to their author.

He then goes on to say:

> Because of the strange invasion of my person by the thoughts of another, I
> am a self who is granted the experience of thinking thoughts foreign to him.
> I am the subject of thoughts other than my own. My consciousness behaves
> as though it were the consciousness of another. ([130], p. 1214)

This idea that in a reading encounter with a script authored by someone else (actually a token of a script-type) we can become a "subject of
thoughts other than [our] own" I shall dub the *Poulet Effect*. Let me assure
the reader that it matters not a whit that Poulet is obviously overstating it,
and mistaking metaphor for literal truth. That, in fact, is what I like about
it. It is an overstatement of an insight—an insight concerning the overlap,
without true identity—of our thoughts and beliefs and opinions with the
forms of their expression. For the exaggeration of this insight is of exactly
the same kind as an exaggeration concerning the symbolic processing powers of machines by some proponents of AI. The exaggeration contained in
the Poulet Effect teams up, I believe, in a fascinating manner, with the absence of Ziff/Sartre disambiguation asymmetries attending the relationship
a programmer enjoys to the execution or results of a program "authored"
by him or her. An illustration of this odd combination of distinctions at
work surfaces when considering an answer to the following question: Does
a computer programmer stand to his or her programs and their execution
plus end results in the way that some Sartrean novelist, for example, stands
to his or her compositional labors? The answer is a resounding "No." For
that's the main point of programming. You let the computer do it! And
this was the point being dramatized by Simon, Shaw, and Newell [125]
in their early computer simulation labors of cognitive processes with their
program, the *Logic Theorist* (LT), which they listed as co-author of a little

paper on their successes with some theorems in *Principia Mathematica*. LT came up with some elegant results unanticipated by its authors. (No privileged access to the processes by which they came about!) So even though you author the program, you neither wish to nor can track all its moves—its manipulation of the symbols which are its medium—in anything like the way a novelist, say, tracks the occurrence of the words he or she is responsible for making upon the page. And because of this, the Ziff/Sartre disambiguation asymmetries do not obtain, or do not obtain in the same pervasive fashion. But there, nonetheless, at the end of it all, after re-entry into ordinary English, are the results of the computer's machinations looking very like those inscriptions we've come to take for granted as our own. Hence they look for all the world just like those sentences we've produced which involve an extension of ourselves into the medium of our language. And, should we pick them up and read them, we could, indeed, be as easily transported *via* psycholinguistic illusion into enjoying the Poulet Effect except with the following ironic twist: that the illusion of thinking the thoughts of another, would not be an illusion of thinking the programmer's thoughts.

The programmer, *sans* Ziff/Sartre disambiguation asymmetries, would have turned the "thinking" over to the machine itself. And so the illusion could only be the illusion of sharing the machine's thoughts, which are not literally thoughts, but only "thoughts." Rather they are strings of symbols which when interpreted properly may be used as expressions of thoughts, and thus candidates for derivative but not intrinsic intentionality.

But the illusion might persist undetected. This can happen because (1) we have a natural sense of our own thoughts being realized from time to time in a notational medium; and we have a sense of notational patterns similar to those we create (ones generated by computers) as also having thoughts realized in them—the computers receiving credit for them, since the programmer perforce assumes a detached role (no Ziff/Sartre disambiguation asymmetries with respect to the computer's outputs). The idea that no one in particular needs to be credited with the results simply gets overlooked. (2) So too, our encounter with those computer generated patterns may be parallel to our encounter (as readers) with the writings of others (involving, perhaps, a Poulet Effect from time to time). This supports an interpretation of the strings of symbols churned out by the computer as being in some sense mental. So the idea of a mentalized notation being processed and utilized for certain purposes, for which the programmer takes a back seat so far as the ascription of credit is concerned, results in the computer, somewhat by default, becoming the obvious recipient thereof. Hence a contribution to the "very idea" (Haugeland) of AI. Other factors contribute to the "very idea" of AI, however, and some reside in the fact that mindless mimicry was possible—in the fact that there could be MUSAIs which were recipients only of derivative or observer-relative ascriptions of intentionality, but that they nevertheless did really do what they were used to mimic (paying bills, playing in a robot rock band, etc.). This takes on more interest when it is realized that not all aspects of mentality are prone to such imitations, and that for some of these, the distinction between original or intrinsic and derivative does not arise.

7 Why There is no Chinese Room Type Counterexample to a Theory of Artificial Pain (or Strong AP) and the Lack of the Distinction between Original (or Intrinsic) and Derivative Non-Intentional Aspects of the Mind

In stark contrast to the bolder claims made on behalf of AI over the years, no one so far as I know, has yet had the audacity to propose that anything like a pain (or a feeling of tiredness, or moods such as a free floating anxiety, or the having of a blue after-image, etc.) has actually been realized in some mechanistic model. There is no extant theory of Artificial and *Strong Non-Intelligent* Mental States for philosophers to whomp on. But why the more modest stance with respect to modeling these aspects of the mental? A few philosophers have at least broached the issue of what it could be like for a robot or a computer to be in pain: e.g., Ziff and the Smarts in their articles discussed earlier, Putnam on privacy and pain-reporting in his classic "Minds and Machines," [13] Daniel Dennett in his 1978 article "Why You Can't Make a Computer that Feels Pain" [14], Hubert and Stuart Dreyfus in *Mind Over Machine* [45], and John Haugeland in *Artificial Intelligence– The Very Idea* [77]. After remarking on our common prejudice that "robots have no feelings" and on the presupposition "that thought and feeling are separate things" and "that understanding and affect are fundamentally distinct and disparate," Haugeland (in his chapter called "Real People" which follows the chapter called "Real Machines") writes:

> And insofar as it addresses only cognition, Artificial Intelligence seems to rely on the same assumption. But that just underscores the essential questions: *Could* AI accommodate feelings? Does it *need* to? ([77], p. 230)

and, with respect to AI systems,

> ... it's hard to imagine that these systems actually feel anything when they react to impinging stimuli. Though the problem is general, the intuition is clearest in the case of pain: many fancy systems can detect internal damage

---

[13] In Anderson [1], pp. 72–97. Relevant to the last section of this paper Putnam develops analogs to our notions of privacy and direct access to psychological states (and bodily malfunctions—pains?) for machines. I am interested in whether his examples could be used to cook up a case of presumed artificial pain (AP) which a Searle-like Chinese Room counterexample might be germane to. I don't think so, but I don't pursue the idea. Searle (in conversation) seemed to think it might be so used.

[14] In *Brainstorms* [41], pp. 190–229.

or malfunction and even take corrective steps; but do they ever hurt? It seems incredible; yet what exactly is missing? The more I think about this question, the less I'm persuaded I even know what it means (which is not to say I think its meaningless). ([77], p. 235)

And,

Moods, it seems to me, are the toughest of all, if only because they are so peculiar. Since they're not generally localized to any particular stimulus or condition, they can hardly be conceived as inputs ("melancholy here now" or some such). But since they're also not localized in topic or content, it's equally difficult to attribute their cognitive relevance to any determinate cognitive component within them. Yet moods do profoundly affect what and how we think, in their own nonvoluntary, nonrational, and oddly pervasive way ... I suspect that moods may turn out to be an important problem for cognitive science ... ([77], p. 246)

But for the most part these features of the mind have not attracted much attention in recent years. In AI and cognitive science, and the philosophy of mind in general, the focus instead has been on very "thinky" aspects of our existence, or what Putnam, for his own purposes, describes in his recent *Representation and Reality* ([136], p. 6) as "the oldest pattern of explanation of our mental workings there is: explanation in terms of beliefs and desires." The widespread interest in intentional aspects of the mind and theories of mental representation has inspired brilliant work and lively discussions which have overshadowed the topics mentioned by Haugeland.

My own attraction to these pervasive and less cognitive pockets of our lives has been motivated by the belief that they are possibly half of who we are, obviously interact with cognition, and would eventually need to be accounted for in any viable theory of the latter. They are an important part of what having "the right stuff" amounts to. Dennett in his "Why You Can't Make a Computer that Feels Pain," reacting to some of my earlier remarks on the topic writes:

The triumphs of artificial intelligence have been balanced by failures and false starts. Some have asked if there is a pattern to be discerned here. Keith Gunderson has pointed out that the successes have been with task oriented, *sapient* features of mentality, the failures and false starts with *sentient* features of mentality, and has developed a distinction between program-receptive and program-resistant features of mentality. Gunderson's point is not what some have hoped. Some have hoped he had found a fall-back position for them: *viz.*, maybe machines can *think* but they can't *feel*. His point is rather that the task of getting a machine to feel is a very different task from getting it to think; in particular it is not a task that invites solution simply by sophisticated innovations in *programming*, but rather, if at all, by devising new sorts of *hardware*. This goes some way to explaining the recalcitrance of mental features like pain to computer simulation, but not far enough. ([42], p. 190)[15]

---

[15] Dennett then sets out to take the discussion "far enough," with the upshot of his investigation being,

My reason for harking back to this is that I now believe that the *conditions* which make possible a bona fide distinction between original (or intrinsic) and derivative intentional mental aspects, can be better understood by seeing how such conditions fail to obtain in the case of other less cognitive mental phenomena—program-resistant ones—and that this, in turn, sheds light on them.

Searle in a Chinese Dental Surgeon's Chair: A Counterexample to a Theory of Artificial Pain? In Searle's Chinese Room example, Chinese inscriptions do get manipulated by Searle, but supposedly no thinking by Searle, in Chinese, concerning the meanings of the inputs he receives or the concatenations he constructs, occurs. The outputs, in Chinese, which he produces, are no more intelligible to him than the inputs or stock of characters he has to work with. To a Chinese convert to Western Orthodox Turing Tests for Intelligence in Machines, the "program"—in this case Searle plus his rule book for manipulating Chinese inscriptions—would appear to behave like a reader-writer who comprehends Chinese. But he really doesn't. This, in paraphrase, is Searle's point—coupled with the claim that the situation maps onto various typical alleged strong AI models. For my purposes it is entirely beside the point to attempt to adjudicate between his contentions and the myriad of objections they have given rise to. I wish only to use the Chinese Room example as a type of thought experiment—*however it is assessed!*—which seems to have no literal counterpart in connection with other aspects of the mind: e.g., non-intentional (program-resistant) ones.

Consider the sort of pain one feels when one needs root canal surgery, or any other comparably excruciating pain. And now imagine that someone proposes a machine model of the having of that sort of pain—i.e., artificial pain (or AP) and, moreover, it is alleged to be a model of *strong* AP, i.e., the machine or robot is said to actually feel some pain. And now suppose we add a Searle-as-skeptic to the scene who wishes to expose the whole enterprise for the toothacheless sham he supposes it to be. We might first imagine him (imagining himself) ensconced in a Chinese dental surgeon's chair in a locked office, but then what? How could we (he) fill in

---

But if, as I have claimed, the intuitions we would have to honor were we to honor them all do not form a consistent set, so there can be no true theory of pain, and so no computer or robot could instantiate the true theory of pain, which it would have to do to feel real pain.

But this skepticism has only to do with a theory involving "ordinary concept of pain," and he adds,

Physiological perplexities may defy the best efforts of theoreticians, of course, but philosophical considerations are irrelevant to the probability of that. If and when a good physiological sub-personal theory of pain is developed, a robot could in principle be constructed to instantiate it. ([42], pp. 228–229)

In what follows I shall make some suggestions about what, if any, "philosophical considerations" *could* be relevant to the latter sort of theory of pain envisioned by Dennett.

further details so that a parallel dialectic to the Chinese Room example can develop? What could go on in the dental surgeon's chair vis-à-vis Searle and observers providing inputs and outputs of whatever imagined sort, that could at least *seem* to give the lie to a proposed *strong* AP model in the way Searle's mimicking an alleged *strong* AI program in the Chinese Room seemed to him (and others) to give the lie to such a project?

Obviously, a lot of yelling and shouting or moaning and groaning, even in "appropriate contexts," would be neither a sufficient nor necessary condition for a subject being in pain. So it seems safe to assume at the outset that spoken or written tokens of these emanating from our AP theorist's robot could not be at the *heart* of what was being claimed when it was claimed that the robot or machine actually instantiated pain, even if the capacity for yelling and shouting conveniently tagged along as part of the AP robot's endowments. The theory is a theory about pain, and not pain reporting. It has nothing to do with linguistic or symbolic behaviors whatsoever, whether observable or only internalized. The distinction between really thinking *in Chinese* and only seeming to do so, obviously has no counterpart in the case of pain. For one isn't in pain *in* Chinese or English or *in* anything at all. (Specifying a nationality for the dental surgeon is blatantly superfluous.) Is there any shred of an analogy to be found with the Chinese Room example (the Chinese aspect aside) for a proposed expose of a *strong* AP theory? We'll make a stab at it.

Let the *strong* AP model assume the form of a robot equipped with a purported analog of a human brain and a tooth that's gone blooey. We can also imagine Searle, say, skeptical of the claim, and (imagining himself) equipped with enough neurophysiological savvy and technique that he is able to manipulate his own neurological conditions so that finely tuned parallels between the presumed toothache-relevant "neurological" conditions of the robot and Searle seem established. (Maybe he turns a funny dial temporarily implanted in his head for the purposes of checking out simulated neurological conditions in proposed *strong* AP models.) The proponent of the AP model has speculated that a successful modeling of the having of the type of pain that calls out for root canal surgery has occurred. But Searle, with his supposed knowledge of the detailed parallels between what's going on in his brain as he sits in the chair and the robot's "brain," might be well aware that such parallels are insufficient for the production of the pain in question, since, luckily, *he* doesn't feel any. And this (if we wink at the methodological simplicity of the case) could be taken to show that a proposed model of a brain productive of a certain pain was inadequate. But such a tactic would not in any systematic way undercut the vision of that type of biosimulation project; maybe the parallels were not as intact as they were thought to be—and so on and so forth. *Notice: this latter sort of objection, unlike the Chinese Room objection to strong AI, is not any sort of philosophical or even methodological objection at all. It is simply a debatable, indirect inference, that some proposed replication of conditions sufficient to give rise to a type of pain seem not to have been established. It in no way suggests that, in principle, such a replication could not succeed. It only suggests (in its simplistic way) that on a given occasion a replication failed.*

There could be, to shadow Dennett's remark (see footnote 15), various physiological perplexities which would mitigate against the formulation of a "good physiological sub-personal theory of pain" (and there also might be technological barriers to instantiating pain as described by that theory in a robotic replication). But, as he claims, "philosophical considerations are irrelevant to the probability of that." There are, of course, philosophical considerations which bear on the question as to how we could ever come to know that a pain was actually instantiated in an artifact—the problem of "other minds" for robots. But that is an altogether different matter. The point here, is that the sort of claim that issues from our imaginary case, (involving, obviously, a rather dizzy methodology) is simply one, based on evidence however impeccable or faulty, that certain *physiological* conditions were not replicated in a model. If things had gone the other way, for example, and Searle *had* felt an excruciating pain in his tooth, we are supposing that the claim (however risky) would have been, instead, that certain *physiological* conditions had been replicated in the model. But neither contention is philosophical; they are simply inferences regarding the presence or absence of certain physiological conditions.

The foregoing helps us to see why we are not inclined even to entertain a distinction between original and derivative pain, which in turn may have implications for how we might conceptualize a *complete* mechanistic (not necessarily computational) model of the mind.

In the Chinese Room example Searle supposedly mimics an AI computer program, and does so without understanding or thinking in Chinese. Nevertheless it makes perfectly good sense to attribute to his outputs in Chinese, or to those of the AI system he is a debunking simulation of, derivative or observer-relative intentionality. But in the case of the Chinese Dental Surgeon's Chair example, where the mechanistic model of brains productive of pain doesn't pan out, there is nothing on the order of derivative pain which remains as residue to attribute either to Searle or to the type of brain-model he is the supposed instantiation of.

Consider the calculations of a pocket calculator which can plausibly be said to have meaning in an "observer-relative" sense, but not in an original way. Now what would it be like to have an analog to that with respect to pain—e.g., a pocket agonizer? What could a pocket agonizer be like? Could it, like the pocket calculator—which doesn't literally intend to arrive at the calculations it arrives at, but only derivatively, as a result of our imposed interpretations, arrives at them—arrive at only derivative pains and not original ones? What would that involve?

The difference between a pocket calculator and a pocket agonizer is that it's difficult to imagine a pocket agonizer as (1) a simulation of human pain and (2) actually ... actually what? Actually having or producing pain? Certainly not.

There is no clear idea of what a simulation of the having of a pain—a state of agony, for example—could be, other than the simulation of pain *behavior* or the *behavior* that might accompany agony, *or* a replication in a model brain of the neurophysiological conditions underlying pain (or constituting it if some form of the identity theory of mind and brain is correct), or, we can add to the list, an abstract *representation* (say in computer program form) of neural connections in a brain with pain. And neither the simulation of pain behavior, nor the model brain, nor an abstract representation of a brain, would provide examples of pain in the (merely) derivative or observer-relative sense.[16]

---

[16] The oddity of the idea can be made clearer by considering simulation.

The contrast between a real pain and the foregoing sort(s) of simulation of pain is on a different conceptual footing from intentionality (or meaning) and the simulation of intentionality (or meaning). That is, the difference between a simulation of pain (whatever that might involve) and real pain, is different from the difference between a simulation of intentional problem-solving behavior, for example, and real intentional problem-solving behavior. For the simulation of the tasks involved in the latter may result in such tasks really being performed:

Suppose someone proposes a pocket calculator as a simple model of human calculators. But how *good* a model is it, we ask? And the proposer says, "Oh, there are big differences. It (the pocket calculator) is solar powered or battery powered, or you have to plug it in—different basic energy sources, hardware, different architecture, etc. Also, it can do percentages and square-roots with a rapidity that we couldn't hope to emulate, and it does them using different algorithms, etc. So, no, however it is we perform calculations, they are very unlike, in many ways, how a pocket calculator performs them, even though we must admit that the calculator can and does come up with an impressive number of computational results which are just the results we would come up with in our own additions, subtractions, multiplications, divisions, etc., which is, of course, what was aimed at in the designing and manufacturing of them in the first place." Nevertheless—and this is the primary point—*however unconvincing the pocket calculator may seem as a simulation of human calculating processes, there is no doubt that the pocket calculator does calculate (just as an automatic teller really does dispense money for you from your checking account).*

The automatic teller, a partially developed MUSAI after all, really does dispense money, even though it doesn't see itself as doing that, doesn't understand what money is, places no interpretation on what it does, has no self-styled semantics, as it were. But it does genuinely dispense money, and in pretty much the same sense that the pocket calculator genuinely performs calculations for you. So even if you label the calculations or the money dispensing *derivative* in order to underline the fact that what is being done receives its significance (its interpretation, its intentional thrust, what it is about) from the "outside," nevertheless there is a sense in which its behavior, what is done, is, as it were, very real, which is precisely why they inform the visions of AI.

One could easily set up a a cassette-carrying pocket agonizer that had various buttons for whimpers, moans, excruciating cries, and the like, such that when pushed would cause it to emit convincing simulacra of whimpers, moans, excruciating cries, etc., just as Descartes long ago imagined. But it would not be the case, as Descartes was well aware, that therefore the pocket agonizer was *really* in some agonizing state.

But it's not only that the pocket-agonizer as we've imagined it lacks real pain—or original pain—it is also that it seems to lack derivative pain, (or derivative agony).

It's not that there is after all some sense—albeit a derived sense—in which the pocket agonizer is in pain if we impose a . . . a what? A kind of feeling upon it? Upon its outputs? The sounds it emits? Or what?

The utter peculiarity of the very idea of derivative pain (or agony) can be put in relief by attempting another rendition of the quote from Haugeland I fussed with earlier (see footnote 7), substituting the relevant sensation and feeling terms for 'meaning' and 'mean' along with other alterations (e.g., 'sentient' for 'semantic'):

> . . . a sentient engine's tokens (states?) only involve a sensation such as pain because we give it to them; their sensations, e.g., pains, like that of smoke signals and writing [what are the analogs of smoke signals and writing for sentient aspects of the mind?], is essentially borrowed, hence *derivative*. To put it bluntly: pocket agonizers don't feel anything by their tokens (states?) (any more than books do) [another analog to pseudo-meaning involving pseudo-sentience, please!] they only feel what we say they do.

We can only bumble around with the Haugeland quote; we can't really twist a parallel one out of it for non-intentional mental aspects such as pain. For non-intentional mental phenomena do not give rise to detached externalized versions of themselves in the way that intentional phenomena do, such as thoughts and the sentences which express them and which *via* their tokens can be separated off from their creators (and which can occur in English or Chinese, etc.). A pain, or the having of an after image, or a free-floating anxiety, does not, like a thought or other intentional mental acts, involve anything like an extension of ourselves into a medium, which then is detachable from us. Instead we are, as it were, the medium in which they occur. And there they stay put. They are indexical. They have a singular occurrence in space and time. They are in this way more like artifacts such as the Mona Lisa, than they are like a Picasso print, or "The Wasteland." Their existence does not spread out, as it were, via the vehicles for their expression. If we excise the nasty tooth and torch the Mona Lisa, the pain is gone and the art work ceases to exist. But although Diderot died, and an irate critic burned a copy of "The Wasteland," both the former's thoughts and Eliot's poem continued to persist. Pains do not proliferate themselves in copies, or tokens of a type. They are not a *tokening* phenomenon. They (and many other program-resistant phenomena) are, if we stretch Nelson Goodman's famous distinction between *autographic* and *allographic* works of art, autographic.[17] They cannot, as Poulet said of Diderot's thoughts, "sleep with everybody without ceasing to belong to their author." They belong only to the one who bears them. They are isolated there. Nothing else could be a genuine example of *them*. To have the same type of pain as someone else involves nothing like what we have called the Poulet Effect. We talk of sharing another's pain, but that, if said of the kind of pain one feels when in need of root canal surgery, is highly metaphorical, whereas thinking *Diderot's* thoughts by reading what he wrote is, though less than literal truth, much more than metaphor. This does not mean, however, that by imparting to a machine manipulations of token expressions of such thoughts, we thereby achieve the goals of *strong* AI. To think so would be to mistake derivative intentionality for original. Some of the seductiveness behind such thinking was suggested in the previous section. What I mean to stress here is that for non-intentional mental aspects there is no comparable allure to mislead anyone in any quest for *strong* AP. For there are no examples of detached derivative pain "tokens," as it were, to tempt us as material for pain simulation in the form of programs capable of receiving, processing, and producing them. Though there are types of pain, each example of each type of pain is itself a real (or original) pain, and that is all there is to pain.

So one way to phrase the problem of constructing a general model of the mind—an AI one, or any other—is to ask how those mental aspects which give rise to the distinction between *original* and *derivative* versions of themselves (as in the case of intentional phenomena) can be integrated with those aspects of the mind which do not. How do the pains, moods, anxieties, fears, and various sensations not analyzable in terms of intentionality or problem solving or internalized or externalized cognition, and which so vividly color and constrain the content of our day by day experiences, blend into our psychological portrait? For obviously they are somehow integrated in us,[18] and constitute a significant part of what we

---

[17] See *The Languages of Art* [67], esp. pp. 113–122, and pp. 195–198. Goodman writes (p. 113):

> Let us speak of a work of art as autographic if and only if the distinction between original and forgery of it is significant; or better, if and only if even the most exact duplication of it does not count as genuine. If a work of art is autographic, we may also call that art autographic. Thus painting is autographic, music nonautographic, or *allographic*.

Compare: just as nothing else counts as the Mona Lisa, so too nothing else counts as the pain felt by Elmer when in need of root canal surgery. So too, just as my copy of "The Wasteland" counts as Eliot's (genuine) achievement, I am privvy to the (genuine) thoughts of Diderot in reading his work, etc. (Obviously there are disanalogies as well: what could count as a forgery of Elmer's pain? etc.)

[18] Relevant to the integration problem, the Dreyfuses in *Mind over Machine* [45] discuss the problems of using computer simulations of distributed associative

see ourselves as being, and what our now only imagined USAIs would have to partake of in order to have all the right stuff.[19]

---

memory systems to capture human intuitive capacities for remembering faces, etc. They write:

> Can experts describe for storage in computers their memories of typical lived situations so the computers can likewise be experts? Light and shadow on a face can easily be digitized, but how can we enter into a computer the pattern of saliences, expectations, and emotional colorings, such as hopes and fears, that characterize a remembered whole situation? It is just because no one has the slightest idea how such could be stored in distributed associative systems that cognitivists feel justified in a adopting the implausible view that what we remember are descriptions. (p. 94)

The problem of vision strikes me as conceptually complex in that it seems to straddle both program-receptive (problem solving) aspects of the mind—problems of recognition, etc.—and program-resistant ones—e.g., the sheer capacity for sight. And the theoretical situation seems even more hair-raising if it is true that other program-resistant features (fears, etc.) impinge on the recognition abilities in the way the Dreyfuses suggest. But I suspect these problems, are, alas, not peculiar to vision, but extend in general to attempts to explain all sapient aspects of ourselves.

[19] I wish to thank Fred Stoutland and other members of the Saint Olaf College philosophy faculty for some useful comments on this paper.

Bibliography

[1] Anderson, A. R., ed. 1964. *Minds and Machines*. Englewood Cliffs, NJ: Prentice-Hall.

[2] Asher, N., 1986. Belief in Discourse Representation Theory. *Journal of Philosophical Logic* 15(2):127–189.

[3] Asher, N. 1987. A Typology of Attitudinal Verbs and their Anaphoric Properties. *Linguistics and Philosophy* 10(2):125–197.

[4] Austin, J. L. 1962. *Sense and Sensibilia*. New York: Oxford University Press.

[5] Austin, J. L. 1970. *Philosophical Papers*, 2d ed. New York: Oxford University Press.

[6] Barwise, J. 1986. Noun Phrases, Generalized Quantifiers, and Anaphora. Report No. CSLI-86-52. Stanford: CSLI Publications. Also in *Generalized Quantifiers: Linguistic and Logical Approaches*, ed. E. Engdahl and P. Gärdenfors. Dordrecht: D. Reidel.

[7] Blackburn, S. 1975. The Identity of Propositions. In *Meaning, References and Necessity*, ed. S. Blackburn. New York: Cambridge University Press.

[8] Boer, S., and Lycan, W. 1986. *Knowing Who*. Cambridge, MA: MIT Press.

[9] Brody, J. E. 1989. Personal Health: Most Studies Indicate Presence of Aluminum Is the Effect, Not the Cause, of Diseased Brains. *The New York Times, National Edition*, April 6, 1989, p. 22.

[10] Burge, T. 1978. Belief and Synonymy. *Journal of Philosophy* 75:119–138.

[11] Burge, T. 1979. Individualism and the Mental. In *Midwest Studies in Philosophy, IV: Studies in Metaphysics*, ed. P. French, T. Uehling, and H. Wettstein. Minneapolis: University of Minnesota Press.

[12] Burge, T. 1982. Other Bodies. In *Thought and Object*, ed. A. Wood-field. New York: Oxford University Press.

[13] Burge, T. 1982. Two Thought Experiments Reviewed. *Notre Dame Journal of Formal Logic* 23:284–293.

[14] Burge, T. 1986. Cartesian Error and the Objectivity of Perception. In *Subject, Thought and Context*, ed. P. Pettit and J. McDowell. Oxford: Oxford University Press.

[15] Burge, T. 1986. Individualism and Psychology. *Philosophical Review* 95:3–45.

[16] Burge, T. 1986. Intellectual Norms and Foundations of Mind. *Journal of Philosophy* 83:697–720.

[17] Burge, T. 1986. On Davidson's "Saying That." In *Truth and Interpretation*, ed. E. LePore. Oxford: Basil Blackwell.

[18] Burge, T. 1988. Individualism and Self-knowledge. *Journal of Philosophy* 85:649–663.

[19] Bylebyl, J. J. 1970. *Cardiovascular Physiology in the Sixteenth and Early Seventeenth Centuries*. Ann Arbor: University Microfilms.

[20] Carnap, R. 1947. *Meaning and Necessity*. Chicago: University of Chicago Press.

[21] Chastain, C. 1975. Reference and Context. In *Mind, Language and Reality*, ed. K. Gunderson. Minneapolis: University of Minnesota.

[22] Chomsky, N. 1965. *Aspects of the Theory of Syntax*. Cambridge, MA: MIT Press.

[23] Chomsky, N. 1980. *Rules and Representations*. Oxford: Basil Blackwell.

[24] Chomsky, N. 1982. *Lectures on Government and Binding*. Dordrecht: Foris.

[25] Chomsky, N. 1986. *Knowledge of Language: Its Nature, Origin, and Use*. New York: Praeger.

[26] Church, A. 1943. Review of Quine's "Notes on Existence and Necessity." *Journal of Symbolic Logic* 8:45–47.

[27] Church, A., 1950. On Carnap's Analysis of Statements of Assertion and Belief. *Analysis* 10:97–99.

[28] Church, A. 1951. A Formulation of the Logic of Sense and Denotation. In *Structure, Method and Meaning: Essays in Honor of Henry M. Sheffer*, ed. P. Henle, H. Kallen, and S. Langer. New York: Liberal Arts Press.

[29] Church, A. 1954. Intensional Isomorphism and Identity of Belief. *Philosophical Studies* 5(5):65–73. Also in *Propositions and Attitudes*, ed. N. Salmon and S. Soames. Oxford: Oxford University Press, 1988.

[30] Churchland, P. M. 1984. *Matter and Consciousness: A Contemporary Introduction to the Philosophy of Mind*. Cambridge, MA: MIT Press.

[31] Davidson, D. 1963. The Method of Extension and Intension. In *The Philosophy of Rudolf Carnap*, ed. P. Schilpp. La Salle: Open Court.

[32] Davidson, D. 1965. Theories of Meaning and Learnable Languages. *Proceedings of the 1964 International Congress for Logic, Methodology, and Philosophy of Science*. Amsterdam: North Holland. Also in *Inquiries into Truth and Interpretation*. New York: Oxford University Press, 1984.

[33] Davidson, D. 1967. Truth and Meaning. *Synthese* 17:304–323. Also in *Inquiries into Truth and Interpretation*. New York: Oxford University Press, 1984.

[34] Davidson, D. 1968. On Saying That. *Synthese* 19:130–146. Also in *Inquiries into Truth and Interpretation*. New York: Oxford University Press, 1984.

[35] Davidson, D. 1969. True to the Facts. *Journal of Philosophy* 66:748–764. Also in *Inquiries into Truth and Interpretation*. New York: Oxford University Press, 1984.

[36] Davidson, D. 1973. Radical Interpretation. *Dialectica* 27:313–328. Also in *Inquiries into Truth and Interpretation*. New York: Oxford University Press, 1984.

[37] Davidson, D. 1974. Belief and the Basis of Meaning. *Synthese* 27:309–323. Also in *Inquiries into Truth and Interpretation*. New York: Oxford University Press, 1984.

[38] Davidson, D. 1976. Reply to Foster. In *Truth and Meaning: Essays in Semantics*, ed. G. Evans and J. McDowell. Oxford: Oxford University Press. Also in *Inquiries into Truth and Interpretation*. New York: Oxford University Press, 1984.

[39] Davidson, D. 1984. *Inquiries into Truth and Interpretation*. New York: Oxford University Press.

[40] Davidson, D. 1987. Knowing One's Own Mind. *Proceedings and Addresses of the American Philosophical Association* 60(3):441–458.

[41] Dennett, D. 1978. *Brainstorms*. Cambridge, MA: MIT Press.

[42] Dennett, D. 1987. *The Intentional Stance*. Cambridge, MA: MIT Press.

[43] Donnellan, K. 1972. Proper Names and Identifying Descriptions. In *Semantics of Natural Language*, ed. D. Davidson and G. Harman. Dordrecht: Reidel.

[44] Dretske, F. 1981. *Knowledge and the Flow of Information*. Cambridge, MA: MIT Press.

[45] Dreyfus, H. L., and Dreyfus, S. E. 1986. *Mind over Machine*. New York: Macmillan.

[46] Dummett, M. 1973. *Frege: Philosophy of Language*. London: Duckworth.

[47] Dummett, M. 1981. *The Interpretation of Frege's Philosophy*. Cambridge, MA: Harvard University Press.

[48] Evans, G. 1980. Pronouns. *Linguistic Inquiry* 11(2):337–362.

[49] Evans, G. 1981. Understanding Demonstratives. In *Meaning and Understanding*, ed. H. Parret and J. Bouveresse. Berlin and New York: De Gruyter.

[50] Evans, G. 1982. *The Varieties of Reference*. Oxford: Oxford University Press.

[51] Evans, G., and McDowell, J., eds. 1976. *Truth and Meaning: Essays in Semantics*. Oxford: Oxford University Press.

[52] Field, H. 1977. Logic, Meaning, and Conceptual Role. *Journal of Philosophy* 74:379–409.

[53] Field, H. 1978. Mental Representation. *Erkenntnis* 13:9–61.

[54] Fine, K. 1989. The Problem of *De Re* Modality. In *Proceedings of the Conference "Themes from Kaplan"*, ed. J. Almog, J. Perry, and H. Wettstein. Oxford: Oxford University Press.

[55] Fodor, J. 1987. *Psychosemantics*. Cambridge, MA: MIT Press.

[56] Fodor, J. Substitution Arguments and the Individuation of Beliefs. Forthcoming.

[57] Forbes, G. 1987. Review of Nathan Salmon's *Frege's Puzzle*. *The Philosophical Review* 96(3):455–458.

[58] Foster, J. A. 1976. Meaning and Truth Theory. In *Truth and Meaning: Essays in Semantics*, ed. G. Evans and J. McDowell. Oxford: Oxford University Press.

[59] Frege, G., 1892. On Sense and Reference. In *Translations from the Philosophical Writings of Gottlob Frege*, ed. P. Geach and M. Black. Oxford: Basil Blackwell, 1952.

[60] Frege, G. 1918. Thoughts. In *Propositions and Attitudes*, ed. N. Salmon and S. Soames. Oxford: Oxford University Press, 1988. Originally appeared in English in *Mind* 65(1956):289–311.

[61] Frege, G. 1979. *Posthumous Writings*. Ed. H. Hermes, F. Kambartel, and F. Kaulbach. Trans. P. Long and R. White. Chicago: University of Chicago.

[62] Frege, G. 1980. *Philosophical and Mathematical Correspondence*. Ed. G. Gabriel, H. Hermes, F. Kambartel, C. Thiel, and A. Veraart. Chicago: University of Chicago Press.

[63] Frege, G. 1984. *Collected Papers on Mathematics, Logic, and Philosophy*. Ed. Brian McGuinness. Oxford: Basil Blackwell.

[64] Freud, S. 1949. *Outline of Psycho-Analysis*. Trans. James Strachey. London: Hogarth Press.

[65] Gabel, P., and Feinman, J. M. 1982. Contract Law as Ideology. In *The Politics of Law: A Progressive Critique*, ed. D. Kairys. New York: Pantheon Books.

[66] Goldman, A. 1976. Discrimination and Perceptual Knowledge. *Journal of Philosophy* 73:771–791.

[67] Goodman, N. 1968. *The Languages of Art*. New York: Bobbs-Merrill.

[68] Grice, P. 1989. *Studies in the Ways of Words*. Cambridge, MA: Harvard University Press.

[69] Groenendijk, J. and Stokhof, M. 1990 Dynamic Predicate Logic. To appear in *Linguistics and Philosophy*.

[70] Gunderson, K. 1983. Interview with a Robot. *Analysis* 23:136–42.

[71] Gunderson, K. 1984. Leibnizian Privacy and Skinnerian Privacy. *Behavioral and Brain Sciences* 7(4):628–629.

[72] Gunderson, K. 1985. *Mentality and Machines*, 2d ed. Minneapolis: University of Minnesota Press.

[73] Gunderson, K. 1989. Leibniz's Walk-In Machine, Perception, and the Perils of Physicalism. In *Science, Mind, and Psychology*, ed. C. W. Savage and M. L. Maxwell. Lanham, MD: University Press of America.

[74] Haliday, M. and Hasan, R. 1976. *Cohesion in English*. New York: Longman.

[75] Hart, H. L. A., and Honore, H. M. 1959. *Causation in the Law*. New York: Oxford University Press.

[76] Haugeland, J. 1981. Semantic Engines: An Introduction to Mind Design. In *Mind Design*, ed. J. Haugeland. Cambridge, MA: MIT Press.

[77] Haugeland, J. 1985. *Artificial Intelligence–The Very Idea*. Cambridge, MA: MIT Press.

[78] Heidelberger, H. 1975. A Review of Dummett's *Frege: Philosophy of Language*. *Metaphilosophy* 6:35–43.

[79] Heim, I. 1982. *The Semantics of Definite and Indefinite Noun Phrases*. Ph.D. Thesis. University of Massachusetts, Amherst.

[80] Higginbotham, J. 1986. Davidson's Program in Semantics. In *Truth and Interpretation*, ed. E. LePore. Oxford: Basil Blackwell.

[81] Hornsby, J. 1977. Saying Of. *Analysis* 37(4):177–185.

[82] Jackendoff, R. 1987. *Consciousness and the Computational Mind*. Cambridge, MA: MIT Press.

[83] Johnston, M. 1988. The End of the Theory of Meaning. *Mind and Language* 3:28–42.

[84] Kadmon, N. 1987. *On Unique and Non-unique Reference and Asymmetric Quantification*. Ph.D. Thesis. University of Massachusetts, Amherst.

[85] Kamp, H. 1984. A Theory of Truth and Semantic Representation. In *Truth, Interpretation and Information: Selected Papers from the Third Amsterdam Colloquium*, ed. J. Groenendijk, T. Janssen, & M. Stokhof. Dorsrecht: Foris.

[86] Kamp, H. 1986. What Should Intensional Logic Be For? Lecture delivered at the APA Western Division Meeting, St. Louis.

[87] Kamp, H. 1986. Comments on H. Sluga: Reading, Writing, and Understanding. APA Pacific Division, Los Angeles.

[88] Kamp, H. 1987. Comments on R. Stalnaker: Belief Attribution and Context. In *Contents of Thought*, ed. R. Grimm and R. Merrill. Tucson: University of Arizona.

[89] Kamp, H. and Reyle, U. n.d. *From Discourse to Logic, I*. Forthcoming, Kluwer.

[90] Kaplan, D. 1969. Quantifying In. In *Words and Objections: Essays on the Work of W. V. Quine*, ed. D. Davidson and G. Harman. Dordrecht: Reidel. Also in *Reference and Modality*, ed. L. Linsky. Oxford: Oxford University Press, 1971.

[91] Kaplan, D. 1975. *Demonstratives*. unpublished manuscript.

[92] Kaplan, D. 1979. On the Logic of Demonstratives. In *Contemporary Perspectives in the Philosophy of Language*. ed. P. French, T. Uehling, and H. Wettstein. Minneapolis: University of Minnesota Press.

[93] Kaplan, D. 1986. Opacity. In *The Philosophy of W. V. Quine*, ed. L. E. Hahn and P. A. Schilpp. La Salle: Open Court.

[94] Kobes, B. 1986. Individualism and the Cognitive Sciences. Unpublished dissertation, University of California at Los Angeles.

[95] Kripke, S. 1972. *Naming and Necessity*. Cambridge, MA: Harvard University Press.

[96] Kripke, S. 1979. A Puzzle About Belief. In *Meaning and Use*, ed. A. Margalit. Dordrecht: Reidel. Also in *Propositions and Attitudes*, ed. N. Salmon and S. Soames. Oxford: Oxford University Press, 1988.

[97] Kripke, S. 1979. Speaker's Reference and Semantic Reference. In *Contemporary Perspectives in the Philosophy of Language*, ed. P. French, T. Uehling, and H. Wettstein. Minneapolis: University of Minnesota Press.

[98] Kuhn, T. S. 1962. *The Structure of Scientific Revolutions*. Chicago: University of Chicago Press.

[99] Lashley, K. 1956. Cerebral Organization and Behavior. In *The Brain and Human Behavior*, ed. H. Solomon, S. Cobb, and W. Penfield. Baltimore: Williams and Wilkins.

[100] LePore, E. and Loewer, B. 1981. Translational Semantics. *Synthese* 48:121–133.

[101] LePore, E., and Loewer, B. 1988. Dual Aspect Semantics. In *Representations*, ed. S. Silvers. Dordrecht: Kluwer Academic Press.

[102] LePore, E., and Loewer, B. In press. What Davidson Should Have Said. In *Information Based Semantics and Epistemology*, ed. E. Villanueva. Oxford: Basil Blackwell.

[103] LePore, E., and Loewer, B. In press. You Can Say That Again. *Midwest Studies in Philosophy*.

[104] Lettvin, J. Y., Maturana, H. R., McCulloch, W. S., and Pitts, W. H. 1959. What the Frog's Eye Tells the Frog's Brain. *Proceedings of the IRE* 47:1940–1951.

[105] Lewis, D. 1969. *Convention*. Cambridge, MA: Harvard University Press.

[106] Lewis, D. 1972. General Semantics. In *Semantics of Natural Language*, ed. D. Davidson and G. Harman. Dordrecht: Reidel.

[107] Lewis, D. 1979. Attitudes De Dicto and De Se. In *Philosophical Review* 88:113–143. Also in Lewis, D., *Philosophical Papers, I*. Oxford: Oxford University Press, 1983.

[108] Lewis, D. 1981. What Puzzling Pierre Does Not Believe. *Australasian Journal of Philosophy* 59:283–289.

[109] Lewis, D. 1983. New Work for a Theory of Universals. *Australasian Journal of Philosophy* 61:343–377.

[110] Lewis, D. 1983. Postscripts to "Radical Interpretation." In *Philosophical Papers*, Vol. I. Oxford: Oxford University Press.

[111] Linsky, L., ed. 1952. *Semantics and the Philosophy of Language*. Urbana: University of Illinois Press.

[112] Linsky, L., ed. 1971. *Reference and Modality*. Oxford: Oxford University Press.

[113] Loar, B. 1976. Two Theories of Meaning. In *Truth and Meaning: Essays in Semantics*, ed. G. Evans and J. McDowell. Oxford: Oxford University Press.

[114] Loar, B. 1987. Subjective Intentionality. *Philosophical Topics* 15(1): 89–124.

[115] Loar, B. 1988. Social Content and Psychological Content. In *Contents of Thought*, ed. R. Grimm and D. Merrill. Tucson: University of Arizona Press.

[116] Lycan, W. 1973. Davidson on Saying That. *Analysis* 33:138–139.

[117] Lycan, W. 1987. *Consciousness*. Cambridge, MA: MIT Press.

[118] Marr, D. 1982. *Vision*. San Francisco: W. H. Freeman.

[119] Marx, K. 1963. *Karl Marx: Early Writings*, ed. T. B. Bottomore. London: Watts and Company, Ltd.

[120] McDowell, J. 1981. Engaging with the Essential. *Times Literary Supplement* (January 16, 1981):61–62.

[121] McDowell, J. 1984. *De Re* Senses. In *Frege: Tradition and Influence*, ed. Crispin Wright. Oxford: Basil Blackwell.

[122] McGinn, C. 1982. The Structure of Content. In *Thought and Object*, ed. A. Woodfield. Oxford: Oxford University Press.

[123] Millikan, R. 1984. *Language, Thought and Other Biological Categories*. Cambridge, MA: MIT Press.

[124] Namier, L. 1957. *The Structure of Politics at the Accession of George III*, 2d ed. London: Macmillan.

[125] Newell, A., and Simon, H. 1956. The Logic Theory Machine. *IRE Transactions on Information Theory* IT-2(3):61–79.

[126] Owens, J. 1989. Contradictory Belief and Cognitive Access. *Midwest Studies in Philosophy XIV*, ed. P. French, T. Uehling, and H. Wettstein. Notre Dame: University of Notre Dame Press.

[127] Peacocke, C. In press. What are Senses?

[128] Perry, J. 1977. Frege on Demonstratives. *Philosophical Review* 86: 474–497.

[129] Perry, J. 1980. Belief and Acceptance. *Midwest Studies in Philosophy* 5:533–542.

[130] Poulet, G. 1971. The Phenomenology of Reading. In *Critical Theory Since Plato*, ed. H. Adams. New York: Harcourt Brace Jovanovich.

[131] Putnam, H. 1954. Synonymity and the Analysis of Belief Sentences. *Analysis* 14:114–122. Also in *Propositions and Attitudes*, ed. N. Salmon and S. Soames. Oxford: Oxford University Press, 1988.

[132] Putnam, H. 1970. Is Semantics Possible? In ed. H. Kiefer and M. Munitz, *Language, Belief, and Metaphysics*, Albany: State University of New York Press. Also in *Philosophical Papers*, Vol. II. Cambridge: Cambridge University Press, 1975.

[133] Putnam, H. 1973. Meaning and Reference. *Journal of Philosophy* 70:699–711.

[134] Putnam, H. 1975. The Meaning of 'Meaning'. In *Language, Mind and Knowledge*, ed. K. Gunderson. Minneapolis: University of Minnesota Press. Also in *Philosophical Papers*, Vol. II. Cambridge: Cambridge University Press, 1975.

[135] Putnam, H. 1979. Comments. In *Meaning and Use*, ed. A. Margalit. Dordrecht: Reidel.

[136] Putnam, H. 1988. *Representation and Reality*. Cambridge, MA: MIT Press.

[137] Quine, W. V. 1943. Notes on Existence and Necessity. *Journal of Philosophy* 40:113–127. Also in *Semantics and the Philosophy of Language*, ed. L. Linsky. Urbana: University of Illinois Press, 1952.

[138] Quine, W. V. 1951. *Mathematical Logic*. New York: Harper and Row.

[139] Quine, W. V. 1953. Reference and Modality. In *From a Logical Point of View*. New York: Harper and Row.

[140] Quine, W. V. 1956. Quantifiers and Propositional Attitudes. *The Journal of Philosophy* 53(5):177–187. Also in *The Ways of Paradox*. New York: Random House, 1966.

[141] Quine, W. V. 1960. *Word and Object*. Cambridge, MA: MIT Press.

[142] Quine, W. V. 1963. *From a Logical Point of View*. New York: Harper and Row.

[143] Quine, W. V. 1966. *The Ways of Paradox*. New York: Random House.

[144] Quine, W. V. 1969. Reply to Davidson. In *Words and Objections*, ed. D. Davidson and J. Hintikka. Dordrecht: Reidel.

[145] Ramsey, F. P. 1960. General Propositions and Causality. In *The Foundations of Mathematics and Other Logical Essays*, ed. R. B. Braithwaite. Paterson, NJ: Littlefield, Adams, and Company.

[146] Ramsey, F. P. 1960. *The Foundations of Mathematics and Other Logical Essays*, ed. R. B. Braithwaite. Paterson, NJ: Littlefield, Adams, and Company.

[147] Richard, M. 1983. Direct Reference and Ascriptions of Belief. *Journal of Philosophical Logic* 12:425–452.

[148] Richard, M. 1986. Attitude Ascriptions, Semantic Theory, and Pragmatic Evidence. *Proceedings of the Aristotelian Society* 87:243–262.

[149] Richard, M. 1988. Taking the Fregean Seriously. In *Philosophical Analysis: A Defense by Example*, ed. D. Austin, Dordrecht: Reidel.

[150] Richards, B. 1974. A Point of Reference. *Synthese* 28:361–454.

[151] Rosch, E., and Lloyd, B. 1978. *Cognition and Categorization*. Hillsdale, NJ: Lawrence Erlbaum Associates.

[152] Russell, B. 1911. Knowledge by Acquaintance and Knowledge by Description. Chapter X of *Mysticism and Logic and Other Essays*. London: Longmans, Green and Company. Also in *Propositions and Attitudes*, ed. N. Salmon and S. Soames. Oxford: Oxford University Press, 1988.

[153] Russell, B. 1918. The Philosophy of Logical Atomism. In *Logic and Knowledge*, ed. R. C. Marsh. London: George Allen and Unwin, 1956. Also in *The Philosophy of Logical Atomism*, ed. D. Pears. La Salle: Open Court, 1985.

[154] Salmon, N. 1979. Review of Leonard Linsky's *Names and Descriptions*. *Journal of Philosophy* 76(8):436–452.

[155] Salmon, N. 1981. *Reference and Essence*. Princeton: Princeton University Press, and Oxford: Basil Blackwell.

[156] Salmon, N. 1986. Reflexivity. *Notre Dame Journal of Formal Logic* 27(3):401–429. Also in *Propositions and Attitudes*, ed. N. Salmon and S. Soames. Oxford: Oxford University Press, 1988.

[157] Salmon, N. 1986. *Frege's Puzzle*. Cambridge, MA: MIT Press.

[158] Salmon, N. 1989. Illogical Belief. In *Philosophical Perspectives 3: Philosophy of Mind and Action Theory*, ed. J. Tomberlin. Atascadero, CA: Ridgeview.

[159] Salmon, N. 1989. Tense and Singular Propositions. In *Themes from Kaplan*, ed. J. Almog, J. Perry, and H. Wettstein. Oxford: Oxford University Press.

[160] Salmon, N., and Soames, S., eds. 1988. *Propositions and Attitudes*. Oxford: Oxford University Press.

[161] Sartre, J.-P. 1971. Why Write. In *Critical Theory Since Plato*, ed. H. Adams. New York: Harcourt Brace Jovanovich.

[162] Scheffler, I. 1955. On Synonymy and Indirect Discourse. *Philosophy of Science* 22(1):39–44.

[163] Schiffer, S. 1978. The Basis of Reference. *Erkenntnis* 13:171–206.

[164] Schiffer, S. 1987. The 'Fido'-Fido Theory of Belief. *Philosophical Perspectives* 1:455–480.

[165] Schiffer, S. 1987. *Remnants of Meaning*. Cambridge, MA: MIT Press.

[166] Schiffer, S. 1988. Reply to Mark Johnston. *Mind and Language* 3:58–63.

[167] Searle, J. R. 1980. Minds, Brains, and Programs. *The Behavioral and Brain Sciences* 1:417–424.

[168] Searle, J. R. 1980. Intrinsic Intentionality. Reply to criticisms of Minds, Brains and Programs. *The Behavioral and Brains Sciences* 3:450–456.

[169] Searle, J. R. 1983. *Intentionality: An Essay in the Philosophy of Mind*. Cambridge: Cambridge University Press.

[170] Searle, J. R. 1984. Intentionality and its Place in Nature. *Synthese* 61:3–16.

[171] Searle, J. R. 1984. *Minds, Brains and Science*. Cambridge, MA: Harvard University Press.

[172] Searle, J. R. 1987. Indeterminacy, Empiricism and the First Person. *Journal of Philosophy* 84:123–146.

[173] Segal, G. 1988. A Preference for Sense and Reference. *The Journal of Philosophy* 89:73–89.

[174] Smith, A. D. 1988. Review of Nathan Salmon's *Frege's Puzzle*. *Mind* 97(385):136–137.

[175] Smith, E., and Medin, D. 1981. *Concepts and Categories*. Cambridge, MA: Harvard University Press.

[176] Soames, S. 1987. Direct Reference, Propositional Attitudes, and Semantic Content. *Philosophical Topics* 15(1):47–87.

[177] Soames, S. 1987. Substitutivity. In *On Being and Saying: Essays for Richard Cartwright*, ed. J. J. Thomson. Cambridge, MA: MIT Press.

[178] Stalnaker, R. 1984. *Inquiry*. Cambridge, MA: MIT Press.

[179] Stalnaker, R. 1987. Belief Attribution and Context. In *Contents of Thought*, ed. R. Grimm and R. Merrill. Tucson: University of Arizona.

[180] Stillings, N. 1987. Modularity and Naturalism in Theories of Vision. In *Modularity in Knowledge Representation and Natural-Language Understanding*, ed. J. Garfield. Cambridge, MA: MIT Press.

[181] Temin, M. 1975. The Relational Sense of Indirect Discourse. *The Journal of Philosophy* 72:287–306.

[182] Thomason, R. H. 1979. Home is Where the Heart Is. In *Contemporary Perspectives in the Philosophy of Language*, ed. P. French, T. Uehling, and H. Wettstein. Minneapolis: University of Minnesota Press.

[183] Turing, A. M. 1950. Computing Machinery and Intelligence. *Mind* 59(236):433–460.

[184] Wagner, S. 1986. California Semantics Meets the Great Fact. *Notre Dame Journal of Formal Logic* 27(3):430–455.

Subject Index

Name Index

CSLI Publications

Reports

The following titles have been published in the CSLI Reports series. These reports may be obtained from CSLI Publications, Ventura Hall, Stanford University, Stanford, CA 94305-4115.

The Situation in Logic–I Jon Barwise CSLI–84–2 (*$2.00*)

Coordination and How to Distinguish Categories Ivan Sag, Gerald Gazdar, Thomas Wasow, and Steven Weisler CSLI–84–3 (*$3.50*)

Belief and Incompleteness Kurt Konolige CSLI–84–4 (*$4.50*)

Equality, Types, Modules and Generics for Logic Programming Joseph Goguen and José Meseguer CSLI–84–5 (*$2.50*)

Lessons from Bolzano Johan van Benthem CSLI–84–6 (*$1.50*)

Self-propagating Search: A Unified Theory of Memory Pentti Kanerva CSLI–84–7 (*$9.00*)

Reflection and Semantics in LISP Brian Cantwell Smith CSLI–84–8 (*$2.50*)

The Implementation of Procedurally Reflective Languages Jim des Rivières and Brian Cantwell Smith CSLI–84–9 (*$3.00*)

Parameterized Programming Joseph Goguen CSLI–84–10 (*$3.50*)

Shifting Situations and Shaken Attitudes Jon Barwise and John Perry CSLI–84–13 (*$4.50*)

Completeness of Many-Sorted Equational Logic Joseph Goguen and José Meseguer CSLI–84–15 (*$2.50*)

Moving the Semantic Fulcrum Terry Winograd CSLI–84–17 (*$1.50*)

On the Mathematical Properties of Linguistic Theories C. Raymond Perrault CSLI–84–18 (*$3.00*)

A Simple and Efficient Implementation of Higher-order Functions in LISP Michael P. Georgeff and Stephen F.Bodnar CSLI–84–19 (*$4.50*)

On the Axiomatization of "if-then-else" Irène Guessarian and José Meseguer CSLI–85–20 (*$3.00*)

The Situation in Logic–II: Conditionals and Conditional Information Jon Barwise CSLI–84–21 (*$3.00*)

Principles of OBJ2 Kokichi Futatsugi, Joseph A. Goguen, Jean-Pierre Jouannaud, and José Meseguer CSLI–85–22 (*$2.00*)

Querying Logical Databases Moshe Vardi CSLI–85–23 (*$1.50*)

Computationally Relevant Properties of Natural Languages and Their Grammar Gerald Gazdar and Geoff Pullum CSLI–85–24 (*$3.50*)

An Internal Semantics for Modal Logic: Preliminary Report Ronald Fagin and Moshe Vardi CSLI–85–25 (*$2.00*)

The Situation in Logic–III: Situations, Sets and the Axiom of Foundation Jon Barwise CSLI–85–26 (*$2.50*)

Semantic Automata Johan van Benthem CSLI–85–27 (*$2.50*)

Restrictive and Non-Restrictive Modification Peter Sells CSLI–85–28 (*$3.00*)

Institutions: Abstract Model Theory for Computer Science J. A. Goguen and R. M. Burstall CSLI–85–30 (*$4.50*)

A Formal Theory of Knowledge and Action Robert C. Moore CSLI–85–31 (*$5.50*)

Finite State Morphology: A Review of Koskenniemi (1983) Gerald Gazdar CSLI–85–32 (*$1.50*)

The Role of Logic in Artificial Intelligence Robert C. Moore CSLI–85–33 (*$2.00*)

Lecture Notes

The titles in this series are distributed by the University of Chicago Press and may be purchased in academic or university bookstores or ordered directly from the distributor at 5801 Ellis Avenue, Chicago, Illinois 60637.

An Introduction to Unification-Based Approaches to Grammar Stuart M. Shieber. Lecture Notes No. 4

The Semantics of Destructive Lisp Ian A. Mason. Lecture Notes No. 5

An Essay on Facts Ken Olson. Lecture Notes No. 6

Logics of Time and Computation Robert Goldblatt. Lecture Notes No. 7

Word Order and Constituent Structure in German Hans Uszkoreit. Lecture Notes No. 8

Color and Color Perception: A Study in Anthropocentric Realism David Russel Hilbert. Lecture Notes No. 9

Prolog and Natural-Language Analysis Fernando C. N. Pereira and Stuart M. Shieber. Lecture Notes No. 10

Working Papers in Grammatical Theory and Discourse Structure: Interactions of Morphology, Syntax, and Discourse M. Iida, S. Wechsler, and D. Zec (Eds.) with an Introduction by Joan Bresnan. Lecture Notes No. 11

Natural Language Processing in the 1980s: A Bibliography Gerald Gazdar, Alex Franz, Karen Osborne, and Roger Evans. Lecture Notes No. 12

Information-Based Syntax and Semantics Carl Pollard and Ivan Sag. Lecture Notes No. 13

Non-Well-Founded Sets Peter Aczel. Lecture Notes No. 14

Partiality, Truth and Persistence Tore Langholm. Lecture Notes No. 15

Attribute-Value Logic and the Theory of Grammar Mark Johnson. Lecture Notes No. 16

The Situation in Logic Jon Barwise. Lecture Notes No. 17

The Linguistics of Punctuation Geoff Nunberg. Lecture Notes No. 18

Anaphora and Quantification in Situation Semantics Jean Mark Gawron and Stanley Peters. Lecture Notes No. 19

Propositional Attitudes: The Role of Content in Logic, Language, and Mind C. Anthony Anderson and Joseph Owens. Lecture Notes No. 20

Literature and Cognition Jerry R. Hobbs. Lecture Notes No. 21

Other CSLI Titles Distributed by UCP

Agreement in Natural Language: Approaches, Theories, Descriptions Michael Barlow and Charles A. Ferguson (Eds.)

Papers from the Second International Workshop on Japanese Syntax William J. Poser (Ed.)

The Proceedings of the Seventh West Coast Conference on Formal Linguistics (WCCFL 7)

The Proceedings of the Eighth West Coast Conference on Formal Linguistics (WCCFL 8)

The Phonology-Syntax Connection Sharon Inkelas and Draga Zec (Eds.) (co-published with The University of Chicago Press)

Books Distributed by CSLI

Titles distributed by CSLI may be ordered directly from CSLI Publications, Ventura Hall, Stanford University, Stanford, California 94305-4115.

The Proceedings of the Third West Coast Conference on Formal Linguistics (WCCFL 3) ($9.00)

The Proceedings of the Fourth West Coast Conference on Formal Linguistics (WCCFL 4) ($10.00)

The Proceedings of the Fifth West Coast Conference on Formal Linguistics (WCCFL 5) ($9.00)

The Proceedings of the Sixth West Coast Conference on Formal Linguistics (WCCFL 6) ($12.00)